Planning Under Pressure

Planning Under Pressure
The strategic choice approach

Second edition

John Friend
Stradspan, Doncaster

Allen Hickling
Allen Hickling & Associates, Warwickshire

Butterworth-Heinemann
Linacre House, Jordan Hill, Oxford OX2 8DP
A division of Reed Educational and Professional Publishing Ltd

$\mathcal{R}$ A member of the Reed Elsevier plc group

OXFORD   BOSTON   JOHANNESBURG
MELBOURNE   NEW DELHI   SINGAPORE

First published 1987
Reprinted with revisions 1988
Second edition 1997

British Library Cataloguing in Publication Data
Friend, J. K. (John Kimball), 1930 –
    Planning under pressure: the strategic choice approach. – 2nd ed.
    1. Policy sciences   2. Strategic planning
    I. Title   II. Hickling, Allen
    320.6

ISBN   0 7506 2955 X

Printed and bound in Great Britain by Biddles Ltd, Guildford and King's Lynn

Contents

Preface to the second edition

New directions

Our original intention had been to keep our preface to this new edition short. For the first edition included an invited foreword and a lengthy preface, both of which we wished to retain; and, in the reader's interest, we wished to avoid a surfeit of introductory material. Yet, once we came to draft the additional chapters for this edition, we recognised that there were many things we wished to say which fitted better here in a new preface than in the body of the book.

Over the decade since our first edition went to press, both of us have been developing the ideas presented in *Planning under Pressure* in new directions, while continuing to work as independent consultants with different clienteles. So, inevitably, there have been divergences in the directions in which the two of us have been moving. Yet, whenever we meet to compare experiences, we discover intriguing opportunities for synthesis – and it is these that have guided us in drafting the additional chapters for this edition.

In brief, we have agreed that we need make only minor changes in the first nine chapters. However, it was clear to us that the final chapter 10 of our first edition, concerned with horizons for future development as we saw them in the mid-eighties, had now become quite out of date. What we have therefore done is to replace that chapter by three new chapters which, taken together, reflect our experiences over the last decade, and the consequent shifts in our view of opportunities for future development.

The new Chapter 10 – The electronic resource – discusses what we have learnt from our recent experiences in developing computer software for strategic choice, and in introducing this as an additional resource both for decision-makers and for teachers and students of management and planning.

Then the new Chapter 11 – Extensions in process management – reviews a complementary set of experiences in adapting the participatory style of planning discussed in Chapter 9 to ever more demanding challenges; challenges in which the groups involved have tended to become larger and more diverse, in terms of both their cultural backgrounds and the interests which they represent. Here, the concern has been to develop practical ways of helping people to work creatively with each other, as much as with the complexities of the issues that they face.

In the new Chapter 12 – The developmental challenge – we stand back and review the wider implications of these two directions of development – one

leading towards smaller-scale explorations using more tightly-structured prob-
lem-centred methods, the other towards larger-scale interactions using more
loosely-structured people-focused methods. How widely, we ask, should the
boundaries of the strategic choice approach, as presented in this book, now be
drawn? And how does our approach relate to other recent developments in decision support and participatory planning throughout the world?

Our contrasting experiences

Chapter 10 is based largely on the experiences of John Friend over the last decade, while Chapter 11 is based largely on those of Allen Hickling. It does not
seem appropriate for us to dwell on issues of historical development in those
two chapters themselves, so it is important that we should say at least a little
here in this preface about the principal influences at work.

For John Friend, the development of computer software for strategic choice
has been a major programmatic concern since this was identified as a priority
in the final chapter of our first edition. Meanwhile, he has continued to be
involved – more intermittently than Allen Hickling – in various facilitation and
consultancy projects in which the computer has played little or no role.

The decision to start developing software for strategic choice was triggered
in 1987 when John Friend found that he shared this interest with his former
Tavistock colleague John Stringer, then living not far away, and they worked
together on this in the early stages. The development work has subsequently
been sustained through close collaboration between John Friend and his son
Dave, working for him in a software development role.

Originally, the software – which has been named *Strategic Adviser*, or STRAD
for short – was seen as primarily a means of making the philosophy of the
strategic choice approach more accessible to individuals and to small informal
meetings, where the organisational arrangements involved in setting up a workshop with expert facilitation cannot readily be justified. However, the software
development project has also turned out to have wider implications for the
development of the strategic choice approach.

On the one hand, it has led to some significant extensions and refinements
of the specific problem-structuring methods introduced in this book; on the
other hand, it has helped to spread awareness of the strategic choice approach
within other domains of policy in which we ourselves had had little direct facilitation experience at the time when our first edition appeared – not least,
within the domains of industry and commerce as opposed to the world of public policy.

While Allen Hickling's work as a facilitator has also taken him into a diverse
range of contexts, the main thrust of his work has been the development and
co-ordination of major programmes of work in important fields of environmental policy, in local, national and – increasingly – international settings. These
programmes had their roots in his earlier work in facilitating policy-making in

the Netherlands in such areas as management of toxic wastes, estuarial pollution and transport and storage of hazardous petrochemical feedstocks – work which is reflected in several of the illustrations from practice that appear in Chapters 5, 6, 7 and 8.

Since the publication of our first edition, this programmatic interest has led him first into process management roles in the shaping of the first National Environmental Policy Plan for the Netherlands, then into an ambitious programme of projects in which representatives of government, industry and community interests from different nations of the European Union have come together to harmonise their policies for various types of environmentally-sensitive waste. These experiences have in turn led to work with a similar orientation in the Baltic states and other eastern European countries.

Meanwhile, in Britain, a developing relationship with the Environment Council – a national organisation concerned with promotion of environmental awareness and co-operation – has drawn Hickling into facilitation and mediation roles in the management of more acute issues of environmental conflict resolution, in which the stakeholders often set out from deeply opposed positions. In the process, he has worked alongside other consultants with expertise in such fields as negotiation, mediation and consensus-building.

Expanding networks

Over the last decade, the range of people who have become exposed to the principles and methods of the strategic choice approach has been expanding in several directions. This has come about not only through direct collaboration with one or other of us in project work but also through publications – and significantly through the publication of the first edition of this book. We find it particularly encouraging when we come across consultants, planners, managers and academics with whom we, as authors, have had little or no personal contact, yet who have developed enough interest in the methods, and enough confidence in their ability to use them, to start applying them to situations in their own contexts without any reference to ourselves.

The result is that, in our extended Guide to further reading, we are able to point to a number of published applications of strategic choice methods by other people working in such varied fields as third world development, local community action and information systems strategy in commercial enterprises.

Although some of their accounts are tantalisingly brief, others are more extensive. Taken together, they indicate not only that strategic choice methods have now been successfully used in a growing range of contexts – but also, significantly, that many users have sought to explore the scope for combining them with other approaches to participatory planning or problem-structuring that have already demonstrated their value in their respective fields.

In discussing this trend towards synthesis with the work of others, our new concluding chapter speculates about the potential for recogning a new generic field of *developmental decision science*, differing in its orientation from the broad field of systems science – with its various schools – but potentially of comparable significance for coping with complexity in human affairs.

This leads to a review of future prospects and opportunities in terms of eight interlocking themes – research, methodology, facilitation, communication, technology, sponsorship, application and education. Among the opportunities we review here is that of developing computer software for use in what is sometimes called a 'groupware environment' – with use of the fast-expanding capabilities of the internet to overcome constraints of space and time. Although much of the initial momentum here has so far been technology-driven, the scope is now becoming clear for introducing a more process-oriented approach.

Our concluding review leads us – as in the concluding section of our first edition – to the educational challenge, now seen as part of a broader *developmental challenge*. How can learning of the type presented in our book be made as accessible as possible to new generations of decision-makers, so that they can build on it in their own ways? Here, both of us can draw on recent training experiences of our own – in the case of Hickling, in running facilitation courses for the Environment Council and other clients, and in the case of Friend in contributing to courses in the management of sustainable development, in his capacity as honorary professor with the Centre for Development Planning Studies at the University of Sheffield.

We both recognise the scale of the longer-term challenge for facilitation skills are not easy to develop in students whose life experience is so far limited; yet academic staff will only be able to help develop such skills to the extent that they can draw upon a reservoir of first-hand facilitation experience in their own cultural context. We are aware of scattered successes in meeting this kind of challenge in many parts of the world. One of our wider aspirations is to help in building a broader cross-cultural momentum in this direction – not only through this book but also through an intensifying web of collaborative projects covering research, development and exchange of experiences on a global scale.

The authors' preface to our first edition – reprinted here – contains a long list of acknowledgements to people from whom we had drawn inspiration at that time. We could now extend that list considerably. However, we shall refrain from doing so here, because many of the newer names will be found in our revised Guide to further reading or in our expanded section on Points of contact.

If the last ten years provide any guide, we can look forward to a continuing expansion and diversification of these global networks, through electronic and other channels, into the start of the new millennium and well beyond.

John Friend
Allen Hickling

Preface to the first edition

Historical perspective

Twelve years have passed between the conception and completion of this book. For a book concerned with planning under pressure, that may seem a surprisingly long time. But the twelve years of gestation have seen much in the way of development both in the practice and the theory of the general approach to planning about which we write. Over this period, we have found ourselves collaborating with users in many kinds of organisations, public and private, throughout the world. So several thousands of managers, planners and policy-makers have now become exposed to the strategic choice approach; and there are hundreds of these who have played a part alongside us in its development. There have been many interim publications too; some of them reporting on particular research and application projects, others emanating from training programmes designed to introduce the essentials of the approach to prospective users in particular countries.

The origins of the approach – and of this book – are to be found in the work of IOR – the Institute for Operational Research. IOR was formed in 1963, as a unit of the Tavistock Institute of Human Relations in London, as the result of a joint initiative on the part of the Councils of the Tavistock Institute and the national Operational Research Society. Its dual aims were to extend the realm of application of operational research towards broader policy issues, and to build stronger links between OR and the social sciences. These are aims that have remained to the fore through many subsequent organisational changes, with the impetus now being maintained through an extensive network of individuals and groups in several parts of the world.

The first book on the strategic choice approach was published in 1969 (Friend and Jessop, 1969/77), followed tragically soon by the death of its co-author Neil Jessop, the first Director of IOR. The first experimental applications of the approach to practical planning problems were conducted in 1970, in collaboration with six teams of British local government officers; and the first training courses for managers were launched in 1971 at a Coventry hotel. Many other colleagues from the IOR Coventry and London offices had become involved in these early experiences. Then, in 1973 we were also joined in Coventry by Ray Bunker – the contributor of our foreword – who was revisiting the county of his birth on sabbatical leave from the University of Sydney in Australia. As a professional planner, he readily agreed to make it his task to visit as many as possible of the planners and other professionals who had taken part in our experiment in application three years earlier, in order to discover what influence, if any, the experience had had on the organisations and individuals taking part.

At that stage, it appeared that the impact on individuals had been generally more substantial than that on organisations. But the extent of that impact was both variable and elusive; and if dissemination was to proceed further, an obvious next aim was for us to produce a readable, accessible 'how to do it' guide to the approach. So, the understanding at the end of 1973 was that the three of us would work on this task together. Soon, however, the time came for Bunker to return to Australia – sailing by the long sea route, with prospects of plenty of writing time on the voyage. Then time scales became extended and, gradually, the idea of Bunker remaining a co-author became a less practical one – to be replaced by the idea of his providing some introductory remarks from his varied experiences as planning practitioner, consultant, teacher and researcher.

Meanwhile, another prospective co-author had emerged: Alan Sutton, an IOR colleague who became closely involved with the two of us in developing training programmes in Canada, and subsequently in a major government-financed project in Britain to apply strategic choice methods to the exploration of policy alternatives in County Council Structure Plans. But then Sutton too receded as a prospective co-author when, in 1977, he moved to a new base in Western Canada; so, the responsibilities of authorship reverted to the two of us.

Shifting pressures

Work on this book continued during the later seventies – but in a sporadic way as we were both working under high pressure on IOR consulting and research projects for clients in Britain and overseas. For one of us, Hickling, the thrust continued to be on practical applications of the strategic choice approach; but for the other, Friend, it shifted towards research on the organisational and inter-organisational dimensions of complex planning processes, bringing a contrasting perspective to our training activities and our continuing work on the manuscript of this book.

The late seventies were, for both of us, a difficult time in terms of continuity of our project work. In 1980, Hickling set up as an independent consultant; Friend continued to work part-time at the Institute while also taking up an Honorary Senior Visiting Fellowship at the Management Centre of the University of Bradford. Around this time we were both becoming immersed in quite different ventures as well. Hickling, having recently relinquished the management of the village stores and post office adjoining his home, launched a company called Endless Games, through which to enter the burgeoning market of fantasy role-playing games. Meanwhile, Friend, from a new home location in West Yorkshire, found himself working in partnership with his wife to set up a countryside interpretive centre, as an initiative in environmental education run on small business lines.

For both of us, the involvement in work on planning processes continued; and with it our efforts to bring the book to completion. The members of Pergamon's advisory committee for the Urban and Regional Planning Series – of which Friend was a long-standing member – offered a judicious blend of encouragement and exhortation, supported by the editorial staff. We met together whenever we could, usually at least once a month, to progress the writing work. These meetings took place in all kinds of locations – not only in offices but in hotels and restaurants, at motorway service stations, in airport lounges and railway buffets. We met often at our respective homes; indeed, we have photographs of our working one sunny day in an English country garden, with flip charts hung among the greenery climbing up the walls of the cottage behind. Meanwhile, our children grew up and started to go their separate ways; and our wives continued to tolerate our joint writing endeavours with surprising good humour, while developing their own careers in their respective fields of creative art.

The breakthrough finally came in the latter half of 1985. By this time, we had both disposed of most of our other entrepreneurial interests and Friend was again working full time from the Tavistock Centre in London. Hickling was now fully stretched in some challenging applications of the strategic choice approach for Dutch governmental agencies, while Friend was becoming drawn into running strategic choice workshops in new fields ranging from community health planning to information technology strategy within the firm. A high point came during the new year break in January 1986, when a conjunction of circumstances allowed a brief reunion, at Hickling's home, of key people who had been associated with the earlier stages of preparation of the book – including both Ray Bunker and Alan Sutton, who was now resident again in Europe. This was not only a convivial occasion, it also saw a significant step forward in the consolidation of our ideas about technology, organisation, process and product, as presented in Chapter 4. There were still to be six agonising months of meetings, long telephone calls and redraftings before we were finally able to commit our finished text to the publishers. It was far from easy, but the sense of relief was overwhelming.

Complementarities

Our different experiences and work patterns over the twelve years, along with different and complementary personal skills, have led us to recognise differences and complementarities in our respective contributions to the writing process. For much of the time, the main load of drafting and co-ordination has fallen on one of us, Friend, as and when pauses in the pressures to maintain a continuing flow of project work have allowed. Yet the endeavour has been a joint one, which neither of us could have brought to fruition without the other. For Hickling's immersion over this period in practical applications of the strategic choice approach provided an all-important base of experience against which to judge the realism of the advice we wished to offer and the most practical way of presenting it; and the interdependence of our contributions became more and more apparent during the final nine-month period of intensive collaboration in the writing process.

We found during this period that some significant differences had developed between us on matters of emphasis and terminology; and we had to work long and hard at these before reaching agreement on simple, practical ways in which they could be overcome. We recognised too that there were differences in our styles of presentation – written, verbal, graphical – but we agreed that these stylistic differences could be a source of strength rather than weakness, if only we could achieve a creative synthesis between them. Some clues to the complementarities between our perspectives can be found in our respective biographical notes. Among the many facets of his early work experience, Hickling admits to operating as a semi-professional magician; Friend, meanwhile, admits to having graduated in the abstract discipline of mathematics before embarking on his early career in industrial operational research. So, a background of magic comes together with a background in logic; a contrast which, at first sight, seems to sum up neatly enough the main differences in our backgrounds and their influence on our respective styles.

But the potential for creative collaboration would not have existed had we not been capable of meeting each other at least half way. For, in the late sixties, when Friend was struggling to adapt his ingrained belief in rationality, quantification and logical rigour to the untidy social and political realities of decision-making on Coventry City Council, Hickling was taking his postgraduate degrees at the University of Pennsylvania, to become both Master of Architecture and Master of City Planning. It was here that he became exposed to the influence of Ackoff and others in the field of operational research; and it was through the convergence of this experience with Friend's searing experiences of decision-making in Coventry – together with a shared inclination towards use of graphics in expressing ideas and their relationships – that the basis for a productive collaboration was forged.

The logic/magic tensions surfaced repeatedly when Friend's writing tended to become laboured, in the attempt to pin down more formally aspects of the strategic choice approach which had hitherto developed in quite an intuitive way. Sometimes, this led to proposed changes in terminology or technique which did not fit well with Hickling's evolving base of experience in the field; so we found we had to make many fine adjustments – a little more magic here, a little more logic there. In retrospect, the opportunity which the writing task has provided for us to consolidate, review and modify the concepts and methods of the strategic choice approach has been an important one for both of us. The hope now must be that the fruits of this labour will be of as much value to our readers, whether they be practitioners, students, teachers or researchers.

The demand for an authoritative, practical guide to the strategic choice approach has been expressed to us often enough since 1973 and, indeed, earlier.

Our hope now is that this volume will succeed in meeting the demand and thereby help in sustaining the momentum of application, teaching and development of ideas. If the past is any guide, the practice of strategic choice is likely to continue to evolve in different ways in different places in response to different demands and pressures. So, we hope that this book can provide a significant milestone in maintaining the wide-ranging collaborative endeavour on which the advance of the strategic choice approach has been built over the last twelve years.

Acknowledgements

There have been enough references to other people already in this preface for us to have gone some way towards the important and congenial task of acknowledging the contributions by others in this work. The contribution of the late Neil Jessop was seminal and has been acknowledged more fully in the second edition of *Local Government and Strategic Choice* (Friend and Jessop, 1969/1977). The far-reaching contributions of Raymond Bunker and Alan Sutton over the twelve-year writing period have already been mentioned in earlier sections. Another major contribution to be acknowledged is that of Andreas Faludi who, from his Chair in Planning at the University of Amsterdam, has persistently sought to encourage development of the comparatively neglected academic perspectives of the strategic choice approach, and the study of its relatedness to other bodies of planning theory.

Others who have contributed to the development of the approach over the years include many past and present members of IOR and Tavistock Institute staff – Eric Trist, Hugh Murray, Paul Spencer, John Stringer, John Luckman, Don Bryant, James Morgan, Michael Luck, Chris Yewlett, Ken Carter, Hadley Hunter, John Pollard, Brian Quarterman, Gloria Overton, Martin Elton, David Millen, Peter Spink, Michael Floyd and Michael Norris – the last of whom has contributed many incisive comments in recent years. Other significant collaborators and sources of ideas in Britain and elsewhere have included Russell Ackoff, Felix Wedgwood-Oppenheim, Jonathan Rosenhead, Peter Fishburn, John Power, Fritz Scharpf, Bill Ogden, Harry Lash, Robin Fried, Arnold de Jong, Luc Wilkin, Fernand Debreyne, Hans Mastop, Angela de Melo, Robert Glass, Nathaniel Lichfield, Morris Hill, Martin Payne, Doug Spencer, Don Miller, Obbo Hazewinkel, Bram Breure, Paul de Jongh, Fernando Galvão, Maximino Losehiavo de Barros, Moacyr Parahyba, Ken Bowen, Peter Bennett, Colin Eden, Sue Jones, Stephen Cropper, Christine Huxham, Jim Bryant and Tsunekazu Toda. But even to list the academic, international and other affiliations of these and other individuals would take up too much space – let alone to describe the rich and varied nature of their contributions.

Contributors to the typing of successive chapter drafts have also been numerous over the twelve years since this book was conceived – but special acknowledgement must go to Betty Fox, for long the key resource person in IOR's

Coventry office; to Ann Jamieson at the Tavistock Centre; and to Jayne Moore who, working from her home, was finally able to commit the text to disk in a way that we could scarcely have conceived in the dim and distant days of 1973.

Foreword to the first edition

When Neil Jessop's and John Friend's seminal work *Local Government and Strategic Choice* appeared in 1969, I was teaching in the Department of Town and Country Planning at the University of Sydney. I was so impressed that I reviewed it for the then *Journal of the Australian Institute of Planners,* and it has had a marked influence on my work since.

I had the profit and pleasure of spending a sabbatical year with John Friend, Allen Hickling and their colleagues in 1973. This book appears many years afterwards, and it is enlightening to turn back to my impressions of the strategic choice approach at that time. These impressions followed not only from extensive discussions with the authors of this present book, but also from a programme of visits to most of the planners, managers and others who had then begun to use the approach. We generally agreed that the process of strategic choice would benefit from being presented as more cyclic rather than lineal and sequential; should be extended to address policy questions of major significance; and could be applied and used in fields of activity other than urban and regional development. This present book shows how much developmental work has taken place in these directions since the early 1970s.

It would be a pity if the comprehensiveness and thoroughness of this book led to the neglect of opportunities to use the strategic choice approach in partial or informal ways. This is particularly important in working situations where it is difficult to use the approach deliberately and deliberatively, because policies and problems have to be shaped and addressed through a diffuse process of negotiation with many different people and groups. One major example of this style of working was the joint Commonwealth-States study of soil conservation in Australia which I co-ordinated as a Commonwealth public servant in the mid-1970s.

This study had become static and rigidly programmatic. It was dominated by the current technology of soil conservation and by construction of capital works to arrest land degradation with little consideration of any national interests or priorities. The study had been in progress for two or three years and, in the circumstances of that time, it was not feasible for me to introduce strategic choice explicitly to all the various groups of intergovernmental officers who were involved in different ways. But the study was able to conclude with a principal recommendation, agreed to by all parties, about the need for mutual commitments to raise the level of soil conservation effort. This, of course, was supported by a series of statements about what that meant in terms of substance and priorities. These conclusions were then supported by a series of sub-sidiary recommendations which defined the principles of resource allocation needed to support an enhanced soil conservation effort; the organisational re-quirements of this expanded programme; and the dynamics of its continued development and modification. Inter-governmental relations were a particu-larly important part of this operation, and the recommendations were struc-tured to express these.

In effect, the study was changed from one dominated by the heavily struc-tured characteristics of traditional planning, towards an emphasis on the quali-ties of the strategic choice approach as expressed in this book. This soil conservation study accordingly represents an example of the approach being introduced informally but effectively to address the crucial aspects of process and organisation in policy-making and programme/project development and operation.

In an educational context, the strategic choice approach can be used in quite comprehensive and explicit ways. At the most ambitious level, I believe that it can be used as the major structuring element in the design of courses in town and country planning. More pragmatically, I have used it both as a means of illuminating different philosophies of planning, and as a vehicle for problem-solving in planning exercises. Either it can be taught carefully and comprehen-sively along the lines shown in this book; or students can be thrown into the deep end in dealing with a planning situation, after only a brief introduction to strategic choice. In a recent exercise of this latter kind, at the South Australian Institute of Technology, I defined the broad attributes of a planning situation, divided students into three groups and asked them to develop different solu-tions. Each group acted as a professional planning group advising the local coun-cil and taking the problem through a series of progressive decisions over three or four months. To encourage their imagination and to save time on the labori-ous collection of data and information, I asked them to write up the exercise as three different short stories, inventing information along the way which was supportive of, and consistent with, the progressive series of decisions of differ-ent kinds. The three answers showed the leading importance, respectively, of cash flow to the development agency; of an opportunity to accommodate a major metropolitan showground facing relocation; and of the resolution of land use conflicts with adjoining activities. Along the way the students learned a lot about the roles and relationships of decision-makers and decision-takers.

The way strategic choice is used in teaching depends on the educational en-vironment. In the example cited above, the students were in the third year of an undergraduate course: but ideally the students should be introduced to the con-cepts of strategic choice in the first year, and the approach built up throughout the course.

Finally, I believe the stage of development of strategic choice in this book is not the final one. One of its greatest contributions has been to break down the rigidities attending planning, problem-solving and policy-making. I feel that too many people see implementation of plans and policies as simply the routine carrying out of decisions. Yet, I am convinced that aspects and instruments of implementation often need to be shaped, adapted, or accepted as given, right from the beginning of addressing a problem. Otherwise, we will continue to have too many ineffective policies and too many pigeonholed plans.

Raymond Bunker

A quick access guide

How should you start reading *Planning under Pressure*? Your choice will depend on the nature of your interests; the time at your disposal; and the extent of any prior familiarity you may have with the strategic choice approach.

The purpose of this quick access guide is to help you in making your decisions about selective reading. It does so first by outlining the principles on which the book is designed, then by making some suggestions to help you establish your priorities.

The figures

One of the first things to be noticed on flicking through the pages of this book is the number and positioning of the illustrations. There are 97 full-page figures, all boldly numbered. Some figures are professionally drawn, while others are drawn freehand – deliberately so, in order to stress the spontaneous way in which the methods are usually used in practice. Other figures again take the form of photographs, illustrating the approach in use in a workshop setting, or reproductions of windows from computer screens.

In the margins of most of the figures will be found various key words and symbols. These are designed to help the reader in making rapid cross-references within the text. Their meaning will be explained in the next section.

The structure of the book

Three of the twelve chapters present the main characteristics of the strategic choice approach at a general level:

- **Chapter 1** describes its *Foundations*, which are based on first-hand experience of the challenges facing decision-makers in group situations;
- **Chapter 4** draws out the general *Orientations* and shifts of attitude which are central to this approach;
- **Chapter 9** discusses the *Practicalities* of applying the approach in practice, based on cumulative experience over more than 25 years.

Both Chapter 4 and Chapter 9 are organised with reference to a general view of four complementary aspects through which any approach to planning can be described, and compared to others. These four aspects, expressed through the mnemonic **A-TOPP**, are as follows:

$$Approach \quad = \quad \begin{array}{l} \textit{Technology} \\ \textit{Organisation} \\ \textit{Process} \\ \textit{Product} \end{array}$$

In most of the figures of these two chapters, you will see that the aspect of the approach which is currently in the foreground is highlighted in the lower left-hand corner.

The intervening chapters are grouped into two sets:

- **Chapters 2 and 3**, which together introduce the basic *concepts* and *methods* of the strategic choice approach;
- **Chapters 5, 6, 7 and 8**, which expand on these basic concepts and methods, emphasising the practical *skills* involved in applying them to the complexities of decision-making in practice.

The structure of these six chapters reflects a general view of four complementary *modes* of decision-making. This view is presented in diagrammatic form in Figure 8, and is explained more fully on page 19. The four basic modes are:

Shaping   *Designing*   *Comparing*   *Choosing*

In these six chapters, a small motif of four circles, based on the framework of Figure 8, appears in the corner of each figure to identify the mode which is currently in the foreground.

Throughout these chapters the concepts, methods and skills are introduced gradually through the development of a case example – the South Side story – in which they are applied to a semi-fictitious yet realistic situation of planning under pressure in the public domain.

At the end of the book will be found three new chapters which replace the single *Horizons* chapter which reviewed future prospects at the end of the first edition. Chapter 10 describes briefly – with illustrations – how computer software has now been developed as an additional form of support in applying the approach in practice, making it more accessible to individuals and small informal management groups. Chapter 11 describes some important extensions in process management, which have helped in adapting the approach to large and challenging multi-cultural projects. Finally, Chapter 12 reviews the altered horizons of future development as they appear at the time this edition goes to press.

Reading priorities

The guidelines that follow are organised according to the results you may reasonably expect to obtain from different reading strategies. They are presented broadly in terms of increasing levels of comprehensiveness.

For a **first quick appreciation of the approach**, we recommend a fast reading of Chapter 1, then a skim through the figures of the next three chapters – glancing at the definitions of key concepts that appear below the figures in Chapters 2 and 3. This can be followed by reading through the review of the main orientations of the approach which appears on pages 103 to 105 of Chapter 4.

For a **basic grasp of the main principles, concepts and methods**, we recommend a fuller reading of the first four chapters. To reinforce your understanding, you then have the option of trying out the short exercises which appear at the end of Chapters 2 and 3. If you are interested in a clearer understanding of the challenges of applying the approach in practice, you can then skim through Chapter 9; and, if you are interested in using the computer as a tool, you can then browse through Chapter 10.

For a more **thorough appreciation of how you can apply the approach**, we recommend first a familiarisation with the concepts introduced in Chapters 2 and 3, then a browse through Chapters 5, 6, 7 and 8, using Chapter 4 as your point of departure. Having developed a feel from these chapters of the kinds of skill which are involved in applying the approach in practice, we suggest you now read Chapter 9 – especially the section on selectivity and adaptiveness. Then you can either proceed to Chapters 10 and 11, for a fuller appreciation of different contexts of application; or you can return to work through Chapters 5 to 8 in more depth.

For a fuller feel of the **realities of using the strategic choice approach in practice**, we recommend careful examination of the twelve *illustrations from practice* which appear on the end pages of Chapters 5, 6, 7 and 8; then a study of the four management checklists relating to technology, organisation, process and practice which are presented in Figures 83, 85, 86 and 88 of Chapter 9, and the further developments in process management described in Chapter 11.

For speculation about **directions for future development** as they appear on the threshhold of a new century, we recommend that you turn at any stage of your reading to Chapter 12.

If you are **already familiar with the first edition** of this book, then a reading of Chapters 10, 11 and 12 – plus the expanded Guide to further reading – should bring you fully up to date.

Supplementing your reading

As with any other approach to planning, one cannot expect to prepare oneself for all the challenges encountered in practice through reading books alone.

For a fuller understanding of what the strategic choice approach can offer you, it is important that you should start to try out the methods on some of the current decision problems that you face. You may perhaps find that you can make a start by testing them on some of the decisions you need to make in managing your personal affairs, or in developing your career, in the face of all the many uncertainties which are characteristic of this level of planning. However, there is always more to be learnt from the experience of applying the methods alongside other people when working on areas of shared concern. In such relatively small-scale explorations, it has been found that the STRAD software can offer a valuable supplementary learning tool.

Over the last decade, we have found it encouraging that many readers of the first edition have felt sufficiently motivated – and sufficiently confident in their practical skills – to experiment for themselves in planning and facilitating strategic choice workshops. In several cases, indeed, they have gone on to report their experiences in published papers – references to which will be found in the Guide to further reading.

We hope that their accounts will provide inspiration to readers of this second edition and encourage them to try putting the principles, concepts and methods of the strategic choice approach into practice in their own contexts. Should you do this yourself, then we hope that you too may feel inclined to share what you have discovered through a published account of your own, so adding further to the pool of experience that has been forming over the years.

1 Foundations

A philosophy of planning

There are many possible ways in which to approach the challenge of planning in an uncertain world.

The approach to be introduced in this chapter is one in which planning is viewed as a continuous process: a process of choosing strategically through time. This view of planning as a process of strategic choice is, however, not presented as a set of beliefs which the reader is expected to embrace uncritically at this stage. That would be too much to expect – especially of an introductory chapter, which is intended merely to open the door for the more specific concepts, methods and guidelines to be offered in those that follow. People involved in any kind of planning activity of course build up their own sets of beliefs about the practice of planning in the course of their working lives: beliefs which they will not wish to set aside lightly. Yet experience in applying the approach offered here has shown that its fundamentals can usually be accepted without much difficulty by those planners or managers whose working philosophy draws more on their own practice than on taught beliefs. This is because, in essence, the approach sets out to do no more than to articulate, as clearly as possible, the kinds of dilemma that experienced decision-makers repeatedly face in the course of their work, and the often intuitive judgements they make in choosing how to respond.

In practice, such judgements may sometimes be accompanied by a sense of discomfort or even guilt. For the decision-makers may feel they are departing from certain principles of rational behaviour which they have been taught to respect. Indeed, the view of planning as strategic choice is found to offer more of a challenge to such idealised principles of rationality than it does to the intuitive judgements and compromises that seem characteristic of planning practice. If this point can be accepted, the reader should be able to relax in following the ideas put forward in this chapter, and view them as offering perspectives that can help make sense of current practice – without necessarily demanding any revolutionary change in familiar ways of working.

The craft of choosing strategically

It is important to emphasise that the view of strategic choice presented here is essentially about choosing in a strategic *way* rather than at a strategic *level*. For the idea of choosing at a strategic level implies a prior view of some *hierarchy* of levels of importance in decision-making; while the concept of strategic choice that will be developed here is more about the *connectedness* of one decision with another than about the level of importance to be attached to one decision relative to others.

It is not too surprising that these two senses of the word *strategic* have tended to fuse together in common usage. For it is often the more weighty and broader decisions which are most obviously seen to be linked to other decisions, if only because of the range of their implications and the long time horizons over which their effects are expected to be felt. This, in turn, can lead to a view that any process of strategic decision-making should aspire to be comprehensive in its vision and long-range in its time horizon, if it is to be worthy of its name.

But such a view of strategic choice can become a restrictive one in practice; for it is all too rarely that such idealistic aspirations can be achieved. The approach to strategic choice to be built up in this chapter is not only about making decisions at a supposedly strategic level. It goes beyond this in addressing the making of *any* decisions in the light of their links to other decisions, whether they be at a broader policy level or a more specific action level; whether they be more immediate or longer term in their time horizons; and no matter who may be responsible for them. This concept of strategic choice indicates no more than a readiness to look for patterns of connectedness between decisions in a manner that is selective and judgemental – it is *not* intended to convey the more idealistic notion that everything should be seen as inextricably connected to everything else.

So this view of planning as a process of strategic choice implies that planning can be seen as a much more *universal* activity than is sometimes recognised by those who see it as a specialist function associated with the preparation of particular sorts of plans. At the same time, it allows planning to be seen as a *craft*, full of subtlety and challenge; a craft through which people can develop their capacity to think and act creatively in coping with the complexities and uncertainties that beset them in practice.

Organisational contexts of strategic choice

This relatively modest interpretation of the word *strategic* means that the view of planning as strategic choice is one that can be applied not only to decision-making in formal organisational settings, but to the choices and uncertainties which people face in their personal, family and community lives. For example, any of us might find ourselves involved in a process of strategic choice in addressing the problem of where and when to go on holiday next year, or how to sell an unwanted vehicle, or how to deal with a difficult request from a relative or friend. Of course, the craft of choosing strategically becomes more complicated where it involves elements of *collective* choice – of negotiation with others who view problems and possibilities in different ways. Indeed, most of the more demanding problems to which the strategic choice approach has been applied have involved challenges of collective decision-making, either in organisational or inter-organisational settings; and this can have the effect of blurring many of the familiar distinctions of task and discipline around which organisational structures are usually designed. For the skill of choosing strategically through time is one that can become just as essential to the manager or executive as to those in more formal planning roles. This point is illustrated schematically in Figure 1, through which is presented a view of planning under the practical pressures of organisational life. It is a view in which an organisation's arrangements for making plans, and those for making day-to-day decisions, tend to merge together into a less clearly bounded process through which progress is sustained. This is a process of choosing strategically in coping with difficult problems, amidst all the complex realities – or perceptions of reality – which contribute to organisational life.

The larger and more complex the organisation, the more it is to be expected that decision-making responsibilities will have become differentiated according to a multitude of operational, managerial or entrepreneurial roles. The more likely it is too that specialised plan-making functions will have been developed in an effort to maintain a co-ordinated, longer-term view isolated from everyday management pressures. However, no plan-making activity will remain valued within an organisation unless it can provide support for the more difficult and important of the decisions people face; and it is a common experience that carefully prepared plans can quickly lose their relevance under the pressures of day-to-day events. The combined pressures of urgency, competition for resources and turbulence in the world outside can soon lead to disenchantment and confusion in the arrangements for making plans; while the pressures of complexity, conflict and overload can lead to vacillation and inconsistency in the making of day-to-day decisions. To counter the resulting personal and organisational stresses, those responsible for organisational guidance sometimes look towards some overarching framework of *policies* or aims. But, in practice, such policy guidelines can often be difficult to agree – especially when working in inter-organisational settings – and their contributions towards sorting out the predicaments of day-to-day management can be disappointingly small.

The making of generalised policies is therefore given its place in Figure 1; but it is not given pride of place. Instead, the emphasis is on the more subtle process of making progress through time by choosing strategically; and on the creative management of multiple *uncertainties* as a crucial means towards this end. And progress through time can itself take many forms. Immediate progress can take the form of intervening, or negotiating with others, as well as taking decisions on matters where direct action is possible. Meanwhile, progress in building a base for later decisions can also take different forms – not only investigations but also clarification of values and cultivation of working relationships with other decision-makers.

So the term 'planning' will be used in this book to refer generally to this more loosely defined process of *choosing strategically,* in which the activities of

Figure 1   Planning Under Pressure: A view of the realities

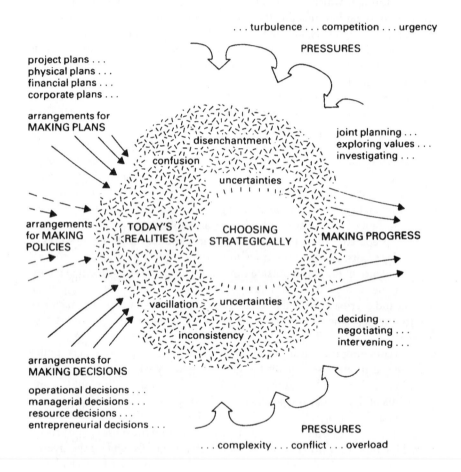

. . . turbulence . . . competition . . . urgency

PRESSURES

project plans . . .
physical plans . . .
financial plans . . .
corporate plans . . .

arrangements for
MAKING PLANS

joint planning . . .
exploring values . . .
investigating . . .

disenchantment

confusion

uncertainties

arrangements
for MAKING
POLICIES

TODAY'S
REALITIES

CHOOSING
STRATEGICALLY

MAKING PROGRESS

vacillation   uncertainties

inconsistency

deciding . . .
negotiating . . .
intervening . . .

arrangements for
MAKING DECISIONS

operational decisions . . .
managerial decisions . . .
resource decisions . . .
entrepreneurial decisions . . .

PRESSURES
. . . complexity . . . conflict . . . overload

FOUNDATIONS

making plans, decisions and policies can come together in quite subtle and dynamic ways. But with a wide variety of ways of making progress to be considered, the process can soon begin to appear as one not so much of planning but of scheming – to introduce a term which has a similar literal meaning but which carries very different undertones in its everyday usage. Whereas the notion of planning may invoke a sense of idealism and detachment, the notion of scheming tends to suggest working for sectional advantage in an often devious way. So there is a case to be made that people involved in planning must learn to become effective schemers; and furthermore that it is possible to exercise scheming skills in a responsible way. Those who are troubled about social responsibility in planning – and that includes both the authors of this book – may wonder whether there must always be a divide between responsible planners and irresponsible schemers – and if so, whether it must always be the latter who will win. As Chapter 10 will demonstrate, the concept of *responsible scheming* need not be considered a contradiction in terms. Indeed, it is towards the search for a theory and a practice of responsible scheming that the strategic choice view of planning can be said to be addressed.

It is, however, one thing for an individual to embrace a philosophy of planning as strategic choice; and quite another thing for a group of people working together to share such a philosophy as an unequivocal foundation for their work. Experience has shown that there are some settings where a sense of shared philosophy can indeed emerge – either where a set of close colleagues has learnt to work together as a coherent team, or where they discover that a common professional background allows them to proceed on shared assumptions as to how decisions should be made. Yet those whose work involves cutting across organisational boundaries must expect often to find themselves working alongside people with whom they do not share a philosophical base. So it is important to think of the philosophy presented in this chapter as a helpful frame of reference in making use of the more specific concepts and methods to be introduced in this book, rather than as a necessary foundation from which to build.

Indeed, it is a common enough experience, when working with strategic choice concepts, that people of quite diverse backgrounds can make solid progress towards decisions based on shared understandings, with little or no explicit agreement at a more philosophical level. Often it is only through the experience of working together on specific and immediate problems that they find they are beginning to break through some of the philosophical barriers which may have inhibited collaboration in the past.

Dilemmas of practice

The view of strategic choice presented in this book gained its original impetus from the experience of a particular research project, which offered unusually extensive opportunities to observe the kinds of organisational processes indicated in Figure 1.

Figure 2   Judgements of balance in strategic choice

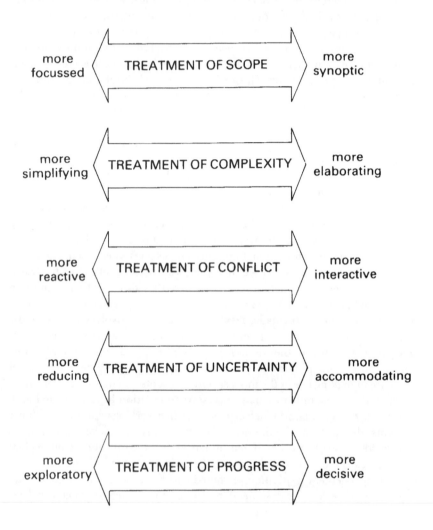

more focussed   TREATMENT OF SCOPE   more synoptic

more simplifying   TREATMENT OF COMPLEXITY   more elaborating

more reactive   TREATMENT OF CONFLICT   more interactive

more reducing   TREATMENT OF UNCERTAINTY   more accommodating

more exploratory   TREATMENT OF PROGRESS   more decisive

FOUNDATIONS

The setting of this research was the municipal council of a major English city – Coventry – which, between 1963 and 1967, agreed to act as host to a wide-ranging project on the processes of policy-making and planning in local government, viewed as a microcosm of government as a whole. This seminal research was supported by a grant from the Nuffield Foundation, and has been more fully reported elsewhere (Friend and Jessop, 1969/77). Over the four-year period, the research team was able to follow a wide range of difficult issues including the review of the city's first development plan; the redesign of its urban road network; the reorganisation of its school system; the renewal of its housing stock; the finance of public transport; and the scheduling of capital works. The researchers were able to hold many discussions with the various politicians, administrators, planners and professional experts involved, and to observe the processes of collective decision-making in which they came together – not only in the departmental offices and the formal meetings of Council and its committees, but also in the smoke-filled rooms of the opposing political groups.

Through these experiences, some impressions of the persistent *dilemmas* of decision-making in such complex circumstances gradually came to the fore. Among the clearest impressions were:

- that people held different and continually shifting views about the **shape** of the issues they faced and, not least, about how closely or widely the boundaries of their concern should be drawn;
- that there were persistent pressures for them to arrive at commitments to action in an **incremental** or piecemeal way, however committed they might be in theory to the idea of taking a broader, more, comprehensive view of the issues before them;
- that there was a continuing dilemma of balancing **urgency** against **uncertainty** in decision-making through time;
- and that there were persistent difficulties in distinguishing the **technical** from the **political** aspects of the decision process, even though the entire organisational structure was built around the maintenance of distinctions of this kind.

These impressions of the practical difficulties of choosing strategically in organisations facing complex problems have been strengthened and extended by many other experiences since the conclusion of the Coventry project – not only in the world of local government but in other public sector organisations, in industry and commerce, in voluntary organisations, and in the increasingly wide range of problem situations where these different domains of decision-making tend to converge. On the strength of this broader experience, a view is presented in Figure 2 of five broad dimensions in which difficult choices of *balance* tend to arise in the management of a continuing process of strategic choice. There is a choice between:

- a more **focused** and a more **synoptic** treatment of problem *scope*;
- a more **simplifying** and a more **elaborating** treatment of *complexity*;
- a more **reactive** and a more **interactive** treatment of *conflict*;
- a more **reducing** and a more **accommodating** treatment of *uncertainty*;
- and a more **exploratory** and a more **decisive** treatment of *progress* through time.

The practical task of choosing a position in each of these five dimensions is not one of making a firm and lasting commitment to one extreme or the other. It is more a task of maintaining an appropriate *balance* in continually shifting circumstances, shifting from time to time in one direction or another, according to the – often intuitive – judgements of those involved. In the chapters that follow, the picture presented in Figure 2 will be used as a point of reference in building more structured frameworks of ideas through which to expand further on the view of planning as a process of strategic choice. These frameworks will give deeper significance to the various contrasts which, at this stage, can only be indicated in outline terms.

In later chapters, fuller interpretations will be offered of other related aspects of the dilemmas of practice observed in Coventry and elsewhere, which are not brought out so clearly in the comparatively broad set of balances presented in Figure 2. In particular, later chapters will have more to say about the issues of urgency and incrementality, and about the relationship of the political arena to the technical domain. This is a dichotomy which, in Coventry City Council, could be seen as the fundamental organising principle on which the formal structures of accountability were designed; but it is a relationship with far wider implications for decision-making, even in contexts where such distinctions may become more blurred.

Responding to difficulty in making decisions

The view of planning as a process of strategic choice is, above all, a dynamic one. However, in building up a view of the way this process works, it is useful to begin with a more static picture. This picture, which is quite simple yet also quite general in its application, has as its focus any situation in which one or more decision-makers are experiencing *difficulty* in choosing how they should act in response to some particular *decision problem* with which they are currently concerned. A snapshot view of such a decision situation is presented in Figure 3. The decision problem itself is depicted as a cloud, to indicate that its shape will often be in some degree obscure. However, what makes it problematic to the decision-makers is that they are experiencing some pressure to arrive at a decision, yet it is not clear to them what course of action they should choose.

Where a group of people find themselves collectively in such a situation, then it is often found that different members of the group will advocate different ways of responding; so some degree of conflict of opinion may emerge. Three types of response which are repeatedly offered in practice are indicated by the three different 'bubbles' shown emerging from the central cloud in Figure 3.

Very often, people will see the way out of their present difficulties in terms of explorations of a more or less technical nature. The suggestions offered typically include various forms of costing or forecasting exercises, surveys, technical analyses, research studies; or, in some circumstances, proposals for investment in more ambitious forms of mathematical or economic modelling. Whatever the form of investigation, however, the purpose is to reduce the difficulties of making decisions by investing in a process of *exploration* into particular aspects of the decision-makers' working environment about which it is felt that too little is currently known.

Other people, meanwhile, may see the way out of the difficulty in terms of other, less technical, kinds of exploration designed to establish more clearly what policy values should guide their choice of action. Typically, they may call for investment in activities designed to clarify goals, objectives, aims or policy guidelines, whether through formal or informal channels. In some situations, this may mean simply consulting decision-takers who bear more direct responsibility for organisational policy; in others it could mean deliberately seeking fuller involvement in the process by a range of affected interest groups or their representatives.

A third response is to seek the way out of the difficulty by moves to extend the current agenda of decision-making concern. People advocating this response will often argue that the decision problem currently in view is one that cannot realistically be addressed in isolation, because it is connected to one or more other decision problems which lie ahead. So the demand here is likely to be for some form of co-ordination, negotiation or planning exercise that will allow the current decision problem to be explored alongside others within a broader, more synoptic problem focus.

Each of the three kinds of demand – most typically expressed as demands for *more information,* for *clearer objectives* and for *more co-ordination* – can be regarded as a different kind of attempt to manage the current state of **uncertainty** over what should be done about the current decision situation. Indeed, it is possible to go on to identify three general *categories* of uncertainty along the lines indicated below, which are distinguished by the different forms of response that can be made. These three types of uncertainty play an important part in the philosophy of planning as a process of strategic choice; they can be formally described as follows:

- Uncertainties about the working Environment: **UE** for short
- Uncertainties about guiding Values: **UV** for short
- Uncertainties about Related decisions: **UR** for short

It is important to stress that the idea of uncertainty in strategic choice is

Figure 3 Three types of uncertainty in decision-making

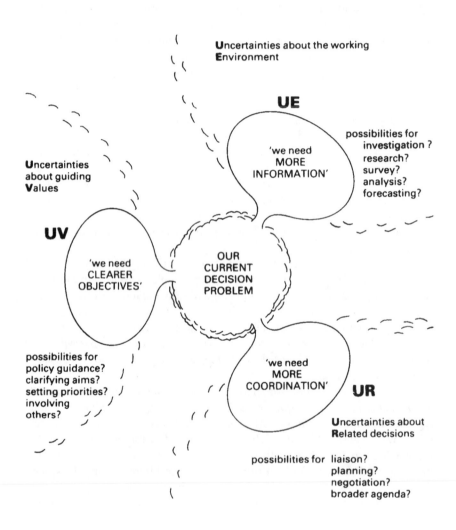

Uncertainties about the working
Environment

UE

'we need
MORE
INFORMATION'

possibilities for
investigation ?
research?
survey?
analysis?
forecasting?

Uncertainties
about guiding
Values

UV

'we need
CLEARER
OBJECTIVES'

OUR
CURRENT
DECISION
PROBLEM

possibilities for
policy guidance?
clarifying aims?
setting priorities?
involving
others?

'we need
MORE
COORDINATION'

UR

Uncertainties about
Related decisions

possibilities for liaison?
planning?
negotiation?
broader agenda?

FOUNDATIONS

normally viewed in *relative* rather than absolute terms. It is treated as an attribute of particular situations and people rather than something with an objective reality of its own. In practice it is often far from easy for people to agree which of the three kinds of uncertainty are most crucial in a particular decision situation; and, therefore, how much attention should be given to each possible form of response. For instance, members of a city planning team, considering whether to recommend approval of an application to build a new hotel, might see possibilities either for calling for deeper investigation of its traffic implications; or for seeking clearer guidance on the Council's policies in relation to this particular kind of development; or for initiating a wider review of tourism possibilities within the city as a whole. They might of course want to move in all three directions more or less at the same time; however, this is not always possible where there are pressures to make a speedy decision. Nor will it necessarily be desirable to invest resources in all possible ways of responding to uncertainty – especially if some of them are expected to be less effective than others, in terms of reducing the feelings of uncertainty among the decision-makers involved.

Managing uncertainty: a dynamic view

So, in practice, it may be far from easy to judge how uncertainty is to be *managed* at any moment, even in situations where the sources of that uncertainty have been clearly identified.

To consider further the possible ways of managing uncertainty through time, it becomes necessary to move to a more *dynamic* view. Such a view is presented in Figure 4, which builds on the 'snapshot' picture of Figure 3 by introducing the reality that any form of investigative, policy clarifying or co-ordinating initiative must take some time to carry through. Indeed, explorations in some of these directions may, in practice, take longer to carry out than others. However, the intended consequence of pursuing any chosen exploratory path is to make the decision situation less difficult to deal with once the outcome of the exploration is known – in other words, to lessen the feelings of uncertainty being experienced by the decision-makers, and thus to increase the level of *confidence* with which they can act. In practice, however, it will not often be realistic to expect that the feelings of uncertainty surrounding a difficult decision problem can be made to vanish altogether, however much effort may be invested in exploratory activities. In terms of the symbolism used here, the process can be pictured as one whereby the original cloud becomes smaller in its dimensions and, by implication, less obscure.

Sometimes, of course, feelings of uncertainty may be reduced through time without any conscious action on the part of the decision-makers. Expected events may or may not unfold; trends may become more apparent; the intentions of other parties may be revealed; policy positions may become more clear cut. In general, however, uncertainty can only be reduced at a cost – whether this be

Figure 4   Opportunities for managing uncertainty
            through time

merely the cost of delay when there may be urgent issues to be settled, or whether it also includes more direct costs in terms of money, skills or other scarce resources.

So the management of uncertainty through time is rarely simple in the types of judgement it entails. It is the raising of these judgements to a more conscious level that is one of the most distinctive characteristics of the strategic choice approach.

Interconnected agendas of decision-making

Of the three exploratory routes indicated in Figure 4, it is the co-ordinative (UR) route which is of most far-reaching significance in developing the idea of planning as strategic choice.

The demand to move in this direction arises when there is a sense that the present agenda of decision-making is too restricted – that the decision problem currently in view is significantly influenced by uncertainties to do with intended actions in other fields of choice. Such a concern for a wider view will often lead to an extension in the time frame as well, because the pressures for decision may be less immediate in some of these related areas. The concern for co-ordination may also shift the process in the direction of some form of liaison or joint working with other sections or departments, and sometimes, also, with other decision-makers quite outside the organisational framework within which the current problem is being addressed.

The concern for co-ordination in dealing with related fields of choice does not, however, inevitably mean transcending organisational boundaries in this way. At a more modest level, it may simply be a matter of the same decision-maker recognising that an issue to be dealt with today should be considered in relation to some other issue to be dealt with next week. In the case of the hotel development mentioned earlier, for instance, it could be that a proposal to develop an indoor leisure centre is known to be pending on a neighbouring site, suggesting that either proposal could affect the other.

In general, the pursuit of the co-ordinative (UR) route implies forging a relationship between one decision process or planning process and others, in the manner indicated in Figure 5. The dynamic view is here taken a step further than in Figure 4, by showing the fuller implications of a shift from a more limited to a broader decision focus. The investment in 'more co-ordination' can be seen as shifting the focus, temporarily at least, from the original decision problem to a broader and more complex problem within which it is contained.

Incremental progress in planning

One of the most important points about this shift to a broader problem focus is that it does not automatically mean that those involved should be aiming for

Figure 5   Extending the problem focus

PROGRESS
TOWARDS
COMMITMENT

MODIFIED
DECISION
PROBLEM

POLICY GUIDANCE?

INVESTIGATION?

UE

A BROADER
PLANNING
PROBLEM

UE

OUR
CURRENT
DECISION
PROBLEM

UV

UV

UR

UR

PRESSURES
FOR DECISION

PRESSURES FOR DECISION ON OTHER
RELATED AGENDAS (varying time horizons)

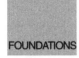

early decision in respect of all the related choices now brought into view. It is perfectly possible that the shift to a broader focus will help to reduce uncertainty in the original decision problem and so enable firm commitment to be agreed, without leading to simultaneous commitments in any or all of the other related areas. Indeed, the issue of balance between exploratory and decisive progress has already been highlighted (Figure 2) as one of the main areas of judgement in strategic choice; and it is a balance of critical importance in managing uncertainty through time.

The broader the focus of the problem within the larger cloud in Figure 5, the more it is likely to be thought of not simply as a decision problem but as a *planning problem* because it contains elements of both immediate and longer-term decision. But the distinction is not so much an absolute one as one of degree. This point is made in Figure 5 by showing the three kinds of uncertainty surfacing again at the broader level of the more complex planning problem. Indeed, if uncertainties of type UR again appear important at this level, this may trigger off concerns to move to an even broader level of concern, and to begin to explore the shape of an even larger and more obscure cloud. But this process of continually enlarging the scope of the problem will always have its limits in practice; and, if useful pointers to action are to emerge, then the focus of concern must be kept within manageable bounds.

It is not hard to see how planning procedures conceived with ambitions towards comprehensiveness can develop their own internal momentum. Such tendencies can be found in corporate planning procedures for the guidance of large and diffuse commercial enterprises, and also in exercises in the production of land-use plans or economic planning frameworks, through which public agencies endeavour to set a context for the actions of other parties. The danger is always that such activities will become separated from other management processes and so cease to exercise any real influence on the more immediate decisions they were designed to inform. This risk of disengagement between arrangements for planning and for management has already been suggested in the keynote diagram (Figure 1); it is a risk that can be confronted directly from the perspective of planning as a process of strategic choice.

Human settings for decision-making

The shift from a 'snapshot' view of decision-making (Figure 3) to a more dynamic, multi-level picture (Figures 4 and 5) implies that the imagery of the cloud should itself be conceived in more realistic, multi-dimensional terms. To extend the metaphor, clouds in reality are not flat: they have length, depth and breadth; their edges may be blurred; they progress across the sky, changing shape as time passes; they dissolve, they merge, they break up; and, in so doing, they assume new and often unpredictable forms.

With such a picture in mind, it is possible to look more closely at some different kinds of human context for decision, as a step towards a closer examina-

Figure 6   Two contexts for sequential decision-making

tion of the processes of thought and communication which go on 'within the cloud'. Figure 6 begins by looking at an organisational context of the most simple and restricted kind: an individual sits on a chair (symbolising a defined organisational role), with successive matters for decision arriving in an 'in' tray on a table (symbolising an agenda). The matters are dealt with in sequence, agreed rules are applied, and decisions are then transferred to the 'out' tray one at a time.

If the rules are unambiguous in their bearing on the issue currently being dealt with, then the cloud representing the thought process of the decision-maker is a small one, and quickly evaporates, to be replaced by the next. Indeed, the symbolism of the cloud can be replaced by the more mechanistic image of the black box – and the decision-maker at the table is at risk of being superseded by an electronic counterpart. Of course, the cloud may sometimes become larger, when a more complex case arrives. The decision-maker now experiences uncertainty and, as in the case of the public official dealing with the application to build a new hotel, this uncertainty may be in part due to awareness of links to other related cases – as symbolised perhaps by some matters marked for further attention in a 'pending' tray.

Figure 6 then demonstrates another context of sequential decision-making, by contrasting the situation of a single decision-maker sitting at his or her small table with that of a collective decision-making body – a committee or management board – grouped around a larger table. Such a group will often have a pre-circulated agenda, presenting an ordered list of issues to discuss and where possible resolve, corresponding to the 'in' tray of the single decision-maker. Among the occupants of the roles symbolised by the chairs around the larger table, there will usually be someone in a 'chairing' role, responsible for ensuring that the business is dealt with in an orderly and expeditious way. In place of the 'out' tray, there will usually be a running record of decisions kept by a committee secretary or clerk; while the occupants of at least some of the other chairs around the table will sometimes be recognised as having different representative or expert roles to play.

The decision-making process is now not purely one of cogitation within an individual's head; it embraces processes of communication, verbal and non-verbal, among the members of the group. For the observer of the process, the elongated cloud above the large table in Figure 6 takes on additional substance, in that it becomes possible to follow the dynamics of information sharing, negotiation and – if decisions are to be reached – compromise between conflicting views. For instance, if the issue of permission to build a new hotel has been brought up on the planning committee's agenda, there may be a variety of financial, aesthetic, engineering and commercial considerations to be exposed and shared. Further, there may be various conflicts of interest to be managed; for instance, there could be conflicts between the committee's responsibilities to the local community and the relationships of some members with the developer, who could perhaps be a well-known and influential local figure.

However, many decision processes in practice fail to conform to either of

Figure 7   A process of simple choice

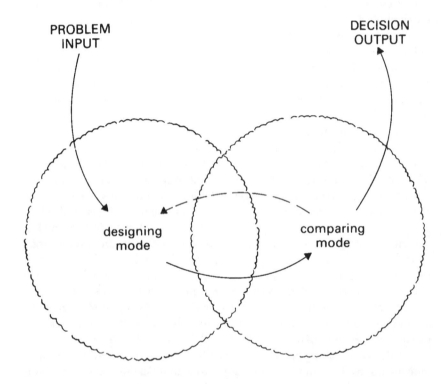

PROBLEM
INPUT

DECISION
OUTPUT

designing
mode

comparing
mode

these tidy, sequential models. If the issues are complex and their boundaries unclear, then organisational responsibilities too are likely to be diffuse and probably confused. Communications may take place not just around tables but on the telephone, in corridors, in small back rooms. The inputs and outputs can no longer be seen as falling into any clear sequence, and the image of the single cloud may have to be replaced by one of several separate clouds which continually come together, drift apart, coalesce or disappear. For instance, the hotel developer, in making his or her own investment decisions, may have a series of meetings with planners and other public officials, as well as finance houses, landowners and other commercial interests. The developer as well as the committee members will have uncertainties to manage in some or all of the three categories of UE, UV and UR; and the extent to which the different planning processes can be linked may begin to raise a host of difficult administrative, political, ethical and legal issues.

Modes of decision-making

In developing further the view of planning as a process of strategic choice, it is helpful to see the process within any 'cloud' as continually shifting between different and complementary 'modes' of decision-making activity. In the simple situation of sequential decision-making, where the nature of the problem inputs and the expected decision outputs is well defined, this movement can be seen in terms of only two complementary modes: the one concerned with *designing* possible courses of action, and the other with *comparing* them in the light of some view of what their consequences might be. This relatively simple view is indicated in Figure 7.

The process may not in practice be strictly linear because a comparison of the consequences of any pair of alternatives – for instance a straight 'yes' or 'no' to the application to build a hotel – may reveal that either response could have undesirable consequences and so trigger off a search for some other compromise solution. So it becomes necessary to allow for the possibility of a feedback loop returning from the comparing to the designing mode. So, in Figure 7 the single 'cloud' is shown as tending to change shape into two smaller clouds – clouds which may still not be clearly separable in practice, insofar as the interplay between designing and comparing may become rapid and difficult to trace.

This picture has much in common with other, more orthodox models of decision-making processes, which tend to present stages or activities in logical sequence, having a beginning and an end, while allowing for elements of feedback or recycling in between. However, the more diffuse, continuous kind of process which is characteristic of the making of complex decisions in practice involves coping with multiple problem inputs and multiple decision outputs, with no clear sequential relationships between the two. To represent this kind of process, it is necessary to move to a rather more elaborate picture of the process within the cloud, introducing two additional modes as shown in Figure 8.

Figure 8   A process of strategic choice

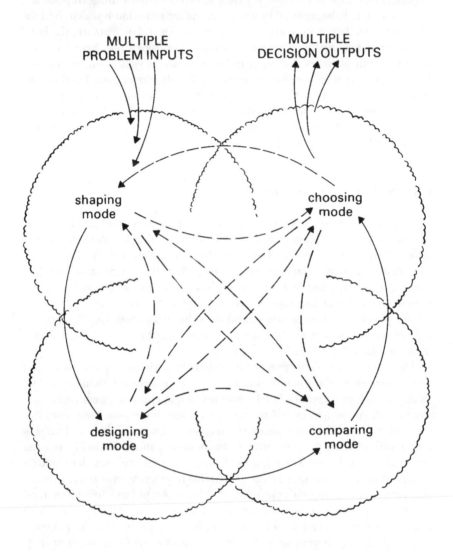

The two further modes of decision-making activity which make their appearance in Figure 8 are both of a more subtle and political kind. One of these is concerned with the *shaping* of problems; a mode within which judgements about the possible connections between one field of choice and another can have a crucial role to play. The other, referred to as the *choosing* mode, is concerned with the formation of proposed commitments to action progressively through time. Here it has to be kept in mind that the more complex the shape of the problem, the wider the choices that have to be faced. There will be choices, not only about what courses of action are preferred, but also about what degree of commitment is appropriate at this stage; which decisions should be deferred until later; and what explorations could be set in train in response to different types of uncertainty.

So instead of two partially overlapping foci within the cloud, there now appear four, with a variety of possible directions of movement between one mode and another. The most orthodox progression might appear to be from shaping problems, through designing possibilities, to comparing their consequences and then on to a final choosing of actions. However, such a progression is likely to be neither straightforward nor realistic, insofar as the process is to be seen as a continuous and incremental one, with no clear beginning and no single end. For the choice of actions to deal with some parts of the problem situation will leave other choices open for the future, creating opportunities for future reshaping of problems as unexpected events occur and new connections begin to appear.

Challenges to management and planning norms

Already, the ideas presented here can be seen to pose some direct challenges to long-established management and planning norms: norms which have indeed been under sustained challenge from other sources, yet remain extremely persistent in the design of formal management and planning procedures – often for reasons of organisational stability and accountability which cannot be lightly criticised. Among the more deeply-established norms in any management system are those of *linearity, objectivity, certainty* and *comprehensiveness*. These can be summarised as follows:

- aim for **linearity** – 'Tackle one thing at a time';
- aim for **objectivity** – 'Avoid personal or sectional bias';
- aim for **certainty** – 'Establish the full facts of the situation';
- aim for **comprehensiveness** – 'Don't do things by halves'.

Such norms may usually be adequate enough for the functionary sitting at a desk, working to highly constrained terms of reference. However, even here the system of rules can rarely be exhaustive in representing the situations that could arise; so feelings of uncertainty about how to act will sometimes surface and with them will arise difficulties in conforming to the norms of linearity and objectivity in their pristine forms. When a shift is made from decision-making to plan-making, the same four norms tend to show a remarkable persistence, even though the language may change. Yet the experience of working on difficult and complex planning problems is that the norms of linearity, objectivity, certainty and comprehensiveness keep on breaking down. So, in this book, they will be replaced by less simple prescriptions of the following form:

- don't aim for linearity – learn to work with **cyclicity**;
- don't aim for objectivity – learn to work with **subjectivity**;
- don't aim for certainty – learn to work with **uncertainty**;
- don't aim for comprehensiveness – learn to work with **selectivity**;

These alternative prescriptions may appear to be less straightforward to interpret in practice than the more familiar norms. But experience demonstrates that they offer a much more effective guide for people in attempting to choose strategically in practice. What is more, once they are stated and developed more fully, they can help people cope constructively with any sense of residual guilt they may feel in failing to apply simple management and planning norms when they encounter problems of a more complex kind.

Implications for a technology of strategic choice

There are many forms of management and planning technique which have been devised to help people deal with difficult decision problems. Indeed, systematic methods of designing courses of action, and comparing their likely consequences, have reached a considerable level of sophistication in some professional fields. For instance, systematic methods have been developed for assessing investment proposals in the light of predictions of not only their economic but also their social and enviromental implications, while there are various computer-aided methods which can help generate a range of alternatives within some of the better understood fields of technological design. Meanwhile, mathematical programming techniques can allow analysts to conduct a systematic search for better solutions within a complex, multi-dimensional field, provided certain stringent assumptions about the structure of the problem can be met.

As yet, however, there has been much less investment in the development of techniques to support the two modes of decision-making which appear in the upper part of Figure 8 – even though these two modes take on special significance in confronting decision problems of a less clearly-structured kind, where it becomes necessary to cope with multiple inputs and outputs in a highly flexible, cyclic and, necessarily, subjective way.

Just as a distinction can be drawn between the two lower, more technical, modes in Figure 8 and the upper, more political modes, so another kind of distinction can be drawn between the two modes to the left of the diagram and the two modes to the right. Whereas the former two modes are primarily addressed towards the task of opening up the field of choice facing the decision-makers, the latter two modes can be seen as addressed towards the complementary task of narrowing that field down again in order to work towards agreement on action.

This distinction will be used as a basis for the organisation of the next two chapters. These will introduce and illustrate a series of basic concepts and techniques which have been developed, tested and modified progressively through repeated application to a range of applied planning problems. Together, these concepts and techniques can be seen as constituting an *appropriate technology* for strategic choice: appropriate in the sense that it is not intended as an advanced technology for use primarily by the expert. Rather the technology is designed to support the interactive work of groups of people who have different perspectives to contribute to a problem; who face quite daunting challenges in communicating with each other; yet who may appreciate the importance of working quickly and informally under the pressures of day-to-day events.

So, the concepts to be introduced in the next two chapters will only occasionally be worth applying with a high level of analytical sophistication by specialists in a back-room setting. Indeed, the more complex and unclear become the issues and their relationships, the more problematic become the more political modes of shaping problems and choosing actions, and the more vital it becomes that any technology of strategic choice be capable of use in a flexible and relatively non-technical way.

Implications for chapter structure

The emphasis in the chapters that follow will therefore be on quite simple and *transparent* concepts and techniques – most of them involving graphical forms of representation. These are intended to aid the processes of communication between people whose perspectives, attitudes and experiences may differ, as much as to help individuals in structuring their own personal thought processes. Working on these principles, Figure 9 presents a preview of the way in which the content of the nine chapters that follow will relate to the four modes of strategic choice which were distinguished in Figure 8. This picture can be used in conjunction with the Quick access guide at the beginning, by the reader who wishes to refer at any moment to the principles of structure on which this book has been designed.

Chapter 2, which is concerned with concepts and techniques for working into complex problems, will begin with the shaping mode, and will introduce some simple concepts which can help in structuring areas of choice and the interconnections between them. It will then move down to the designing mode, to introduce some further ideas to help in organising views about the options

Figure 9   A structure for subsequent chapters

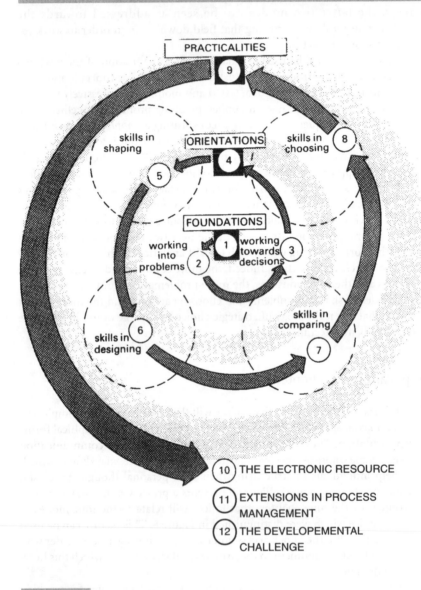

available and the patterns of compatibility or incompatibility between them. Chapter 3 is concerned with the complementary process of working towards decisions; it will begin with some concepts intended to help in comparing the foreseeable consequences of alternative courses of action, taking uncertainty explicitly into account. It then moves on to introduce further concepts addressed to the explicit management of uncertainty and the choice of incremental actions through time, drawing on the UE/UV/UR framework which has already been introduced. Together, the two chapters provide a foundation for the discussion, in later chapters, of the many different ways in which the basic concepts and methods can be brought into play in practice.

2 Working into problems

Introduction

The aim of this chapter is to introduce a set of basic concepts and methods which, taken together, offer a means of helping people to structure complex decision problems in terms of inter-related elements of choice. These concepts and techniques are addressed in particular to the work of the shaping and designing modes as set out on the left hand side of the general process diagram (Figure 8). This means that they are concerned both with the shaping of problems and with the designing or formulation of possible courses of action in response to those problems. A further set of concepts and techniques for comparing those possible courses of action and for choosing between them will then be described in Chapter 3, to complete this introduction to a basic 'technology' for strategic choice.

The basic concepts to be introduced in this chapter will include those of the decision area; the option within a decision area; and the decision scheme, consisting of a set of mutually consistent options drawn from a set of interconnected decision areas. These and other concepts will be introduced in turn, illustrated by example and more formally defined. Taken together, they offer a quite general and flexible basis for the formulation of complex decision problems; and, more specifically, for the use of an analytical method known as Analysis of Interconnected Decision Areas – AIDA for short. The essentials of the AIDA method will be explained in this chapter, but some of the more important variations on it will be deferred for discussion in later chapters.

The approach to structuring of complex problems to be introduced here is quite simple in its essence. Yet, because it involves trying to express complex realities in simple and comprehensible terms, it can demand subtle and shrewd judgements of those participating in the process; judgements of a kind which are often made intuitively by individuals, yet are rarely exposed to argument in the normal course of debate. The nature of these judgements will become more apparent as this chapter unfolds.

For the purpose of introducing the basic ideas as simply and clearly as possible, this chapter will begin to develop a case example to be known as the *South Side Story*. It is a story of a group of decision-makers faced with a set of linked investment and locational decisions which impinge on a residential community of around 7000 people, living on the fringe of a larger urban area long dominated by heavy industry, but now in a state of economic and environmental decline.[1] The story is one which will be developed gradually in this and later chapters, as further concepts are introduced and the skills and judgements involved in applying them in practice are discussed.

For purposes of exposition, the various concepts and techniques will at this stage be introduced sequentially and in an orderly way. However, it has to be kept in mind throughout that in practice the process of strategic choice is normally much more flexible and adaptive. The process can shift rapidly from one mode to another, with a continued readiness to 'recycle' through earlier stages of analysis as new insights emerge and the level of understanding grows.

The concept of the decision area

The concept of a **decision area** provides the most fundamental element in the approach to problem structuring to be described in this chapter.

In essence, this concept offers no more than a means of describing and labelling any problem situation where people see an opportunity to choose between different courses of action. To begin with a simple example, you, the reader, may even now be thinking about a choice as to whether to read the remainder of this chapter or to skip ahead to the next. Or a person lying in bed may be conscious – even if only dimly – of a choice about what to do when a bedside alarm sounds: whether to get up, to ignore it, or to silence it by whatever means may be available. On a less personal note, a bank manager may encounter a decision area when judging what level of interest to charge a particular client for a loan; while the local authority planners mentioned in the last chapter found themselves faced with a decision area as to whether or not to approve the proposal for a new hotel. Meanwhile, the developer in question might face a range of decision problems, to do with timing, choice between alternative locations, scale, design, financial backing and other important commercial matters. These could either be expressed as a single, rather complex decision area or – as would be more usual when using strategic choice methods – as a set of different decision areas, the mutual relationships of which would have to be explored.

Implicit in each of these situations is an opportunity for decision-makers, whether alone or in association with others, to act in at least two alternative ways.[2] Also implicit in each situation is some sense of pressure or concern to arrive at a commitment to some preferred course of action amongst those believed to be available – even though it is only to be expected that some decision

1   The South Side Problem as presented here is closely – though by no means exactly – modelled on one of the first successful experiences in applying strategic choice methods to urban development problems.

2   Purists sometimes point out that the word 'alternative' applies logically to an 'either/or' situation , so it is not strictly correct to talk of a set of more than two different courses of action as 'alternatives'. However, this need not be treated as a serious source of difficulty here, as in the chapters that follow the comparison of alternatives will usually be treated as essentially a pairwise process.

areas will carry a greater sense of urgency to act than others. It is this sense of pressure to act that creates a *decision problem* for those concerned – it being useful to distinguish the idea of a decision problem from that of other types of problem or puzzle which may be picked up and worked on casually as a diversion by anyone looking for interesting ways of passing their time.

To illustrate the concept of the decision area through the example of the South Side Story, it is now necessary to set the scene a little more fully, by describing how the pressures to act have arisen in this case. At this stage, the context will be taken as one in which South Side comes within the administrative boundaries of a large urban municipality – the city of Dockport, serving around a quarter of a million people in all. South Side itself is an old-established neighbourhood with a strong sense of community among the residents – though they have been steadily declining in number as older housing has been cleared and local employment opportunities have dwindled. This population base is likely to be reduced further over the next few years by the impending closure of the local steelworks, which has been a source of many jobs – but also of severe local air pollution that has lessened the attraction of South Side as a residential area. Although many of the older houses which remain in South Side are scheduled to be demolished in the next two or three years, others could have a prolonged life if designated for improvement, with financial aid from governmental grant aid programmes.

Suddenly, however, a new note of urgency has arisen for the municipality in considering what to do about South Side – and, in particular, in addressing the problem of how far to invest in its continued viability as a residential community. For a proposal has just been published by a transportation agency to route a new arterial highway carrying industrial and other traffic directly through the neighbourhood. As might be expected, this heightens the sense of anxiety about the future among the local residents and traders. In response, the municipality calls for an early report on the problem from a specially-formed internal working party of planners, engineers, accountants and legal and valuation experts. From their initial discussions, it will be supposed that a list of seven potentially important decision areas emerges, as indicated in Figure 10.

In this list, it will be noticed that each decision area has not only been described with some care, but also given a brief label for purposes of future reference. The question marks – though they can be treated as optional in practice – are here added as a reminder that each decision area is supposed to represent an *opportunity* for choice rather than any particular *outcome* of the decision process. This is a point that is also stressed in the more formal definition accompanying Figure 10.

As the example shows, any list of decision areas can be quite diverse in the types of opportunity for choice which it contains. The first decision area in the list concerns choice of alignment for a road; the second concerns choice of location for a proposed local facility; two others concern choice of land use for particular sites; while the last in the list concerns a choice of timing.

There can also be variations between decision areas in the level of generality

Figure 10   The concept of a decision area

South Side
example

DECISION AREA	LABEL
which route to choose to take the new arterial road across South Side ?	ROAD LINE?
where to locate the local shopping centre for South Side ?	SHOP LOC'N?
whether or not to declare West Street a housing improvement area ?	WEST ST?
what land use to specify for the area of cleared housing in the centre of South Side	CENT'L SITE?
what level of investment to indicate for the continued life of South Side as a residential area ?	DIST LIFE?
what land use to specify for the disused gasworks site ?	GAS SITE?
when to schedule the closure of Griffin Road school ?	GRIFF SCHL?

Shaping

CONCEPTS

A **decision area** is an opportunity for choice in which two or more different courses of action can be considered.

at which they were expressed. Whereas the fifth decision area concerns choice of policy stance in relation to investment in South Side as a whole, the third concerns a much more specific choice of action in relation to one particular street. It is one of the inherent strengths of the decision area concept that it allows different types and levels of choice to be considered together within a common analytical framework.

Links between decision areas

As soon as a set of opportunities for choice has been formulated as a list of decision areas – even if only in a tentative way – it will usually begin to become apparent that some of them at least can be viewed as *interconnected,* in the sense that there is a case for considering them jointly rather than attempting to come to decisions taking each of them one at a time.

For example, an appreciation of the local geography of South Side might make it apparent that it could be unwise to consider the choice of use for the central site without any reference to the choice of location for the future local shopping centre. This implies a belief that the choices made if the two decision areas were considered together could *differ* from those that might emerge if each were looked at in isolation, on separate 'agendas' of decision-making. This might be the case if the choice of particular uses for the central site made some conceivable locations for the shopping centre physically impossible, or vice versa: it could also be the case if certain choices in either decision area seemed likely to make some choices in the other less attractive in terms of costs, implications for local residents or other consequences with which the working party could be concerned. More obviously, there could be an interconnection between the two decision areas if one of the possible locations for the shopping centre were the central site itself.

However, not every pair of decision areas in a list is likely to be directly linked in any of these ways. For instance, there may be no direct reason for supposing that the choice as to whether or not to improve West Street cannot be arrived at independently from the choice of location for the shopping centre, or the choice of use for the central site.

Using labelled circles to represent the decision areas and connecting lines to represent the presence or absence of direct links between them, a picture of mutual relationships can be built up graphically as shown in Figure 11. Here the connecting line, or **decision link,** represents no more than a working assumption that, at least at the present stage of understanding of the problem, it makes sense to look into the mutual relationships between the two decision areas CENT'L SITE? and SHOP LOC'N?. Meanwhile, the absence of a link between WEST ST? and either of the other decision areas represents a working assumption that this choice can be dealt with independently from the other two.

The idea of a decision link forms a second 'core' concept in the strategic

Figure 11   The concept of a decision link

A **decision link** is a relationship between two decision areas expressing a belief that it could make a difference to consider them jointly instead of separately.

choice vocabulary, and is more formally defined in a statement appearing below Figure 11. The term *decision link* is usually abbreviated simply to *link* for working purposes, because it is usually clear from the context that the word is being used in this special sense. It is important to note at this stage that the concept of a decision link implies no particular view about the *sequence* in which the linked decisions should be taken, or about possible causal relationships. People who may be versed in other approaches to the mapping of decisions or systems are sometimes tempted to add arrowheads to decision links, to suggest directions of influence or precedence between one choice and another. However, it has not been found helpful to introduce such conventions into the approach being discussed here, which is purely concerned with the logic of *mutual* connectedness between one decision area and another.

Another caution concerns the tendency to interpret the concepts of decision area and decision link too narrowly in terms of familiar forms of relationships. In dealing with land use or locational problems in particular, there is a tendency for planners to focus on spatially defined decision areas and to look for links in terms of geographical adjacency or similar relationships. But decision areas and relationships between them can be used to reflect all kinds of non-spatial considerations as well, as the further unfolding of the South Side Story will make clear. For this reason, no physical map of South Side is introduced at this stage: but any reader who may find it helpful to form some view of the geographical layout of South Side may like to glance briefly at the sketch map at the end of this chapter (Figure 18).

The decision graph as a representation of problem structure

In any situation where a complex problem can be expressed in terms of a set of several decision areas, some but by no means all of which may be directly connected by decision links, then it is possible to use the graphical connections introduced in Figure 11 to build up a wider view of the structure of that problem in the form of what is called a **decision graph.**[3]

A decision graph is, in effect, no more than a two dimensional 'map' showing a set of decision areas and a set of links which connect some pairs but not others. Figure 12 gives an example of a decision graph for the set of seven decision areas so far identified within the South Side decision problem. This indicates that there are eight decision links in all, out of the total of 21 which would be theoretically possible if each of the seven had been directly linked to each of the other six.

This particular decision graph reflects an agreed view, among people who can be supposed to have specific knowledge of the realities of the South Side situation, that some decision areas are more directly interconnected than others. For instance, it shows several links connecting the four decision areas concerned with ROAD LINE?, SHOP LOC'N?, CENT'L SITE? and DIST LIFE? –

3 In some earlier writings this was referred to as a strategy graph.

Figure 12 The concept of a decision graph

South Side
example

Shaping
CONCEPTS

A **decision graph** is a diagrammatic representation of a set of decision areas and the relationships between them expressed as decision links even though ROAD LINE? and DIST LIFE? are only linked indirectly through the other two. The WEST ST? and GRIFF SCHL? decision areas, in contrast, are comparative outliers, each being directly connected to only one of the other decision areas. Indeed, had it not been for the sudden introduction of a choice to be made about the road line, as a result of a highway planning exercise over a wider area, the WEST ST? decision area would have been completely disconnected from the SHOP LOC'N? and CENT'L SITE? decision areas, as was earlier suggested (Figure 11). This is a relatively simple example of a common occurrence not only in urban planning but in other fields, where the introduction of new decision areas can introduce additional complexity into a hitherto much simpler pattern of decision links.

Where a decision graph includes a larger number of decision areas than the example of Figure 12, then it may be quite important to explore ways of rearranging it to bring out its underlying structure more clearly. It is important to note that there is no set rule to guide the positioning of each decision area on the graph: the map is a *topological* one, the meaning of which would not be changed if the relative positions of the decision areas were altered. The essential information conveyed by Figure 12 would be exactly the same if the WEST ST? decision area were shifted from the left to the right of the picture. However, it might then show some awkward crossovers between decision links, unless other decision areas were to be repositioned at the same time.

The value of any decision graph lies essentially in the picture it presents about the structure of relationships between elements of a complex problem; a picture which can be modified through time and challenged wherever there is disagreement between participants in the process. In this way the participants can proceed, through as many iterations as need be, towards deeper examination of possibilities for action and their consequences, either within the graph as a whole or within selected decision areas or clusters within its structure.

The choice of a problem focus

The possibility of focussing on a selected cluster of decision areas within a larger decision graph offers an important field of judgement in a process of strategic choice. Indeed, it can mark a critical point of transition from the work of the shaping mode to that of the designing mode – especially where the decision graph is so large and complex in its structure that it is difficult to think of designing possible ways forward while keeping the full set of interconnected decision areas in view.

Any focus for the examination of possible ways forward which has been deliberately selected to include some but not all the decision areas in a decision graph can be referred to as a **problem focus**. It is important to note here that the scope of this problem focus can be changed, repeatedly if so desired, as work on the problem proceeds. There are many different considerations that can be taken into account in choosing a problem focus, and these will be discussed more

Figure 13   The concept of a problem focus

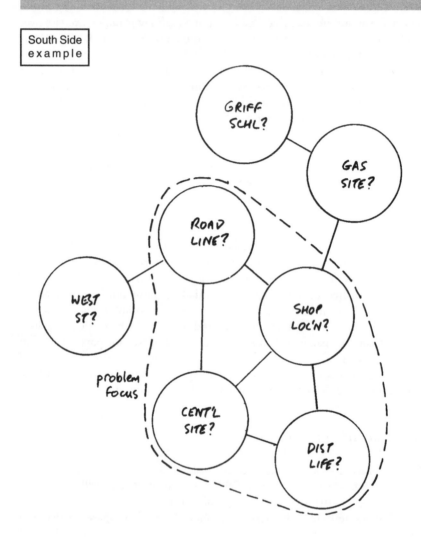

South Side example

A **problem focus** is any subset of the decision areas in a decison graph which is selected for closer examination

fully in Chapter 5. At this stage it is the general *concept* of the problem focus
that is important, as a means of managing the transition from the shaping to
the designing mode.

In Figure 13, one possible problem focus has been selected for the South
Side problem, by exercising a degree of selectivity within the decision graph of
Figure 12. The comparatively isolated WEST ST?, GAS SITE? and GRIFF SCHL?
decision areas have here been excluded, and a boundary indicating the limits of
the resulting problem focus has been drawn around the other four. In the case
of a decision graph of comparatively simple structure such as this, the step of
choosing to concentrate on these four may seem a somewhat obvious one to
take, working on the basis of the structural information alone (Figure 12). But
it is not hard to see that the judgement could become more difficult if there
were many more decision areas and connections to consider, and if it was thought
important to take into account other reasons for focussing – such as the relative
urgency and importance of different decision areas.

Even in this simple example there are several other choices of focus that
could have been made. It could have been decided to focus only on the triangular cluster of ROAD LINE?, CENT'L SITE? and SHOP LOC'N? decision areas,
on the grounds that each has at least three decision links joining it to other
decision areas, whereas DIST LIFE? has only two. It could also have been decided deliberately to keep all seven decision areas within the problem focus, or
even to restrict it to only one decision area in the first instance – SHOP LOC'N?
being one possible candidate because of its pivotal position on the graph. The
narrower the focus, the less work there will be to do in the designing mode,
especially if the alternatives within the decision area or areas concerned can be
considered clear cut. So the more rapid can be the progress forward into the
comparing mode. However, this is not to suggest that the case for choosing a
broader focus will not re-emerge later, once the uncertainties involved in working within the narrow focus have taken clearer shape.

Options within decision areas

Despite all the information about the structure of a decision problem that may
be contained within a decision graph, or even within a particular problem focus within a decision graph, this form of problem representation does nothing
in itself to indicate what range of possible actions is likely to be open to the
decision-makers. To make progress in this direction, it is necessary to move into
the more technical domain of the designing mode, which takes its place in the
bottom left-hand corner of the general process diagram (Figure 8). This is where
the analytical method of *Analysis of Interconnected Decision Areas (AIDA)* begins to have an important part to *play*.[4]

4 The AIDA method was first developed in the course of a seminal IOR/Tavistock Institute
project on communications in the building industry, conducted in parallel with the Coventry local government study. Fuller references will be found in the Guide to further reading at
the end of this book, but see in particular Luckman (1967).

Figure 14   The concept of a decision option

South Side
example

DECISION AREA	OPTIONS	OPTION LABEL
ROAD LINE ?	– northern route – southern route	– NORTH – SOUTH
SHOP LOC'N ?	– Main Street – King Square – gasworks site	– MAIN – KING – GAS
CENT'L SITE ?	– industry – housing – open space	– IND – HOUS – OPEN
DIST LIFE ?	– 10 year horizon – 20 year horizon – 40 year horizon	– 10 YR – 20 YR – 40 YR

options in further decision areas excluded from problem focus :

WEST ST ?	– improve West Street – no action	– YES – NO
GAS SITE ?	– shopping – open space – housing – industry	– SHOP – OPEN – HOUS – IND
GRIFF SCHL ?	– schedule for early closure – keep open a few more years	– EARLY – LATER

The term **decision option** – usually referred to in practice simply as an **option** – will be introduced at this point to describe any one course of action within a decision area, out of whatever range of possibilities may be seen as available. In the South Side case it will be supposed, for the sake of example, that the members of the local working party are able to agree that the range of choice in each of the seven decision areas can be represented by a set of two or more possible options, as indicated in Figure 14.

In practice, of course, it may sometimes be necessary to list more options than indicated in this example if a fully representative picture of the range of possibilities within a decision area is to be presented. Indeed, there may be a good deal of debate about these options among participants who may have different appreciations of the problems before them. During such a debate, different perceptions could well emerge not only about the number of options in each decision area, but also about the terms in which they should be expressed. For instance, it could be asked why the set of options for public investment in the continued life of South Side as a residential district should be limited to the range of 10-year, 20-year and 40-year horizons. Why not 5 years, or 15, or 100? And why express the range of possibilities in terms of time horizons at all? Could not the alternative policies perhaps be expressed in some broader, more flexible but still meaningful way, such as a choice of short, medium and long term strategies?

It is also important to check that the options within a decision area are *mutually exclusive*. For instance, if industrial use of the central site did not necessarily rule out the possibility of housing or open space on part of the site, then mixed use options might have to be introduced; or perhaps the decision area itself could be reformulated in some way, to enable the options available to be expressed in a different form. Questions about whether the options within a decision area can be considered both representative and mutually exclusive can be well worth discussing if they help to focus critical attention on what is meant by the decision area in question, and to suggest possibilities for reformulation of the problem in more realistic ways.

Once the set of options within a decision area is agreed to be adequate as a base for further analysis, it can be a useful practical step to give them short labels, as in Figure 14. So long as these labels do not suppress too much of the information contained in their full descriptions, they can save a great deal of time and space when it comes to examining combinations of options from different decision areas.

Compatibility of options in interconnected decision areas

Once options have been identified, the question arises of what possibilities for choice are to be found, not merely within each decision area taken separately, but within linked pairs or sets of decision areas within the selected problem focus. It therefore becomes necessary to introduce assumptions about how far

Figure 15   The concept of an option bar

South Side
example

COMPATIBILITY TABLE FOR OPTIONS FROM
FIRST TWO DECISION AREAS - ROAD LINE ?
& SHOP LOC'N ?

ROAD LINE ?

	-NORTH	-SOUTH
SHOP LOC'N? - MAIN	•	✕
-KING	•	✕
-GAS	✕	•

[• represents a COMPATIBLE combination

✕ represents an INCOMPATIBLE combination or OPTION BAR]

EXTENSION TO INCLUDE A THIRD
DECISION AREA - CENT'L SITE ?

	ROAD LINE ?		SHOP LOC'N ?		
	- NORTH	-SOUTH	-MAIN	-KING	-GAS
CENT'L SITE? -IND	•	✕	•	✕	•
-HOUS	•	✕	•	•	•
-OPEN	•	•	•	•	•

Designing

CONCEPTS

An **option bar** is a representation of an assumption that two options from different decision areas are incompatible with each other.

options from different decision areas can be combined. For instance, the ROAD LINE? decision area in South Side contains two options while the SHOP LOC'N? decision area contains three; if each option in the first decision area could be freely combined with each option in the second, this would give a total of 2 x 3 = 6 possible combinations from which to choose. In practice, however, the range of possibilities may be more restricted, because of various kinds of *constraint* which may be encountered in trying to combine particular options in one decision area with particular options in other decision areas. For example, a knowledge of local geography in South Side might make it sensible to assume that the choice of the southern road line would rule out the choice of both the Main Street and the King Square shopping locations, because either would mean that the majority of residents would be cut off from their neighbourhood shopping centre. Such a combination could be seen as violating what might be recognised as an important design principle – if not altogether destroying the centre's economic viability. A similar check on other combinations of options from these two decision areas, followed by a testing of options in the CENT'L SITE? decision area against those in each of the previous decision areas, might generate further assumptions on incompatibilities as shown in Figure 15. Such a table is sometimes known as a *compatibility matrix*. When other decision areas are added, it can be extended further in a stepwise fashion to form a triangular array, until each pair of the decision areas within the present problem focus is covered. Each relationship of incompatibility between a pair of options from different decision areas, as indicated by a cross in any particular cell of the table, is known as an **option bar**. In the South Side example, there are altogether three option bars connecting the ROAD LINE? and SHOP LOC'N? decision areas, which rule out three of the six conceivable combinations of options; then there are a further three option bars ruling out certain further combinations once the CENT'L SITE? decision area is added.

As in the identification of options within a decision area, it is quite normal for different participants to hold different views as to which combinations of options are feasible and which are not. Again, such differences can be used as a point of departure in working towards a clearer shared view of the structure of the specific decision problem which the decision-makers face.

Building up an option graph

Where there are many decision areas and options to consider, and so the number of possible combinations is large, it can become a correspondingly laborious matter to check each option in each decision area for compatibility with each option in every other decision area in a systematic way. This itself is one good argument for choosing a limited problem focus of no more than four or five decision areas within a complex decision graph. However, in building up a series of two-way tables such as those in Figure 15, it is usually found that crosses representing option bars appear in only a minority of the cells. This can greatly sim-

Figure 16   The concept of an option graph

Designing

CONCEPTS

An **option graph** is a diagrammatic representation of the compatibilities and incompatibilities of options within a problem focus.

plify the analysis of which combinations are possible and which are not.

The same kind of information can be built up by graphical methods, through an extension of the kinds of conventions used to develop the decision graph. This involves constructing what is known as an **option graph,** in which decision areas are represented by circles, as in the decision graph, but the set of options available within each decision area is specified within each circle as in the example of Figure 16. This allows the structure of relationships between specific options to be represented by drawing in connecting lines between those pairs of options from different decision areas where option bars have been identified.

It can avoid clutter in the option graph to use abbreviated labels for the options within each decision area and also to write the name of the decision area itself outside, rather than inside, the circle. The pattern of option bars can then be built up gradually, scanning the whole graph for possible incompatibilities rather than working logically through the combinations one at a time – and concentrating on pairs of decision areas which are directly connected through decision links. This kind of approach can provide a more open means of building up a picture of incompatibilities than the matrix approach – especially where there are several participants with different kinds of insight to offer.

Although the picture of Figure 16 may look quite complex and hard to interpret at a glance, it is worth noting that it includes only ten option bars in all, as compared to the much larger number of combinations of pairs of options from different decision areas – in this example, thirty-five – which remain feasible. This observation helps to explain the convention of using connecting lines in an option graph to represent *incompatible* combinations rather than *compatible* ones. When first encountered, this convention can be found surprising and counter-intuitive. Nevertheless, a little experience soon shows that it is normally far more economical to use links between options to represent the few incompatible pairs of options than the many compatible pairs. Not only does this make the picture of criss-crossing lines less impenetrable to the eye; more importantly, it allows new option bars to be introduced gradually as new reasons for incompatibility suggest themselves, and makes it much easier to keep track of the logic within the option graph.

It is only to be expected that the pattern of option bars in an option graph will bear some resemblance to the pattern of decision links within the corresponding part of the decision graph – if only because one obvious way in which a pair of decision areas can be interconnected is through some restriction on the extent to which options within them can be combined. However, the correspondence will not necessarily be precise: for instance, a pair of decision areas may be seen as linked on the decision graph not because there are any combinations of options which are incompatible, but because there are some combinations which appear to bring particular advantages or disadvantages in terms of costs or other consequences. So decision links do not necessarily imply option bars. Nor is it inconceivable that option bars will be identified to connect pairs

Figure 17   The concept of a decision scheme

South Side
example

Designing

CONCEPTS

A **decision scheme** is any feasible combinaion of options containing one from each of the decision areas within a problem focus.

of options from decision areas which were not thought to have been linked when the decision graph was first drawn; it is always possible that deeper reflection will bring insights into the problem structure which were not apparent at first sight.

Generating feasible decision schemes

At this point the core concept of a *decision scheme* will be introduced to describe any combination of options, one drawn from each of the decision areas within a problem focus, which is *feasible* in the sense that it does not violate any of the option bars included in the current formulation of the decision problem. Even where the number of option bars in an option graph is quite limited, it can be far from easy to see what range of possible decision schemes is available simply by looking at the option graph itself. Instead, it is necessary to embark on a logical procedure for testing the feasibility of different combinations of options from the decision areas, considered not just two at a time but in sets of three or more taken together.

This means first arranging the decision areas within the current problem focus according to some chosen sequence, and then proceeding logically through that sequence in the manner illustrated in Figure 17. Here the various feasible combinations of options from the four selected decision areas for South Side are built up by proceeding through a systematic branching process. The combinations are presented in the form of a tree-like display somewhat similar in format to the 'decision tree' used in classical decision analysis. However, the aim here is not to provide a framework for analysing contingencies and probabilities, but simply to display all available decision schemes for further examination. To emphasise this difference, the alternative phrase *option tree* will be adopted here.

In Figure 17, for example, the path through the tree which combines the NORTH road line with the GAS shop location is eliminated at an early branching point, because of an option bar linking these two options directly. At a later stage, the NORTH–KING–IND route is terminated because there is an option bar between the KING and IND options, while further on again, the NORTH–MAIN–IND–20YR route is ruled out because of an incompatibility between a 20 year district life and the main street shop location. So, in progressing along each branch of the tree, it is necessary to check the compatibility of each new option not only with the option in the immediately preceding decision area, but also with all the others further back. In this example, indeed, the entire branch which begins NORTH-MAIN-OPEN is eliminated, not because of incompatibilities involving any pair of these three options, but because of two different types of option bar which are encountered once the final DIST LIFE? decision area is added.

In this example, the systematic development of the tree shows that there are, in all, nine feasible decision schemes, each of which has been given an alphabetic label for reference purposes. Sometimes there will be only a few feasible decision schemes, or even none at all; on other occasions, there may be so many that they become difficult to compare at all without some further filtering process.

The process of working systematically through the branches of a tree can provide important opportunities for learning. It can, of course, become time-consuming if the number of decision areas and options is much larger than in this example. In such circumstances, computer methods can sometimes be helpful, both as a check on the logic of the process and a means of testing rapidly the effect of different assumptions on options and option bars. There are various alternative ways of setting out the kind of information contained in Figure 17. In this example, the closed branches are included and terminated by a cross to help demonstrate the logic of the process; they could however, have been omitted so allowing the range of available choices to be presented in a more compressed form. If desired, the set of feasible schemes could have been presented as a straight list rather than in the form of a tree; the advantage of the branching format is essentially in the *structural* information it conveys. Also, the arrangement of the set of decision schemes could be changed, either by working through the decision areas in a different sequence or by introducing comparative considerations to bring to the fore those schemes which might be considered more desirable. But this latter possibility means moving on to the perspective of the comparing mode, and will be left for further consideration in Chapter 3.

Analysing interconnected decision areas: Concluding review

This chapter has introduced a set of basic concepts which provide a foundation for the general method of problem structuring that has become known as Analysis of Interconnected Decision Areas, or AIDA for short. The most fundamental concepts of the AIDA method – those of the decision area, the option and the option bar – together form the basic elements required as input to build an option graph as a representation of the structure of choices within a problem or part of a problem; and, from this, to find out what range of possible 'solutions' or decision schemes is available. Among the other ideas introduced in the earlier sections of this chapter were those of the decision link, the decision graph and the problem focus – all of these being intended to help people in debating the overall shape of the problem before the more specific AIDA methods are brought into play.

The AIDA method of problem structuring does, of course, have its limitations in representing complexity of certain kinds; and these limitations will be discussed further in later chapters. In particular, it is not always easy to adapt the method to decision problems which are most naturally expressed in terms of adjustments to the levels of a set of more or less continuous control variables. However, decision problems can only be seen in terms of this kind of 'control model' in comparatively stable operating contexts, where the overall shape of the problem can be seen as more or less invariable through time. In such a case, it may be possible to use more sophisticated and specialised forms of analysis concerned with the systemic relationships among the decision variables particular to that operational setting. Nevertheless, even such 'well structured' problems can often be embedded in wider problem settings with a more volatile structure, to which a more open-ended approach to problem structuring, of the kind described n this chapter, can usefully be applied. For the strategic choice approach has no claims to be a 'systems approach' in the commonly accepted sense: rather, it is a *process* approach in which the elements are choices which are normally supposed to be of a transient nature, and the relationships between elements are not therefore expected to assume any systemic form.

Relating the concepts and methods introduced in this chapter to the five basic dimensions of balance in strategic choice (Figure 2), the first of them – to do with the treatment of scope – has begun to be addressed by the concepts introduced to guide the work of the shaping mode: the decision area, the decision link, the decision graph and the problem focus. The second dimension of balance – to do with the treatment of complexity – has begun to be addressed by the general concepts of the decision option, the option bar, the option graph and the decision scheme, introduced to guide the work of the designing mode. But there is more to be discussed about the treatment of scope and of complexity in strategic choice in later chapters. Meanwhile, the treatment of conflict, uncertainty and progress – while touched upon in some places in this chapter and Chapter 1 – has scarcely begun to be discussed in terms of basic concepts and techniques. It is the introduction of such concepts and techniques that will be the purpose of Chapter 3.

Some excercises

At this stage, some readers may be glad of an opportunity to test their ability to make use of the concepts introduced in this chapter. To this end, the chapter concludes with a short set of exercises, all of them based on simple variations in the formulation of the decision problem faced in the South Side story as described so far.

1. If every pair of decision areas in Figure 12 which is not shown as directly interconnected were to be connected up, how many additional decision links would there be?

2. Suppose in Figure 12 that two additional decision links were added, one to connect ROAD LINE? to DIST LIFE? and the other to connect WEST ST? to SHOP LOC'N?. Could the positions of the various decision areas be altered to make the structure of the decision graph clearer, in particular by avoiding any crossovers between the connecting links?

3. How many different ways can you see of choosing a problem focus within the decision graph as modified in Question 2, so as to include three fully

Figure 18 South Side: Some local orientation

South Side
example

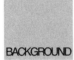

PROPOSED NEW ARTERIAL ROAD

north line

to steelworks
and river

south
line

→
from
Dockport
central area
5 km

Main Street

West Street
housing

CENTRAL
SITE
(cleared)

King
Square

to the
sea

MAIN BLOCK OF
OLDER HOUSING
STREETS (what life?)

NEWER
HOUSING
ESTATE

possible sites
for future
South Side
local shopping
centre

Griffin Road
School

gasworks
site

to Eastwell 2km

←————— 1 kilometre —————→

BACKGROUND

interlinked decision areas?

4. Suppose the 40YR option for DIST LIFE? were to be eliminated as no longer available for some reason. How many of the nine feasible decision schemes in Figure 17 would this remove?

5. If an extra option bar were to be added to Figure 16, to rule out the combination of the 40YR option in the DIST LIFE? decision area with the OPEN option in the CENT'L SITE? decision area, how many of the nine feasible decision schemes in Figure 17 would have to be ruled out as not feasible?

6. Which of the decision schemes in Figure 17 – *beyond* those eliminated by Question 5 above – would be cut out if option bars were to be added between the NORTH option in the ROAD LINE? decision area and *both* the 10YR and 20YR options in the DIST LIFE? decision areas.

7. How many additional decision schemes would be added to the list of nine in Figure 17 if the option bar ruling out the SOUTH option in the ROAD LINE? decision area in combination with the IND option in the CENT'L SITE? decision area were to be *removed?*

Finally, two more open-ended questions which, unlike those above, have no one answer. First, examine Figure 18, which shows the spatial relationships between the locations and alignments assumed in the formulation of decision areas and options in this chapter.

8. Do the spatial relationships shown in this map lead you to question the reasoning behind any of the decision links shown in Figure 12, or to suggest that any new ones should be included?

9. Do these same spatial relationships suggest that there could be a case for questioning the arguments behind any of the option bars shown in Figure 16 or for adding any further option bars?

3 Working towards decisions

Introduction

The aim of this chapter will be to complement Chapter 2 by introducing a further set of basic concepts and methods, designed to guide work within the comparing and choosing modes. Taken together, the various core concepts introduced in the two chapters will form a skeleton for an *appropriate technology* of strategic choice: a skeleton which will be built upon further in Chapters 5 to 8, where a range of variations on these concepts and methods will be discussed.

The transition from the last chapter to this one involves a shift of focus; a shift from a concern with designing possible courses of action to a concern with discriminating among those possibilities in order to make progress towards decisions. As in Chapter 2, the intention will be to introduce a limited set of core concepts in as simple and basic a form as possible. However, they are concepts which address evaluative issues more directly than the concepts introduced to guide the work of the shaping and designing nodes; and these evaluative issues can become quite subtle and complex.

The first three concepts to be introduced are those of the comparison area, the relative assessment and the advantage comparison. All of these terms have their counterparts in everyday use; but they are expressed here in language which is designed to encourage a more explicit consideration of uncertainty than is found in some other approaches to evaluation.

These concepts apply generally to any situation where there are different courses of action to be compared, whether there be only two alternatives to consider or a much wider range of possibilities to be scanned. Also, the concepts are designed to apply whether or not there are numerical or other acceptable scales of measurement in view – recognising that consequences can often be subtle and far-reaching in their impact, so that an attempt to reduce assessments to a single unambiguous scale may not always be an appropriate way of dealing with the complexities and uncertainties encountered in practice.

The fourth concept to be introduced – that of the working shortlist – does however mean introducing more simplified scales of assessment to narrow down the range of possible alternatives. This is especially useful when working with several linked decision areas, generating a wide range of feasible combinations of options to be compared. So it is at this point of the chapter that the basic concepts about comparing come together with those about designing feasible decision schemes through AIDA, which were introduced towards the end of

Chapter 2. In the second half of Chapter 3, four further basic concepts will be introduced, designed to guide the work of the choosing mode: these are the concepts of the uncertainty area, the exploratory option, the action scheme and the commitment package. It is in introducing these later concepts that the emphasis on management of uncertainty through time will come directly to the fore, in the spirit of the view of planning as a continuous process of strategic choice which was presented in Chapter 1.

Formulating a set of comparison areas

The task of comparing any pair of alternative courses of action necessarily involves forming some view of what the consequences, effects or implications might be if either course of action were to be pursued rather than the other. It is possible to conceive of circumstances in which it may be sufficient to consider implications in relation to only one dominant area of concern. For example, a person choosing a painting to hang on a bedroom wall might be content to compare and choose solely on the basis of personal aesthetic judgement – at least in circumstances where that person lived alone and the set of alternative paintings available were all offered at the same price, with the same physical dimensions. Or a developer's comparing competitive tenders for a building project, might conceivably be content to compare on the grounds of quoted cost alone – but only in the somewhat artificial circumstances that all tenders met the brief in an identical way and no other comparative information was available with which to discriminate between contractors in terms of their reputations for reliability or quality of work.

These two examples indicate how rarely in practice it is realistic to restrict attention to a single dimension of comparison taken on its own. Indeed, the more far-reaching the implications of a decision problem, the wider the set of participants likely to become involved. So the less practicable it can become to reduce their concerns to a single basis for comparison, whether this be expressed in monetary or other terms.

The approach to comparison to be developed here can therefore be described as essentially a *multi-criteria* approach – to adopt a phrase which has lately become fashionable in relation to more specific mathematical methods of comparison. The concept of a *criterion* is of course familiar enough, not only to decision scientists but also to many practising planners and managers. However, the word is one which can convey subtly different meanings to different people – for instance, it conveys to many people an expectation of a defined scale of measurement, even though dictionary definitions tend to suggest the idea of comparison with some preset standard or norm. For this reason, the concept of criterion will here be replaced by a more general concept of a **comparison area**, which will be more carefully defined within the context of the strategic choice approach.

In essence, a comparison area can be seen as simply a description of some area of concern to the participants in a decision process, within which they may wish to consider what the consequences of alternative courses of action might be. Figure 19 illustrates this concept by presenting descriptions of four different comparison areas which could be seen as important in addressing the decisions facing the South Side Working Party, in the planning situation that was outlined in Chapter 2. As in the earlier listing of decision areas, each of these comparison areas is specified in terms of both a brief label, for quick reference, and a fuller and more careful description of what it embraces. By convention, the brief label is followed by a colon (:), so as to distinguish a comparison area from a decision area, the label of which is followed by a question mark (?). The fuller description can serve an important practical purpose, as a means of checking that the same comparison area is being interpreted in a similar way by different participants; and it can of course always be modified later as understanding grows.

It is often helpful to include, within the fuller description of a comparison area, not only an indication of the *types* of effects or consequences that it covers, but also some indication of their *incidence* in terms of community sectors or interest groups, or perhaps over different time horizons. This can be especially significant where the participants see themselves as accountable to more than one 'constituency' of affected interests. Indeed, different participants in a decision process will sometimes be recognised as representing different sectors or groups. Questions of incidence and perceived equity can sometimes become quite crucial to the politics of comparing and choosing; and they can indeed emerge as major sources of uncertainty in the UV category, the management of which can become critical to the guidance of the overall decision process.

In order to keep the number of comparison areas manageable, they can if desired be formulated so as to bring together several different elements under a single more general heading. For instance, in Figure 19, the familiar heading of CAPITAL: is used to bring together expenditures on both construction works and property acquisition. In other situations, however, there might also be compensating capital receipts to consider, from the disposal of surplus land or buildings which, according to accounting convention, might be considered either within the CAPITAL: or the INCOME: comparison area.

Sometimes, too, different comparison areas can be combined. For example, it might be agreed that for working purposes the CAPITAL: and INCOME: comparison areas in Figure 19 should be combined into a broader comparison area simply called FINANCE:. These examples merely serve to demonstrate the general point that there may be much scope for *choice* in the way a set of comparison areas is formulated. Indeed, where there are several participants, it can be valuable to encourage open debate over this choice, leading to elaboration or simplification of the set of comparison areas as work proceeds and the level of shared understanding grows.

Figure 19   The concept of a comparison area

South Side
example

COMPARISON AREA	LABEL
differences in capital outlay on construction works and property acquisition :	CAPITAL :
differences in net flows of income to this authority :	INCOME :
differences in local employment opportunities :	JOBS :
differences in confidence and quality of life for South Side residents :	RESIDENTS :

Comparing

CONCEPTS

A **comparison area** is a description of any field of concern in which it is desired to compare the consequences of alternative courses of action.

Assessing consequences within comparison areas

Once a set of comparison areas has been chosen, it can be put to use as a framework for comparing alternative courses of action in the light of people's assessments of what their differing consequences might be. The idea of a **relative assessment** will be treated as another core concept in the strategic choice vocabulary; but it will often be abbreviated to the single word **assessment** so long as the context is clear. The idea of a relative assessment is intended to cover not only any consequences or implications of a direct and immediately foreseeable kind, but also any consequences or implications which may be more gradual, indirect and hard to pin down in any tangible way.

There are two important qualities to bear in mind in making a prior assessment of the consequences of some proposed future course of action, as opposed to a retrospective assessment of the consequences of some course of action already carried through. Firstly, any assessment of future consequences will always be to some degree *conjectural,* in that it will involve elements of speculation or guesswork as to what might follow *if* that course of action were to be set in train. Secondly, such an assessment will be essentially *comparative* in the sense that, whether explicitly or otherwise, it involves contrasting the consequences of pursuing that course of action with those that might follow from choosing some other course instead. This point applies even if that other course were to take a passive stance and aim to preserve the status quo – which is a common baseline for many kinds of assessment in practice.

Figure 20 presents some examples of relative assessments within each of the four comparison areas for South Side. Two different examples of relative assessments are presented here, both from within the range of nine possible decision schemes which was developed earlier (Figure 17). First, Scheme B is assessed relative to Scheme A – the difference between these two alternatives being only in the choice of option for use of the Central Site. Then, Scheme H is assessed also in relation to the same baseline of Scheme A, recognising that the comparison in this case is likely to be rather less straightforward because Schemes H and A differ in the options selected in each of the four decision areas.

It will be noticed in this example that the *forms* in which the relative assessments are presented differ from one comparison area to another. Even though the capital and income assessments are both expressed in monetary units, the capital assessments are expressed as lump sums and the income assessments as annual flows, in keeping with familiar accounting conventions.

Differences in jobs are also expressed in numerical terms, but this time expressed in non-monetary units of the net number of local jobs created. However, the assessments of the consequences for the South Side residents are expressed here purely in terms of words – illustrating a very common situation in practice where there is no accepted numerical scale to which to refer.

The example of Figure 20 also illustrates some of the different ways in which feelings of *uncertainty* can be expressed. In one case – the assessment of capital

Figure 20　The concept of a relative assessment

South Side
example

DECISION AREAS				DECISION SCHEME	COMPARISONS	
ROAD LINE?	SHOP LOC'N?	CENT'L SITE?	DIST LIFE?		COMPARISON AREA	RELATIVE ASSESSMENT

NORTH — MAIN — IND — 10YR │ scheme A

A = baseline for comparison

assessments of B relative to A:

1st comparison: B vs A

CAPITAL: about 250k * less

↓

INCOME: 10k-30k * less per year

NORTH — MAIN — HOUS — 10YR │ scheme B

JOBS: 100-200 local jobs fewer

RESIDENTS: probably more confidence

assessments of H relative to A:

2nd comparison: H vs A

CAPITAL: 200k * less to 400k * more

↓　　↓　　↓　　↓

INCOME: 40k-100k * less per year

SOUTH — GAS — OPEN — 20YR │ scheme H

JOBS: 40-160 local jobs fewer

RESIDENTS: much less confidence

[↓ indicates change of option relative to scheme A]

[* k = 1000 units of this national currency - e.g. £, $, Fr....]

Comparing

CONCEPTS

A **relative assessment** is a name for any statement about the consequences within a comparison area of pursuing one course of action instead of another.

outlay for Scheme B relative to Scheme A – a single estimate only is presented; but the word 'about' is inserted to convey the information that there is felt to be at least some uncertainty over the extent of the difference. In other places, a range of figures is presented; this conveys additional information about the degree of uncertainty experienced – which may well differ between one relative assessment and another. By moving to a more elaborate format of presentation than that in Figure 20, it would be possible to go into these feelings of uncertainty in more depth, distinguishing between different contributory factors, spelling out underlying assumptions and indicating contingencies which could have a significant effect on the levels of assessment presented. These possibilities will be discussed further in Chapter 7; for the time being, it is enough to stress that there is a wide field of choice in the level of elaboration or simplification employed in presenting relative assessments in practice.

Judging comparative advantage between alternatives

Because the set of comparison areas is designed to reflect fields of direct concern to decision-makers, any statement that one alternative differs from another within a particular comparison area will usually convey a sense of positive or negative *value* in the current decision situation; it will be seen as either good or bad, nice or nasty. For example, from the comparison of Scheme B with Scheme A in Figure 20, it will almost certainly count as an *advantage* to B that it should incur about 250 thousand monetary units less than A in capital outlay, but a *disadvantage* that it should yield less income. Again, it is likely to be considered a disadvantage to Scheme B that it should create fewer jobs, but an advantage that it should generate more confidence among the residents of South Side.

Sometimes, there may be some conflict of opinion as to whether a relative assessment should be viewed in a positive or a negative light; and often, there will be some doubt as to whether advantages in some comparison areas should be seen as outweighing disadvantages in others. Such a state of doubt appears to surround the comparison of Schemes A and B for South Side, because the overall balance of advantage across the four comparison areas is by no means clear. However, Scheme H appears to offer no advantages compared to A in any of the four comparison areas, if the same sense of positive and negative values is applied – unless perhaps further investigation of the uncertainty about the CAPITAL: assessment could reveal that H has indeed an advantage over A in this one comparison area.

Various methods of economic analysis have been developed which allow assessments in different comparison areas to be brought together by being expressed in commensurate terms. For instance, annual flows of income can be converted to capital equivalents by forms of discounted cash flow analysis which reflect market rates of return. Some economists have also developed methods for computing monetary values for other quantitative indicators, such as num-

Figure 21 The concept of an advantage comparison

South Side
example

DECISION AREAS

| ROAD LINE? | SHOP LOC'N? | CENT'L SITE? | DIST LINE? | DECISION SCHEME | COMPARISON AREA | COMPARISON RELATIVE ASSESSMENT |

NORTH — MAIN — IND — 10 YR | scheme A

comparison B vs A (as in figure 20)
↓
NORTH — MAIN — HOUS — 10 YR | scheme B

A = baseline for comparison
assessments of B relative to A:

CAPITAL: about 250k * less

INCOME: 10k-30k * less per year

JOBS: 100-200 local jobs fewer

RESIDENTS: probably more confidence

ADVANTAGE COMPARISON B vs A

[KEY: ◄───► = range of belief about comparative advantage. ◇ = best guess]

Comparing

CONCEPTS

An **advantage comparison** is a name for any statement of belief about the balance of advantage between alternatives in one or more comparison areas.

bers of jobs created. But such conversions can have the effect of suppressing underlying uncertainties of value judgement which, from a strategic choice perspective, it may be important to expose to debate.

It is more in keeping with the philosophy of strategic choice to turn to an openly judgemental scale of comparison, in which uncertainties of value judgement can be exposed alongside any other uncertainties that have arisen in assessing the nature or magnitude of the consequences in the various comparison areas. Such an approach is illustrated in Figure 21, which introduces a non-numerical scale of **advantage comparison** as a basis for translating relative assessments within diverse comparison areas into a common framework. The adjectives 'negligible', 'marginal', 'significant', 'considerable' and 'extreme' are intended to represent an ascending scale of advantage to the decision-makers in either direction. However, the way in which these words should be interpreted – and indeed the judgement as to what the relative widths of the various bands of the scale should be – can be left open to the discretion of the users in the particular organisational and political context in which they are working.

For example, Figure 21 interprets the assessment that Scheme B will involve 'about' 250 thousand monetary units less capital outlay than Scheme A as representing somewhere between a significant and a considerable advantage to B in relation to the decision situation currently faced in South Side. In another context, the judgement made might be quite different: for example a central government setting a national budget might well regard such a difference as negligible, while a small business, or an individual managing a family budget, would probably consider it extreme. In each row of Figure 21, the convention is adopted of representing the range of uncertainty over where the advantage lies by a pair of arrowheads, with the current 'best guess' marked in between – frequently, but not necessarily, positioned at the mid-point of the range. As the example suggests, this range of uncertainty can vary considerably from one comparison area to another.

It is important to recognise that the range is intended to embrace uncertainties encountered both in assessing alternatives *within* each separate comparison area and also in judging how these assessments should be transferred to the common advantage comparison scale. For instance, in the South Side case, there may be considerable uncertainty not only over how large the difference in local jobs created might be, but also over how much weight should be attached to any such difference in policy terms. Turning to the impact on South Side residents, uncertainty arises partly because there is no clear numerical yardstick for assessment of different levels of confidence in the future of the area, and partly because some decision-makers may place a higher policy value on residents' confidence than others.

The value of a common judgemental scale, however crude, is that it provides a framework within which assessments in different comparison areas can be balanced and merged. For example, taking the four 'best guess' points in Figure 21, it can be argued that a considerable advantage to Scheme B in terms of capital should outweigh a (merely) significant advantage to A in terms of income: and that the advantage of B to local residents should roughly balance out the advantage to A in terms of jobs, leaving a slight overall advantage to B when all four comparison areas are viewed together.

However, this overall balance of advantage can become more difficult to judge when notice is taken of the uncertainties that surround the various placings on the advantage comparison scale. In the illustration presented in Figure 21, the combined effect of these uncertainties is to make it by no means clear to which alternative the overall balance of advantage for the decision-makers will lie. Some approaches to the more careful analysis of how such uncertainties affect the balance of advantage will be discussed in Chapter 7. However, the most important point about the particular format of advantage comparison illustrated here is that it allows many different sources of uncertainty to be brought together in a common perspective: a perspective which is designed to reflect the political realities of the situation within which the alternatives in question have to be compared. This kind of advantage comparison between specific alternatives will therefore form an important point of reference when it comes to considering methods of working in the choosing mode.

Restricting the focus for comparisons among decision schemes

Where there are only a few alternative courses of action to consider, it may not be difficult to compare each with every other, using the same kind of methodical approach to pairwise comparison which was illustrated in Figures 20 and 21. This is usually feasible enough when comparing a set of three or four options within a single decision area, or when the focus of comparison is limited to only a few feasible decision schemes.

However, this pairwise approach to comparison can become much more time consuming where there are many possible combinations of options available. For example, there are 36 possible pair comparisons that might be made among the nine decision schemes for South Side (Figure 17), because each of the nine can be compared with each of the eight others – the resulting number of comparisons being reduced from 72 to 36 when it is remembered that pairwise comparison is a two-way process. If the number of possible schemes was doubled to 18, the number of possible comparisons would increase more than fourfold, to 153. In general, the longer a list of schemes grows, the more essential it becomes to choose some more manageable set of schemes within the list – in everyday terms, a shortlist – before attempting to compare alternatives more thoroughly in a pairwise manner. The term **working shortlist** will be added to the basic strategic choice vocabulary to describe any shortlist formed for such a purpose. In effect, it serves the same kind of simplifying purpose when people are working towards decisions as does the idea of problem focus when they are working into complex problems.

One way in which a long list of decision schemes can be reduced is to focus only on those which come within acceptable limits in terms of one or more chosen dimensions of evaluation which the decision-makers see as of particular importance. So it might be decided to place a constraint on the maximum level of capital cost – if capital is regarded as a scarce resource – or the minimum level of income to be generated by a scheme. Or it might be agreed, in the South Side case, to exclude any schemes involving a net loss rather than a gain of local job opportunities compared to the status quo.

Introducing such a constraint normally means resorting to a simplified scale of assessment, on which each scheme can be represented by a single point, with all information about uncertainty set aside for this purpose. This then allows the set of schemes to be rearranged, or ranked, in an unambiguous order of preference so far as that particular scale is concerned, allowing all schemes above or below the agreed threshold to be set aside. Often the chosen scale will be a numerical one, but this is not essential: for instance, a non-numerical scale with seven points labelled 'very high', 'high', 'fairly high', 'medium', fairly low', 'low' and 'very low' provides quite an acceptable scale for ranking purposes, because it is quite clear which assessment comes before which other in the sequence.

A simplified scale for purposes of ranking or shortlisting can be defined either within a single comparison area, or to span more than one comparison area where there is some common scale through which they can be linked. For example, a monetary scale can be used to span both capital and recurrent costs, provided there is some agreed convention for converting running costs into capital equivalents or vice versa. In general, however, the use of any such composite scale as a shortlisting device can mean a considerable sacrifice of information in the interests of simplification. Indeed, any approach to shortlisting can mean sacrificing much information about *uncertainty* which could be important later on. For instance, potentially significant information about South Side was presented earlier (Figure 20) through the use of qualifying words such as 'probably' and through using lower and upper limits in place of single-point estimates. Any shortlisting process can also mean loss of much information about the *multi-dimensional* nature of consequences both within and between the chosen comparison areas. Such losses of information can be quite justifiable as a means of focussing the process of comparison where there are many schemes to consider; but only so long as the possibility is not forgotten of re-introducing that information at a later stage in the decision process.

The use of simplified scales in forming a working shortlist is illustrated in Figure 22. This example introduces two contrasting scales for the purpose of choosing a more limited focus for comparison within the set of nine schemes already generated for South Side.

In this example, the scale of expected capital cost is expressed in standard monetary units, defined as in Figure 20. The assessment for each of the nine schemes has here been built up by a straightforward addition of capital estimates for each option, each measured against the same baseline which supposes there to be no capital investment at all. An alternative approach would, of course, have been to make a separate estimate for each of the nine schemes seen

Figure 22 The concept of a working shortlist

South Side
example

SCALE ASSESSMENTS
with preference rankings

DECISION AREAS				DECISION SCHEME	SCALE OF EXPECTED CAPITAL OUTLAY k = 1000 units of this currency	SCALE OF RESIDENTS' CONFIDENCE R↔RRRRR lowest highest
ROAD LINE?	SHOP LOC'N?	CENT'L SITE?	DIST LIFE?			

expected capital outlay shown against each option

NORTH 1400k

MAIN +100k — IND +450k — 10 YR +0 — Scheme A — 1950k 2ⁿᵈ= — RRR 4ᵗʰ=
MAIN +100k — HOUS +200k — 10 YR +0 — scheme B — 1700k 1ˢᵗ — RRRR 2ⁿᵈ=

KING +400k — HOUS +200k — 10YR +0 — scheme C — 2000k 4ᴿ= — RRR 4ᴿ=
KING +400k — HOUS +200k — 20YR +100k — scheme D — 2100k 7ᵗʰ= — RRRR 2ⁿᵈ=
KING +400k — HOUS +200k — 40YR +150k — scheme E — 2150k 9ᵗʰ — RRRRR 1ˢᵗ

OPEN +50k — 20YR +100k — scheme F — 1950k 2ⁿᵈ= — RR 7ᵗʰ
OPEN +50k — 40YR +150k — scheme G — 2000k 4ᴿ= — RRR 4ᴿ=

SOUTH — GAS — OPEN 1350k +550k +50k — 20YR +100k — scheme H — 2050k 6ᴿ — R 8ᴿ=
SOUTH — GAS — OPEN — 40YR +150k — scheme I — 2100k 7ᵗʰ= — R 8ᴿ.

schemes selected for inclusion in working shortlist on basis of rankings UNDERLINED

Comparing

CONCEPTS

A **working shortlist** is any subset of a set of decision schemes in which it is intended to compare alternatives more closely.

as a composite entity. Indeed, this might have been judged preferable if there were believed to be significant capital savings or costs associated with particular *combinations* of options from different decision areas.

The second scale, relating to confidence among local residents, is developed in a different way. The lowest score is awarded to the scheme or schemes judged to have the most negative effect on residents' confidence – in this case Schemes H and I – while the highest score is awarded to the scheme or schemes judged to have the most positive effect – in this case Scheme E. Then intermediate numbers of points are awarded to each of the other possible schemes. Of course, these scores too could have been built up cumulatively by options, in the same way as the numerical scale of capital cost – but it has been supposed here that the scoring of each scheme viewed as a whole offers a more realistic alternative in the particular circumstances of South Side.

Figure 22 shows not only the scores of the nine schemes on each of the two scales, but also the two sets of *rankings* obtained in this way, with tied rankings in some cases. Inspecting this information, it appears that Scheme B shows particular promise, having a high ranking in terms of both indices. In choosing a working shortlist for closer comparison, other apparently promising schemes might also be included, such as Scheme A and Scheme E – which is the most promising in terms of residents' confidence, even if the least promising in terms of capital outlay. Another candidate could be Scheme C, which is moderately well placed in both respects. But a fuller comparison of B with A, C or E might throw up disadvantages in other comparison areas, which might suggest that the focus of comparison should be shifted yet again. Furthermore, some schemes which are apparently poorly placed according to the scales of Figure 22 might well be brought back into consideration later because of types of advantage excluded from the shortlisting process at this stage.

Exploring areas of uncertainty

All the time comparisons of alternatives are being made, the participants will usually also be subject to practical pressures, political and administrative, to move in the direction of decisions: or, in terms of the general process model (Figure 8), to shift upwards from the comparing into the choosing mode. At such times, attention will shift from the comparison of alternatives under uncertainty to the conscious management of that uncertainty from a decision-making perspective.

So it is at this point that the concept of an **uncertainty area** will be introduced. This will be regarded as another core concept in the strategic choice vocabulary; similar, in some respects, to the concepts of decision area and comparison area as already introduced. All three concepts can be seen as expressing *areas of concern* to the participants in a planning process, and as offering wide scope for discretion and judgement in the way they are formulated. Indeed, circumstances often arise where what was at first expressed as an area of con-

Figure 23　The concept of an uncertainty area

South Side
example

UNCERTAINTY AREA	LABEL	TYPE	
? attractiveness of central site to employment-intensive industries	?SITEJOBS	UE	identified as major influences on advantage comparison of A and B in relation to JOBS: comparison area
? policy value to us of job creation	?VALJOB	UV	
? decision on future use of steelworks site	?STEELSITE	UR	identified as major influences on advantage comparison of A and B in relation to RESIDENTS: comparison area
? policy value to us of meeting residents concerns	?VALRES	UV	
? decision on density of new housing developments	?HOUDENS	UR	
? future trends in regional housing market	?HOUMKT	UE	identified as influencing comparison of A and B in relation to INCOME:
? policy decision on level of infrastructure provision on new industrial sites	?INDINFR	UR	identified as influencing comparison of A and B in relation to both INCOME: and CAPITAL:

Choosing

CONCEPTS

An uncertainty area is a description of any source of uncertainty which is causing difficulty in the consideration of a decision problem.

cern of one type may with advantage be reformulated in terms of any one of the other types.

An uncertainty area can be formulated at any moment in a process of strategic choice where doubts arise over the choice of *assumptions* on which the designing or comparing of alternatives should proceed. Such assumptions can be of many kinds, but they can be grouped broadly according to the three categories of uncertainty that were introduced in general terms in Chapter 1: UE for Uncertainties about the working Environment; UV for Uncertainties about guiding Values; and UR for Uncertainties about Related decisions (Figure 3).

In the UE direction, participants in a process of strategic choice may experience personal doubts, or may differ among themselves, as to the assumptions they should make about external circumstances or trends. In the UV direction, they may experience doubts or disagreements as to the values that should influence them, especially when they are seeking to compare alternatives across different comparison areas which reflect the concerns of diverse interest groups. In the UR direction, they may have difficulties agreeing what assumptions to make about the choices that are expected to be made in future in other decision areas outside the current scope of the problem on which they are working: decision areas over which they might conceivably have some influence, even if that influence may be quite limited or indirect.

In Figure 23, the concept of the uncertainty area is illustrated through seven examples which reflect various doubts and disagreements seen as relevant by members of the South Side Working Party, at a moment when they are trying to judge the balance of advantage between the two decision schemes labelled A and B. This list of uncertainty areas might be part of a considerably longer list built up at successive stages of the process. Here, however, those listed are all seen as having *relevance* to the particular task of judging whether the overall balance of advantage lies to A or B. This is a judgement that can be approached by focussing on the information about uncertainty that was presented in the advantage comparison analysis of Figure 21 – though that analysis on its own gives no information about what the main *sources* of uncertainty are.

As in the listing of decision areas, and indeed also of comparison areas, the convention is here adopted of giving each uncertainty area both a fuller description and a briefer label for quick reference. The convention of placing the question mark before rather than after the label is intended merely as a means of distinguishing uncertainty areas from decision areas. Indeed, it allows either kind of area to be quickly transformed into the other whenever it seems sensible to do so.

The list in Figure 23 begins by identifying five uncertainty areas which are seen as between them creating difficulty in judging the balance of advantage between Schemes A and B in the JOBS: and RESIDENTS: comparison areas. These two comparison areas are examined first because they appear (Figure 21) to hold the widest range of doubt when all the four assessments are translated into terms of the advantage comparison scale.

Looking first at the JOBS: assessment, the range of 100 to 200 local jobs fewer for Scheme B relative to Scheme A may reflect in the main a feeling of uncertainty about the attractiveness of the Central Site to employment–intensive industries – which can be expressed as an uncertainty area of type UE. However, once the attempt is made to translate this assessment into terms of comparative advantage, a substantial degree of doubt may also arise as to what weight the participants should give to the creation of new jobs in this locality, relative to other consequences of the choice before them; so this is a doubt that can be expressed as an uncertainty area of type UV.

Turning to the RESIDENTS: comparison, Figure 23 again shows a substantial area of uncertainty of type UV, concerned with the policy value that the municipality should attach to meeting the concerns of local residents. However, the main uncertainties in assessing the actual impact on local residents of choosing Scheme B rather than A can in this case be seen as of type UR rather than UE, because they are to do with two related areas of decision outside the current problem focus. One of these is concerned with the future use of a nearby site, which is expected to be vacated soon by a major steel making corporation. Some residents of South Side have been campaigning for redevelopment of this site for light industry rather than other purposes; if this case is conceded, it is thought their concern about the use of the Central Site will be less acute than if the site is put to any alternative use. The other uncertainty area relates to the recommendations of the municipality's own housing planning team over density of any future housing development on the Central Site itself: if the density is high enough and the cost low enough to make homes on this site available to local people, then it is judged that residents' confidence in the future of their community will be increased.

Finally, the list of Figure 23 includes two further uncertainty areas which impinge on the INCOME: and CAPITAL: assessments – in one case impinging on them both. However, a glance back to Figure 21 suggests that these uncertainty areas will not be so critical to the overall comparison of Schemes A and B as those affecting the JOBS: and RESIDENTS: assessments. So no attempt need be made at this stage to look for further uncertainty areas which affect these two financial dimensions of the overall evaluation frame.

Identifying exploratory options

Once a list of uncertainty areas has been developed, the question arises of what, if anything, should be done about them. For each uncertainty area that seems to be relevant to a particular comparison of alternatives, there is always the possibility of *accepting* the current level of uncertainty over what assumptions to adopt, and looking for ways in which it can be accommodated. However, there may also be a possibility of initiating some kind of *exploratory action* which offers a hope that current feelings of uncertainty can be significantly *reduced* before decisions have to be made.

Any course of action designed to alter the current state of doubt within an

uncertainty area can be called an **exploratory option**. The idea of an exploratory option is of central significance to the work of the choosing mode, so it
will be considered as another core concept in the strategic choice vocabulary. In
effect, the identification of any exploratory options that could be adopted in
response to a particular uncertainty area can be seen as extending the problem
formulation by introducing an additional decision area; a decision area concerned with whether or not any investment should be made in the reduction of
current levels of doubt within the uncertainty area concerned.

This point is illustrated in Figure 24, which gives examples of exploratory
options relating to each of the first three uncertainty areas from the list in Figure 23 – supposing these to be judged the most important at the present moment in the decision process. In each case, one possible exploratory option is
identified and is compared with the 'null option' of taking no exploratory action in relation to the uncertainty area in question. The nature of any exploratory action to be considered will tend to vary with the type of uncertainty area
addressed. As originally suggested (Figure 3), uncertainty areas of type UE will
suggest possibilities for exploration in the form of research, surveys, analytical
work or forecasting exercises. Uncertainty areas of type UV will suggest possibilities for exploration in the form of policy soundings or exercises designed to
clarify objectives or goals; while uncertainty areas of type UR will suggest possibilities for exploration in the form of liaison, negotiation, joint planning or
co-ordinating initiatives to deal with relationships between the decisions currently in view and others relating to different agendas and decision-making
powers.

Sometimes, it is not initially clear which of the categories UE, UV or UR
describes a particular uncertainty area best. The step of considering possible
exploratory options may itself help to make this classification clearer. However,
there may be cases where two or more quite different kinds of exploratory options seem to be available. This may sometimes lead to the possibility of splitting the uncertainty area into two or more separate elements, which will be
discussed further in Chapter 8.

In assessing the consequences that might flow from pursuing any exploratory option, there are in general three dimensions of evaluation which will be
of importance to the decision-makers. Firstly, they will be concerned with assessing any changes in the level of *confidence* with which decisions can be made,
arising from a reduction in the state of uncertainty surrounding key assumptions. Secondly, they will be concerned with assessing any *resources* which may
be used up in pursuing that exploratory option; such an assessment might cover
not only such tangible resources as money and scarce skills, but also less tangible resources such as personal energy and goodwill, which may also be in short
supply. Lastly, they will be concerned with questions of the *delay* involved in
pursuing any exploratory option; this may be a critical consideration where
there are pressures for early action to be taken into account.

These three dimensions of evaluation can be viewed as different kinds of
comparison area within which relative assessments of the impacts of different

Figure 24 The concept of an exploratory option

South Side
example

UNCERTAINTY AREA	EXPLORATORY OPTION	COMPARISON OF EXPLORATORY OPTIONS	
		COMPARISON AREA	RELATIVE *ASSESSMENT
? SITE JOBS (UE)	commission consultants to do market survey	CONFIDENCE:	slightly more confidence in advantage comparison A:B
		RESOURCES:	estimated fee 20k
		DELAY:	allow 3 months from commissioning to reporting
? VAL JOB (UV)	informal soundings with leading members of policy group	CONFIDENCE:	much more confidence in advantage comparison A:B
		RESOURCES:	some demands on time of busy policy-makers
		DELAY:	allow 1-2 weeks to contact and discuss
? STEELSITE (UR)	liaison with joint steelworks site planning team	CONFIDENCE:	more confidence in advantage comparison A:B
		RESOURCES:	perhaps ½ day spent in meeting; also preparation time
		DELAY:	allow 1 month

* relative to option of taking no exploratory action i.e. null option

Choosing

CONCEPTS

An **exploratory option** is any course of action conceived as a means of reducing current feelings of uncertainty within some uncertainty area.

exploratory options can be made – the aim being to judge whether or not to invest any exploratory effort towards the reduction of doubts within any of the uncertainty areas currently in view. For example, the information presented in Figure 24 suggests that the proposed informal soundings among policy-makers, directed towards the UV-type uncertainty area ?VALJOB, could yield better returns in terms of confidence, for a lesser cost, than the commissioning of a market survey directed towards the UE-type uncertainty area ?SITEJOBS – and furthermore that they could do so with less serious consequences in terms of delay to the decision-making process.

Choices in the timing of decisions

Because exploratory actions invariably take at least some time to carry through – ranging perhaps from a few minutes in the case of a quick telephone call, to several years in the case of a major research study – the consideration of how to manage uncertainty also means confronting difficult choices about the *timing* of commitments within a continuous planning process. For there is little point in taking actions to improve the confidence with which decisions can be made unless those decisions are deferred until the outcomes of those explorations are known.

However, if the problem involves consideration of choices in several interrelated decision areas, it does not necessarily follow that commitments to decisive action must be deferred in *all* those decision areas until any agreed exploratory actions have been followed through. There may be some decision areas in which the participants' preferred course of action will be little affected, if at all, by the outcomes of these explorations; and, furthermore, there may be some decision areas in which the external pressures for early commitment are much more intense than in others.

So, in practice, a choice arises in relation to each decision area within the current problem focus, not merely as to which option should be pursued, but also as to whether commitment in that decision area should be made now, or should be deferred until some later time. This means that the *extent of commitment* within the present problem focus has itself become a matter of choice for the participants. So at this point they must strike a balance between a more exploratory and a more decisive approach to progress through time (Figure 2). This is a type of judgement which is often confronted in practice by decision-makers, even though it has as yet received comparatively little attention in the development of planning methods.

As a means of dealing with this element of choice in the timing of decisions, the core concept of an **action scheme** will now be introduced.[1] This term will be used to describe any course of proposed action in which commitment to a specific option is indicated in one or more of a set of decision areas, while commit-

1   The term 'action set' was used in the same sense in earlier writings on strategic choice.

Figure 25 The concept of an action scheme

South Side
example

set of possible ACTION SCHEMES within more urgent decision areas		choices remaining open in other decision areas		DEZISION SCHEME	COMPARISON OF FLEXIBILITY for each action scheme	
		DECISION AREAS			Total count of available decision schemes	ROBUSTNESS INDEX = count of schemes with residents' confidence score at least RRR *
ROAD LINE?	DIST LIFE?	SHOP LOC'N?	CENT'L SITE?			

NORTH - 10YR I	MAIN — { IND scheme A HOUS scheme B } KING — HOUS scheme C	[3] 3
NORTH - 20YR II	— KING — { HOUS scheme D OPEN scheme F }	[2] 1
NORTH - 40YR III	— KING — { HOUS scheme E OPEN scheme G }	[2] 2
SOUTH - 20YR IV	— GAS — OPEN scheme H	[1] 0
SOUTH - 40YR V	— GAS — OPEN scheme I	[1] 0

* see Figure 22

Choosing

CONCEPTS

An **action scheme** is a course of action involving commitments within only some of the more urgent decision areas within a problem focus.

ment in others is explicitly deferred until later in the process. An illustration of the way in which this concept can be applied to the South Side problem situation appears in Figure 25.

In this illustration, five possible action schemes for South Side are compared. Each is based on a different combination of options in the ROAD LINE? and DIST LIFE? decision areas – it being supposed that these are the areas of choice in which pressure for commitment is currently most intense. The patterns of subsequent choice associated with each action scheme are displayed by a straightforward rearrangement of the branching sequence through which the original set of nine decision schemes was developed. So the same set of nine decision schemes appears as in the original array (Figure 17), but this time in a slightly modified order because the DIST LIFE? decision area has been brought further forward.

Of the five action schemes, there are two which, in effect, leave no flexibility of future choice at all, because of the structure of option bars. The choice of either of these action schemes implies commitment in each of the remaining three decision areas as well; however, each of the other three action schemes leaves open a future choice of between two and three of the original nine decision schemes.

This illustrates the important general point that action schemes which embody the same level of intended commitment in the more pressing decision areas can differ from each other in terms of the *flexibility* of future choice which is retained. Such flexibility may be of considerable practical value to the participants, especially where they are beset with doubts about what course of action will be the most advantageous in the longer term. One simple, yet practical, means of comparing action schemes for flexibility involves the use of what is called a *robustness* index; a 'robust' action being seen as one which is preferable to others in that it leaves open a wider range of acceptable paths for the future. The underlying assumption is that the more paths left open which meet some specified level of acceptability, as viewed under current circumstances, the better equipped the decision makers will be to respond to unexpected circumstances should they arise in future.

This idea of robustness is not a difficult one in its essentials but its interpretation in practice can sometimes call for a considerable degree of care. This is firstly because the threshold of acceptability may not be easy to define and, secondly, because – in a strategic choice problem formulation – flexibility in some decision areas may be valued more highly than flexibility in others. These points can be illustrated with reference to Figure 25, where the five action schemes are compared in terms of two different indices of flexibility. The first is based on a straightforward count of all schemes still left open, while the second is based on a count of only those schemes which pass above a particular threshold of acceptability in terms of residents' confidence (Figure 22). Both these indices assume that flexibility in the SHOP LOC'N? and CENT'L SITE? decision areas are valued equally highly; an assumption which could, however, be modified by giving them different weightings if that was felt to be more realistic.

Developing a commitment package

To conclude this discussion of work within the choosing mode, a final core concept will be introduced, bringing together the various dimensions of the choices people face in considering how to move forward at any moment in a continuous planning process. This is the concept of the **commitment package** – conceived as a balanced assemblage of proposed steps forward which may embrace a set of proposed immediate actions; a set of explorations to deal with important areas of uncertainty; and a set of understandings about the ways in which any deferred choices should be addressed. Any commitment package will, therefore, contain a considered set of proposals as to how to move progressively forward towards commitment through time: a set of proposals which can be compared against other alternative sets of proposals and, if agreed, can be adopted as a basis for incremental progress in a continuous planning process.

Figure 26 presents an example of one possible commitment package that might be considered as a basis for making progress in the South Side problem situation. It takes into account not only the analysis so far presented in this chapter, but also the political realities of the situation in which the South Side Working Party is currently operating. The basic format that is used here – some variations and extensions of which will be discussed in Chapter 8 – involves dividing the overall tableau into rows corresponding to the various decision areas, and also into columns corresponding to the different types of proposal that could be included in relation to each.

In the format of Figure 26, the heading of **Immediate Decisions** is used to register not only the set of substantive *actions* to which commitment is now proposed – in other words, the proposed action scheme – but also any *explorations* which it is proposed should now be set in train to create an improved basis for future choice. Such proposals for exploration reflect a deliberate choice of exploratory options to deal with some but not necessarily all of the more important uncertainty areas which have been identified. So the set of immediate decisions is in effect conceived as an incremental step forward, not just in relation to the substantive decision problem, but also in relation to the associated problem of how to manage uncertainty through time.

Under the second main heading of **Future Decision Space**, the format of Figure 26 allows not only for an indication of which options in which decision areas are to remain open, but also for any further proposals relating to the arrangements by which future decisions should be made. In relation to these *deferred choices,* proposals may be made as to the future time horizons at which decisions should be made – proposals which may reflect not only the time scales involved in undertaking relevant exploratory actions but also any procedural considerations arising from the particular administrative and political context in which the participants are working. In South Side, for example, the proposed informal soundings and liaison activities, designed to cope with uncertainty in deciding a use for the Central Site, might be expected to take no more than a month; but it might be two months before the next scheduled meeting of the decision-making group at which a formal decision on this matter could be taken.

The practicalities of the organisational context in which decisions are to be taken can also play an important part in the second sub-division of future decision space, concerned with what is here called *contingency planning*. This heading recognises that it will often be important to prepare in some way for particular contingencies of a foreseeable kind, which could have a crucial effect on future decisions – including possibilities that particular assumptions which seem to offer a firm basis for proceeding in present circumstances might be overturned by subsequent events.

In considering what proposals to enter in the last two columns, it may become necessary to probe certain basic assumptions relating to the terms in which decision areas were formulated for purposes of analysis. For example, in South Side it could be important to realise that even a firm commitment now to the northern road line may be more in the nature of a *recommendation* to an autonomous highway authority than a matter to be decided on the authority of the municipality of Dockport alone; so some preparation might be advisable for the contingency of that recommendation being turned down. Also, it might be important to recognise that the option of declaring a 10-year commitment to the continued life of South Side as a residential community does not imply an irrevocable commitment to the demise of that community ten years hence; there might be the possibility of an extension in that life at some later time, given certain conditions which might be anticipated now, even if only in general terms.

It will be noticed that the example of an action scheme incorporated in Figure 26 differs from the examples compared earlier (Figure 25) in that it proposes current commitment in three rather than two decision areas. The scope for future choice within the problem focus is in this case reduced to the two Schemes A and B; so the proposals for exploratory action in this commitment package are focussed on the comparison of these two schemes, drawing on the earlier analysis of uncertainty areas and exploratory options (Figures 23 and 24).

A final point illustrated by Figure 26 is that the design of a commitment package offers a point at which aspects of a decision problem that were deliberately omitted from a problem focus or a working shortlist can be brought back into view. In the South Side case, it will be noticed that the West Street decision area has now resurfaced, even though it had been deliberately left out of the problem focus chosen for most of the designing and comparing work. Despite the judgement that this decision area can be treated in an isolated way, the same judgements about immediate or deferred choice arise in this case; and the same general ideas about management of uncertainty apply.

Choosing incrementally under uncertainty

Summarising at this point, this chapter has followed the same principles as Chapter 2 in presenting a set of core concepts and methods – this time designed

Figure 26 The concept of a commitment package

COMMITMENT PACKAGE

DECISION AREAS	IMMEDIATE DECISIONS		FUTURE DECISION SPACE	
	ACTIONS	EXPLORATIONS	DEFERRED CHOICES	CONTINGENCY PLANNING
ROAD LINE?	NORTH	—	—	IF recommendations not accepted, THEN appeal
DISTRICT LIFE?	10 YEARS	—	—	IF a major developer appears, THEN be ready to extend life
SHOP LOCATION?	MAIN STREET	—	—	—
CENTRAL SITE?	—	informal soundings with leading members of policy group AND liaison with joint steelworks site planning team	in 2 months: decide use of central site [industry OR housing]	—
WEST STREET?	—	investigate designs and costs for possible improvement scheme	in 6 months: decide whether to improve West Street [yes OR no]	—

to help when working in the comparing and choosing modes. As before, the aim has been to introduce these concepts and methods at as simple a level as possible. So the chapter began by introducing some core concepts about comparing alternatives, starting with the concept of the comparison area and then introducing those of the relative assessment, the advantage comparison and the working shortlist, before turning to other concepts to assist work in the choosing mode. These later concepts were those of the uncertainty area, the exploratory option, the action scheme and the commitment package, the last of these offering a general framework within which to build commitments incrementally through time.

As may already be appreciated, these ideas cannot always be applied in practice in such a straightforward way as in the South Side case example as presented here. But the difficulties encountered in practice lie not so much in the concepts themselves as in the realities of the situations to which they are applied; and these difficulties remain to be addressed whatever methods of working it may be decided to apply.

In principle, there is nothing in the concepts introduced here which should make them incompatible with more formalised methods of technical, economic or environmental evaluation of the kind sometimes employed on problems which are seen as of enough importance to justify the investment involved. The key point emerging from the strategic choice philosophy is that there are always *choices* open to participants in the way in which the processes of comparing and choosing are to be addressed. Referring to the five dimensions of balance that were presented in Figure 2, choices of scope arise in agreeing the range of comparison areas to be included; choices in the treatment of complexity arise in judging how much elaboration or simplification there should be in the assessment of consequences; choices in the treatment of uncertainty arise in judging how far to invest in exploratory actions; and choices in the treatment of progress arise in the design of a commitment package. Choices in the treatment of conflict arise too, in deciding how far people should work on these issues in an interactive, as opposed to a reactive, way; and this raises issues which will be discussed further in Chapter 4.

It is important to emphasise that these various balances need not remain unchanging through time within a continuously evolving process of strategic choice. It is found in practice that this means approaching the work of the comparing and choosing modes in a spirit of *dynamic comparison,* within which attention is continually fluctuating between comparison of many alternatives at quite a rough and ready level, taking little explicit account of uncertainty, and deeper comparison of a selected few alternatives within which issues of managing uncertainty can be more consciously addressed. The broader level of comparison leads to restricted shortlists of alternatives to be examined more closely at the deeper level: while the deeper level in turn affords opportunities to examine critically the simplifying assumptions introduced in any such shortlisting process.

In Chapters 7 and 8, the skills appropriate to management of such a process

Figure 27   South Side: Some considerations of scale

administrative boundary

MUNICIPALITY

OF

DOCKPORT

Total
population
230,000

WEST STREET
HOUSING AREA
160 dwellings
c. 500 residents.

MAIN STREET SHOPPING AREA
17 existing traders within area
identified in Figure 18 as a
possible future shopping centre *

MAIN BLOCK OF
OLDER HOUSING STREETS
800 dwellings
c. 2800 residents

NEWER
HOUSING
ESTATE
650 dwellings
c. 2400
residents

SOUTH SIDE NEIGHBOURHOOD AREA
- about 7,400 residents and 28 traders in all

EASTWELL NEIGHBOURHOOD AREA
about 18,500 residents and 70 traders in all

* profitability of several South Side
traders known to be in decline

of dynamic comparison, and the conscious management of uncertainty within that process, will be examined more closely in the light of working experience in a range of different contexts. In particular, the concept of the commitment package will be developed more fully, with reference to organisational contexts where the participants cannot always be considered as a cohesive team, and the politics of incremental action can therefore become subtle and complex.

For simplicity of presentation in this chapter, the participants in a process of strategic choice have been assumed to share a common framework of account-ability and a common view of the task they face. Yet the more difficult and far-reaching become the problems to be addressed, the wider and more diffuse the interests on which they are likely to impinge; and the more unrealistic it may become to think of those involved in the process as having the same level of internal cohesion as has been assumed in the case of the South Side Working Party. Therefore, the more it is to be expected that the choices to be made about the treatment of conflict will involve skilled judgements as to how the politics of organisational and inter-organisational relationships should be addressed.

Some exercises

This chapter – like Chapter 2 – will conclude with a few simple exercises based on variations of the South Side story. These are designed to help the reader begin to develop a working familiarity with the basic concepts and methods introduced here, so most of the questions are of a quite specific and sharply-focussed form. However, some of them do call for elements of inven-tiveness as well as interpretation, in that the information about South Side pre-sented in the text and the diagrams will not always be enough to give the re-quired answer. This merely means that the reader will be faced with some real-istic problems of managing uncertainty in addressing even some of the simpler of the exercises which appear below.

1. Working solely on the information presented in Figure 19, which of the four comparison areas might be broken down into more narrow comparison areas covering different sub-categories of consequences within the general headings as defined?
2. Working from information in Figure 20, what set of relative assessments could you make for Scheme H if you used Scheme B rather than Scheme A as a baseline? (Where you are not sure how to express this assessment in any comparison area, try to find some way of expressing the uncertainty you feel.)
3. Suppose that the relative assessments for income and jobs were at the same levels as shown in Figure 20, but in favour of Scheme B rather than A. Could there then be any grounds for hesitation in expressing an overall preference between A and B? If so, what would these grounds be?
4. Turning from Figure 20 to Figure 21, could the value judgements implied in

converting the four relative assessments to a common advantage comparison scale lead you to modify your response to Question 3?

5. Does the advantage comparison of Figure 21 suggest that either scheme is likely to be preferable to the other in terms of a strictly financial evaluation covering both capital and income assessments?

6. Suppose in Figure 22 that the expected capital cost index were + 200k rather than + 400k for the King Street shop location, and 1200k rather than 1350k for the south road line. How might this modify your choice of working shortlist?

7. Can you infer anything from Figure 22 about the way in which residents' confidence is expected to be influenced by choice of the location for the shopping centre?

8. Would you judge that any of the three exploratory options compared in Figure 24 has a clear advantage over any one of the others as a response to the difficulty of judging comparative advantage between Schemes B and A? If so, on what assumptions does your judgement depend?

9. In Figure 25, suppose the most urgent decision areas are now DIST LIFE? and CENT'L SITE?. Which combination of options in these two decision areas leaves open the widest range of choice of schemes, first in total and secondly when the constraint of at least RRR on the residents' confidence index is applied?

10. Can you modify the commitment package of Figure 26 to reflect the proposal that choice should be left open in the SHOP LOC'N? as well as the CENT'L SITE? decision areas, as in the first action scheme listed in Figure 25? Referring if you wish to the sketch map of Figure 18, can you make a guess as to the sorts of explorations that might be recommended to prepare for this deferred decision?

11. In Figure 27, some further information is introduced about the numbers of people, dwellings and traders affected by decisions on the South Side problem. In what ways might this extra information help you in answering any of the questions posed above? What further types of information might you look for if you were a member of the South Side Working Party, assuming time is short and pressures of decision are intense?

Answers to these questions will be found at the end of the book.

4 Orientations

Building on the foundations

Taken together, the first three chapters present a set of foundations for the approach to planning under pressure which has become known as the strategic choice approach. Chapter 1 presented a view of the realities that people face when attempting to choose strategically under the manifold pressures of organisational life. It was argued that the key to a realistic approach lay in the idea of conscious management of uncertainty through time; an idea which was seen as posing a fundamental challenge to the familiar, if sometimes implicit, norms of linearity, objectivity, certainty and comprehensiveness which have traditionally been valued in the design of formal management and planning systems. In Chapters 2 and 3, this approach was extended by introducing a set of core concepts which could be seen as laying foundations for a *technology* of strategic choice, with reference to a view of *process* in which four complementary modes of working – shaping, designing, comparing and choosing – were seen as interrelated in a dynamic way.

The aim of this chapter will be to pause and take stock of what has been covered so far. It will do this within a general framework for reviewing alternative approaches to decision-making and planning, in which the considerations of *organisation* and of *product* are given due weight alongside those of *technology* and *process* which were the main focus of concern in the introductory chapters. This will provide a broad base from which more pragmatic advice on the use of the strategic choice approach will be developed in Chapters 5 to 9. So, in essence, this chapter offers a philosophical bridge between the three introductory chapters and the five that follow.

Review of the core concepts

Before addressing this main task, it will be useful briefly to take an overall view of the set of sixteen core concepts which have been introduced in the last two chapters. Figure 28 brings these concepts together and shows how they relate to the four complementary modes of shaping, designing, comparing and choosing presented earlier (Figure 8).

Because the essence of the process of strategic choice is that work should proceed in an adaptive and exploratory fashion rather than in a rigid sequence,

Figure 28   A vocabulary of strategic choice

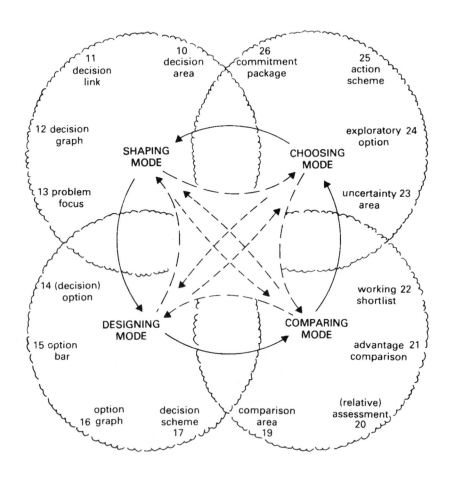

NUMBERS refer to earlier Figures in which
definitional statements and examples appear.

there is no fixed order in which the sixteen core concepts should be applied in practice. The particular sequence in which they were introduced in Chapters 2 and 3 was chosen merely for ease of exposition, recognising that some linear sequence has to be followed when introducing any set of ideas for the first time.

Starting with the *shaping mode,* a complex and possibly ill-defined decision problem can be structured in terms of a set of **decision areas**, some pairs of which are directly interconnected through **decision links**. This leads to a picture of a network of relationships among decision areas, referred to as a **decision graph,** within which a choice of **problem focus** can be made.

Turning to the *designing mode,* a representative set of **decision options** is identified within each decision area, and **option bars** are specified wherever it is assumed that pairs of options drawn from different decision areas are mutually incompatible. The resulting **option graph** can be seen as a form of map, indicating which combinations of pairs of options are available within the current problem focus. The corresponding set of feasible **decision schemes** can now be developed by arranging the decision areas in some chosen sequence and then moving systematically through all possible branches in the resulting tree-like pattern.

Moving on to the *comparing mode,* **comparison areas** are formulated for comparing alternative options or schemes, and within these **relative assessments** are made, representing judgements as to what their consequences might be. Such assessments can be balanced against each other through **advantage comparisons** between pairs of selected alternatives, allowing value judgements and feelings of uncertainty to be expressed in a common decision-centred framework. Wherever there are many schemes available, the use of simplified numerical or other scales within some comparison areas becomes important as a means of choosing a limited **working shortlist.**

In the work of the *choosing mode,* sources of doubt are expressed in the form of **uncertainty areas**, leading towards the identification of **exploratory options** whereby some of these doubts might be addressed. Timing considerations are now introduced, leading to the consideration of **action schemes** which may contain proposals for early action in some but not necessarily all decision areas. Such proposals can be brought together with explorations in response to uncertainty, and arrangements relating to deferred decisions, within the framework of a **commitment package,** designed as an incremental step in a continuing process of decision-making through time.

In distilling the essentials of a technology of strategic choice into this basic vocabulary of sixteen core concepts, the guiding principle has been to avoid specialised and esoteric words. Instead, words in common usage are linked together in pairs in such a way as to give them a heightened meaning. Formal definitions have already been recorded underneath the appropriate illustrations (Figures 10 to 17 and 19 to 26) – so the figure references attached to the sixteen core concepts in Figure 28 can be used as a quick cross-reference whenever clarification is required.

Figure 29 Orientations and guidelines in strategic choice

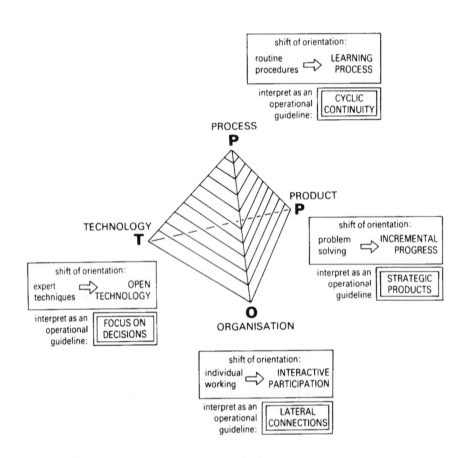

shift of orientation:

routine procedures ⇒ LEARNING PROCESS

interpret as an operational guideline: CYCLIC CONTINUITY

PROCESS
P

PRODUCT
P

TECHNOLOGY
T

shift of orientation:

problem solving ⇒ INCREMENTAL PROGRESS

interpret as an operational guideline STRATEGIC PRODUCTS

shift of orientation:

expert techniques ⇒ OPEN TECHNOLOGY

interpret as an operational guideline: FOCUS ON DECISIONS

O
ORGANISATION

shift of orientation:

individual working ⇒ INTERACTIVE PARTICIPATION

interpret as an operational guideline: LATERAL CONNECTIONS

Approach

A-TOPP

ORIENTATIONS

Technology, organisation, process and product

In any approach to the challenge of addressing complex decision problems, people and their judgements become involved. In general, the wider the scope of the problem, the wider is likely to be the range of participants and of possible relationships between them. So the more it is to be expected that questions of appropriate organisation will come to the fore. Furthermore, if the process is to be effective for the participants and those to whom they are accountable, judgements will arise as to what the most appropriate forms of its product might be. These judgements too are, likely to increase in complexity as the scope of a problem widens.

The four headings of **Technology, Organisation, Process** and **Product** together provide a useful framework through which to summarise at this stage the general *orientations* of the strategic choice approach. This will be done by contrasting them with the emphases of more traditional approaches to management and planning; approaches which still have a persistent influence on thinking in both commercial and governmental organisations. The mnemonic **A-TOPP** (Approach – Technology, Organisation, Process and Product) will be used here in referring to this framework for comparison, with the overall concept on an **Approach** seen as covering all the other four elements.[1] It is not only the strategic choice approach that can be examined in terms of the four elements of technology, organisation, process and product: so too can any other approach, whether it is one which has been consciously designed with reference to particular principles or beliefs – such as the norms of linearity, objectivity, certainty and comprehensiveness described in Chapter 1 – or whether it has evolved pragmatically in response to particular local circumstances and constraints.

Orientations of the strategic choice approach

The four elements within the A-TOPP framework – Technology, Organisation, Process and Product – are represented in Figure 29 as the four vertices of a tetrahedron. The solid structure of the tetrahedron itself is intended to represent the idea of an overall approach viewed in a relatively complete, multidimensional way. The picture as a whole is intended to convey the message that each aspect of the approach can be selected in turn as the focus of attention – yet none of them can ever be viewed entirely in isolation from the other three. In Figure 29, the tetrahedron has been positioned so that the process vertex appears on top. But the whole structure stands on the base formed by the other

1 This framework evolved from one first developed by Hickling; it was later applied to the comparative analysis of approaches in a study of methodologies of regional planning by a joint Birmingham University/Tavistock Institute research team (Hart, Hickling, Norris and Skelcher, 1980)

three vertices, and the tetrahedron could just as easily be tipped over to bring any other vertex to the top, resting firmly on the base provided by the other three.

In Figure 29, the emphases which are characteristic of the strategic choice approach in each of the four 'corners' of the A-TOPP framework are first expressed in terms of general statements of *orientation*. This is to bring out the essential contrasts with more conventional approaches which tend to be well entrenched in decision-making arrangements set up to deal with comparatively clearly structured, bounded problems. There is no intention here to suggest that these well-tried methods should be abandoned altogether; it is more a case of advocating a shift of emphasis, so that a more appropriate balance can be struck.

In terms of *technology*, the strategic choice approach involves a shift away from a reliance on the kinds of *expert techniques* of solution-finding and evaluation which are characteristic of more routine decision-making arrangements. Rather, the orientation is towards what can be described as an **open technology** intended to be freely accessible to participants who have differing and complementary contributions to make. In situations where the very shape of a problem may be obscure and, indeed, a matter of possible controversy, the relevance of what may be called 'black box' technologies becomes considerably reduced. It is no longer enough to produce outputs of advice through the application of well-established methods, the nature of which need not be disclosed because they are considered so well validated by past exercises of a similar kind. Such 'black box' methods may still have their place; but it will be a place of limited significance in the wider process. For in problems of complex and ill-defined shape, it is likely that many different types of choice will become intermeshed – for instance, choices about finance, about timing, about location, about technological or marketing matters, about people and their roles and about contractual or procedural considerations. Such matters are, in turn, likely to cut across the preserves of many different experts; and it is only through an emphasis on open technology – a technology to support communications and interaction across these boundaries – that any momentum of joint working on complex problems can be sustained.

In terms of *organisation,* an orientation towards **interactive participation** is indicated as being characteristic of the strategic choice approach. This is in contrast to the emphasis on *individual working* on assigned tasks which is characteristic of organisational arrangements for working on more clearly structured, recurrent problems. There is, of course, a direct link between the emphasis on participative forms of organisation and that on open technology. Both stress the idea of people working together in an exploratory way, so as to transcend established boundaries of responsibility and specialist expertise. Again, the shift of emphasis is not intended to suggest that the clear assignment of tasks to specific individuals or organisational units no longer has its place. For this latter emphasis remains appropriate in situations where predictable types of issues have to be processed in a consistent and efficient way. So the question is not whether such organisational arrangements should be replaced, but how they can be complemented in circumstances where more challenging situations of strategic choice arise.

In terms of *process,* the shift of emphasis is from reliance on *routine procedures* for dealing with issues which fall into clearly recognisable categories, towards an acceptance that people should be engaged in a **learning process** about issues which no one person can claim to understand in full. Again, the emphasis on a learning process has a clear alignment with the emphasis on open technology and on interactive participation; for in responding to complex decision problems, people must be prepared to learn from each other, recognising that there may be a variety of complementary sources of insight and experience upon which to draw. Again the emphasis on a learning process is not intended to suggest that routine procedures no longer have a part to play: it is simply that they become less appropriate to the more complex challenges of a process of *strategic* choice.

Finally, in terms of *products,* the emphasis is shifted from the conventional idea of *problem-solving,* towards an orientation to **incremental progress** through time. Where problems are of a bounded nature, it is reasonable to look for equally clear and definitive 'solutions'. But there will always be some instances where it is not such a straightforward matter to decide what should be done. Action must sometimes be postponed, referred elsewhere, or entered into in a partial or qualified way. In a process of strategic choice, this kind of progressive commitment becomes more the rule than the exception.

Interpreting the orientations into more specific guidelines

None of the four phrases used to describe the general orientations of the strategic choice approach – open technology, interactive participation, learning process, incremental progress – can be considered as exclusive to the strategic choice approach as presented in this book. Other people – practitioners as well as consultants and scholars – have argued for the adoption of these or similar orientations in responding to complex problems. So, as general prescriptions, such statements now have quite a familiar ring. In particular, the virtues of participative forms of organisation have been widely proclaimed, both in industry and the public sector, while the idea of public planning as a learning process has now almost passed into the realm of accepted conventional wisdom.

However, it has proved far from easy for people to give effect to such changes of orientation in practice. They can all too easily remain as pious exhortations, which evoke a cynical response from those who consider themselves to be realists in the art of decision-making under the practical pressures of organisational life. So the challenge is to find ways of interpreting the four broad orientations into more concrete operational terms. This is a challenge which is rarely faced in relation to technology, organisation, process and product considered in *combination;* however, it is the challenge to which the strategic choice approach is explicitly addressed.

In Figure 29, a first step in this direction is taken by interpreting each statement of preferred orientation into a more specific **operational guideline** which reflects more directly the philosophy of planning as a process of strategic choice. So the orientation towards an open technology is interpreted in terms of a *focus on decisions;* the orientation towards interactive participation is interpreted in terms of an emphasis on *lateral connections;* the orientation towards a learning process is interpreted in terms of *cyclic continuity;* and the orientation towards incremental progress is interpreted in terms of a guideline of *strategic products.*

Each of these guidelines calls for further explanation. This is done in the next four sections of this chapter, drawing on particular aspects of the philosophy of strategic choice as already presented. However, the value of these guidelines does not rest merely on their philosophical content. They are intended to give the statements of orientation a more practical slant; and they serve to draw attention to practical issues that arise in the *management* of the strategic choice approach, as applied to complex planning situations. So the next four sections will not only offer more precise meanings for the operational guidelines offered here under the four headings of technology, organisation, process and product; they will also indicate the nature of the practical management choices which they imply.

Guidance in technological choice

If any technology of strategic choice is to be truly *open,* then it must offer a means of bridging the differences in perception that can exist between participants who view the world from different professional, organisational or cultural perspectives. The adoption of a **focus on decisions** offers one pragmatic means of drawing the attention of participants towards matters which, individually or collectively, they feel to be important in their current planning task. It is only to be expected that they will frequently see the decisions before them in very different terms. They may disagree about the importance of one decision relative to another, or they may have differing views about the level of specificity or generality at which matters for decision should be expressed. Indeed, they can have different views about many aspects of decision-making; but such differences can provide a constructive focus for debate – with appropriate guidance – and thus help the participants in moving towards a more realistic sharing of views.

The centrality of the decision perspective is reflected in the focus on a current decision problem which was originally adopted as a starting point in developing a view of planning as a process of conscious management of uncertainty through time (Figure 3). In subsequent diagrams of Chapter 1, the symbolic shape of the 'cloud' representing this decision problem was variously expanded, pulled apart and examined from a range of contrasting perspectives. Then, in

Chapter 2, the decision perspective was given more concrete expression by adopting the *decision area* as the fundamental unit of analysis, accepting that it could be used to represent choices about many different kinds of things – investment, location, alignment of roads, to mention only a few of the types of choice which were introduced in the telling of the South Side story. It is by the clearer articulation of such choices and their relationships that the form of the cloud representing a current decision problem can be made less obscure. So the adoption of a decision perspective offers one important means – now widely tested and adopted in practice – by which the orientation towards an open technology can be given practical expression, and the *transparency* of complex planning problems thereby increased.

It has to be recognised, however, that the focus on decisions is not the only possible emphasis that can be adopted in introducing an open technology. Other writers and practitioners have embraced with equal conviction the idea of a *systems perspective* as a key to a more effective approach to complexity in planning. However, in its more traditional forms, the adoption of a systems approach can be criticised as focusing attention on some forms of structural relationships at the expense of others, thus working against the spirit of an open technology. Such a comment would apply for example to the modelling of corporate planning problems in terms of systems of financial relationships only, or the modelling of cities in terms of systems of land-use/transport interactions alone.

Recently, some advocates of systems thinking have moved towards what is sometimes called a *soft systems* approach. This recognises that complex phenomena can be examined from many different perspectives, and that much can be learned by subjecting different views of the purposes, boundaries and inter-relationships of systems to structured analysis and debate.[2] So the adoption of a 'soft' systems approach offers an alternative means of giving expression to the emphasis of an open technology. It does, however, focus attention on relationships of a comparatively stable, enduring form, as opposed to the ever-changing relationships between decisions – expressed at various levels and carrying varying degrees of urgency – which provide the primary focus for the strategic choice approach. The approach developed in this book is, above all, intended as an instrument to help people plan under the pressures of the continuously evolving realities they face; which is not to say they cannot also benefit from standing back occasionally to reach out for a broader, more systemic view.

In pursuing the particular expression of an open technology presented here, it is important to see the scope of an *appropriate* technology for strategic choice as embracing not only a set of basic concepts and analytical methods, but also the choice of the physical settings in which people work, the equipment they use and the media through which they communicate with each other. In the more conventional settings of sequential decision-making (Figure 6) – the clerk

2 See in particular Checkland (1981) and Ackoff (1974).

Figure 30 Technological choice: settings and equipment

INTERACTIVE SETTING – EQUIPMENT: PAPER, COLOUR PENS . . .

REFLECTIVE
SETTING: HIGH
TECHNOLOGY

Technology

A-TOPP

ORIENTATIONS

REFLECTIVE
SETTING: LOW
TECHNOLOGY

sitting at a desk, the committee sitting around a long table – such aspects of technology are well established by convention and therefore rarely considered in a conscious way. Background information is presented verbally or in documentary form; while working on a problem, pens and paper may be used by individuals so that notes can, be taken, and action points recorded. In the case of the individual decision-maker, dealing with relatively bounded and recurrent issues, the electronic work station has been beginning to change this familiar pattern. On the other hand, most *collective* decision processes continue to rely on the simplest of technological equipment: and there are good arguments for this, in so far as full rein can be given to peoples' capacities to interact with each other through verbal discourse and debate – freely augmented by those non-verbal signals through which a wider range of reactions and emotions can be expressed.

However, there are alternatives available to the technology conventionally used to support processes of communication and of interaction; and some of these have been found to give fuller expression to the orientation towards an open technology of strategic choice. One alternative setting which has been found to be particularly effective is reflected in the main sketch of Figure 30. This shows a group of people relating to each other not by sitting facing each other from fixed positions around a table, but in an alternative setting which allows them to communicate and interact in a more flexible way. The basic technology in this kind of setting consists of:

- large sheets of paper that can be arranged around the walls of a room, which has to be large enough for people to move around freely;
- a simple, non-permanent means of sticking paper to walls;
- a liberal supply of marker pens of several contrasting colours.

These materials are not, in themselves, very sophisticated; but many decision-makers are unaccustomed to their use, other than in relatively formal presentations. Used together, they have been found to play an important part in encouraging interactive working in groups. More specifically, they can encourage flexibility in use of the various graphical methods for expression of decision problems and their implications which have been introduced in earlier chapters.

It has to be recognised, however, that successful group interaction is not automatically assured merely by creating an appropriate setting and providing appropriate equipment and tools. It is always possible that one or two members of a group will tend to dominate the process, with others reacting by becoming alienated or withdrawn. Therefore, among the variations in strategic choice technology that will be offered in the next five chapters, some suggestions will be offered for helping members of a group to become more fully involved. For example, this can be done by creating opportunities for people to draw up individual lists of decision areas or uncertainty areas, before attempting to merge these into a shared picture on larger sheets of paper ranged around the walls of the room.

Figure 30 includes a reminder that it is not exclusively when they are working in groups that people can draw on the basic concepts and methods of the strategic choice approach. As several experienced decision-makers have found, ideas such as the UE/UV/UR classification of uncertainty can also be helpful to them when they are reflecting alone on difficult problems – as in the symbolic armchair – or when engaged in informal discussions with one or two colleagues who share an awareness of the basic language and ideas. It is in such individual and small group settings too that the computer can most readily play a role in augmenting the technology of communication and interaction; for, as will be demonstrated in Chapter 10, it can then be used as a facilitation tool in guiding decision-makers through the various paths which are open to them in an exploratory yet disciplined way.

However, within the overall technology of the strategic choice approach, it is important to regard the computer as no more than an optional resource. Even at the time this second edition goes to press, the majority of the recorded applications of the approach have made little or no use of computer methods. Yet as the technologies of human-machine interaction and telecommunications continue their rapid advance, new opportunities will inevitably continue to arise for harnessing electronic resources to the support of strategic decision processes; not least, where those processes involve collaboration or negotiation through global communication networks.

The latest state of progress in developing software for strategic choice will be reviewed in Chapter 10, and the longer-term opportunities will be discussed in Chapter 12. What has to be emphasised at this point is that computer methods should in no way be regarded as an *essential* element in the technology of the strategic choice approach.

In pursuing the emphasis on an open technology, the general rule is continually to aim for simplification rather than elaboration, so that high levels of effective communication and interaction can be sustained. However, it is important to remember that there are always choices of *balance* to be made in this and other dimensions of the approach (Figure 2). It is only realistic that the appropriate point of balance at any moment should be judged in the light of the participants' local appreciation of their own present problem situation, and the pressures within which they must work.

Guidance in organisational choice

Turning at this point to the organisational dimension of the A-TOPP framework, the recommended orientation towards **interactive participation** is by no means as straightforward to interpret in practice as might at first appear. For the wider the scope of the problem being addressed, the broader the range of organisational and other interests likely to have a stake in that problem. Then the harder it becomes to reconcile the desire that all these interests should be adequately *represented* with the desire to encourage interactive working. For the larger and more diverse the group, the more difficult it becomes for all to feel involved, and for progress to be sustained.

In addressing the choice of organisational arrangements to deal with complex planning problems, the conventional approach is to focus attention on the design of comparatively stable, clearly structured frameworks of hierarchical guidance. These usually incorporate elements of conscious forecasting and direction-setting as well as managerial control, and are shaped to fit closely the established management structure of the corporation concerned. The intention is – at least in theory – for historical inertias to be questioned; for people to come together to work across departmental boundaries on selected major issues; and often also to involve representatives of other significant interest groups, such as employees, residents or public service clients.

However, the basic management structures of most corporate organisations can still be seen as designed primarily as a means of responding efficiently to certain recurrent *categories* of decision problems, for which clear policy guidelines and rules of delegated responsibility can be defined. Where problems are of a more fluid, indistinct shape, experience shows that formal planning arrangements which reflect the established corporate structure can quickly break down. It is then that more informal, adaptive approaches take over – with the impetus usually coming from those points in the management system where the pressures for decision are most intense. It is in the face of repeated pressures of this kind that organisational arrangements for planning based on the hierarchical control structure begin to lose credibility, because their contribution to the making of key management decisions becomes increasingly hard to demonstrate.

So, to express the decision-centred philosophy of the strategic choice approach, an alternative guideline to the design of organisational arrangements is required. As an operational guideline, intended to reflect the orientation towards interactive participation as against individual working, the idea of a focus on **lateral connections** will now be introduced. The significance of this term in relation to a decision perspective is made more clear in Figure 31, which is an extension of the view of three contrasting responses to uncertainty in decision-making as first presented in Chapter 1 (Figure 3).

Figure 31 starts from the situation of an individual or working group currently concerned with some particular decision or planning problem – whether it be complex or more limited in scope – and experiencing some degree of *difficulty* in deciding what should be done. Different aspects of this current difficulty can be analysed in relation to the three basic categories of uncertainty – UE, UV and UR – and each of these types of uncertainty can be seen as having organisational implications of a somewhat different kind. In each direction, too, there may be various levels of investment to consider, reaching out increasingly far beyond the particular organisational setting in which the problem is currently being addressed. The possibilities may range from the level of quick

Figure 31 Organisational choice: levels of response to uncertainty

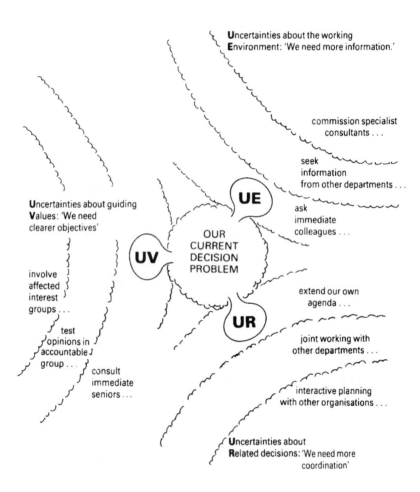

Uncertainties about the working Environment: 'We need more information.'

commission specialist consultants . . .

seek information from other departments . . .

UE

ask immediate colleagues . . .

OUR CURRENT DECISION PROBLEM

Uncertainties about guiding Values: 'We need clearer objectives'

UV

involve affected interest groups . . .

test opinions in accountable group . . .

consult immediate seniors . . .

extend our own agenda . . .

UR

joint working with other departments . . .

interactive planning with other organisations . . .

Uncertainties about Related decisions: 'We need more coordination'

Organisation

A-TOPP

ORIENTATIONS

and informal contacts with people who are relatively close in organisational terms, to the level of more deliberate, and possibly formal, approaches to others who are organisationally more remote.

When working outwards in the *UE direction*, the concern is essentially to acquire additional *information* relevant to the decision-makers' working environment. Some kinds of information can be acquired easily enough by means of informal enquiries from close colleagues; others may involve somewhat more formal approaches across departmental or corporate boundaries; while others again may mean initiating substantial survey, assessment or forecasting exercises, perhaps involving formal contractual arrangements with specialist consultants.

Turning next to the *UR direction*, there may again be several possible levels of investment in outward linkage to consider. However, the people approached now appear not merely in the role of knowledge providers, but also in the role of decision-makers in related fields. So any communication across boundaries will tend to take on a rather different flavour, involving more explicit elements of *negotiation* in so far as each party may be in a position to help the other in reducing some of the uncertainties that they face. The organisational options to be considered in the UR direction can range from occasional bilateral exchanges – whether by telephone or other means – to more interactive working arrangements calling for substantial time commitments by the parties concerned.

Turning finally to the *UV direction*, the most familiar and straightforward means of seeking to reduce uncertainty about guiding values involves referring upwards within a hierarchy to a superordinate point of authority. Beyond this, there may be a possibility of referring for guidance to a meeting of some collective body – a Board, Council or Committee – in which formal authority resides; accepting that at this level there may be many competitive pressures on its agenda and only limited discussion time available. Beyond this again, there may be opportunities to launch special consultative exercises to probe the value positions of interest groups which have a major stake in the present decision problem, whether by use of existing representative channels, by convening open meetings, or by some combination of the two.

The successive levels of response shown in Figure 31 are intended to give no more than a broad indication of the opportunities for working across organisational boundaries that might emerge at any moment in a planning process. Some more specific examples were presented in Chapter 3 (Figures 24 and 26), and further illustrations will appear in Chapter 8. Sometimes it will be appropriate to refer upwards or downwards within a hierarchy, especially as a means of addressing significant areas of uncertainty of the UV type. However, the main orientation in strategic choice is essentially towards building connections in a *lateral* way, working outwards from a specific problem focus rather than downwards from a point of central authority.

Often, there will be choices to be faced as to whether particular connections should be activated through formal or informal channels. In particular, there is always the possibility that conscious investment in building close working relationships with particular individuals will provide a foundation for quick and informal consultation later, when particular issues or circumstances arise. In managing a process of strategic choice, it is generally the choices about lateral working in the UR direction that pose the most subtle challenges; for, as was earlier indicated (Figure 5), it is in this direction that the boundaries of the decision problem itself become enlarged. So, the question now emerges as to how far the range of people involved in interactive working can be extended without the momentum of progress being lost.

Taking these considerations together, the significant areas of management choice in organisational terms can be seen as extending beyond the formal *structuring* of arrangements for internal co-ordination, as the hierarchical command perspective of planning organisation might suggest. For there are also important choices to be made about arrangements for bilateral *linking* and multilateral *grouping* in response to particular problems as they arise. The choices about linking relate to the informal cultivation and activation of networks of inter-personal working relationships by specific participants in the process. On the other hand, the choices about grouping relate to judgements as to when and how to initiate interactive group working with others, or to enlarge the boundaries of an existing interactive process. It should not be forgotten too that choices may arise as to when and how to disband a group which has outlived its usefulness, or otherwise to modify the lattice of arrangements through which a process of interactive working is pursued.

In confronting such choices, it has to be recognised that invitations to participate in interactive group processes will not always be welcomed without reservation. Resistances may be encountered because of fears about loss of autonomy, or straightforward time pressures, or conflicts of interests, or various other factors of a broadly political kind. Factors such as these can contribute to making the emphasis on interactive participation more difficult to interpret in practice than it might appear. The point to be underlined is again that there are always choices of *balance* to be considered. Not least, there is always a balance to be struck between the extremes of reactive and interactive working (Figure 2). This is a balance which must be expected to change through time in an adaptive, evolutionary way – and which can only realistically be judged by those directly involved in the process.

Guidance in process choice

To talk of a process of strategic choice as being essentially a **learning process** may seem to be no more than to repeat a statement which, applied to planning, has now become so widely accepted as to have become little more than a cliché. But this orientation, like the corresponding orientations towards open technology and interactive participation, has proved to be very difficult to put into practice in a satisfactory way. This is because the question of *what* it is most important to learn in relation to complex problems can be by no means easy to answer with any confidence in advance. Often, it is only after interactive work has begun on such a problem that the participants can begin to form any kind of informed, coherent view as to what the most serious obstacles to progress are, and therefore what course their learning process should take.

Most of the more conventional approaches to planning and complex decision-making have advocated a process based on clearly specified sequences of steps or stages, following the norm of linearity which is widely accepted in the design of procedures for dealing with more recurrent, clearly structured decision problems. Following this principle, specific timetables are laid down for consecutive stages of the planning process, covering such activities as survey, formulation of objectives, design of alternatives, evaluation and plan preparation. In those situations where the aim is to add a more purposive direction-seeking emphasis to an existing system of corporate management and control, such steps are then fitted into a periodic – often annual – planning cycle. Arrangements of this kind have the virtue of apparent predictability: this can be important in organisational settings where substantial human, financial or other resources are being committed to the planning task, creating a demand that their use be subject to due procedures of accountability. However, the risk is that the requirement to adhere to a pre-ordained sequence of activities will constrain people to concentrate their effort on learning the wrong things at the wrong times, so far as the more important pressures for decision are concerned. Instances frequently arise, both in business and in public planning, where lengthy and expensive exercises in survey, forecasting or evaluation are carried out to a prearranged timetable, yet turn out to yield results of little relevance to the more crucial problems of the day.

So, in describing the process emphasis of the strategic choice approach, the general orientation towards a learning process will be interpreted more specifically in terms of an operational guideline of **cyclic continuity**. In this, the conventional representation of a process in terms of a linear sequence of stages is replaced by a more flexible set of possibilities for movement between one *mode* of decision-making and another. It may be useful for some purposes to follow an agreed sequence of progression to ensure that all modes are considered in a methodical way; but to maintain the emphasis on a learning process in a complex and evolving problem situation, decision-makers must be prepared to adopt a much more flexible approach. Often the shape of a problem is only dimly perceived, and there are many partially-formed viewpoints to be exchanged. Then the participants have to be ready at any time to move 'backwards' to modes in which substantial work has already been done, so as to challenge and modify past assumptions. Equally, they must be ready to skip 'forwards' to modes where it might seem premature to work in any depth, according to a more conventional sequential view. Indeed, the very concept of a decision area implies a readiness to look ahead to what is *to be* decided at various points in the future, effectively skipping forward from the shaping to the choosing mode.

In Figure 32, the guideline of cyclic continuity is expressed more specifically in terms of the types of *process management choice* which it implies. Starting

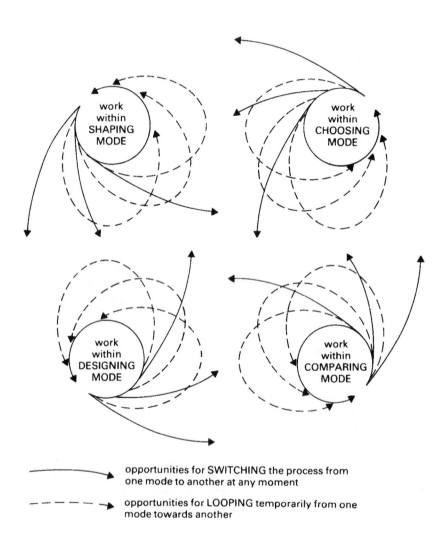

Figure 32   Process choice: opportunities for movement between modes

opportunities for SWITCHING the process from one mode to another at any moment

opportunities for LOOPING temporarily from one mode towards another

Process

A-TOPP

ORIENTATIONS

from the view of a process of strategic choice as involving a continuing inter-play among four basic modes of activity, there are two types of choice that can be made in considering how to direct the learning process. First, there are choices about when and how to *switch* out of the primary mode of the moment and into any of the others, for a spell of deliberate working within that other mode. Then there are those more frequent, often informal, choices that people make about when and how to *loop* briefly outwards from the primary mode of the moment in the direction of another mode, to deal with some limited source of difficulty, before returning to pick up again the momentum of work already established in the primary mode.

Much of the advice to be offered in the next four chapters relates to forms of switching and looping judgement that people can consider when working in each of the four modes. Therefore, each of the next four chapters will end with a diagram which elaborates the relevant 'corner' of Figure 32 by summarising the types of switching and looping judgements that can be made when working in that particular mode.

The broader significance of the guideline of cyclic continuity is that, when people are consciously following the strategic choice approach, the conventional linear process of agenda control, as regulated through an appointed chairper-son, no longer need apply. Instead, it becomes replaced by a more subtle, adaptive process of *route finding* with many possible paths among which to choose. In this process, both switching and looping judgements have to be made continually. Brief loops out of the primary mode of the moment towards another mode are often made subconsciously; however, in group working it can be a significant contribution to the learning process if they can be more consciously recognised and discussed. Switching judgements, on the other hand, have a wider significance in the management of the process as a whole. So it is all the more important that they should be openly debated within a group, if a conscious emphasis on an interactive learning process is to be maintained. More specific advice on how to manage such switches of mode in the course of interactive group working will be given in Chapter 9, reflecting accumulated practical experience as to how best to sustain the emphasis on *relevant* learning at all times.

The significance here given to switching and looping judgements does not mean that more conventional *scheduling* decisions can be ignored in the management of a process of strategic choice. Each participant in the process has inevitably to make at least some advance arrangements to organise his or her working life, in which there will usually be other relatively fixed commitments to fulfil. So periods of interactive working will often have to be scheduled in advance, even if the organisation of work within such a period is kept as flexible as possible by following the precept of adaptive route-finding in place of that of linear agenda control.

In practice, problems can arise in reconciling the demands of cyclic continuity with expectations of linear procedure, not only in the advance scheduling of work but also in accounting to other people retrospectively for the way in which any conclusions or recommendations have been reached. To argue that a particular set of proposals has been arrived at as a result of a cyclic, adaptive, learning process may be to do no more than describe the realities that underlie any process of working at complex problems. But it is only natural that those not directly involved should wish to see some kind of rational argument by which the conclusions offered can be justified, without becoming drawn into the full subtleties of the learning process. The requirement for some degree of 'post rationalisation' can be a vital one in some circumstances, and it will be the subject of further discussion in Chapter 9.

Guidance in product choice

The shift in orientation of the strategic choice approach in relation to the *products* of the process is expressed (Figure 29) in terms of a shift away from an emphasis on definitive resolution of problems at specified end points of the process, and towards a more subtle emphasis on making **incremental progress** through time. Where problems can be treated as simple and discrete, it may make sense to deal with them in accordance with some linear schedule or agenda, with the aim of settling each item of business in full before moving on to the next. When people encounter issues which are more interrelated and complex, the tendency is often to translate this desire for complete solutions into a concern with the production of *substantive plans* at as comprehensive a level as possible. The conventional wisdom is that such plans should be *implemented* in an equally complete manner through more specific operational decisions, budgets and programmes, after they have been steered through the required procedures of authorisation within the organisation.

However, it is a common experience for people to encounter very considerable difficulties in attempting to conform to such principles in practice. Indeed, the more comprehensively they may seek to view the scope of a strategy or plan in terms of the range of substantive issues it should cover, the more these difficulties tend to proliferate. It is in such circumstances that the alternative orientation towards incremental progress comes into its own.

Within the strategic choice approach, the operational guideline which is offered as a more specific interpretation of this idea is that of generating a balance between different kinds of **strategic products** through time. The spirit of this idea is captured in the concept of the commitment package, as introduced towards the end of Chapter 3 (Figure 26). The structure of the commitment package is designed to help people in thinking and talking about what level of *balance* between commitment and flexibility is appropriate at any moment of a continuous process. This entails their weighing up the various urgencies and uncertainties impinging on the choices with which they are currently concerned, and also considering how foundations for the making of future decisions can be built. Such considerations are of only marginal value in a conventional problem-solving approach, but are of profound importance in a process of strategic choice where the need for continuity is explicitly recognised.

The concept of the commitment package provides a particularly clear expression of the principle of treating *commitment as a variable* rather than as something to be conceived in all-or-nothing terms. Yet a commitment package is essentially a product of the work of the choosing mode; and it is important to recognise that there are also products of work in the various other modes of strategic choice which can make a direct contribution to progress in a broader sense. A wider view of the various types of strategic product which can contribute to the momentum of progress in strategic choice is offered in Figure 33.

Figure 33 presents a two-dimensional framework for identifying different types of strategic product, first in terms of a distinction between products of **substance** and those relating to the **process**; and, secondly, in terms of a distinction between **visible** products and those of a more **invisible** or intangible form. The essence of the distinction between substance and process can be illustrated by referring again to the commitment package framework (Figure 26), the aim of which is, essentially, to present the products of work in the choosing mode in a clearly visible form.

Within a commitment package, the products which relate most directly to the *substance* of the decision problem are those appearing in the first column, concerned with immediate actions – it being recognised that these actions may take various forms, including statements of policy and agreement on responsibilities, budgets and deadlines, as well as the commitment to here-and-now actions under the direct control of those involved in the process. There is also a substantive content within the right-hand half of the commitment package framework – that relating to the future decision space. For this includes information about decisions which have been deferred or are seen as contingent on future events.

The existence of *process* elements within a commitment package is implicit in its very nature as an incremental step in a continuing process. Those parts of a commitment package which are most directly process-related include the arrangements for managing uncertainty, along with any proposed arrangements for scheduling; for future decision-making procedures; and for linking with other people with a part to play in the wider process.

There are also other kinds of visible products which are not directly represented in the commitment package framework. These include any documented evidence of progress made through work done in the shaping, designing and comparing modes. Work done in these modes can lead to clearer expressions of the participants' shared views about:

    the nature of the decision problems they face;
    the range of options or schemes available;
    the consequences of different alternatives;
    the uncertainties that make it difficult to express preferences between them.

It is common in planning for such kinds of information to be assembled as

**Figure 33   Product choice: a classification of
              strategic products**

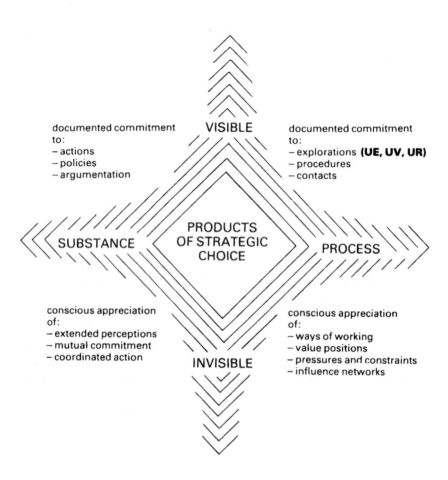

documented commitment
to:
– actions
– policies
– argumentation

VISIBLE

documented commitment
to:
– explorations **(UE, UV, UR)**
– procedures
– contacts

SUBSTANCE

**PRODUCTS
OF STRATEGIC
CHOICE**

PROCESS

conscious appreciation
of:
– extended perceptions
– mutual commitment
– coordinated action

INVISIBLE

conscious appreciation
of:
– ways of working
– value positions
– pressures and constraints
– influence networks

Product

A-TOP**P**

ORIENTATIONS

part of a reasoned *justification* of recommended courses of action. There are various conventional forms – written, diagrammatic, numerical – in which such information about problems, opportunities, criteria, constraints and sources of uncertainty can be assembled and documented whenever important moments of formal commitment to policies and actions arise. But the various concepts and conventions illustrated in Chapters 2 and 3 are specifically intended to help people build up a visible record of progress in all modes in a more continuous way. This is of particular importance when work is proceeding interactively in groups. There is still a task of *interpreting* visible products expressed in such ways into forms which are intelligible to those not directly involved; but there are practical ways of addressing this task, and these will be discussed further in Chapter 9.

Important as these various visible products may be, it is vital also to recognise that any process of strategic choice generates *invisible products* which can have a profound influence in the longer term. First, in terms of the *substance* of problems, people can expect to extend their perceptions in ways that cannot be fully reflected in any documented evidence of progress that is produced. Such extended perceptions may embrace all aspects of substantive progress already discussed at the more visible level, including problems, opportunities, effects and uncertainties.

Such personal shifts in perception will generally be in the direction of increased *sharing* of views among those involved in interactive working; or increasing intersubjectivity, to use a term which others have found useful in relation to group processes (Eden, Jones, Sims and Smithin, 1981). Moves in this direction can be of considerable significance beyond the boundaries of the group involved in the interactive working process; for they can affect the ways in which individuals seek to influence the views and behaviours of colleagues, superiors and associates within their wider working environment.

Also, more realistic perceptions of the external political realities surrounding a problem can be an important invisible product of a process of strategic choice. However, such a product must be seen as relevant as much to future *process* as to the substance of particular problems; so this leads naturally into the discussion of the final quadrant of the product classification of Figure 33. Among the important invisible products which relate more to process than to substance is fuller understanding of:

- other peoples' values;
- their ways of working;
- the pressures and constraints acting on them.

In most cases, this is backed up by extensions to the communications networks of individuals involved in the interactive working.

In interactive working, it is important to consider how far the full range of visible and invisible products can be expressed in more accessible forms, so that

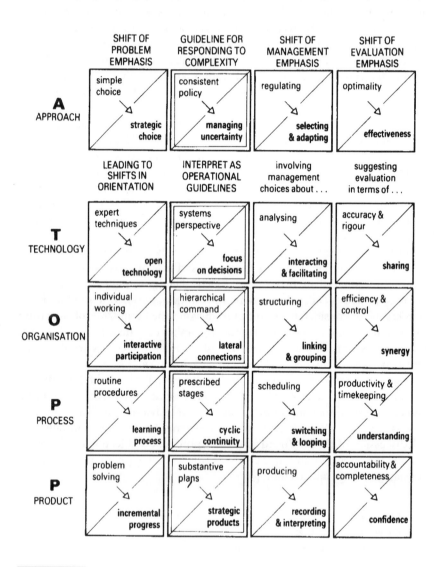

	SHIFT OF PROBLEM EMPHASIS	GUIDELINE FOR RESPONDING TO COMPLEXITY	SHIFT OF MANAGEMENT EMPHASIS	SHIFT OF EVALUATION EMPHASIS
A APPROACH	simple choice → strategic choice	consistent policy → managing uncertainty	regulating → selecting & adapting	optimality → effectiveness
	LEADING TO SHIFTS IN ORIENTATION	INTERPRET AS OPERATIONAL GUIDELINES	involving management choices about . . .	suggesting evaluation in terms of . . .
T TECHNOLOGY	expert techniques → open technology	systems perspective → focus on decisions	analysing → interacting & facilitating	accuracy & rigour → sharing
O ORGANISATION	individual working → interactive participation	hierarchical command → lateral connections	structuring → linking & grouping	efficiency & control → synergy
P PROCESS	routine procedures → learning process	prescribed stages → cyclic continuity	scheduling → switching & looping	productivity & timekeeping → understanding
P PRODUCT	problem solving → incremental progress	substantive plans → strategic products	producing → recording & interpreting	accountability & completeness → confidence

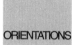

they can be better understood at a collective level. This raises important management choices in the areas of *recording* and *interpretation*. Recording is simply a question of keeping track of progress as it is made. Various methods for recording progress on the substance of problems – and the more visible aspects of progress on the process side – have already been illustrated through the telling of the South Side Story in Chapters 2 and 3; but recording of invisible progress in terms of process is often less straightforward. However, conscious efforts to document shifts in understanding of others, and in communication networks, can be important if these aspects of progress are not to become lost.

It is important to recognise that any conscious documentation of progress requires a process of *interpretation* as well as recording. This must involve the translation of jargon used in group working – whether verbal or graphical – if progress is to be reviewed in terms accessible to others rather than in terms which are intelligible merely to those directly involved. This is important enough in the documentation of visible products, but is even more essential in attempting to document progress at the more invisible level. It is especially important, from a longer term perspective, that people should be helped to recognise invisible products through explicit review of the directions in which progress is – or is not – being made. Some practical advice on these aspects of the management of strategic products will be presented in Chapter 9.

Orientations of strategic choice: A general review

The various points made under the four headings of Technology, Organisation, Process and Product are summarised in Figure 34. This is intended to form a point of reference in following the more concrete guidance to be offered in the next five chapters. The first two columns do little more than present in a more compact form the contrasts in orientation which were highlighted earlier (Figure 29), where the structure of a tetrahedron was introduced to convey the essential unity of the A-TOPP framework.

So, in general terms, the strategic choice approach is interpreted in terms of shifts of emphasis from conventional ideas about technology, organisation, process and product towards the four preferred *orientations* of open technology, interactive participation, learning process and incremental progress. These comparatively general, exhortative statements are then translated in the second column of Figure 34 into the four *operational guidelines* of focus on decisions, lateral connections, cyclic continuity and strategic products. All these can be seen as linked to the more general guideline of the conscious *management of uncertainty*, which distinguishes the strategic choice approach as a practical means of responding to complex problems. Each of these four guidelines can be contrasted with more conventional guidelines for responding to complexity which, in practice, are often disappointing in their effects. These more conventional guidelines – systems perspective, hierarchical command, prescribed stages and substantive plans – have all been used as points of reference in discussing the strategic choice alternatives in the four preceding sections. So these too are brought within the comparative framework in the second column of Figure 34, linked to a more general guideline of consistent policy at the level of overall approach.

The third column of Figure 34 extends this framework to indicate the main areas of *management choice* which it is important to bear in mind when attempting to follow the recommended operational guidelines in practice. Again, these areas of management choice have already been introduced in the preceding sections of this chapter; but it will be helpful to gather them together here.

- In terms of *technology*, it is important to keep in view choices about ways of **interacting and facilitating** as well as about methods of analysis as such.
- In *organisational* terms, the important choices concern ways of **linking** and **grouping** across sectional or organisational boundaries, as well as about the design of more formal co-ordinating structures.
- In *process* terms, there are choices of **switching and looping** to be considered while working interactively, as well as the more familiar choices about scheduling of meetings and deadlines.
- In terms of *products,* there are choices to be made about ways of **recording** and **interpreting** progress, as well as the more familiar choices about production of formal reports which emphasise substantive actions and policies.

All these aspects of management choice can be seen as describing different facets of a more general task of managing the strategic choice approach. This means maintaining a spirit of *selectivity and adaptiveness* in planning and decision-making, as contrasted with a more familiar emphasis on the regulation of more simple decision-making tasks. Yet another level of contrast is added by the fourth and final column of Figure 34, which introduces a set of contrasting emphases in terms of the continuous *monitoring* of the quality of a process of strategic choice. In brief, the message is that judgements about the use of limited resources have to be approached not just in terms of some clearly defined criterion of optimality, but more in terms of a broader concept of **effectiveness**. In the successive rows of the framework, this concept is seen as embracing such concepts as *sharing, synergy, understanding* and *confidence,* in addition to more conventional indicators of success.

These evaluative issues will be discussed more fully in Chapter 9. They remain relevant whether the concern is to make quick prospective judgements about what to do next in the course of an interactive process, or to review progress in a more reflective vein. The important point is that it is not necessary to discard completely such traditional concerns as accuracy and rigour in technology; efficiency and control in organisation; productivity and timekeeping in process; or accountability and completeness in product. It is merely that other crucial considerations have to be explicitly considered as well. Indeed, this point applies to all the contrasts offered in Figure 34; to advocate a shift in emphasis from the top left section of each square towards the bottom right is not to be taken as implying that these more conventional emphases do not have their place. It has to be recognised that all organisations require a base of stability and predictability on which their more adaptive activities can be built; and the concern here is that this should be effectively complemented rather than undermined.

The concern with identifying areas of choice and evaluation which emerges in the third and fourth columns of Figure 34 may suggest that some of the core strategic choice concepts such as those of the decision area and the comparison area could be applied in structuring the management of the process of strategic choice itself. There is no reason in principle why this should not be possible. However, any explicit use of strategic choice methods for this purpose must not distract the participants from the real problems of substance that they face. So it is suggested that Figure 34 be treated as background rather than foreground in reading the chapters that follow. Working on the well-established principle that there is nothing so practical as a good theory, this framework can be referred to as and when required, as a broad philosophical context within which all the practical guidance offered in the next five chapters should make sense.

5 Skills in shaping

Introduction

This chapter offers some practical guidance on approaches to the shaping of complex decision problems. It does so by building on the basic concepts of the shaping mode which were presented in the first half of Chapter 2 – the concepts of the *decision area*, the *decision link*, the *decision graph* and the *problem focus*. Each of these ideas is quite simple in its essence. Within the overall technology of strategic choice, they together provide a foundation for the more technical activities of generating options and exploring their mutual compatibility which distinguish the work of the designing mode.

The importance of work in the shaping mode arises from all the difficult and subtle judgements that can be involved in expressing practical problems in terms of decision areas and linkages between them, and then in agreeing a problem focus on which to work within the resulting decision graph. This can be an especially challenging task in situations where the nature and scope of the choices to be made are far from clear cut and where there are many participants in the process, each with a different understanding of what is at stake.

Experience has repeatedly shown that it can be worthwhile spending a substantial amount of group time working to achieve more satisfactory formulations of a decision graph. This may mean changing the 'map' of decision areas and their connecting links several times, as the level of shared understanding grows. Indeed, such a process of recycling is of value not only when a group of people is still in the early stages of working together. It can also be well worthwhile for the group to return and carry out further work in the shaping mode after they have consciously moved ahead and invested effort in the work of the designing, comparing and choosing modes. This point is inherent in the guideline of cyclic continuity in the process, which was emphasised in Chapter 4 and gave rise to the various switching and looping opportunities indicated in Figure 30. Taking a longer time perspective, the idea of the commitment package demonstrates how incremental progress towards commitment will usually mean deferring choice within some of the decision areas within a decision graph. Any such deferments will, in turn, create opportunities for the reshaping of decision areas and their relationships at future points in time – when other quite new areas of choice may possibly have come to the fore through the unfolding of external events.

In Chapter 2, it was suggested that the choice of problem focus within a wider decision graph marked an important point of transition between the work of the shaping and the designing modes. There are, however, many different considerations which can be taken into account in this process of 'cutting a problem down to size'. Some of these considerations – urgency, degree of importance, level of interconnectedness, degree of influence on the part of a particular set of decision-makers – may be much more important in some decision contexts than in others. Indeed, their importance can vary with the passage of time, even within the same decision context. So the whole process of problem-shaping can be seen as one in which a continuing tension must be expected between the desire to expand the boundaries of a problem to encompass all conceivable elements of choice, and the desire to keep its dimensions more manageable so as to secure a sense of progress towards action.

Approaches to building up a set of relevant decision areas

Given some agreement to carry out work in a difficult but as yet unstructured problem field, the task of beginning to build up a set of decision areas to represent the choices within that field is one that can be organised either at an individual or a group level. It is broadly akin to the process of 'agenda building' which is, literally, no more than the construction of a list of things to be done, or matters to be addressed. However, in strategic choice, the task is not simply to arrange these things to be done into some appropriate order so that they can be tackled sequentially. This is because some of them at least are likely to be interrelated, in a way which implies that they should perhaps be grouped or clustered so that they can be examined together.

Wherever an individual or group is working to a reasonably well-defined remit, as in the problem of looking into the implications of the proposed new road through South Side, then it may not be too difficult to decide where the process of building up a list of decision areas should begin. For example, among the seven decision areas listed in Figure 10, it might be that the first four at least would suggest themselves fairly readily to anyone familiar with the local planning context. Yet in other circumstances, where the remit may be broader or looser, and the elements of choice less clear or less urgent, difficulties are to be expected in agreeing the way in which even the most basic elements of choice should be expressed.

Such difficulties may, of course, arise even where an individual is working alone: but where people are working as a group they can be expected to surface rapidly in the form of debates and disagreements between one person and another. Usually, the different members of the group will bring different kinds of perception to bear, rooted in different kinds of experience, different bases of professional or technical knowledge and different responsibilities to people outside the group, apart from any deeper differences in ways of construing the world around them. Such differences can be valuable in so far as they can help the group develop a more rounded appreciation of the choices which they face.

In South Side, for example, it might be expected that any engineers in the group might see the relevant choices in terms of road alignments, construction techniques and other technical matters to do with elevations, access roads, surface drainage arrangements or bids for resources on capital programmes. Urban planners might see them in terms of opportunities to specify intended uses or other controls relating to particular areas of land; economists might see them in terms of investment levels, amortisation of fixed assets, balance between private and public expenditures and incomes. Then again lawyers, administrators, project co-ordinators, politicians and any other participants in the process might all have their subtly different perspectives on the range and content of the choices to be considered.

In a group setting, one good way to start the process of building up a set of decision areas is simply to begin with a large sheet of blank paper on the wall, on which an initial list of issues or matters of concern is recorded by one participant in such a way as to be clearly visible to all the others. Figure 35 gives an example of the kind of tentative list that might be built up by the South Side Working Party at the outset of its work, before any kind of sorting or grouping of decision areas has been attempted. What matters at this stage is primarily to encourage the involvement of as many participants as possible in the listing of an initial set of elements, however imperfect it may seem. The spirit called for is one of organised brainstorming, in which ideas put forward by one participant can trigger off new directions of thought by others.

An alternative way of starting is to ask each participant to spend a few minutes writing down a list of a few decision areas he or she believes to be important, before the interactive group process begins – or at least before it has built up a momentum of its own. If each individual uses a separate sheet of paper or card to record each suggested decision area – and if these sheets are not too large – then the results can be shared by spreading all the sheets prepared by the participants out on a table top or, perhaps, merely on a patch of clear floor space in the centre of the room. Wall space can, of course, be used for displaying these sheets of paper, provided there is a simple, non-permanent means of sticking paper to the wall.

This kind of approach can be helpful in generating an initial sense of involvement by all participants in a group. Of course, it is also likely to lead to a degree of redundancy in the information generated, because some of the more obvious decision areas are likely to be thought of independently by different people. But this kind of redundancy may be no bad thing at an early stage in a group process, both because any area of choice which is identified by many people can be given more weight on that account, and because the elements of a problem may be perceived in subtly different ways by different participants. Such differences can then provide a focus for constructive debate when it comes to the point of formulating decision areas in more precise terms.

In this kind of activity, it is only to be expected that doubts will arise as to whether some suggested elements of a problem should be considered as decision areas at all. Some areas of choice may seem to lie largely outside the direct

Figure 35 Building up a tentative list of decision areas

South Side
example

DECISION AREA | LABEL

initial quick
listing by
group working
collectively

road line across South Side? — ROAD LINE?
shopping centre location? — SHOP LOC'N?
use of central site? — CENT'L SITE?
use of gasworks site? — GAS SITE?
closure of Main Street? — MAIN ST?
timing of construction of new road? — ROADTIM?
policy on rehousing? — REHOUS?

further
additions
suggested
after
individual
reflection

traffic management in South Side? — TRAF MGT?
West Street improvement? — WEST ST?
closure of Griffin Road school? — GRIFF SCHL?
investment in life of district? — DIST LIFE?
re-routeing of local bus services? — BUS ROUTES?
cutbacks in municipal spending? — CUTBACKS?
extent of further housing clearance? — HOUSCLEAR?
policy on housing repair? — HOUSRPR?
policy on contracting out design work? — DESIGN WK?
procedure for property acquisition? — PROPACQ?

Shaping SKILLS

The building up of an unstructured list of decision areas such as this can be a useful step when a group is just starting work. The list can be extended, altered or restructured as understanding grows, with some entries transferred to lists of comparison areas or uncertainty areas. Individuals can be invited to list their own suggestions either at the start or later in the process.

sphere of influence of the participants, in which case they might perhaps seem better expressed as uncertainty areas. Other 'decision areas' offered may seem more in the nature of statements or choices to do with generalised aims, criteria or desiderata, in which case there would be a possibility of reserving them to be introduced later as comparison areas. As will be seen later, comparison areas and uncertainty areas can always be transferred to separate sheets of paper on the wall, for further consideration when the process moves into other modes. However, there is no reason why they should not be included in a single unstructured list of problem elements in the first instance, with a view to further rearrangement when the group decides to move ahead.

Sorting decision areas by categories and levels

Where the problem to be tackled has no clear boundaries, and especially where many participants are involved, it is not uncommon for the process of generating decision areas to develop a momentum of its own. Each new addition to the list can then prompt further suggestions; so that the process begins to appear a never-ending one. But once the list of decision areas reaches around fifteen or twenty – as in the example of Figure 35 – then questions will begin to arise as to whether it is useful to continue any further in this way. Participants may then well begin to ask whether, before thinking of any further additions, those decision areas already on the list should not be sorted or rearranged in some way, to identify possible overlaps and gaps in the problem formulation as it has shaped up so far.

One obvious way in which to begin to restructure a list of decision areas is to introduce some framework of *categories* of choice which are felt appropriate to the present decision setting. In a setting such as that of the South Side Working Party, for example, it might be felt that the decision areas in the list could be rearranged into broad fields of choice to do with transport, with land use, with finance and, perhaps, with other familiar functional areas such as housing, education, legal or personnel matters. In an industrial management context, the key functional areas might well be different, with categories such as production, marketing, purchasing, maintenance and product development forming the most natural frame of reference for the participants.

The differentiation of *levels* of choice offers another obvious means of sorting decision areas, especially where either the nature of the remit or the diversity of the participants leads to the generation of a list of decision areas some of which are expressed in more generalised terms than others. For example, in the list of Figure 35, the decision area about 'cutbacks in municipal spending' could be seen as impinging not just on South Side but on the population of the municipality as a whole; while that on investment in the continued life of the South Side district could be seen as clearly broader than that to do with the comparatively local West Street improvement issue.

Figure 36 illustrates one approach to the sorting of decision areas both ac-

Figure 36 Sorting the decision areas by categories and levels

South Side
example

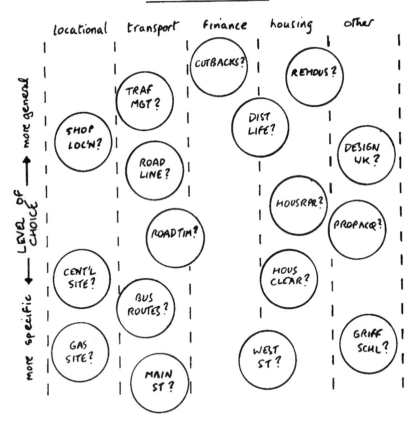

CATEGORY OF CHOICE

locational   transport   finance   housing   other

LEVEL OF CHOICE
more general ← → more specific

- CUTBACKS?
- TRAF MGT?
- REHOUS?
- SHOP LOC'N?
- DIST LIFE?
- DESIGN WK?
- ROAD LINE?
- ROADTIM?
- HOUSRPR?
- PROPACQ?
- CENT'L SITE?
- HOUS CLEAR?
- BUS ROUTES?
- GAS SITE?
- WEST ST?
- GRIFF SCHL?
- MAIN ST?

Shaping It can be useful to rearrange decision areas by fields or levels – or both – whenever an unstructured list seems to be becoming too long or unwieldy. This can help in redefining or clustering similar decision areas; in considering the possibility of a multi-level problem structure; and in choosing a problem focus where there **SKILLS** are many decision areas.

cording to category and to level of generality at the same time. Each decision area is here positioned, vertically, in relation to a spectrum ranging from the most specific operational choice to the most generalised choice of policy orientation. It is also located, horizontally, according to some set of functional categories which, for this purpose, need not be very precisely defined. These two dimensions can be marked out either on a large sheet of paper on a wall, or on a sufficiently large area of floor or table space, depending on the preferences of the group and the facilities of the room in which they are working. The use of floor or table space, with decision areas represented by movable cards, sheets of paper or discs, has the advantage that their positions can be shifted around easily, until the participants agree that the resulting layout represents a good enough 'map' as a basis for further shaping work. Of course, the same flexibility can be achieved on a wall, provided the technical problems of adhesion and easy re-positioning can be dealt with – but refinements in this direction are by no means an essential adjunct to the approach.

The main purpose of this sorting and positioning procedure is to build a broad picture of the overall *balance* of the set of decision areas so far generated; a picture within which it is possible to search for both overlaps and gaps. There may, for example, be very good reasons why, in Figure 36, there should be several comparatively specific transport decision areas, whereas the only financial decision areas seem to appear at the more generalised level: but at least it becomes possible to debate whether there are overlaps that should be eliminated or important gaps to be filled. Overlaps are, of course, especially likely to arise where some or all of the decision areas have been generated by individuals independently, rather than as part of a group process. Often, overlaps will point towards opportunities for more careful reformulation of decision areas, using the kind of guidelines to be discussed in the next section.

Where decision areas seem to be poorly balanced between levels, a useful way of proceeding is to review whether any of the comparatively specific decision areas can be thought of in terms of choices of *means* towards more general *ends,* or whether some of the more general ones can be thought of in terms of choice of ends, suggesting more specific choices of means. For example, the general CUTBACKS? decision area might, on reflection, suggest more specific choices to do with the relative severity with which any particular departmental budget or capital programme was to be cut back in a coming annual review cycle; while the specific issue of closure of the Griffin Road School might, on reflection, suggest broader areas of decision to do with educational re-organisation policy in a wider area.

This kind of ends/means investigation is likely, in practice, to cut across whatever divisions were agreed as a basis for organising decision areas into functional categories. For instance, choices about the closure of the Griffin Road School might be seen as leading towards broader policy choices beyond the field of education – especially if possible non-educational uses were being kept in view for the buildings or site, with implications for other policies and budgets.

Experience tends to indicate that categories are often simplest to distinguish in the middle range of the generality/specificity spectrum, while tending to converge both at the broad policy level, and in some cases at the level of specific local impact. So the vertical divisions in Figure 36 can be thought of as rather like lines of longitude on a globe, which gradually converge as they are extended upwards or downwards towards the polar regions where they meet.

As in the construction of an initial tentative list, one outcome of this process of sorting by levels and categories may be a growing recognition that some decision areas may be better expressed either as comparison areas or as uncertainty areas, so may be best set aside for later consideration in this light. Also, as in the preliminary listing process, it is important not to spend too long in re-sorting decision areas according to categories and levels; this is because of the connections *across* levels and categories which are of more fundamental importance to the work of the shaping mode.

Reformulating decision areas

For a group to establish momentum, it is good practice to formulate decision areas loosely and informally in the first instance, without worrying about the finer points of how they should be worded or the specific nature of the choices which may be available within each. However, this can mean bypassing definition issues which can be of much importance in practical terms; and it can be well worthwhile returning to consider such issues more carefully once the participants in the process feel satisfied that they have built up a good enough set of decision areas to form the basis of an initial decision graph. This kind of pause for reformulation of individual decision areas will be particularly important where there appear to be overlaps between somewhat similar decision areas; overlaps which could be overcome by more careful formulation of what is meant, so that the decision areas can either be merged or else more clearly distinguished from each other.

There are two kinds of difficulty which often arise in the initial listing of decision areas, especially among people who have not previously been accustomed to thinking explicitly in decision area terms. One is that decision areas are confused with options within decision areas: for instance, the decision area described as 'West Street Improvement' could be read as the specific proposal to improve rather than the area of choice as to whether to improve or not. It is this kind of scope for misunderstanding that makes it useful to maintain the discipline of writing a question mark at the end of both the full description and the full label of every decision area.

The other source of confusion encountered in practice is a tendency to express decision areas in terms of choice of preferred state, rather than choice of preferred action. For instance, depending on the powers at the disposal of the decision-makers, it may be one thing to consider whether the vacant central site in South Side should be in residential or industrial use at some future time; yet quite a different thing to consider which zoning should be indicated on a local plan to be prepared and published as a guide to future development decisions. So 'choice of zoning' may be a more realistic phrasing than 'choice of use', when considered in relation to the levels of influence which the public decision-makers in South Side can actually bring to bear. The choice of *action* within their control may relate strictly speaking to the action of setting down a policy statement in print, accompanied by the action of shading a map in one tone rather than another; this act may have some influence over the way the land is used, but perhaps by no means the only influence once market pressures and other policy influences come to bear.

In some contexts, refinements in the expression of a decision area may not matter very much: but in others they may be crucial. In essence, the attempt to express decision areas in more careful and realistic terms involves looping outwards from the shaping mode towards the designing mode. It means thinking about options within decision areas, in order to arrive at a clearer view of the nature of the decision areas themselves. Figure 37 illustrates this point by offering some more careful formulations for five of the seventeen decision areas for South Side which were tentatively listed in Figure 35. These same five decision areas will also be found in the set of seven decision areas first presented to illustrate the general concept of a decision area (Figure 10). For that purpose, they were defined with more care than in the tentative listing of Figure 35, but with less precision than in Figure 37. This illustrates the general point that there is often considerable scope for debate and judgement in the way any particular decision area is expressed.

The closer formulation of decision areas can be seen not just as a means of reaching a clearer understanding of problems, but as a check against wishful thinking – in particular, against the illusion that the participants are in a position to choose between end states, in situations where in reality they may have only limited opportunities for intervention or influence in relation to the decisions of others. So this kind of probing can lead into subtle distinctions between decision areas in terms of decision-making agencies and roles. In a situation such as that of South Side, for instance, there could be an important distinction between professional officers, who are expected to offer *recommendations* on particular matters, and a politically accountable council or committee, which has the power and the responsibility to accept, modify or reject these recommendations as a basis for executive *action*. Such distinctions can become crucial when turning to the work of the choosing mode, and when considering the design of commitment packages in particular. This means that any attempt to formulate decision areas more clearly in action terms can be seen as a form of looping outwards in the direction of the choosing mode.

Of course, too much reflection on such subtleties may inhibit progress in the construction of a decision graph. So again it is important to avoid becoming too deeply immersed in this kind of activity. However, in moving ahead it is important to record any progress which is made in the more exact formulation of decision areas – as in the example of Figure 37 – so that it is available for reference if and when required.

Figure 37 Refining the expression of decision areas

South Side
example

BRIEF INITIAL FORMULATION (as in figure 35)	MORE CAREFUL FORMULATION
ROAD LINE? road line across South Side?	which route to reserve on the South Side local plan map for the proposed new arterial road?
SHOP LOC'N? shopping centre location?	which site to designate in the South Side local plan as the location for a more concentrated local shopping centre?
CENT'L SITE? use of central site?	what type of land use to specify in the South Side local plan for the central area of cleared housing land?
DIST LIFE? investment in life of district?	what public statement to issue about level of intended investment in the continued life of South Side as a residential district?
WEST ST? West street improvement?	whether or not to propose to the Housing Committee that the West Street area be added to the priority list for improvement area status?

Shaping

SKILLS

It is worth giving some thought to the more careful formulation of particular decision areas if they appear to overlap with other decision areas, or if they appear at any time to be emerging as part of a problem focus for the design and comparison of alternatives. The operational meaning of decision areas can become especially crucial when it comes to the design of possible commitment packages.

Introducing links between decision areas

As was emphasised in Chapter 2, the drawing of a decision link between any pair of decision areas represents no more than a working assumption that it could make a difference if the choices available within those two decision areas were to be considered together rather than independently.

As in the generating of the decision areas themselves, it is useful to treat the introduction of decision links and the resulting build-up of a decision graph as a creative group process, in which one person begins by suggesting one or two obvious linkages, stimulating other participants to join in and suggest others. Where the number of decision areas is large, it can be advisable to defer this process until they have been arranged in terms of categories and levels, as in the example of Figure 36. However, it is more usual in practice to start from a set of decision areas which has not been arranged in this way, but can be extended and rearranged freely as the group interaction gathers momentum. Whichever approach is used, it is important to follow a *selective* approach to the introduction of decision links, omitting any which seem less significant than others. This is because a decision graph can become hard to understand if it shows virtually every decision area as joined up to every other. Indeed, as soon as the pattern becomes as complex as this, it can quickly lose any value it might have had as a guide to the understanding of problem structure within the group.

Once the decision graph begins to take shape, a useful way to proceed is to look at each decision area in turn and ask which of the other decision areas – if any – are likely to affect it to a significant degree. It is only to be expected that doubts will arise from time to time over whether the connection between one decision area and another is clear enough or important enough to be shown as a link on a decision graph; and it is only to be expected that participants will disagree with each other over judgements of this kind. Where this happens, progress can be sustained by adding a broken line to the graph, to indicate an uncertain or debatable decision link, as shown in the example of Figure 38. Sometimes, indeed, it may be worth expressing more than one level of doubt about the status of decision links, for instance by distinguishing between broken lines and more tentative dotted lines which identify links of even more dubious status.

As more and more links are added to a decision graph, it usually becomes apparent that it would be helpful to redraw it with some of the decision areas moved across to different positions, so as to avoid or reduce the confusion caused by criss-crossing lines and thus to bring out the underlying structure of relationships more clearly.

If the aim were merely to represent the inherent structure of relationships within the graph – its topological structure to use mathematical language – there would be no need to spend time altering the positions of decision areas to avoid inelegant features of graphic design. However, because the purpose of the decision graph is primarily to facilitate communication within a group, the attempt to 'clean up' its representation can be well worthwhile in practice. A

Figure 38 Building up a picture of decision links

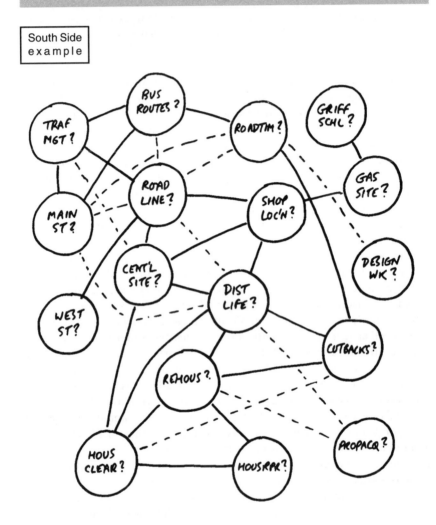

South Side example

Shaping

SKILLS

It is important to begin introducing links between decision areas at a comparatively early stage of work in the shaping mode, recognising that many of the decision links will be only tentative at this stage. The pattern of decision links can if preferred be generated by using non-graphical methods; for example, an alternative matrix format.

confused and untidy picture with many bent or intersecting lines can obscure aspects of problem structure which, with a little rearrangement, could be brought out much more clearly; and this in turn can help members of a group to identify possible clusters of decision areas which they might wish to explore more closely within an agreed problem focus. So it is worth at this point introducing some simple guidelines for rearrangement and clustering of decision areas within a decision graph.

Rearranging a decision graph

There are various working rules, some of them simple and obvious enough, which can be used as an aid to the reshaping of a complex decision graph. First, it is usually not hard to pick out any decision areas which have no more than one decision link connecting them to the rest of the graph, as in the case of WEST ST? in Figure 38. Sometimes, indeed, there may be one or two completely isolated decision areas which were originally seen as important when drawing up a preliminary list, but then turned out to have no links to other decision areas at all. There may also be 'chains' of decision areas – such as that connecting GRIFF SCH? and GAS SITE? to SHOP LOC'N? in Figure 38 – which have only limited connections with the rest of the problem structure. So a useful preliminary step in the restructuring of a graph is to identify such comparatively isolated parts and set them aside, as a step towards exploring more carefully the configuration of the decision areas that remain. Typically, there will be several 'triads' of three fully interlinked decision areas in a decision graph of any size. In Figure 38, for example, there are seven such triads, if only solid links are counted, and several more if broken links are counted as well. It will be less common to find totally connected clusters of four or more decision areas. However, in Figure 38 it is possible, with perseverance, to pick out three such clusters by eye, if broken as well as solid lines are counted. All three, it may be noted, incorporate the same ROAD LINE? decision area, which emphasises its importance to the overall problem structure.

Figure 39 presents the result of one attempt to re-draw the graph so as to bring out some of these structural features more clearly. Through the use of visual judgement and graphical dexterity alone, some of the decision areas have been shifted in position, mainly to reduce the number of criss-crossing lines, while preventing the more isolated decision areas from cluttering up the middle of the picture. Also, to identify closely linked clusters more clearly, boundary lines have been drawn round two clusters of four decision areas and one of five. Not all of these clusters include *totally* interconnected sets of decision areas, and there is no need to be rigid in this respect. What the clustering in Figure 39 does reveal is that there are three closely connected clusters which in this case connect up in a chain: an observation which offers an important aid in comprehending the overall structure of this particular graph.

It is not easy, nor perhaps too helpful, to try to codify more precisely the kind

Figure 39   Rearranging a decision graph

South Side
example

Shaping   Where the structure of a decision graph is difficult to make out visually
because there are too many decision links connecting decision areas
which are far apart on the graph, it can be important to give time to the
repositioning of at least some decision areas to bring out the underlying
structure more clearly. It is useful to start by identifying more isolated
SKILLS   decision areas and closely connected clusters.

of rules to be used in this kind of structuring process. This is because any attempt to codify creates a need to agree more precisely what status a broken link should be given as compared with a solid link, and this may be to place too much meaning on what is intended as no more than a loose and informal convention for making assumptions about relatedness between decision areas. Yet it is always possible to develop and apply more precise codes of rules for the limited range of situations where this could be a worthwhile aid to the work of the shaping mode. For instance, decision links can always be formulated as yes/ no or zero/one entries in a two-way table or *matrix* of mutual relationships between pairs of decision areas: and question marks or other symbols can then be introduced to represent doubtful links if desired. Then that matrix can be rearranged according to some set of logical rules which, in turn, may indicate how the decision graph could, with advantage, be redrawn.

Resort to such methods is most likely to be worthwhile in circumstances where a graph is so complex that visual inspection offers few clues to its underlying structure, so that any attempt to disentangle it without resort to a computer is likely to involve judgements of an arbitrary and therefore misleading kind. In practice, experienced users of strategic choice methods usually stop well short of this level of elaboration in the size of a graph – not least because input of structural information to a computer can mean slowing down the pace of interactive working within a group.

Highlighting more important decision areas

A decision graph may have to be rearranged more than once to bring out its structure as clearly as possible, and to draw attention to closely linked clusters without other decision areas getting in the way. However, this kind of structural information on its own cannot be expected to bring out all those characteristics of a problem situation which might be significant in choosing a more restricted problem focus or foci within which to switch to the work of the designing mode. In particular, the participants will often be aware that some decision areas are more important to them than others; in the sense that they represent choices where there is more at stake. Also, there may be some decision areas which may carry particular urgency even if they are not so significant in themselves – and it could be unwise to exclude these from any more restricted problem focus which the participants might choose.

It is always possible, however, to add information on importance, urgency or other considerations to a decision graph, by the simple device of introducing further symbols to highlight those decision areas which are believed to call for particular attention on any such grounds. Figure 40 illustrates how this can be done by simply adding to the graph various kinds of symbol to distinguish decision areas which the participants see as significant to them on different grounds. Here circles are marked in one way to indicate particular *urgency* of decision, and in another way to indicate particular *importance* in terms of their

Figure 40 Highlighting more significant decision areas

South Side
example

consequences. An asterisk is used to indicate decision areas within which there are thought to be comparatively *clear alternatives*, because these offer a prospect of straightforward progress when turning attention to the work of the designing mode. A different convention again is used in Figure 40 to highlight those individual decision areas which have a particularly high level of *connectedness* to other decision areas. The symbols chosen in this illustration are of a kind to allow them to be used in conjunction with each other, if necessary. So, for example, the CUTBACKS? decision area is identified as both urgent and important in its consequences; the ROAD LINE? decision area is identified as both urgent and highly connected; the DIST LIFE? decision area, meanwhile, is identified as important in its consequences and also highly connected, if not thought to be so urgent at this stage.

The identification of highly connected or 'nodal' decision areas is of course one aspect of this process that can be carried out by working from the structural information contained in the decision graph itself. In the graph of Figure 40, it is not too hard to pick out ROAD LINE? and DIST LIFE? as the two most interconnected decision areas, as each has eight links to others, if the more doubtful links are included.

However, judgements about urgency and level of importance have to be made on the basis of information which comes not from the graph itself but from people's perceptions of the particular pressures and responsibilities that they face. It is, therefore, only to be expected that there will be differences of opinion as to relative urgency and importance where the participants are working as a group. There is no reason why different codings should not be used to pick out importance to different sets of interests; and when working with coloured marker pens, contrasting colours can always be used to build a richer picture than can be presented in a black and white diagram, such as that of Figure 40. For instance, one colour could be used to pick out decision areas of particular importance to local people in South Side, and another to pick out those of broader importance to the municipality as a whole, as a means of ensuring that neither perspective is lost sight of when it comes to choice of an agreed problem focus.

It is very much in the spirit of the strategic choice approach that differences of perspective should be debated openly within the group, while in the process of adding information on urgency and impact to the decision graph. In the course of such a discussion, specific arguments may emerge as to why one participant sees a decision area as urgent which another sees as not so urgent; or again, in the case of another decision area, it could emerge that one participant has foreseen that the choice could have serious importance for some sector of the community with which other participants were not so closely concerned. So the highlighting of more critical decision areas on the grounds either of urgency or importance can bring valuable benefits in terms of increased mutual understanding – involving as it does elements of anticipation of timing and evaluative considerations that the participants may wish to explore in more depth when it comes to future work in other modes.

Figure 41   Superimposing organisational boundaries on a decision graph

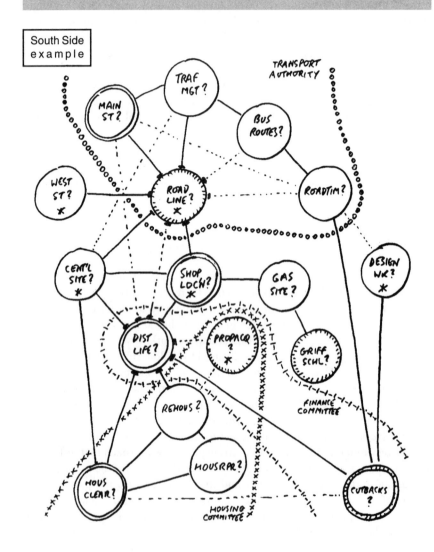

South Side example

It is often important in practice to distinguish between different areas of organisational or departmental responsibility in the manner indicated above, using different coloured boundaries where possible. This can help in considering who should participate in the work of other modes, and in what ways linkages to the work of other parties might be maintained.

Superimposing organisational responsibilities on a decision graph

A further type of consideration, which can be used to differentiate between decision areas within a decision graph, relates to the degree of influence or *control* which the participants expect to be able to exercise. In South Side, for instance, the members of the working party might see themselves as collectively having a direct influence on the decision as to where the shopping centre for South Side should be located and, possibly, also on the choice of designated use for the central site. However, they might recognise that their influence was more limited when it came to recommendations on the line of the road; and their influence might be even more marginal in relation to the high-level corporate budgeting decisions which are implied by the CUTBACKS? decision area. Therefore, they might wish to discuss whether CUTBACKS? would be better reformulated as an uncertainty area instead of a decision area at this stage.

One means of reflecting judgements about relative influence or control is simply to designate another symbol with which to distinguish individual decision areas on a decision graph, along the lines of those used to indicate urgency and importance in Figure 40. This approach is indeed often used in practical applications of the strategic choice approach. However, in many situations it is useful to go further than this by distinguishing several different zones of *organisational responsibility* and influence, and to do this by superimposing a new set of boundary lines on the decision graph as a whole. For example, Figure 41 once more takes the overall decision graph arrived at for the South Side problem and superimposes three new sets of boundaries, to do with transport decisions; housing decisions; and financial decisions – each of these relating to a zone of organisational responsibility which is recognised in this particular decision setting. Such organisational boundaries will sometimes overlap; and both the patterns of overlap and the patterns of decision links across the boundaries can then reveal much about the issues of inter-departmental or perhaps inter-corporate co-ordination that would arise if any particular set of decision areas were chosen as a prospective problem focus.

The kind of information used to develop the graph in this way will often be similar to that used to sort a preliminary list of decision areas into functional categories, as illustrated in Figure 36. So the results of any earlier work in sorting decision areas by categories can be drawn on in the process of superimposing a map of organisational responsibilities onto a decision graph. However, it is important to stress that the decision graph is intended *primarily* as a picture of problem structure rather than organisational responsibilities. Its value in organisational terms is that it can be expected to highlight issues of co-ordination which could have remained hidden had the process of problem formulation been carried through in a more traditional way.

Of course, there is a danger that the introduction onto the same decision graph of information about organisational boundaries, on top of all the other information it contains, will present the participants with too rich and complex a picture for them to comprehend in its entirety. This is why Figure 41 – while

highlighting particular decision areas as in Figure 40 – omits the cluster boundaries which appeared earlier in Figure 39. However, when a decision graph is
being built up on a large sheet of paper on a wall, the risk of confusion can
again be much reduced through the use of contrasting colours to distinguish
different sets of boundaries. For colour distinctions have a much clearer impact
than distinctions among lines containing various patterns of dots, dashes and
crosses, as used in Figure 41. Furthermore, they take less time to draw, which
can be a significant factor where there is a momentum of group interaction to
be sustained.

Considerations in choice of a problem focus

The work done in adding all this further information to a decision graph can
offer a basis either for further rearrangement and reformulation or – once the
participants are satisfied that they have a good enough representation of the
problems before them – for moving on to look more closely at choices within
selected parts of the graph. It is only if the graph as a whole contains no more
than four or, at most, five decision areas that a group – or for that matter an
individual – is likely to find it useful to move into the work of the designing
mode without limiting the problem focus in some way. To attempt to explore
combinations of options within a set of more than five decision areas is to risk
moving into a depth of analysis which can be very time-consuming and, as
experience shows, only rarely productive in terms of the progress to which it
leads.

Indeed, it is advisable to err on the side of too narrow a problem focus in the
early stages of analytical work, by choosing a set of no more than three linked
decision areas – perhaps two, or even only one. Alternatives can then be carefully developed and compared within that focus before attempting to broaden
the problem focus out again, possibly by introducing only one additional decision area at a time.

In the original example used to illustrate the concept of problem focus –
Figure 13 of Chapter 2 – the choice of focus was a simple one. For there were
only seven decision areas in all, and three of those clearly occupied comparatively outlying positions. But, when a set of participants is presented with a
more complex picture, such as that of Figure 41, where should the process of
choosing one or more foci for more intensive analysis begin? This judgement
must inevitably depend on the context, as it is only the participants themselves
who are in a position to judge what weight to give to decision areas they have
marked as urgent compared to those they have marked as important or easier
to influence; and it is only they who will be able to appraise the advantages to
be obtained through working at clusters of issues which cut across departmental or corporate boundaries. Furthermore, it is only they who can weigh these
advantages against any possible political difficulties they foresee, drawing on
their own knowledge of the history of working relationships – good, bad or

indifferent – between the individuals, professions or organisational units concerned.

In some situations, there is a case for adopting not just one problem focus but two or more, on which different groups of people can work simultaneously. This possibility is illustrated in Figure 42. Here it is supposed that it has been agreed in South Side to adopt two overlapping problem foci as a basis for deeper investigation. One of these contains four of the five linked decisions within the transport sphere of responsibility, so is likely to raise comparatively few organisational difficulties. Within this particular problem focus it is quite possible that the work of the designing mode can be treated as a purely technical exercise – though the work of comparing and choosing may still involve challenges of a wider political nature.

The second problem focus – which the reader may recognise as corresponding exactly to the set of four decision areas selected as the original problem focus in Chapter 2 – overlaps with the first focus in that it contains the ROAD LINE? decision area. It includes one urgent decision area and two of high importance, along with one other decision area which is connected to all these three. Three of the four decision areas are marked as containing reasonably clear alternatives; but the fourth, DIST LIFE?, is a broader policy-level decision area which presents more difficulties in this respect. This problem focus, in contrast to the other, does not lie entirely within a well-defined field of organisational responsibility; so it might well be agreed that the South Side Working Party, or some sub-group of those concerned, would afford the most appropriate setting for the next stages of the work.

It will be noticed in Figure 42 that some urgent and important decision areas are still omitted from either focus. So questions will, of course, arise as to what should be done about them – especially the more urgent ones. It may be agreed that some urgent decision areas such as PROPACQ? can best be explored further on their own at this stage, in effect forming a 'focus of one' in terms of the problem focus concept. And it may be that other decision areas such as HOUSCLEAR? and CUTBACKS? raise issues which can hardly be tackled without taking various wider organisational relationships into account. So it might be agreed that any deeper consideration of these issues should be set aside by the members of the South Side Working Party at this stage, accepting that they might wish to return to them in later work.

Summary: Process judgements in the shaping mode

There is not much which is inherently difficult in the concepts of the decision area and the decision link, which have remained as the basic building blocks of the approach to shaping of problems throughout this chapter. Where the challenge lies is in applying these simple concepts to the representation of complex problems, in such a way as to capture as much as possible of the understanding of these problems which is to be found among

Figure 42   Selecting multiple problem foci

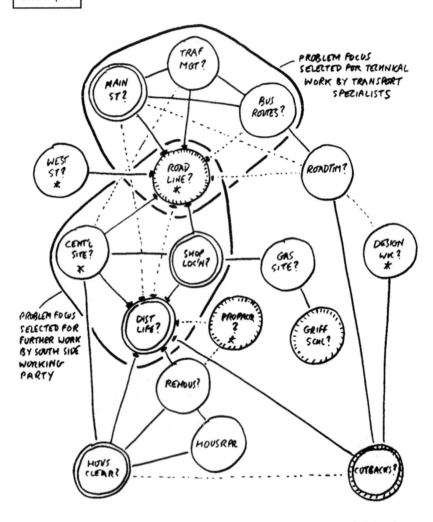

It becomes useful to distinguish more than one problem focus within a decision graph in any situation where it is possible to identify areas for more specialised analysis; where it is desired to define tasks for sub-groups of a large working group; or where there is a concern to schedule a succession of linked analytical tasks over a period of time.

the participants; to bring out differences of view wherever these are significant; and to help them find ways of moving forward towards an agreed collective view.

Because the concepts and tools used when working in this mode are simple in themselves, it is possible to take on board more complexity in the dimensions of the decision problems being looked at than would be the case with more sophisticated methods. So it can be quite realistic in practice to build up a decision graph containing twenty or even more decision areas, within which more limited foci for further analysis can be picked out, using some combination of the methods illustrated in this chapter. This is not, however, to say that it will invariably be useful to build up a graph of that size or complexity. If it is readily agreed that a problem can be represented in terms of only four or five important areas of choice – or indeed only one or two – there is no point in striving to make its representation more complex.

When working in the shaping mode, one of the few opportunities there is for moving to greater elaboration in analytical methods lies in the use of matrix conventions for representing the structure of a decision graph. Such methods were briefly touched on earlier in the discussion of ways of rearranging a complex decision graph and identifying clusters of closely linked decision areas. This kind of approach can normally be useful in a situation, where a decision graph contains such a complex pattern of links that it is unclear from visual inspection alone how it could be rearranged to bring out its inherent structure more clearly; and where there are, therefore, dangers that human bias will play a significant part in its interpretation. Figure 91 in Chapter 10 illustrates the format in which a decision graph is displayed when using the STRAD software, and the accompanying text discusses briefly some of the ways in which the software can help in redrawing the graph and in suggesting possible problem foci. The value of the software is that it can enable changes to be made more freely than when working on flip charts. However, the role of the computer is only to make *recommendations* on possible foci; the final judgement must remain one for the people concerned.

Here, as in other aspects of the strategic choice technology, the essential point is that depth of analysis can be treated as a variable to be controlled. Yet, experience shows that the creativity of the process of shaping problems is best sustained by keeping the level and methods of analysis as simple as possible, especially when working in groups. This is because it keeps the process open and transparent, and provides flexibility for changes in formulation as the work proceeds. For instance, it may be only after a comparatively complex graph has been gradually built up on the wall, by collective effort, that there is a shared basis for discussing what new decision areas might be added, and whether existing ones should be merged or expressed in different ways. The obvious next step will then be to start again on a clean sheet of paper, keeping the earlier version as a secondary record

Figure 43   Process choices when working in the
                shaping mode

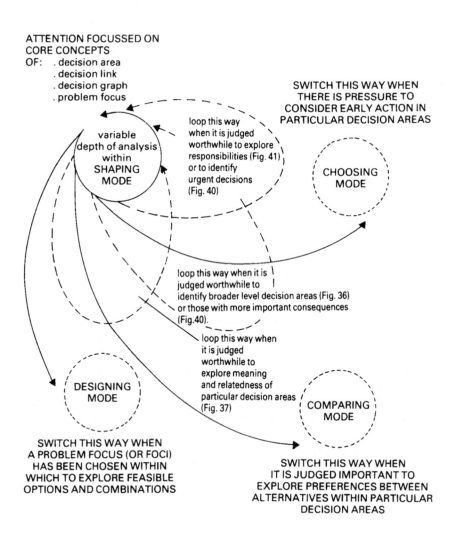

ATTENTION FOCUSSED ON
CORE CONCEPTS
OF: . decision area
       . decision link
       . decision graph
       . problem focus

variable
depth of analysis
within
SHAPING
MODE

loop this way
when it is judged
worthwhile to explore
responsibilities (Fig. 41)
or to identify
urgent decisions
(Fig. 40)

SWITCH THIS WAY WHEN
THERE IS PRESSURE TO
CONSIDER EARLY ACTION IN
PARTICULAR DECISION AREAS

CHOOSING
MODE

loop this way when it is
judged worthwhile to
identify broader level decision areas (Fig. 36)
or those with more important consequences
(Fig.40).

loop this way when
it is judged
worthwhile to
explore meaning
and relatedness of
particular decision areas
(Fig. 37)

DESIGNING
MODE

COMPARING
MODE

SWITCH THIS WAY WHEN
A PROBLEM FOCUS (OR FOCI)
HAS BEEN CHOSEN WITHIN
WHICH TO EXPLORE FEASIBLE
OPTIONS AND COMBINATIONS

SWITCH THIS WAY WHEN
IT IS JUDGED IMPORTANT TO
EXPLORE PREFERENCES BETWEEN
ALTERNATIVES WITHIN PARTICULAR
DECISION AREAS

Shaping

SUMMARY

of the process rather than throwing it away. It is quite common for a group to go through many different formulations of a decision graph, before they can agree it offers a good enough basis for moving ahead. But such recycling of effort will only be creative if there is a shared sense that those involved are continually making progress in terms of mutual understanding of the underlying problem structure.

Figure 43 summarises the main points of this chapter, with reference to the concepts of *switching and looping* as explained in Chapter 4 (Figure 32). The types of judgements to be made within the shaping mode include not only choices of appropriate depth of analysis when working within that mode, but choices of when and how to move on into any of the other modes. Where some subset of linked decision areas has emerged as a useful problem focus, then the obvious next step is to move into the *designing mode* and, whether through AIDA or other methods, to search for feasible combinations of options among the decision areas concerned. But it is always possible that attention will be quickly drawn to just one crucial decision area, where the options are already clear cut; in that case, it may be possible to move directly to an examination of the consequences of those options within the *comparing mode*. Then, if there is little doubt which option is to be preferred, it may be possible to move almost straight away into the *choosing mode*, where a commitment to act on that particular option can be made. This describes the kind of fast route through a decision process which is often followed by an individual working on hunch or experience; but it is less characteristic of groups formed to work on difficult decision problems, the consequences of which for other interests may be profound.

If two or more different problem foci have been identified within a large decision graph, then the process can, of course, be carried forward by agreeing to move from the shaping mode into more than one of these other modes, more or less simultaneously – perhaps by subdividing the working group for this purpose, provided that the case for some continuing linkage between their activities is kept in view.

Apart from indicating the various possibilities for switching out of the shaping mode, Figure 43 also shows three shorter loops which represent brief excursions in the direction of the other three modes, while continuing to work primarily within the shaping mode. For instance, any attempt to formulate decision areas more precisely, in terms of the kinds of alternative actions likely to be available, involves a loop in the direction of identifying options – and therefore towards the task of the *designing mode*. Any attempt to balance a set of decision areas according to some framework of categories or levels, as in Figure 36, means looping in the direction of the *comparing mode*, because the broader levels of choice offer a potential evaluative framework. The highlighting of especially important decision areas within a decision graph can also be seen as a form of looping in the direction of the comparing mode. Meanwhile, the highlighting of more urgent decision areas on the decision graph tends to involve looping out towards the *choosing mode*; so does the superimposing of different organisational domains where responsibilities for action lie.

This brief review of relationships with other modes only serves to emphasise the underlying unity of the process of strategic choice. It is important to stress the value of making these choices of movement between modes in a flexible, evolutionary way, rather than feeling constrained to conform to any more rigid and prescriptive sequence of operations. Some practical guidelines to help in managing this wider adaptive process will be offered in Chapter 9.

Illustrations from practice

On the three double pages that follow, the reader will find a set of three contrasting *illustrations from practice* which have been chosen to supplement the points about skills in shaping which have already been made in this chapter with reference to the South Side problem.

The illustrations are taken from applications in very different contexts – in Brazil, in the Netherlands and in Russia. The first includes photographs of people in action, to give some impression of the way in which decision graphs can be built up and reshaped through interactive group working. The second demonstrates how simple forms of ends–means mapping can be used to generate decision areas and to explore relationships between levels. The third sets the work of the shaping mode in the context of the wider process, by demonstrating how agreement on a problem focus forms a starting point for development of options for closer examination.

Figure 44   Illustration from practice – shaping 1

Shaping   Theme: Group interaction in problem structuring using decision
                     graphs to find a working focus.
           Problem: Policy formulation in a comprehensive development plan
                     for an offshore island.
PRACTICE   Context: Five-day workshop with a local inter-disciplinary planning
                     team, Recife, Brazil, 1984.

Commentary on Figure 44

These photographs were taken during the second day of a five-day workshop held in November 1984 in Recife, in the tropical north-east of Brazil. The task was to apply strategic choice methods to the exploration of alternative landuse, economic, social and infrastructure policies for the offshore island of Itamaracá in the Recife Metropolitan Planning Region. This island, with an area of about 60 square kilometres and a permanent population of around 8,000, was connected to the mainland by a road bridge and had become subject to intense pressures for development, which had to be reconciled with concerns about the conservation of the natural environment and of the islanders' traditional way of life.

The group which participated in the workshop included members of an interdisciplinary planning team from FIDEM, the metropolitan planning agency, two of whom were attached to the island's local municipal council. The process was facilitated by two Brazilians who were already familiar with the strategic choice approach, with John Friend as visiting consultant. The workshop was jointly sponsored by FIDEM, the Federal University of Pernambuco, the State Transportation Department and the British Council.

The two decision graphs on the wall in the top left photograph are shown in detail to the right. The first was developed by focusing on a single important decision area selected from an initial set of about 60; this concerned the choice of road access to the undeveloped north of the island. The group then identified eight other decision areas which were directly linked to this, and some cross-links were inserted (2). On the second decision graph (4), this set of nine decision areas was rearranged to bring out clusters more clearly, and different colour codings and symbols were used to highlight decision areas of special significance on grounds of urgency and importance (the codings being listed on the wall on a sheet below the graph itself).

Of particular interest in this case was the use of different colours to pick out not only decision areas of metropolitan importance, but also those of particular local importance to the islanders themselves. This distinction was made in response to a concern among some members of the group that the analysis might ignore issues about which the residents themselves were concerned. There was a great deal of lively discussion over the choice of a problem focus for further analysis, as shown in the second group photograph (3) – where the second decision graph has just been replaced by a redrawn version showing the pattern of links rather more clearly.

It was later agreed to explore and compare alternatives within a focus of three decision areas chosen with both metropolitan importance and importance to the islanders in view. A later stage in the comparison of alternatives within this focus is illustrated in Figure 69 of Chapter 7.

Figure 45   Illustration from practice – shaping 2

1

2   3

Shaping | **Theme:** Use of ends-means mapping to identify decision areas which are then analysed to find a problem focus.
| **Problem:** Disposal of accumulated polluted silts dredged from the Rhine delta.
PRACTICE | **Context:** Inter-ministerial government working group, Den Haag, The Netherlands, 1985.

Commentary on Figure 45

These papers were made during one of the middle sessions in a series of exploratory workshops held in Den Haag, The Netherlands, in the period May to August, 1988. The project was set up to explore the extent of the problem, and the feasibility of inter-ministerial working in this case. It also formed part of an action-research project aimed at developing ways of managing uncertainty in environmental decision-making.

The problem centred on recent findings about heavy metals in the sediments lying under Holland's extensive water surfaces. Particular urgency created a focus on the Rhine estuary. Here a deep passage has to be kept clear to the harbour of Rotterdam. Unfortunately the sludge is replaced by the river currents almost as fast as it is removed. Thus to stop dredging is no solution – and there is an immediate need for a decision as to where to place the removed sludge. Sources of the pollution are known to extend far up the Rhine and its tributaries so there are international aspects to be taken into account also.

The working group was formed from various directorates of the Rijkswaterstaat (traffic, waterways and water supply) and the Ministry of VROM (housing, physical planning and environment), with Allen Hickling as Process Consultant.

The ends/means mapping (1) provided a way of helping the group to focus at several levels on what could be done to manage the situation. Thus, starting with 'clean underwater soils' (in the rectangle), the first means to be identified included prevention, cleaning and isolation of the toxic sludge. Ends (to the right in the diagram) were very broad, including the elimination of bad effects on flora and fauna. The next level down (to the left in the diagram) brings out possibilities with respect to the technology for cleaning, policy over emissions, approvals – and, of course, the international dimension. These lead to more specific issues of law-making, subsidies, publicity, transportation and so on.

The list of decision areas (2) was one of those developed out of the ends-means activity. The two first words of each line demonstrate the discipline of using 'choice of' ('Keuze van' in Dutch) as the opening phrase of all descriptions of decision areas. In this case they are mostly associated with publicity, claims for damages, various initiatives, and (at the bottom) one which is crossed out because it was thought to be too all-embracing and in need of working out more detail.

This was done in the decision graph (3) next to the list of decision areas. The messiness of the chart is typical of work done when the learning process is going quickly. The analysis to find a working focus was by use of the basic decision-making criteria of urgency, impact, controllability and connectedness. Two candidates for such a focus have been identified – a cluster of three decision areas at the top of the chart, and a set of two at the bottom. In fact the upper one was chosen, together with the very important central decision area concerning different ways of integrating the organisations involved.

Figure 46　Illustration from practice – shaping 3

1

2

3

4

Shaping

PRACTICE

Theme:　Choice of a problem focus, with some help from computer methods, as a starting point for closer work on options.

Problem: Development of food distribution and retailing systems in a major metropolitan area.

Context:　A project in St. Petersburg, Russia, conducted by Danish consultants for the European Commission.

Commentary on Figure 46

These photographs illustrate how the initial shaping of issues can influence the work carried out in later stages of a strategic choice workshop. They come from a two-day workshop in which John Friend was invited to act as facilitator to five members of a project team from the Danish Technological Institute who were coming to the end of a twelve-month contract for the European Commission to help in developing food distribution and retailing policies for the metropolitan area of St. Petersburg in north western Russia.

After an initial listing of 27 issues covering three flipcharts – only the first of which is shown here (1) – 10 of these issues were classified as decision areas, and brief descriptions of these were transcribed to adhesive 'Post-It' notes. These were transferred to another flipchart and rearranged to bring out their interrelationships, using connecting lines to represent decision links and outer rings to represent importance and urgency (2).

One of the team members had received some training in the use of the STRAD software; she was therefore able to enter the resulting decision graph into the computer so as to generate a recommendation for a set of three decision areas which might form the core of a proposed problem focus. This recommendation was then debated critically before a problem focus of four decision areas was selected .

The next photograph (3) shows the later stage of developing options within this set of decision areas – indicating that the focus was at this stage first expanded to five decision areas, then reduced again to three. The letters A, B and C refer to three particular combinations of options (decision schemes) that were then selected for relative assessment in the light of a set of agreed comparison areas, some of which had emerged during the initial listing of issues.

The final photograph (4) shows a format that was adopted in this project, having emerged from an earlier project on community health strategy in London (Friend, 1994), to summarise progress at the end of the first day and to help in setting priorities for the second day. The four quadrants correspond to the four process modes of shaping, designing, comparing and choosing. The note within the main section of each quadrant summarises the progress so far achieved within that mode, while a brief note on further work which it would be useful to do in that same mode appears in the outer corner of each quadrant. In this case, it was agreed that no further shaping work should be necessary on the second day of the workshop.

6 Skills in designing

Introduction

In Chapter 2, the set of concepts for shaping complex problems led into the introduction of a further set of concepts for designing feasible courses of action within any selected problem focus. These further concepts together provided a set of foundations for a design method – Analysis of Interconnected Decision Areas, or AIDA – which could be applied quite generally to any problem that could be expressed in terms of multiple areas of choice, however diverse these might be.

This chapter will build on those foundations by discussing the challenges which can arise in applying the conventions of AIDA to untidy decision problems, and the types of judgement which are called for in meeting these challenges in practice. The chapter will draw on working experience in applying strategic choice methods to problems of many different kinds. Although a number of elaborations of the basic concepts and techniques will be introduced, it is not intended to suggest that these forms of elaboration are always either necessary or desirable: it is simply that they are available to the skilled user of the strategic choice approach, wherever they can be of help in overcoming practical difficulties as they arise.

The principal advantage of the AIDA method of problem formulation is that it can allow many different kinds and levels of choice to be expressed in the same general language. So it offers a means of opening up the process of problem structuring to participants who may see the elements of a decision situation from quite different professional or representative perspectives. Its strength is that it has no inherent bias towards any particular frame of reference, whether financial, locational, engineering, marketing, administrative, political – or, indeed, anything else.

This high level of generality is, however, only achieved at a cost. For it may be necessary to accept quite drastic simplifications when striving to represent complex design choices in terms of once-and-for-all decision areas, with a finite range of discrete options within each. There are, of course, other design methods which offer the possibility of overcoming these constraints – but usually these mean moving to a more specialised frame of reference, so as to view the problem primarily – for example – as one of engineering design; or of land-use planning; or of financial budgeting; or of scheduling a set of interconnected activities through time.

More specialised approaches to problem structuring can, of course, have an important place in practice, especially within management contexts where similar kinds of choice tend to arise recurrently over time. Choices can then often be expressed in terms of repeated adjustments to continuous control variables, rather than choices between discrete options within more transient decision areas. The AIDA approach to problem structuring was not developed with these comparatively well-structured management situations in view. Nevertheless, situations sometimes arise when it can be used to complement, rather than replace, more refined methods of problem structuring within particular specialist frameworks. Indeed, an initial quick analysis of options and relationships within the simplified conventions of AIDA can often form a useful prelude to deeper analysis by other methods. Its particular value can lie in opening up the debate about problem structure to a wider set of participants, and affording a clearer perspective of how far more specialist examination of particular parts of the problem may, or may not, be justified when set against the pressures for decision which the participants currently face.

Identifying sets of options within decision areas

In generating a set of options within a decision area, the most important consideration is that they should be mutually exclusive; that the choice of any one option should foreclose the choice of any of the others. In an idealised, analytical world, such a set of options should, where possible, also be exhaustive: in other words, it should be a complete list of all the possible courses of action available. But in practice, this may be quite an unrealistic condition to impose, and it is usually necessary to settle for a set of options which is agreed to be *representative* of the full range of choice available, rather than one which covers every conceivable possibility.

For instance, in South Side, it might be possible to think of other lines for the new road apart from the northern and southern routes which were identified earlier (Figure 14). It could equally be possible to conceive further locations for the proposed shopping centre, or other quite different uses for the central site. Turning towards the broader policy decision on level of public investment in South Side, this was expressed in terms of choice of time horizon; and the choice of time horizon is one which could, of course, be regarded as a continuous variable, to be extended more or less indefinitely into the future. So the question arises here of whether the particular horizons of ten, twenty and forty years are to be considered sufficiently representative of the full range of alternatives available in practice. It may be that this is readily agreed to be so – perhaps because, in the municipality responsible for South Side, these represent familiar periods of amortisation for different kinds of capital assets. Yet any such assumption can always be challenged, debated and then modified if the participants agree.

Figure 47 illustrates the process of questioning which is involved in reviewing whether or not additional options should be included – a process which can be conducted either purely within an individual's head, or through interactive debate within a group. Whatever the method of search may be, it can be useful in practice to keep a record of possible options which have been considered but excluded, with reasons for the exclusion noted as in Figure 47. These options can always be reintroduced at a later stage if a case for doing so can be made.

The examples of possible additional options which appear in Figure 47 – relating to each of the four decision areas which were chosen as an initial problem focus (Figure 13) – illustrate various types of consideration which can arise in judging whether a proposed set of options is both representative and mutually exclusive. In the case of ROAD LINE?, for instance, the question arises of whether what is sometimes called a *null option* should be included, to reflect the possibility of building no new road at all. In this case, the null option is supposed to be excluded because of the particular brief given to the South Side Working Party: but of course this brief could, at any stage, be changed and the list of options modified accordingly. As will be seen later, the possibility of null options can arise again, more directly, when working in the choosing mode, when possibilities for deferring choice into the future begin to come to the fore.

Another question that can sometimes arise in practice is whether or not an option should be included when it is *uncertain* whether or not the conditions will occur which would make it possible. In Figure 47, this question arises in the case of the football ground as a possible location for the new shopping centre; and the assumption is recorded that this option should be excluded for now, possibly to be reintroduced at a later stage. Turning to the review of the DIST LIFE? decision area in Figure 47, it will be noticed that the 40-year option has been taken to *represent* the 60-year horizon, on the grounds that this possible additional option is believed to be broadly similar to the 40-year option in its consequences, and also in its pattern of option bars. Indeed, this latter test casts doubt on whether it is even necessary to distinguish between the 20- and 40-year options; for a glance back to Figure 16 will show that these two options are identical in their patterns of option bars within the chosen problem focus.

Reformulating decision areas containing composite options

Another situation often encountered in practice is that in which doubts arise as to whether the initial list of options can realistically be considered as *mutually exclusive* – or whether, perhaps, some mixture of one option and another might be possible. For instance, in the case of the CENT'L SITE? decision area in South Side, the question could arise – as is suggested in Figure 47 – of whether it is possible to combine different uses on the same site and, if so, which particular combinations of use might be possible.

If the possibility of such 'composite' options arises, then it can be important

Figure 47   Testing the range of options within a
            decision area

South Side
example

DECISION AREA	OPTIONS	FURTHER OPTIONS?	COMMENT
ROAD LINE?	-NORTH -SOUTH	-MIDDLE ROUTE?	not feasible without massive demolition, so EXCLUDE
		-NO NEW ROAD AT ALL?	possibility not at present being considered, so EXCLUDE (re-introduce later?)
SHOP LOC'N?	-MAIN -KING -GAS	-FOOTBALL GROUND SITE?	only possible if club decides to move. Looks unlikely, so EXCLUDE for now
CENT'L SITE?	-IND -HOUS -OPEN	-MIXED USE OPTIONS?	some possibility that housing in West of site could be combined with either open space or (light) industry in East. Possibly INCLUDE composite options in later design work
DIST LIFE?	-10 YRS -20 YRS -40 YRS	-LONGER SPAN? (eg 60 YRS)	similar to 40 YR option in consequences & option bars, so EXCLUDE
		-SHORTER SPAN? (eg 5 YRS)	politically inconceivable because of promises to residents, so EXCLUDE

Designing   Both when first identifying options within decision areas, and at intervals
             thereafter, it is useful to question briefly whether any additional options
             should be included to make the set of options more representative of
             the full range of choice available. This is often done verbally and
SUMMARY   informally, but a record of arguments for exclusion or inclusion can
             provide a useful point of reference later.

to explore more carefully what the full range of possibilities might be. For instance, if it were possible to mix housing and industrial uses on the central site, could this imply an integrated design in which housing and light industry might be closely woven together throughout the site? Or would physical or other considerations suggest that housing should be sited towards one end and industry towards the other? Would different proportional mixes be possible, and how far could these different possibilities be reflected in the reformulation of options within the decision area?

The answers to such questions might sometimes depend on technicalities such as soil and drainage conditions, or on structural factors such as existing land uses on other adjacent sites. Figure 48 illustrates one simple way of dealing with this kind of complexity, which involves simply dividing up the original decision area into two more specific decision areas. In this example, the composite options within the CENT'L SITE? decision area in South Side have been dealt with by defining two simpler decision areas covering the western and eastern parts of the site respectively.

Whether this is a realistic and a useful way of reformulating the choices available will often depend on an understanding of local realities. In this case, it is assumed that the site is such that a division into two parts along some east/west boundary line makes sense. The new formulation embodies an assumption – which can always be challenged and reviewed at any time – that industrial use in the west is incompatible with housing in the east. Whether the opposite combination is possible is supposed, in this case, to be more doubtful; and this is indicated by a broken line connecting the option of housing in the west to the option of industry in the east. So this example introduces a new convention: a tentative or *uncertain option bar*, represented by a broken line connecting the options in question. So, a broken line is used to express a feeling of uncertainty over the existence of an option bar – just as it was used to express uncertainty over existence of a decision link when working in the shaping mode.

The expansion of a decision area into two or more linked decision areas, in order to arrive at a clearer formulation of composite options, means re-examining any option bars which might have linked the original decision area to others in the wider problem focus. For example, it could be that those bars in Figure 16 which originally excluded the combination of industrial use on the central site with the option of the southern road line, and also with the option of the King Street shopping location, apply to industrial uses at one end of the central site but not necessarily at the other.

Recording assumptions behind the inclusion of option bars

There are many possible grounds for making a judgement that some pair of options from linked decision areas should be viewed as incompatible. Sometimes, the incompatibility will arise from the inherent logic of the situation. For instance, one option within the decision area about the use of the gasworks site

Figure 48 Reformulating decision areas with composite options

South Side
e x a m p l e

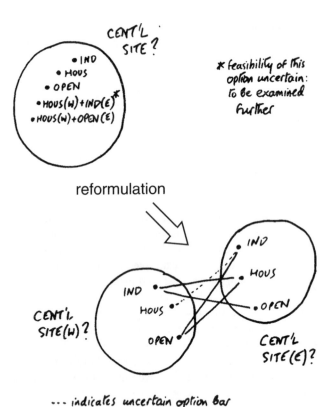

CENT'L SITE?

• IND
• HOUS
• OPEN
• HOUS(W) + IND(E)*
• HOUS(W) + OPEN (E)

* feasibility of this option uncertain: to be examined further

reformulation

IND
HOUS
OPEN

CENT'L SITE(W)?

IND
HOUS
OPEN

CENT'L SITE(E)?

... indicates uncertain option bar

Occasionally, it is helpful to examine the possibility of breaking a decision area down into two or more separate but connected decision areas, especially if the number of possible options is large and some of them appear to be composite in form. Such a reformulation can help in examining whether the set of alternatives indicated is fully representative, and in exploring structural assumptions.

(Figure 10) might relate to its development as the location of the new district shopping centre. This option would then be logically incompatible with any option in the SHOP LOC'N? decision area which involved locating the new centre in Main Street, at King Square or on any other conceivable site apart from the gasworks site itself.

Often, however, option bars are used to rule out combinations which are not so much incompatible in strict logical terms, but agreed to be undesirable on other grounds; perhaps because they may violate some agreed policy, or because they are thought likely to incur consequences which are agreed to be unacceptable. For example, there might be some design configurations for South Side which would present such severe engineering difficulties that they could only be overcome at unthinkable expense – for example, by the construction of a tunnel or deep cutting for the proposed new arterial highway.

The assumptions behind the inclusion of different option bars may be many and varied, and it is important to keep track of these assumptions so that they can be re-examined at any time. Figure 49 illustrates one simple way in which this kind of documentation of assumptions can be handled. This involves attaching a symbol to each option bar, whether as an addition to the information on the option graph itself or as a substitute for the simple cross used earlier (Figure 15) to register an incompatibility in the option compatibility table.

The symbols used in this example are simply letters of the alphabet, with an accompanying key to indicate the nature of the judgement involved in each case. Thus the two option bars marked 'a' are included because these combinations would both involve the unthinkable combination of locating a shopping centre where it would be cut off by an arterial road from its local residential catchment area. The combination marked 'b' is ruled out because it is judged not to be viable in economic terms; and the two combinations marked 'c' are excluded because they would mean permitting housing or industrial development on a restricted site unacceptably close to a busy main road. The more doubtful option bar marked 'd' reflects a more debatable assumption; the assumption that industrial use of the central site might erode the attractiveness of shops at King Square to local shoppers, who might then be able to take their custom to alternative shopping centres further afield.

While assumption 'd' has been picked out as more debatable than the rest, it may also be possible to distinguish in other ways between the levels of conviction with which option bars are to be regarded as imposing unacceptable constraints. This can be important if there are so many option bars as to seriously constrain the range of possible schemes that can be taken forward for comparison; in which case there will be an incentive to relax some of the less stringent of the option bars.

As a guide to this procedure, it is sometimes found useful to adopt a rough-and-ready judgemental scale to differentiate between option bars according to the relative ease or difficulty of breaking the constraints they imply. On a three-point scale, for example, the highest grading – perhaps indicated by three crosses – might indicate very strong grounds for an incompatibility

Figure 49 Recording assumptions underlying option bars

South Side example

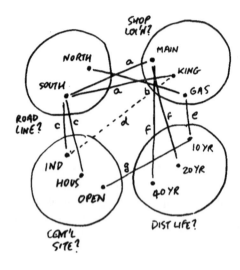

EXPLANATIONS
FOR OPTION BARS:

a shops would be
   cut off from homes

b uneconomic
   combination

c site too near road
   to be developed

d industry on central
   site might make
   King Square
   shopping uneconomic

e shops on gas site
   not a short term
   option

f main street shopping
   not a long term
   option

g. open space use not
    possible in short term

		ROAD LINE?			SHOP LOC'N?			CENT'L SITE?		
		-NORTH	-SOUTH		-MAIN	-KING	-GAS	-IND	-HOUS	-OPEN
SHOP LOC'N?	-MAIN	•	a							
	-KING	•	a							
	-GAS	b	•							
CENT'L SITE?	-IND	•	c		•	d?	•			
	-HOUS	•	c		•	•	•			
	-OPEN	•	•		•	•	•			
DIST LIFE?	-10YR	•	•		•	•	e	•	•	g
	-20YR	•	•		f	•	•	•	•	•
	-40YR	•	•		f	•	•	•	•	•

judgement; the second grading, with two crosses, could indicate an incompatibility which might be broken if there were strong enough grounds for doing so; while the single cross grading could mark a weaker or more doubtful incompatibility. Such symbols for grading the strength of incompatibility could be used instead of more specific reference letters either in a compatibility matrix or an option graph. The procedure for developing a set of feasible schemes can then be repeated, either with or without the 'weaker' option bars, to test what effect different assumptions would have on the range of choice available. It should be emphasised, however, that the grading of option bars offers no more than a crude filtering device which can occasionally be helpful when working in the designing mode. It always carries the risk of suppressing deeper evaluative issues, of a kind which can be subjected to more explicit scrutiny when working in the comparing mode.

Introducing multiple option bars

One of the basic simplifying assumptions of the AIDA design method is the assumption that the majority of important design constraints can be represented as simple option bars: as relationships of incompatibility between pairs of options drawn from pairs of interconnected decision areas. Indeed, it is this kind of simplification which makes AIDA such a versatile and transparent means of exploring complex problems. In most problem situations encountered in practice, design constraints can indeed be represented in this way, at least for working purposes. Occasionally, however, important design constraints arise which can only realistically be represented in terms of a more complex form of incompatibility, involving some combination of options from not just two decision areas but three or more considered together.

Where some combination of three or more options from different decision areas is incompatible, this can be formulated through an extension to AIDA conventions known as a *multiple option bar*. For example, in South Side there could be subtle economic arguments why it should be considered impractical to consider a district life as short as ten years if the particular combination of housing development on the Central Site and a King Square shopping location were chosen – even though a 10-year life might be quite conceivable in combination with either of these options taken on its own. So, a triple option bar could be formulated to connect the particular triad of options combining KING in SHOP LOC'N?, HOUS in CENT'L SITE? and 10YR in DIST LIFE?; and one quite simple means of representing such a triple option bar on the option graph is illustrated in Figure 50. Here, an unlabelled node on the graph is shown linked to each of the three options in different decision areas which are to be excluded in that particular combination.

It is usually not too difficult to add a limited number of triple or even fourfold option bars to a decision graph in the manner shown in Figure 50. But, in general, the introduction of multiple option bars tends to make the structure of a problem

Figure 50   Introducing multiple option bars

South Side
example

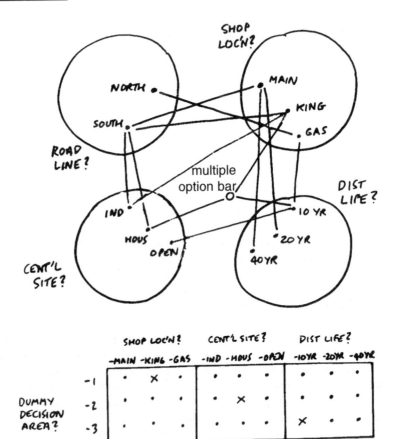

SHOP
LOC'N?

NORTH

MAIN

KING

SOUTH

GAS

ROAD
LINE?

multiple
option bar

DIST
LIFE?

IND

10 YR

HOUS

20 YR

OPEN

40 YR

CENT'L
SITE?

	SHOP LOC'N?			CENT'L SITE?			DIST LIFE?		
	—MAIN	—KING	—GAS	—IND	—HOUS	—OPEN	—10YR	—20YR	—40YR
—1	•	✕	•	•	•	•	•	•	•
—2	•	•	•	•	✕	•	•	•	•
—3	•	•	•	•	•	•	✕	•	•

DUMMY
DECISION
AREA?

Designing

S K I L L S

It is only occasionally in practice that it is worth trying to identify multiple option bars, to rule out particular combinations of options from three or more different decision areas. In practice, they can often be avoided by reformulation of the decision areas. The expression of a multiple option bar as a dummy decision area is useful mainly as a simplifying step where generating schemes by computer.

more difficult to comprehend, and is to be avoided unless it is clearly of pivotal importance to the present problem focus. It is, therefore, comparatively rare – though by no means unknown – for multiple option bars to be introduced during periods of interactive working, when the main concern is to develop a picture of problem structure which can contribute to mutual understanding within the group.

However, circumstances do arise in practice when it is important to explore what effects the introduction of multiple option bars might have on the range of decision schemes available. If the range of choice has already been displayed in the form of a tree, it is not too difficult to filter out those branches in which multiple option bars appear: for instance, it is not hard to see that there is only one of the nine decision schemes for South Side presented in Figure 17 – Scheme C – which would be eliminated if the KING-HOUS-lOYR multiple option bar were introduced.

Multiple option bars can also be introduced into computer programs for developing the range of feasible decision schemes available within any specified formulation of a problem. Even if the program is designed to deal with incompatibilities between pairs of options alone, the higher-order option bars can be handled through the device of the *dummy decision area*.[1] The dummy decision area is defined to include as many options as the number of decision areas which are linked through the multiple option bar – three in the case of the multiple option bar introduced in Figure 50. Each of the options affected in these other decision areas is then excluded by an option bar linked to a different one of the options in the dummy decision area, as shown by the set of three additional compatibility matrices in Figure 50. The dummy decision area has the effect of excluding this particular combination of three options, but no other combinations of two among the three. The three simple option bars can then be used as computer input in place of the triple option bar, and the search for feasible routes through the tree can proceed in the normal way. The dummy decision area can also, if desired, be shown directly on the option graph; in the example of Figure 50, this would involve replacing the unlabelled node by a full sized circle to represent a decision area labelled DUMMY?, including options labelled 1, 2 and 3, each with its appropriate connections to an option within one of the other decision areas. However, this kind of representation has little value in practice, as – unless the dummy decision area can be so labelled to draw out some deeper significance to the substantive decision problem – it is likely to serve more as a distraction than a source of illumination to the participants.

Coalescing decision areas

Wherever there is a high density of option bars connecting the various options within any pair or cluster of decision areas, then the number of feasible

1 Introduced by Hunter in his early work on the development of an AIDA computer program.

Figure 51   Coalescing closely linked decision areas

coalesce to form one decision area

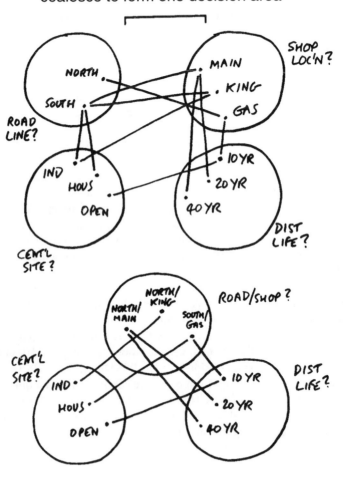

It is usually only worth coalescing two or more decision areas into a single decision area in situations where the number of options and option bars can be significantly reduced by this step, and where the resulting set of composite options can be readily visualised and compared. In many cases, it will be possible to reformulate these composite options at a broader level of generality for subsequent reference.

combinations which remain available within that part of the problem focus is likely to be quite small. There may then be a case for *coalescing* two or more of the decision areas concerned into a single decision area containing a smaller set of composite options. This is, in effect, the converse of the device illustrated earlier (Figure 48), where a single decision area containing composite options was split up into two separate decision areas with option bars connecting particular options within them. An example of the device of coalescing decision areas appears in Figure 51 which is again based on the three closely linked decision areas for South Side considered in Figure 50. Here, there is a high density of option bars between the ROAD LINE? and SHOP LOC'N? decision areas, which has the effect of excluding three of the six possible combinations. Therefore, these two decision areas can be coalesced into one, here labelled ROAD/ SHOP?. This decision area includes the three composite options of NORTH/MAIN, NORTH/KING and SOUTH/GAS, each with its corresponding pattern of option bars linking it to options in the remaining CENT'L SITE? decision area.

In general, it is not likely to be worth coalescing decision areas where the result would be to create a decision area containing more than three or, at most, four composite options; as would be the case, for example, if the ROAD/SHOP? decision area in Figure 51 were to be further coalesced with either the CENT'L SITE? or the DIST LIFE? decision areas, creating a set of seven composite options in the first case, or six in the second. Nor are composite options of much value once they cease to be readily intelligible in design terms. In Figure 51, for example, it is not too hard to look at each of the three options within the ROAD/SHOP? decision area as a coherent physical option for the broad-scale design of a future South Side neighbourhood. But the ability of participants in the decision process to conceive alternatives in this way could easily be lost were any additional dimensions of choice to be introduced as well.

As soon as a first attempt has been made to identify options and option bars within a selected problem focus, various opportunities may be identified both for expanding some decision areas and for coalescing others. Changes in either direction will depend on the judgement of participants as to which aspects of their problems are of greater or of lesser importance, as well as on more analytical considerations to do with the number of options within a decision area and the densities of option bars which connect particular pairs. In general, the aim will usually be to arrive at a design formulation which the participants feel to be *well-balanced* in relation to their current perceptions of the choices before them. In this respect, they are likely to find that their work within the designing mode yields changes in their perceptions of the decision areas and their links, and so contributes to a sense of progress in the work of the shaping mode.

Figure 52 Estimating the number of feasible decision schemes

South Side
e x a m p l e

method of
estimation
(cumulative)

ROAD LINE?
- NORTH - SOUTH

SHOP LOC'N?
- MAIN
- KING
- GAS

SHOP LOC'N?
- MAIN - KING - GAS

CENT'L SITE?
- IND
- HOUS
- OPEN

CENT'L SITE?
- IND - HOUS - OPEN

DIST LIFE?
- 10 YR
- 20 YR
- 40 YR

number of feasible combinations
of options in first pair of
decision areas [= 3]

↓

× number of options in
next decision area × 3

↓

× proportions of feasible
combinations in new
compatibility tables $\times \frac{4}{6} \times \frac{5}{9}$

↓

[= 5.3]

↓

× 3

↓

$\left[\times \frac{6}{6}\right] \times \frac{6}{7} \times \frac{8}{9}$

[= 9.5]

Comparison of estimates with actual numbers of feasible
combinations [as shown in Figure 17]

	ESTIMATE	ACTUAL
FIRST 3 DECISION AREAS [ROAD LINE? SHOP LOC'N? CENT'L SITE?]	5.3	6
FIRST 4 DECISION AREAS [DIST LIFE? added]	9.5	9

Designing

SKILLS

This kind of procedure for obtaining a rough estimate of the range of
feasible schemes is rarely used explicitly in interactive working. It can
however provide a useful quick aid to judgement when deciding whether
or not to extend an option tree by adding further branches - especially
when a tree has grown to a point where it is beginning to become difficult
to comprehend the overall range of choice it contains.

Estimating the range of choice within a problem focus

Once a problem has been expressed in terms of a pattern of options and option bars connecting some set of decision areas, it becomes possible to work out the number of feasible decision schemes by arranging the decision areas in some chosen sequence and then working systematically through the branches of the resulting tree of possibilities, in the manner illustrated in Figure 17. However, it is sometimes useful to make a rough estimate of the number of schemes before embarking on this systematic process; and there is a rule of thumb which is sometimes useful in this respect.[2]

The basis of the rule is simply to work out a series of fractions, one for each pair of decision areas, representing the proportion of option combinations which remain feasible after any option bars are taken into account. Then the total number of combinations which would be available in the option graph, if there were no option bars, is multiplied by each of these fractions in turn. The outcome is an estimate – usually quite a close one – of the number of schemes that could be available were all the combinations to be worked through in full.

Figure 52 illustrates how this process works for the four decision areas in the original South Side option graph of Figure 16. The process of estimation is built up in a stepwise fashion, starting with only two decision areas and adding one more at each stage. At the first stage, the number '3' simply reflects the information that only three of the six combinations in the first small table are still available once the three option bars are taken into account. When the third decision area is added, the number of combinations available in the first two decision areas – three in all – is first multiplied by the number of options in this new decision area, which is also three; the result is then multiplied by the two fractions 4/6 and 8/9 representing the proportions of feasible combinations in the two additional option compatibility tables – to estimate the number of schemes now available for the three decision areas taken together.

The process of estimation indicates that approximately 5.3 out of the conceivable 18 combinations so far are likely to be feasible; this compares with the exact number of six as revealed by the tree of Figure 17. Figure 52 then takes the estimation procedure a step further, showing that the estimate remains quite close – 9.5 compared to 9 – when the fourth decision area is added. It is, of course, quite possible to work directly from the option graph when building up the estimates, if the information is not already set out in the form of compatibility tables. Wherever there are no option bars between a pair of decision areas, the appropriate 'multiplier' fraction is 1; a point which can greatly simplify the computations involved.

This kind of estimating procedure can be carried out by hand, as in Figure 52, or it can be built into an interactive computer program; it can be especially useful as an aid to deciding whether or not to add an additional decision area to

2 This was first suggested by John Luckman and consequently became known as 'Luckman's Lemma'; a lemma in mathematics meaning no more than an unproven rule.

Figure 53   Altering the sequence of decision areas in a tree

South Side
example

(a) sequence as in Figure 17, but closed branches omitted

ROAD LINE?	SHOP LOC'N?	CENT'L SITE?	DIST LIFE?	

```
┌ NORTH ──┬─ MAIN ───┬─ IND ────── 10YR     ┐
│         │          └─ HOUS ───── 10YR     ├ 2 schemes
│         │
│         └─ KING     ┌─ HOUS ──┬─ 10YR      ┐
│                     │         │  20YR      │
│                     │         │  40YR      ├ 5 schemes
│                     │         └─ OPEN ──┬─ 20YR
│                     │                   └─ 40YR    ┘
│
└ SOUTH ── GAS ─── OPEN ──┬─ 20YR          ┐
                          └─ 40YR          ┘ 2 schemes
```

(B) sequence altered to bring broader policy choice forward

DIST LIFE?	SHOP LOC'N?	ROAD LINE?	CENT'L SITE?

```
┌ 10YR ──┬─ MAIN  ── NORTH ── IND or HOUS  ┐
│        └─ KING  ── NORTH ── HOUS         ┘ 3 schemes
│
│ 20YR ──┬─ KING  ── NORTH ── HOUS or OPEN ┐
│        └─ GAS   ── SOUTH ── OPEN         ┘ 3 schemes
│
└ 40YR ──┬─ KING  ── NORTH ── HOUS or OPEN ┐
         └─ GAS   ── SOUTH ── OPEN         ┘ 3 schemes
```

(C) sequence as in (a) but extended to left with ROADLINE? as pivot

WEST ST?	ROAD LINE?	SHOP LOC'N?	CENT'L SITE?	DIST LIFE?

```
YES ┐── NORTH ──┬─ MAIN ───┬─ IND  ──── 10YR              ┐ 2×7
NO  ┘           │          └─ HOUS ──── 10YR              │ schemes
                └─ KING ───┬─ HOUS ──── 10YR or 20YR or 40YR
                           └─ OPEN ──── 20YR or 40YR       ┘
NO ── SOUTH ── GAS ─── OPEN ── 20YR or 40YR              ] 1×2 schemes
```

At any moment when the range of possible decision schemes is set out in the form of a tree, it can be helpful to try changing the sequence of decision areas to explore different structural features. In particular, this makes it possible to focus on more urgent, important or controllable decision areas by bringing them further forward, or to develop combinations on either side of a pivotal decision area.

an option tree in which the range of feasible decision schemes so far has already been estimated or enumerated. The estimation process can also help in making quick assessments of the consequences of adding or removing option bars; if an estimate shows that a problem is so constrained as to be likely to leave open a very small number of feasible schemes, then this may suggest that certain of the more doubtful option bars should be removed in order to open up a wider range of choice. Where there is a large number of decision areas within a problem focus, the procedure can be used to estimate the likely number of schemes to be found either in the formulation as a whole or in particular branches of the tree. In other words, it is a flexible tool which is by no means essential to the strategic choice 'tool box' – but which can sometimes save time, and alter the course which further analysis may take.

Altering the sequence of decision areas in a tree

Figure 17 illustrated one kind of standard format in which it is possible to display the set of decision schemes that is feasible under any chosen set of assumptions about options and option bars. This format indicates those points where option bars have been encountered, by means of the device of displaying 'dead' branches wherever they arise in the development of the option tree. However, various alternative forms of presentation are possible, including a format which simply suppresses information on dead branches, to make the resulting picture more compact (this simplified form was adopted in Figure 22). Another possibility is simply to list the set of feasible schemes in straight tabular form: or to list them using repeat signs wherever the same option in a decision area recurs on successive lines. This gives a presentation which is logically similar to that of the tree, but avoids any use of graphics; so it offers a useful alternative format in the production of formal documents.

A more fundamental choice that arises in developing a set of feasible decision schemes concerns the choice of *sequence* in which the decision areas should be considered. By bringing different decision areas to the fore, different structural features can be displayed. This point is illustrated in Figure 53, which begins by comparing just two of the twenty-four possible sequences available for arranging the four decision areas in the South Side problem focus. The first sequence is that originally used in Figure 17, with the information about dead branches omitted. It draws attention to the information that the majority of feasible schemes involve choice of the northern road line and that, of these, five out of seven involve choice of King Square as location for the shopping centre.

The second sequence illustrated in Figure 53 brings the DIST LIFE? choice to the fore – a rearrangement which might be decided upon in the light of the broad policy significance of this particular choice. To save space, options in the final decision area are this time listed horizontally rather than vertically. This alternative sequence demonstrates that the three branches relating to the 10- 20- and 40-year horizons all allow equal numbers of possibilities in the remaining decision areas. Furthermore, the combinations available under the 20- and 40-year life policies are otherwise identical – a point which might indeed have been spotted from the structure of the option graph, but is demonstrated more clearly in the structure of the option tree.

The third example in Figure 53 illustrates another kind of format, in which an option tree is developed in two directions, both to the left and the right of a selected 'pivotal' decision area. This can be particularly useful in circumstances where a decision graph can be partitioned into two parts which are only connected through a single decision area or decision link. In this example, just one decision area is introduced to the left of the pivotal ROAD LINE? decision area – the WEST ST? decision area, which was linked in the decision graph of Figure 12 to the ROAD LINE? decision area alone and, for that reason, was omitted from the original problem focus (Figure 13). It is supposed here that there is just one option bar which involves the WEST ST? decision area – an option bar which rules out the YES option in combination with the southern road line. This piece of information can be introduced quite simply when the new decision area is added to the left of the tree, adjacent to the only other decision area to which it is directly related.

The wider potential that may sometimes exist for developing a tree separately on either side of a pivotal decision area can be appreciated by glancing back at the larger decision graph of Figure 42, where the ROAD LINE? decision area forms the sole point of overlap between two potential problem foci. If the pattern of option bars in the transport cluster of decision areas was an intricate one, then the range of possible decision schemes within the transport focus could be explored by developing another decision tree branching out to the left of the pivotal ROAD LINE? decision area.

Mention has already been made of the potential of computer methods in developing sets of feasible decision schemes. Computer methods can of course make short work of the multiple basic 'logic-crunching' operations that are involved, as will be discussed further in Chapter 10. When there are only three or four decision areas in focus, it is not too arduous to go through the procedure without computer support. However, experience has shown that it is easy for humans to make errors in this process, so a computer can always provide a useful check. It is of course technically feasible for the computer to handle quite large numbers of interconnected decision areas, but it is another matter to present the results in a form that can be readily absorbed by the participants. Where the power of the computer can be especially useful is in the realm of *sensitivity analysis*, for it can quickly be tested whether different assumptions about the inclusion of any doubtful options or option bars have any significant impact on the range of decision schemes available.

Exploring consistency between levels of choice

There is another variation on the procedure for developing feasible combinations of options from several decision areas, which has been found particularly useful wherever there are some decision areas expressed at a higher level of generality than others. This is sometimes the case where a set of people are reviewing choices of broad policy orientation at the same time as more operational choices which might be consistent with some policy positions but not with others. In such circumstances, the options or combinations at the more operational level can be evaluated not merely according to their anticipated consequences in certain agreed comparison areas, but also according to their *consistency* with different policy orientations which could be adopted at a broader level. An example will help to illustrate how this analysis of consistency between two levels of decision can work in practice. Figure 54 shows an example of a consistency matrix (or table) relating to South Side, in which four of the seven decision areas from the original problem formulation – including the WEST ST? but excluding the DIST LIFE? decision area – have been regarded as forming together the more operational level of choice.

For purposes of exploring relationships between levels the DIST LIFE? decision area has been reformulated here as a broader policy-level choice of investment horizon with only two options – short and long. To this choice is added another choice at the broader policy level concerned with emphasis on public versus private investment – reflecting perhaps a well-recognised ideological difference on the municipal council. There are then four combinations of emphasis at the policy level, which have been expressed as four columns in the matrix of Figure 54. In this case, it is judged that there is an element of doubt over whether a private investment emphasis can be considered compatible with a longer-term investment horizon in view of prevailing economic circumstances. So there is one possible option bar within the broader level of choice, which may possibly eliminate one of the four columns in its entirety.

The main cells of the matrix are then completed by entering a cross wherever an option within a decision area at the more operational level is judged *inconsistent* with a policy orientation represented by a *combination of options* at the broader level. As always, there can be scope for argument as to whether or not particular entries in the table should be included, and any such argument can yield useful products in terms of learning and mutual adjustment among the participants. Any incompatibilities between options among decision areas at the more operational level can also be displayed within this kind of format; and the triangular grid that appears to the left of the main matrix of Figure 54 offers one compact means of adding information of this kind.

The consequences of any set of assumptions about incompatibilities can then be worked out and displayed in terms of a series of separate option trees covering the more operational decision areas, one corresponding to each broader choice

Figure 54 Exploring consistency between levels of choice

South Side example

LEVEL 1
DECISION AREAS (more general)

			PUBLIC		PRIVATE	
INVESTMENT EMPHASIS?			SHORT	LONG	SHORT	LONG
INVESTMENT HORIZON?			✓	✓	✓	?
ROAD LINE?	– NORTH		•	•	✗	•
	– SOUTH		✗	✗	•	•
SHOP LOCN?	– MAIN		•	✗	•	✗
	– KING		✗	•	•	•
	– GAS		✗	•	✗	•
CENT'L SITE?	– IND		•	•	✗	•
	– HOUS		•	•	•	✗
	– OPEN		✗	•	✗	•
WEST ST?	– YES		•	•	•	✗
	– NO		•	✗	•	•

LEVEL 2 DECISION AREAS (more specific)

INVESTMENT ORIENTATION?   ROAD LINE? SHOP LOCN? CENT'L SITE? WEST ST?

- SHORT TERM PUBLIC: – NORTH – MAIN – ⎡ IND —— YES or NO
                                         ⎣ HOUS —— YES or NO

- LONG TERM PUBLIC: – NORTH – MAIN – ⎡ HOUS —— YES
                                         ⎣ OPEN —— YES

- SHORT TERM PRIVATE: – no combinations feasible at level 2

- LONG TERM PRIVATE: – ⎡ NORTH – KING – OPEN – YES or NO
                          ⎣ SOUTH – GAS – OPEN – NO

Designing

SKILLS

Distinctions between broader and more specific levels of choice offer a valuable means of dealing with complexity where the number of decision areas is large. When exploring choices over many interrelated fields of policy, it can occasionally be helpful to introduce a hierarchy of three or even more levels of generality, using feasible combinations at the broader levels as a framework for evaluation at other levels.

of orientation. So it is possible to explore what range of choice is available for any one of the broader policy orientations, and to present the results in the normal branching form. It is often found that a particular choice of orientation will pre-determine the choice of option in some decision areas, while leaving open a range of alternatives in others. In Figure 54, for example, a choice of a shorter term public investment emphasis restricts choice of ROAD LINE? to the northern option, and choice of shopping location to Main Street, while leaving the WEST ST? choice completely open.

Where there are many decision areas it can be useful to draw out such structural features by varying the sequence of decision areas between one branch and the next, to bring any 'no choice' decision areas to the front and to set back any 'free choice' decision areas to the end of the sequence; this will sometimes leave a 'conditional choice' zone in between, the structure of which can be examined more closely. This kind of representation is sometimes referred to as a *decision stream;* it can be especially useful in displaying structural characteristics of problems which include a large number of decision areas, and then seeking reactions from policy-makers before going on to search for compromise schemes which may sometimes be consistent with more than one policy orientation.

This kind of analysis of consistency, between levels of choice, in effect takes the process of strategic choice in the direction of the comparing mode, for it introduces a form of evaluation which stresses the assessment of alternatives not so much directly in terms of their consequences, as in terms of their perceived consistency with different political orientations or aims. In effect, the comparison areas described in Chapter 3 are replaced by the broader-level decision areas – illustrating how one kind of strategic choice concept can be replaced by another in a flexible, adaptive way. This therefore provides a fitting point at which to conclude this chapter, and to review the various points made about skills of working within the designing mode.

Summary: Process judgements in the designing mode

The various points made in this chapter have taken the process of strategic choice into a somewhat more technical domain than those made in Chapter 5 – reflecting a general shift of emphasis in moving from work in the shaping mode to work in the designing mode. It is worth first re-emphasising the general point that work in the designing mode may sometimes be very important, but at other times much less significant. In the extreme case, there will be little designing work to be done at moments where the problem focus has been restricted to a single decision area, and the options within that decision area are not too hard to identify. However, even in these circumstances, it may be difficult to choose between these options because of uncertainties of type UR relating to possible future decisions in related fields; so sooner or later other decision areas may be brought back within the problem focus, and the range of possible combinations may begin to broaden out again.

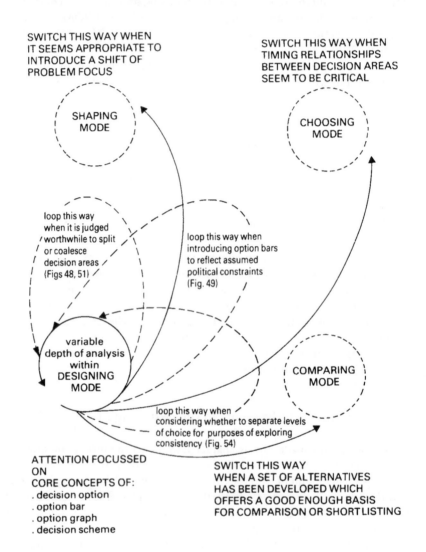

Figure 55   Process choices when working in the designing mode

SWITCH THIS WAY WHEN
IT SEEMS APPROPRIATE TO
INTRODUCE A SHIFT OF
PROBLEM FOCUS

SWITCH THIS WAY WHEN
TIMING RELATIONSHIPS
BETWEEN DECISION AREAS
SEEM TO BE CRITICAL

SHAPING
MODE

CHOOSING
MODE

loop this way
when it is judged
worthwhile to split
or coalesce
decision areas
(Figs 48, 51)

loop this way when
introducing option bars
to reflect assumed
political constraints
(Fig. 49)

variable
depth of analysis
within
DESIGNING
MODE

COMPARING
MODE

loop this way when
considering whether to separate levels
of choice for purposes of exploring
consistency (Fig. 54)

ATTENTION FOCUSSED
ON
CORE CONCEPTS OF:
. decision option
. option bar
. option graph
. decision scheme

SWITCH THIS WAY
WHEN A SET OF ALTERNATIVES
HAS BEEN DEVELOPED WHICH
OFFERS A GOOD ENOUGH BASIS
FOR COMPARISON OR SHORTLISTING

Designing

SUMMARY

When working in the designing mode, as in each of the other modes, the choice of appropriate *level of analysis* is always a matter of judgement. In general, there is a case for inclining towards simplification in the first instance, and only then moving in the direction of further elaboration if or when there seems justification for so doing. In the work of the designing mode, simplicity generally means working within a limited focus of no more than three, four or five decision areas, usually with between two and four options in each. At this level, the number of option bars will usually be manageable and the process of developing a set of feasible decision schemes will not be too complex. The simpler the structure, the more practicable it will be to develop the set of schemes in a way which keeps all the participants involved. But when participants are working in the designing mode, as opposed to the shaping mode, there is more likely to be a case for handling at least some of the complexity in other ways. In particular, a computer can be used in checking combinations in terms of feasibility; in rapidly changing the sequence of a tree to display different structural information; and in testing the consequences of removing or adding option   bars, or options, in terms of the overall range of choice available. But the computer can become a distraction in an interactive group situation; and its benefits in terms of speed and flexibility may be of little value if the momentum of group working is thereby disrupted.

Figure 55 shows the various directions of movement out of the designing mode towards other modes. One frequent direction of movement will be towards the *comparing mode,* to develop a basis of comparison among the various decision schemes that are available. But, as was explained in Chapter 3, there are different levels of comparison from which to choose. If there are only two or three schemes available in all, then it becomes possible to compare them all in considerable depth, taking uncertainty explicitly into account; but if there are many schemes, it may be more practicable to compare them first at a much broader level, to form a more limited working shortlist as illustrated in Figure 22.

Alternative directions of exit from the designing mode take the process into the choosing and the shaping modes respectively. Exit directly into the *choosing mode* will be possible where the participants agree that one course of action in a particular decision area is clearly superior to the others. For example, the participants in the South Side exercise might be so convinced by the advantages of the northern road line, after realising that it presents a far wider choice in other decision areas than the southern alternative, that they agree to make a recommendation for the northern line straight away, without conducting any further analysis. And there are also many circumstances in which an exit from the designing to the *shaping mode* will make sense. In particular, a very restricted range of alternatives within a problem focus may suggest that this focus might easily be extended, whereas a very wide range may suggest it should be narrowed down.

Also, as indicated in Figure 55, there are various ways in which the guidance offered in this chapter can involve more modest process 'loops' in the direction of the other modes. A loop towards the *shaping mode* is implied both in the coalescence of decision areas and in the breaking down of decision areas with composite options into two or more linked decision areas. A loop towards the *comparing mode* is implied in the step of separating out different levels of choice for the development of consistency matrices. It is also implied in the device of annotating option bars to indicate different kinds of arguments for introducing assumptions of incompatibility between options; arguments which in many cases will be grounded in value judgements of a debatable kind. Finally, the re-sequencing of a set of decision areas to bring more urgent decision areas to the fore implies a form of looping towards the *choosing mode,* where the pressures for action begin to dictate the direction in which the process moves.

Illustrations from practice

Following the precedent set in Chapter 5, a set of three diverse *illustrations from practice* is presented on the pages that follow. They have been selected to illustrate some of the more important practical points that arise in relation to the work of the designing mode.

   The first illustration, based on extracts from documents published in connection with a land-use policy plan for an English rural area, demonstrates one way in which information about options and their mutual consistency can be presented clearly for public discussion. The second illustration, from an application in the Netherlands, shows how members of a group can work together in developing a set of feasible schemes from the information contained in an option graph. The third illustration is taken from a group exercise in organisational choice, and anticipates some of the points to be made in Chapter 9 about systematic documentation of the progress made through interactive working on flip charts around the walls of a room.

Figure 56 Illustration from practice – designing 1

1

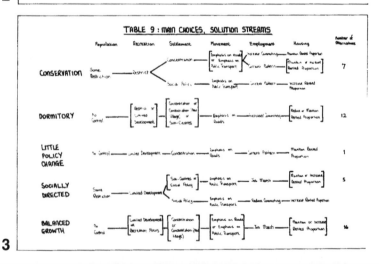

2

3

Designing	Theme:	Presentation for Public Discussion of Policy Options, Incompatibilities and Choices within Orientations.
	Problem:	Preparation of a Structure Plan as a Policy Framework for a Rural Area.
PRACTICE	Context:	Planning Team for Rutland with Various Community Groups, County of Leicestershire, England, 1975–76.

Commentary on Figure 56

These three extracts are taken from documents published by the County Council of Leicestershire in central England as part of the process of preparing a first official Structure Plan for Rutland. Rutland is a predominantly rural district of some 30,000 inhabitants which at that time (1975/6) had recently lost its independent County status (since recovered).

The table at the top is one of a series of six similar tables presented for public discussion in November 1975, as part of a consultation document entitled 'Let's talk about Rutland'. This particular table focuses on employment policy for Rutland, and lists in the first column a set of five possible options for employment, treated as a single decision area. Each row of the table contains notes on the incompatibility of that particular employment option with specific options in other decision areas concerned respectively with population change, housing, movement, recreation, settlement pattern and finance. For presentation purposes, the individual options in these other decision areas were not shown in separate subdivisions of the columns as in the standard format of option compatibility tables. This kind of simplification is most desirable in published documents. It will be noticed that the table does however briefly indicate the arguments on which particular option bars are based, so that the underlying assumptions can be challenged by readers.

Below the table appears an excerpt from a subsequent page of the same document (2), arguing for the exclusion of certain options on the strength of the foregoing analysis – among them the fifth of the employment policy options, excluded on the grounds of its excessive financial implications. After a description of the challenge of policy design and evaluation that remains (paragraphs 9.11 and 9.12), the report then goes on to list out the main options that remain in the various decision areas (only those for the first two decision areas, concerned with population and employment, being included in this extract).

The final illustration opposite is taken from a technical document written to present the analysis on which the submitted Structure Plan was based. The five 'solution streams' had been developed to indicate the range of choice available in the six main decision areas (excluding the financial decision area) for each of five broad policy 'orientations' or emphases which could be clearly envisaged by the County and District Councillors. It was indicated by the planners that the set of policies finally selected might be based on a compromise between orientations rather than the selection of any one orientation in its pure form; and the final decision was to go for a set of policies based on a position part way between the conservation and the socially directed orientations.

Figure 57   Illustration from practice – designing 2

1

2   **3**

Designing	Theme:	Deriving Alternative Schemes from an Option Graph and forming an Option Tree.
	Problem:	Implementation Policy for the Law against Nuisances, in an Environmental Policy Plan for a Municipality.
PRACTICE	Context:	Action-Research with the Project Group, Municipality of Emmen, The Netherlands, 1982.

Commentary on Figure 57

These photographs were taken at a working session of the project group during the second month of a one-year project to produce a Municipal Environmental Policy Plan. This work was undertaken by the Municipality of Emmen in the Province of Drenthe in the north of Holland as part of an action research project sponsored by the Central Government.

The project group was drawn from various parts of the organisation and contained a mixture of administrators, planners, engineers and other professionals. The alderman responsible for the plan was often present for parts of such sessions. Allen Hickling and Arnold de Jong, who were conducting the research, acted as process consultants.

A high level of unemployment in this part of Holland, and around Emmen in particular, had led to the environment receiving very low priority in the recent past. This had been especially the case with respect to industry and commerce. Thus the need for an Environmental Policy Plan was a matter of debate. Environmentalists argued it to be essential if not too late, while others considered it not only unnecessary, but even harmful.

The focus of the work in this sequence of photographs is the implementation of controls of various kinds – legal, planning, and so on (1). It represents a good example of how different levels of choice can be combined in an option graph – although this may be only of value early in a project.

Here there are decisions about whether to produce detailed local plans for the industrial areas; whether to be involved in zoning and the setting of norms; and the thoroughness of the implementation plan to be made for the law about nuisances. At the same time there were more general considerations about the attitude to management of controls, and the relaxation of by-laws.

The process of deriving the decision schemes on the wall is important (2). In this instance there were three members of the group directly involved, and this helped to keep track of the logic. The decision tree itself (3) is typical in that an unexpected number of schemes had to be accommodated, leading to a very asymmetrical layout. This does no harm to the learning process, and was corrected in the official loose-leaf record of the meeting. Here also the reasoning and assumptions underlying the option bars were recorded.

In this case recycling occurred soon after, and the whole problem was broken out into its constituent levels for further analysis.

Figure 58   Illustration from practice – designing 3

Designing

PRACTICE

Theme: Documentation using a photo record of progress in designing alternative decision schemes.

Problem: Organisational choice in developing a programme of a study group of a national society.

Context: Process of OR study group, Operational Research Society, Birmingham, England, 1985.

Commentary on Figure 58

The four illustrations opposite show how even relatively quickly drawn, exploratory flip charts produced in the course of a working session can be incorporated in a documentary record to help the participants recall afterwards something of the spirit of the process in which they were involved. The flip charts are part of a set of 17 generated during a one-day workshop held at the University of Aston in Birmingham by a study group of the Operational Research Society of Great Britain. This study group, called the Process of OR Study Group (PORSG), had been formed several years earlier by a set of members of the Society with an interest not just in the analytical techniques of operational research but in the wider process of carrying out operational research projects in organisations.

Nine members of the study group took part in the workshop, the task of which was to consider possible directions for the future of the group after a period in which its momentum seemed to have been slipping. Allen Hickling had agreed to act as facilitator to the workshop, of which John Friend was also a member. Because only a few hours were available, and because not all those present were familiar with the strategic choice approach, Allen Hickling did not involve the group as a whole in building up the record of progress on the wall; instead he combined the facilitator and recorder roles, attempting to capture the contributions of others on flip charts in a rapid, free-flowing way.

Quite early in the workshop, the initial concerns expressed by participants were structured loosely in the form of an ends/means diagram rather similar to that shown in Figure 45; from this, an initial set of seventeen decision areas was generated. The two wall charts on the right hand side reflect attempts to examine some of the broader decision areas more closely. It will be noticed that some questions arose in discussion about whether the labels of particular options should be changed, and whether or not options could be treated as mutually exclusive.

The more 'finished' option graph in the top left corner incluides a set of three key decision areas concerned with the future of the group; the form of organisation; and the question of expansion of its membership – a further decision area on frequency of meetings having been first included but then set aside. The analysis of this option graph indicated a choice of 14 decision schemes. A debate on preferences was centred on four comparison areas, some of which were treated as constraints; these were concerned with commitment, relevance to others, availability of enough willing people and effect on OR education.

The upshot of the meeting – corresponding broadly to scheme 10a in the tree – was the formation of a committee to work on a promotional strategy with a six-month deadline in view. The committee then went on to devise a programme of joint meetings with regional groups of the Society, thus opening up the debate about the practical process of conducting operational research projects to the wider membership of the Society. The analysis of this option graph indicated a choice of 14 decision schemes. A debate on preferences was centred on four comparison areas, some of which were treated as constraints; these were concerned with commitment, relevance to others, availability of enough willing people and effect on OR education.

7 Skills in comparing

Introduction

In this chapter the aim will be to explore, more fully than was possible in Chapter 3, the subtle judgements that arise when working in the comparing mode. The relevant core concepts were introduced in Figures 19 to 22; they are those of the *comparison area,* the *relative assessment,* the *advantage comparison* and the *working shortlist.* These concepts are all very general ones, which can be adapted to guide the work of the comparing mode at a variety of levels, ranging from the most rough and ready appraisal of 'pros' and 'cons' of some proposed action, to the most elaborate exercises in quantification and predictive modelling.

However, experience so far in applying strategic choice methods to practical decision problems supports the view that it is only very rarely that the more elaborate forms of comparison exercise can be justified. In the first place, it will usually take an exceptionally weighty decision to justify the time and resources called for in collating and analysing large amounts of data: more fundamentally, however, the strategic choice philosophy draws attention to the question of whether extensive investment in analysis will produce a good enough return in terms of the level of confidence with which decisions can be taken, once the full range of uncertainties bearing on that decision has been considered.

So experience indicates that it usually pays to concentrate on quite simple, crude approaches to the comparison of alternatives. Yet it is important to stress that there is always scope for *choice* in the ways alternatives are to be compared. There are choices to be made in the formulation of comparison areas; choices in methods of relative assessment; choices in ways of presenting broader advantage comparisons; and choices in the extent to which simplified numerical or other indices are introduced to narrow down the full range of alternatives to a more limited working shortlist. The guidance offered in this chapter is intended to help users in addressing these choices of evaluative method and style in a more conscious and effective way.

It is important to recognise that the work of comparing alternatives can become very *difficult* in practice, however simple or elaborate the chosen methods of evaluation may be. The difficulties encountered can be political as much as technical, especially where there are many different constituencies of interest which might be affected – some perhaps directly represented in the decision process and others not. Furthermore, the procedural setting itself may be far

Figure 59   Developing a set of relevant comparison areas

South Side
example

DECISION AREA [-options]	RELEVANT COMPARISON AREAS	check relevance to other decision areas within present problem focus :			
		ROAD LINE?	SHOP LOC'N?	CENT'L SITE?	DIST LIFE?
ROAD LINE? [-NORTH -SOUTH]	• CAPITAL OUTLAY • IMPACT ON RESIDENTS • FLEXIBILITY of future development opportunities	: : •	✓ ? ✓	✓ ✓ ✓	? ✓
SHOP LOC'N? [-MAIN -KING -GAS]	• INCOME from rents • CONVENIENCE TO SHOPPERS • CONTINUITY FOR TRADERS • ROAD SAFETY		: : : •	✓ ✓	
CENT'L SITE? [-IND -HOUS -OPEN]	• LOCAL JOBS created • contribution to HOUSING POLICY • VISUAL IMPACT on local environment			• • •	✓
DIST LIFE? [-10 YR -20 YR -40 YR]	• CONFIDENCE of South Side residents				•

Comparing

S K I L L S

In building up a set of comparison areas which are relevant to a specific problem focus, it can be useful to start by examining each of the decision areas in turn, identifying the more important areas of difference between options as indicated here. When working interactively, this kind of activity is usually carried out verbally, and can be combined with the use of various brainstorming methods.

from simple, and may change as the problem focus shifts. For these reasons, the guidance in this chapter will be shaped according to the principle of *dynamic comparison,* which has already been touched upon in the concluding section of Chapter 3. This principle captures the evaluative implications of the wider view of planning as a process of choosing strategically through time: a process in which there may be a succession of 'evaluative moments' as the focus of comparison changes or as new information comes to light, whether through unforeseen circumstances or through explorations deliberately set in train.

Identifying appropriate comparison areas

In general, a set of comparison areas should be chosen to be as relevant as possible to the scope of the decision problem currently in view, and also to the political domain within which decisions are to be made. With problems of any complexity, there is always a danger that these considerations taken together will draw the participants in the direction of quite an elaborate evaluation frame, with a longer list of comparison areas than can be conveniently managed when working under practical pressures. So, as with the definition of decision areas, it can be worth devoting some time and effort to the formulation of an appropriate yet manageable set of comparison areas. Yet again, as with decision areas, people's views on comparison areas may change as a group process builds up momentum and the level of shared understanding grows; so the formulation of comparison areas is better viewed as a continuing matter of concern than as something which should take up a great deal of time in the early stages of an interactive process.

Where a current problem focus is expressed in terms of a set of linked decision areas and a choice of options within each, one practical way in which to begin generating comparison areas is to take each decision area in turn – perhaps starting with those which are believed to be most important – and then to consider what kinds of consequences or effects are thought to be most relevant to the comparison of options within each. One way of organising such a process is illustrated in Figure 59.

In this example, the first question concerns the consequences of choosing between the northern and the southern road line through South Side. It might be immediately apparent that these options are likely to differ in terms of capital outlay and also in terms of impact on local residents. Further discussion might then suggest that there is another important consequence to be considered, relating to the flexibility to pursue further local development options in the future. So the consideration of this one decision area has indicated a set of three different comparison areas straight away. These are listed in Figure 59 using brief and tentative definitions. Such definitions can always be extended later, in the manner illustrated earlier in Figure 19, and can be modified, if need be, as the work proceeds. Some of these comparison areas may, of course, also be relevant to other decision areas as well; this is indicated in Figure 59 by checking off subsequent columns in the table where this is thought to be the case, or where there is some doubt over this point.

Turning to the second decision area – that on location of the shopping centre – an additional set of comparison areas may emerge as important. These again are listed in a tentative way, using the options within the decision area as one source of guidance in reviewing what kinds of comparison areas are likely to be significant. As further decision areas are added, the list is extended further – though it becomes more and more likely that some at least of the relevant comparison areas will have already been generated at an earlier stage. In the example of Figure 59, it will be seen that a set of eleven tentative comparison areas has been generated once the four decision areas within the chosen problem focus have been considered in turn.

But a list of comparison areas generated in this way is unlikely to provide a well-balanced base for comparing alternatives, until some further work has been done on the *structure* of the list. For a start, the list may well be too long for working purposes; furthermore, it may contain a certain amount of repetition or overlap, raising doubts about the level of generality or specificity with which comparison areas should be expressed. For example, in considering the ROAD LINE? decision area, it was at first considered good enough to talk simply of 'impact on residents' without distinguishing one group of residents from another. Further down the list, in comparing options for DIST LIFE?, it was however felt to be appropriate to formulate a rather more specific comparison area concerned with the level of confidence of South Side residents in the future of the area. If the West Street decision area were to be added to the list, then a further question could arise of whether impacts on this more compact group of residents should be considered separately from those on the larger South Side community.

In many practical problem situations, questions will arise about *discrimination* between different affected groups, between different kinds of impact on the same group and, possibly, between different time horizons of impact as well. In the South Side situation, it might indeed be very important that the working party should debate what different *categories* of impact on residents there might be: whether, for instance, it could be important to distinguish the severe and immediate consequences for those few residents facing the possibility of physical demolition of their homes from the less severe but continuing nuisance to others from high levels of traffic vibration and noise.

Developing a balanced evaluation frame

Participants in a decision process do not normally work entirely from scratch when building up a list of comparison areas relevant to each new decision problem that comes up. Usually, each member of a group begins with some preconceptions about a relevant *frame* of evaluation; a frame which may either have evolved as a purely intuitive response to felt political pressures, or may have been articulated more systematically as an expression of formal organisational policies or aims.

One of the more explicit forms that a frame of evaluation can take is a written statement of guiding *objectives* of the type often developed by those responsible for the management and control of large corporate organisations. Such a statement may sometimes be structured in a hierarchical form, with expressions of broad aspirations at one level and expressions of more specific policy intentions at another. In other situations the elements in the framework may be expressed in less aspirational and more pragmatic terms; perhaps in terms of broad problem areas to be addressed, such as poverty or unemployment, rather than in terms of idealistic aims to be achieved. Usually, however, a statement expressed in terms of amelioration of problems can be rewritten in terms of achievement of goals, or vice versa; the underlying sense of purpose may be quite similar in either case.

Underlying such statements of purpose, however, may be more subtle political pressures, relating to the structure of accountability within which the participants are operating. Sometimes, this sense of accountability will differ significantly from one participant to another: one member of the South Side Working Party, for example, might feel a special responsibility for the interests of South Side residents, and another for the interests of unemployed school leavers throughout the wider municipality. Such variations are likely to be influenced by some mix of personal commitments, representational roles and the principles of accountability on which the membership of the working group has been selected.

Figure 60 illustrates how it is possible to use more than one type of evaluation frame as a point of reference in the search to develop a more structured set of comparison areas for a process of strategic choice. In the first list, based on a more *purposive* approach, a set of broad headings and more specific sub-headings is used to develop a framework of *policy* appropriate to the South Side problem; in the second list, a different set of headings and sub-headings is used to identify relevant interests or 'stakeholder' groups, reflecting a concern to be *responsive* to varied political pressures. Either list would probably have to be extended quite considerably before it could be considered to be at all complete in its own terms. Nevertheless, these two examples of evaluation frames are both reasonably typical of their kind. The first is typical of the kind of hierarchically-ordered statement of objectives which is sometimes formally adopted as a set of central guidelines for the work of a corporate organisation; while the second is typical of the range of interests to which a set of publicly accountable decision-makers might see themselves as having to respond. If the setting were one of a commercial rather than a political organisation, the headings might, of course, be different – for example, the interests to be considered might include shareholders, employees, customers, suppliers – but the organising principles would be much the same.

Either type of list could, of course, be used directly as a set of comparison areas within which to evaluate alternative courses of action. However, in ad-

Figure 60   Building a balanced evaluation framework

South Side
example

(1) FRAMEWORK OF POLICY CONCERNS (purposive approach)

ECONOMIC
- restrict municipal expenditure commitments
- increase local wealth / tax base
- create new local employment

SOCIAL
- avoid disrupting established communities
- reduce inequalities in access to welfare facilities

ENVIRONMENTAL
- segregate vehicles and pedestrians
- enhance quality of urban landscape
- reduce level of air pollution around steelworks

(2) FRAMEWORK OF INTERESTS TO BE CONSIDERED (responsive approach)

RESIDENTS
- Dockport urban area as a whole
- South Side district
- local neighbourhoods affected by particular proposals

UNEMPLOYED
- adults
- school leavers

LOCAL TAXPAYERS
- households
- businesses

EXTERNAL INTERESTS
- national taxpayers
- users of inter-city highways

Comparing

SKILLS

Even where a set of comparison areas has been generated initially with reference to a particular problem focus, it can be useful to check the list for balance and coverage by cross-reference to broader evaluation frameworks. Different perspectives can emerge by referring to frameworks expressed in terms of organisational purposes and of political interests, so use of both types of framework can be worthwhile.

dressing any specific decision problem it will often be more helpful to generate comparison areas directly in the first instance, as illustrated in Figure 59. Then the tentative comparison areas generated in this way can be matched against whatever more structured lists of policy concerns and interests may be available, to help generate insights into ways in which the set of comparison areas to be used might be reformulated in a more logical and consistent way.

Although the two types of framework illustrated in Figure 60 are organised on different principles, there will often be more similarities between them than might at first appear. For example, a concern with employment appears in both lists, expressed in different ways, as does a concern with municipal expenditure levels. The value of this kind of cross-reference between contrasting frames of reference is that it illuminates the scope for *choices* in the way comparison areas are expressed. Among them are choices between different levels of specificity or generality, and between levels of aggregation or disaggregation which might be considered appropriate to a particular decision process and a particular 'evaluative moment' within that process.

One particular opportunity for evaluative choice concerns the possibility of reformulating some comparison areas as decision areas, relating to choices of policy orientation at a quite general level. This opens up the opportunity for an alternative approach to evaluation which was introduced in Chapter 6 (Figure 54), based on the exploration of *consistency* between different levels of choice. This can be particularly helpful where there is uncertainty or disagreement about choices of appropriate policy stance: for example, lack of agreement on whether corporate expenditure commitments should be held to their present level, allowed to increase to some degree, or perhaps deliberately reduced. Such matters can often be the subject of long-standing political controversy, which cannot always be addressed too explicitly in a process of strategic choice – but which even so can be accommodated in the analytical work.

Approaches to the comparison of alternatives in terms of flexibility

Whatever the range of policy concerns or interests that may be relevant to a decision problem, there is one particular aspect of comparison that is of fundamental importance to the process of choosing strategically through time. This is the comparison of alternative courses of short-term action in terms of the *flexibility* of future choice which they allow. One approach to this aspect of comparison was illustrated in Figure 25, where five possible action schemes for South Side were compared in terms of the range of longer-term decision schemes left open by each. This range was first presented in terms of a straight count of schemes; but then a *robustness* index was used to indicate how many schemes in each case met a specified threshold of acceptability, reflecting the concerns of one of the more important of the various interest groups affected in this case.

In general, flexibility of future choice tends to be valued positively by decision-makers. This is because the more courses of action are left open for the future, the greater *in general* will be the prospects of successful adaptation to whatever changes in circumstances the future may bring.[1] However, it may not always be realistic to treat flexibility of future choice as one simple comparison area, because the value of such flexibility may differ between one area of future choice and another, and also between one set of interests and another. Indeed, flexibility to one party may sometimes mean restrictions of opportunities to others. In South Side, for example, the opportunities for residents to improve their homes, or to exercise other kinds of choices in their own domestic lives, might become more restricted if certain options for development on nearby sites were not foreclosed.

Where many alternatives are being compared in broad terms, it may be adequate to treat flexibility or some such term as a single broadly defined comparison area, as in the list of Figure 59. At other times, however, it may be important to relate this aspect of comparison more carefully to some evaluation framework which identifies a range of affected interests or policy concerns, as in the two examples of Figure 60. This finer level of flexibility analysis becomes practicable in any situation where opportunities for future choice have been structured in terms of decision areas and options, so that flexibility in some decision areas can be given greater weight than flexibility in others. For example, in the situation of Figure 25, the first of the five short-term action schemes could be regarded with particular favour as it is the only one to leave open the opportunity of developing the central site for industry – an aspect of flexibility which could be viewed as of particular importance to the local unemployed.

Another possibility – which will be discussed more fully in Chapter 8 – is that the preservation of options in some decision areas might be seen as of particular significance as a means of responding to certain specified *contingencies* that might arise in future. For example, the opportunity to zone the central site in South Side for industry might be seen as of particular significance if the contingency of closure of the local steelworks were to occur.

Circumstances sometimes arise in practice where another related aspect of flexibility has to be considered; the flexibility not just to choose between alternative courses of action in future but to *alter* courses of current action at some point in time after an initial commitment has been made. Where decision areas and options have been rigorously defined in terms of immediate action commitments of an irrevocable nature, this possibility should strictly speaking not arise. However, when people are working on problems under pressure, this kind of rigour is not always appropriate. This is a point that is of particular significance in relation to choices of broad policy orientation, which may be publicly adopted at one moment but can be modified or reversed later should circumstances change.

1 This can be seen a essentially an expression of the cybernetic law of requisite variety, first enunciated by Ross Ashby in his 'Introduction to Cybernetics' (Ashby, 1956). At its simplest, the law states that 'it takes variety to control variety'.

One means of approaching this question of flexibility to modify a policy position at some future time is illustrated in Figure 61. This example builds on the comparison of South Side policy orientations presented earlier (Figure 54). Figure 61 starts by presenting the courses of possible action at an operational level which are left open by each of the three possible policy orientations – omitting the short-term private orientation because no schemes at all at the operational level were found to be consistent with it.

Also, it was indicated in Figure 54 that a long-term private investment orientation was believed to be of doubtful feasibility. In such circumstances, one working assumption might be that such an orientation could not be adopted in the short term, yet that the choice of a short-term public investment orientation now could leave open the possibility of a later switch to a long-term private orientation, should a sufficiently interested and influential private investor appear. The full logic of this situation is represented in Figure 61, where POLICY NOW? and POLICY LATER? are formulated as separate areas of choice, in place of the composite decision area which was originally labelled INVESTMENT ORIENTATION?. The choice *now* of an orientation towards short-term public investment can then be compared to the choice *now* of a long-term public investment orientation – or, indeed, any other alternative – in terms of the additional flexibility it offers in terms of its *changeability* to a different policy position in future. However, it should be noted that, in this example, the flexibility available in the 'Level 2' decision areas may be limited if some of them are of high urgency, calling for commitment at or before the time the initial policy is agreed. This kind of difficulty will be considered further in Chapter 8.

Choice of method of assessment within a comparison area

Just as there are different ways in which alternative courses of action can be compared in terms of their relative flexibility, so more generally there are different ways in which alternatives can be compared within any other kind of comparison area. This means that there are always judgements to be made as to how any kind of comparative information should be *presented* to help people make comparisons between specific alternatives – not least where information from varied sources has to be compressed into a compact and intelligible form. Among the practical choices to be faced are choices relating to the use of different forms of language for communication such as words, figures and graphs, as well as choices about the ways in which feelings of uncertainty should be expressed. Some of the differences of approach that can be considered in both these directions were considered in Chapter 3 (Figures 20 and 21).

Underlying such choices of presentation, however, may be deeper choices about the actual techniques or *procedures* to be used in making assessments of alternatives, and the sources of information or judgement on which those procedures should draw. Such choices of assessment procedure can sometimes have an important bearing on the levels of effort and time to be devoted to different

Figure 61   Expressing interchangeability in policy choice

South Side
example

LEVEL 1 (POLICY) CHOICE

INVESTMENT ORIENTATION?

POLICY   POLICY
NOW?   LATER?

LEVEL 2 CHOICES

ROAD   SHOP   CENT'L   WEST
LINE?   LOC'N? SITE?   ST.?

- LONG TERM ————— [no change / possible]   —— NORTH - MAIN - [HOUS - YES / OPEN - YES]
  PUBLIC

- SHORT TERM ——— CONTINUE   —— NORTH - MAIN - [IND - [YES / NO] / HOUS - [YES / NO]]
  PUBLIC

* CHANGE TO ——— [NORTH - KING - OPEN - [YES / NO]
  LONG TERM   SOUTH - GAS - OPEN — NO]
  PRIVATE

* opportunity to change
  to this policy orientation
  may arise later IF
  a major private developer
  should express interest

[note that choices in some of
these level 2 decision areas
may become foreclosed if they
are subject to pressures for
decision before opportunities
for policy change arise]

Comparing

S K I L L S

Where decision areas relate to choices of policy stance or other positions which allow future modification, it can sometimes be useful to compare short-term alternatives in terms of the possibility of changing to other positions at some future time. Such comparisons are usually made informally and interactively, but this example of a more formal comparison illustrates the general principles involved.

comparison areas, and also on the levels of confidence with which assessments can be expressed.

Some procedures of assessment are highly intuitive, while others involve precisely-defined sequences of calculation. For example, to form an assessment of the relative capital outlays involved in different development options for the central site in South Side, there could be a choice of either asking a single financial or engineering expert for a quick 'off the cuff' guess, based on accumulated personal experience; or calling for a more painstaking calculation taking several weeks, in which several different experts might be asked to play some part. However simplified or elaborate the procedure may be, it is important to remember that the range of underlying sources of uncertainty will be the same – the choice being one as to whether or not effort should be invested in exploring them in a conscious way.

Wherever a particular procedure of assessment is thought to be critical to the decisions currently in view, there is always the opportunity to pause and explore its structure in more depth, in a search for a fuller understanding of the pattern of elements and operations on which it is built. One systematic means of conducting this kind of exploration is illustrated in Figure 62. For illustrative purposes, this example is restricted to one comparatively tangible aspect of the assessment procedures in South Side – that of the relative assessment of capital outlays for two of the development options for the central site.

The breakdown of elements and operations in Figure 62 begins by taking two of the apparently straightforward numerical assessments of capital cost which were first presented in Chapter 3 (Figure 22): the estimates of 450k and 200k entered against the industrial and housing options for use of the central site.

The baseline for each of the assessments in Figure 62 is assumed to be the 'null option' of leaving the site in its present derelict state – an option which may be purely hypothetical in so far as it is not considered a realistic alternative within the present South Side problem formulation but, nevertheless, might offer a well-defined starting point for the application of standard cost assessment techniques.

In Figure 62, the assessments of capital outlay for the industrial and housing options are both shown broken down in a stepwise way into various contributory *elements* of assessment. Some of these take the form of other more basic estimates of a quantitative kind – for instance, estimates of the usable site area and the unit cost of site servicing per hectare – while others take the form of non-numerical statements of assumptions which are still worth recording explicitly, especially where they remain open to challenge. For example, one engineer might assume that engineering difficulties on the central site were 'not exceptional'; yet another might cast doubt on this assumption in the light of a somewhat different appraisal of drainage problems or geological conditions. Again, some participants might wish to challenge an underlying policy assumption that industrial sites should be provided with a comprehensive range of infrastructure services before being advertised for rental or sale, whereas only

Figure 62 Uncovering the elements in an assessment procedure

South Side
example

ELEMENTS IN ESTIMATION OF CAPITAL COSTS OF SERVICING CENTRAL SITE FOR ALTERNATIVE USES:	CENT'L SITE?	
	– ind	– hous
estimated cost of servicing this site	450 k	200 k
estimated usable site area	30 ha	25 ha
full area of site	40 ha	40 ha
⊖ estimated extent of buffer zone	–10 ha	–15 ha
⊗ estimated site servicing cost/ha	x 15 k/ha	x 8 k/ha
knowledge of unit servicing costs on other comparable recent sites	11–14 k/ha	6–7 k/ha
predicted rate of cost inflation for site servicing contracts	5% per year	5% per year
extent of any engineering difficulties expected on this site	not exceptional	not exceptional
policy on range of site infrastructure services to be provided by municipality	comprehensive for industrial sites	minimal for housing sites

[simple arithmetical operations]
marked ◯

Comparing

SKILLS

This kind of systematic exploration of the elements contributing to an assessment procedure is not usually worth carrying out unless and until the focus for comparison has been narrowed down to a few alternatives which differ critically in terms of assessments in particular comparison areas, making it important to explore key sources of uncertainty and alternative ways in which they might be managed.

minimal infrastructure should be provided if housing development were being considered.

The breakdown of assessments into contributory operations and elements is a procedure that could, in theory, be pursued almost indefinitely, exposing more and more hidden assumptions all the time. However, this depth of investigation will not normally be justified unless it is suspected that it will expose new areas of uncertainty which might have a critical effect on work within the choosing mode. Under practical time and resource pressures, it is more usual to trust the judgement of the experts; however, the opportunity is always there to ask probing questions about the assumptions underlying any expert assessments, and Figure 62 illustrates one general procedure that can be used to probe systematically the range of assumptions on which particular assessments rest.[2]

Of course, the nature of the assumptions and the underlying procedure of assessment may be quite different in different types of comparison area. For instance, any assessments of annual incomes for the two alternatives in Figure 62 could depend on judgements about the year-by-year build up of incomes over some fixed period of future years, with mounting levels of uncertainty as the time horizon extends. And, wherever there is no obvious numerical unit of assessment on which to rely – as in the assessment of the impact any course of action might have on existing residents of South Side – then the breakdown of contributory assumptions is likely to be a less straightforward matter. But the same principles apply; and the method of stepwise investigation of assumptions illustrated in Figure 62 remains valid even when most or all of the contributory assumptions have to be explored by interrogating an expert whose assessments are based purely on personal experience and informed judgement.

Expressing feelings of uncertainty when assessing alternatives

Because any assessment of the effects of pursuing a course of action involves at least some elements of conjecture, anybody who is asked to contribute towards the process of assessment must expect to encounter feelings of *uncertainty* – whether these feelings are addressed consciously or at a more unconscious level. Referring again to the example of an assessment procedure considered in Figure 62, it might be possible for a local planner to feel very confident about quoting a figure of four hectares for the full area of the central site, accepting that details of boundary demarcation could make a marginal difference. Yet the extent of the proposed buffer zone – assumed to be wider in the case of the housing than the industrial option, so as to provide a higher level of insulation from traffic noise – might be seen as a rather more debatable matter. And the assessment of site servicing costs per hectare might be expected to involve higher levels of uncertainty again – as was indeed suggested in Figure 62 by the fuller

2 Other examples relating to actual planning studies carried out by Coventry City Council were presented in *Local Government and Strategic Choice* (Friend & Jessop, 1969/77 pp69-95).

Figure 63　Eliciting limits of surprise

South Side
example

would it surprise you if it were suggested that the CAPITAL COST PER HECTARE to service industrial development on this site could be:

below 5 k/ha? (YES!)　　　　　above 30k/ha? (YES!)
below 10k/ha? (YES)　　　　　above 20k/ha? (YES)
below 12k/ha? (NO)　　　　　above 18k/ha (NO)

So take range of assessments as [10k/ha to 20k/ha]
point assessment (best guess) as 15 k/ha

would it surprise you if it were suggested that the BALANCE OF ADVANTAGE between schemes A and B in terms of the CAPITAL: comparison area could be:

extreme in favour of A? (YES!)　　　extreme in favour of B? (YES)
considerable in favour of A? (YES!)　considerable in favour of B? (NO)
significant in favour of A? (YES)
marginal in favour of A? (YES)
negligible either way? (YES)
marginal in favour of B? (YES)
significant in favour of B? (NO)

So take balance of advantage in terms of CAPITAL:
to be [significant to considerable] in favour of B

Comparing

SKILLS

This kind of stepwise questioning process is usually carried out verbally, and can be introduced briefly and informally at any stage of interactive working where it is proving difficult to arrive at an assessment either on a numerical or a more judgemental scale. It can be used either to overcome unwillingness to offer any assessment at all, or to probe the level of uncertainty surrounding a point assessment.

breakdown of this element into four different contributory elements, not all of them of a readily quantifiable form.

People who are asked to make assessments under uncertainty – even if they be professional experts in their field – do not always behave in a similar or consistent way. One expert, for instance, might prefer to quote a single estimate of 15k per hectare for industrial servicing costs, as if it were quite incontrovertible, treating any feelings of uncertainty as a purely personal concern. However, another expert might profess such a high state of uncertainty as to be reluctant to offer any figure at all – perhaps for fear of being called to account should any estimate offered later be falsified by events. To overcome such feelings of reluctance in quoting figures – or conversely, to get a sense of the level of uncertainty which surrounds a single apparently confident estimate – it is often worth adopting a simple questioning procedure which has become known as the *surprise limit method*. This method is illustrated with reference to South Side in Figure 63.

The surprise limit method can be applied to any element within an assessment procedure which calls for judgements along some numerical or equivalent scale. It involves asking a series of questions of a person who holds information in that field – the *knowledge source*, in expert systems language – as to what levels on that scale would cause them *surprise*, starting with extreme levels at either end and gradually working inwards until a range of 'non-surprising' possibilities remains.

Figure 63 demonstrates two different levels at which this approach can be applied to the comparison of capital outlays for Schemes A and B in the South Side problem situation. In the first set of questions, it is supposed that an expert – in this case perhaps a civil engineer – starts from a position of reluctance to give any estimate of the capital cost per hectare of servicing the central site for industrial development. So the interrogator begins by taking what is likely to be an unrealistically low level – in this case 5k per hectare – and asking whether it would cause the expert any surprise if the servicing cost per hectare were as low as this. If the expert says 'yes' then the question is repeated with successively higher levels until a level which no longer causes surprise is reached. The same kind of question can also be asked, starting from what is initially judged to be an unrealistically high level and working downwards.

Usually, the questioner works from the two ends more or less alternately, accepting that there will be a tendency to 'overshoot' the limits of surprise from time to time. The process is, therefore, one of gradual narrowing down from both ends until a view is arrived at of the *range* of tenable assumptions in between. Such a procedure, of working by successive approximation towards a feasible range, can usually persuade even the most reluctant expert to give some expression to his or her 'limits of surprise', even when starting from a position of refusal to make any estimate at all. In the opposite situation, where an expert refuses to deviate from a single point on the scale, it becomes possible to test the limits of surprise by working outwards from that point rather than inwards from the extremes. In practice, the procedure is usually conducted purely through verbal questions and answers; it is mainly for illustrative purposes that Figure 63 sets out the successive steps in written form.

The second illustration in Figure 63 shows how the surprise limit method can be applied even when the scale is a non-numerical one. The scale here is the generalised one of degree of *comparative advantage* which was first illustrated in Chapter 3 (Figure 21). The process of asking surprise limit questions in relation to this non-numerical scale is essentially the same as before; this example demonstrates how relative assessments can be arrived at even within comparison areas where there is no basis for comparing alternatives other than in terms of some intuitive sense of level of advantage – marginal, significant or whatever – within the specific setting in which decisions are to be made.

There is, of course, no reason why surprise limit questions should not be addressed to more than one expert. Indeed, the possibility that there may be several different knowledge sources opens the way to the use of systematic approaches such as the Delphi method (Dalkey, 1969) for pooling the judgements of several individuals with differing kinds or levels of expertise to contribute. Such experiments, if used as a background for discussion rather than a substitute for it, can expose all kinds of hidden differences in the assumptions of different individuals. One exercise in which a surprise limit approach was used to explore differences in perception between colleagues in the same team – an administrator, a planner and an engineer – has been fully reported elsewhere (Friend, Power and Yewlett, 1974 p140–158).

Combining advantage judgements across different comparison areas

It can be difficult enough at times to arrive at judgements of the balance of advantage between alternatives within any single comparison area: it can be even more difficult to judge the overall balance of advantage across a set of dissimilar comparison areas. This was illustrated by the comparison in Chapter 3 (Figure 21) of two alternative schemes for South Side across the four comparison areas of CAPITAL:, INCOME:, JOBS: and RESIDENTS:, each represented by a range of points on a common advantage comparison scale. It is at such moments of evaluation *across* comparison areas that major feelings of uncertainty about value considerations tend to come most directly to the fore, and have to be taken into account alongside whatever other feelings of uncertainty may have been encountered in making assessments within the separate comparison areas taken one at a time.

It is never an easy matter to bring diverse sources of uncertainty within a common analytical framework. But it is necessary to do so if it is intended to compare alternative approaches to the management of uncertainty within the choosing mode; and it was as a step in this direction that a broad-based method of advantage comparison under uncertainty was introduced in Chapter 3. The judgement was presented (Figure 21) that Scheme B had the advantage over

Scheme A in terms of capital outlay and probably also in terms of impact on residents; but that Scheme A had the advantage in terms of income and jobs. But the levels of advantage were subject to much uncertainty – uncertainty deriving in part from the process of assessment within each comparison area and, in part, from the value judgements involved in conversion to the common advantage comparison scale. These uncertainties made it all the more difficult in that example (Figure 21) to judge where the overall balance of advantage lay when all four comparison areas were taken into account.

This kind of balancing process is one which people continually have to undertake in practice, if only in an intuitive way. However, once a comparative advantage scale has been used to record an explicit picture of judgements and assumptions, it becomes possible to supplement that intuition – and to carry out checks on its reliability – by resort to rather more systematic methods. One way of doing this is illustrated in Figure 64. In Figure 64, a numerical scale of advantage assessment has been introduced as a means of *calibrating* the distinctions between bands on the original non-numerical scale, and thus as a basis for combining judgements across the different comparison areas. The calibration of the scale is a matter of convenience: the particular numerical scale used in Figure 64 treats the point of no advantage either way as zero, and takes the boundary between the 'significant' and 'considerable' bands as ten points in either direction – one direction being treated as negative and the other positive so as to keep the arithmetic straight.

Such a scale allows the mid-point of the range for each comparison area to be expressed as either a negative or a positive number. These numbers can then be added together to arrive at a rough estimate of the mid-point of the *range of belief* about overall comparative advantage, for any set of comparison areas taken in combination. In the illustration of Figure 64, there is a total of 20 'advantage points' in favour of B to be counted by adding the mid-points of the CAPITAL: and RESIDENTS: ranges, against 19 points in favour of A obtained by adding the mid-points of the INCOME: and JOBS: assessments. The net effect is a marginal single point of net advantage in favour of B when all four comparisons are combined.

But then there is the influence of uncertainty to be considered, which is considerable in this case. A rough rule of thumb, which is good enough for most practical purposes, is that the range of belief for a combined advantage comparison will be a little wider than the range of belief for the most uncertain of the separate advantage comparisons within the individual comparison areas; if there are two comparison areas with an equally wide span of uncertainty, then a span about half as wide again as either of them can be assumed. In the illustration of Figure 64, it will be noticed that the range for both RESIDENTS: and JOBS: extends about 10 points on either side of the mid-point, whereas the range for both CAPITAL: and INCOME: assessments is significantly less. So the rule of thumb suggests that a range of about 15 points on either side of the mid-point will be roughly right as an expression of the total range of uncertainty when all comparison areas are combined. As shown in Figure 64, this

South Side
example

ADVANTAGE COMPARISON B vs A

combined judgment on above four comparison areas :

[calculation of mid point : +12 -7 -12 +8 = +1]

EFFECT OF ADDING A FURTHER COMPARISON IN TERMS OF FLEXIBILITY

combined judgment over all five comparison areas :

+3

means there could be a significant or even considerable advantage to either alternative when all sources of uncertainty are taken into account: so there is a case for some serious thought about how the overall range of uncertainty could be managed, before a preference in the direction of either alternative is expressed.

This kind of procedure for combining advantage comparisons can also be carried out in a step by step way, introducing one new comparison area at a time. This possibility is illustrated in Figure 64 by the introduction of FLEX-IBILITY: as an additional comparison area; the range of positions on the scale being based, in this case, purely on a quick intuitive judgement about the relative flexibility of A and B. In the event, Figure 64 shows that this addition makes only a marginal difference to the mid-point and range arrived at for the other four comparison areas combined.

With practice, it becomes possible to use a non-numerical advantage comparison scale in a quick and informal way, either as a group activity or by asking people to work individually on pre-prepared sheets, then comparing and collating the individual judgements which they make. It usually takes a little experience to arrive at consistent interpretations of the different levels of significance within a particular working situation; for people have to learn to use the successive bands of a comparative advantage scale in a broadly similar way.

For example, in a particular context, it might seem to make sense to rate one alternative as having a 'considerable' advantage over another in each of two comparison areas, but little sense to regard their combined advantage as 'extreme'. In that case, it might be decided to extend the width of the 'considerable' band on the scale until such inconsistencies tended to disappear. Also, methods based on statistical theory can provide a check on any more intuitive rules of thumb by which ranges of uncertainty are combined.[3] However, in interactive group working, such checks are mainly of use on an occasional basis, as a means of building confidence that intuition is not generating results which are at too much variance with logic.

Applying constraints in the choice of a working shortlist

Where there is a large number of decision schemes to be compared, it will usually be quite unrealistic to subject more than a few of them to the kind of carefully structured pair comparison process under uncertainty which has just been discussed; so the need to choose a more restricted working shortlist becomes acute. One approach to the choice of such a working shortlist was illustrated in

3 If a set of variables are independent and can be assumed to follow the normal (Gaussian) probability distribution, then the standard deviation of their sum can be taken as the square root of the sum of the squares of the separate standard deviations. So if the ranges shown in Figure 64 are assumed to represent two standard deviations on either side of the mean, the corresponding distance for the first four comparison areas combined would be the square root of (four squared plus five squared plus ten squared plus ten squared), which is about equal to sixteen.

Figure 65 Applying constraints in generating decision schemes

South Side
e x a m p l e

expected capital costs in k (recalibrated with least cost alternative in each column = 0)

joint assessment

ROAD LINE?		SHOP LOC'N?	DIST LIFE?		CENT'L SITE?		WEST ST?	
- NORTH	50k	- MAIN	-10YR	0	-IND	450k	-YES	150k
- SOUTH	0	- KING	-10YR	300k	-HOUS	200k	-NO	0
			-20YR	400k	-OPEN	0		
			-40YR	450k				
		-GAS	-20YR	650k				
			-40YR	750k				

PROPOSED RULE FOR ELIMINATING HIGH-COST SCHEMES: close any branch when cumulative total for expected capital cost exceeds 500k

SCHEME:

NORTH ——— 50k ——— MAIN -10YR ——— 50k ——— IND ——— 500k ——— YES ——X 650k
NO ——— 500k ——— P
HOUS ——— 250k ——— YES ——— 400k ——— Q
NO ——— 250k ——— R

KING { 10YR ——— 350k ——— HOUS ——X 550k
20YR ——— 400k ——— HOUS ——X 600k
OPEN ——— 400k ——— YES ——X 550k
NO ——— 400k ——— S
40YR ——— 500k ——— HOUS ——X 700k
OPEN ——— 500k ——— YES ——X 650k
NO X (option bar)

SOUTH ——— 0 ——— GAS { 20YR ——X 650k
40YR ——X 750k

PROPOSED WORKING SHORTLIST: compare R,S,P, using R to represent Q

Chapter 3 (Figure 22), where all schemes which were estimated to come above a specified threshold of capital cost were set aside, as were all those which did not meet a specified minimum level on the non-numerical residents' confidence index. The application of such minimum or maximum *constraints* on selected indices of assessment is a useful, if obvious, means of arriving at a working shortlist where there is a very large number of possible decision schemes to be considered. This is especially so where the options within the individual decision areas can be assessed separately on numerical or equivalent scales, and assessments for some at least of the combinations of options can be made simply by adding the option assessments together. In practice a monetary index is often used as a constraint, because there are many situations in which it is politically appropriate to apply some upper limit to the overall cost of a decision scheme. However, in other situations a constraint might be placed on the minimum number of jobs created, or the maximum number of residents to be displaced, or the minimum ratio of annual return to investment. In general, it will, of course, only be worth introducing a constraint on any scale if it corresponds to a concern which is important in the particular context in which the participants are working.

When applying a constraint to a large and complex set of decision schemes, it is not always necessary to work through all possible schemes in full. One means of simplifying the procedure is illustrated in Figure 65. Here, assessments of capital cost are indicated for the set of possible decision schemes for South Side, these being presented in the form of a tree as in Chapter 3 (Figure 22) – but with some adjustments introduced to illustrate particular points. First, the WEST ST? decision area has been added, which increases the total range of schemes. Secondly, the options within the SHOP LOC'N? and DIST LIFE? decision areas are assessed jointly rather than separately – because it is supposed now that there are certain costs associated with choosing options in particular combinations in these two decision areas – and the sequence of decision areas has been modified so as to bring these two decision areas together. Thirdly, the capital cost assessments in each column have been recalibrated so that the alternative with the lowest capital cost is taken as zero and the expected capital cost of every other alternative is assessed as a positive figure relative to this minimum amount. Such recalibration can be useful where it is desired to apply a constraint of expected *relative* cost – but of course in many situations cost limits may be conceived in more absolute terms.

Because only positive cost figures can now appear, it is possible to set a constraint on the maximum cumulative figure which is acceptable at any branching point in the tree. In Figure 65, a capital cost limit of 500k monetary units has been introduced. This has the effect of terminating the branches emanating from choice of the southern road line quite early on, and also closing some of the other branches before the full set of feasible schemes has been developed. In this example, only four feasible schemes remain which do not violate either the option bars or the cumulative capital cost constraint of 500k. These four schemes have been given the labels P, Q, R and S for working purposes, and together they offer one basis for a manageable working shortlist.

If desired, the working shortlist can be further reduced by grouping together schemes which are rather similar in terms of their options, then using one of them to *represent* the other members of that group at this stage in the comparison process. In the example of Figure 65, the judgement has been made that Scheme R can represent Scheme Q within a more restricted shortlist of only three schemes, because the two schemes differ only in terms of the West Street option and R is the less costly of the two.

Often, it can be difficult to judge in practice at what level a constraint should be set, if the purpose is to develop a working shortlist which is neither too large nor too limited to serve as a base for more careful comparison of alternatives. The level of the constraint can, of course, always be raised or lowered in retrospect, if the level first chosen does not have the desired effect. Where computer support is available, then such adjustments can be carried out quickly; indeed, if desired, the level of constraint can be varied automatically in accordance with specified rules. One possibility is to specify in advance the number of schemes required in the working shortlist, leaving the computer to adjust the level of the constraint accordingly. Another possibility is to specify the maximum level of difference to be considered between the least-cost scheme and any other scheme to be included in the list – recognising that, as in the example of Figure 65, the level of cost for the least-cost scheme cannot be known at the outset if there is a possibility that the combination of all the zero-cost options will be excluded by option bars.

Shortlisting across multiple comparison areas

The application of constraints in relation to numerical or similar indices can provide an effective way of reducing the range of schemes where this is very large. But this reduction can carry a cost, because it can mean ignoring for the time being any other comparison areas which cannot be treated in this way; and also because potentially vital information about uncertainty has to be temporarily set aside. So, it is often wise to view the use of constraints as only a crude filtering phase in the formation of a shortlist, leading to an intermediate list of schemes to which other methods of shortlisting can subsequently be applied.

As was also illustrated earlier (in Figure 22) the *ranking* of alternatives according to order of preference in different comparison areas offers another useful reference point in selecting promising alternatives for closer examination. Simple rankings can be deduced quickly wherever decision schemes can be compared in terms of numerical or equivalent indices, with tied rankings wherever the indices for two or more alternatives are the same; and it is not difficult to scan two or more comparison areas simultaneously once the information has been reduced to this form. But a set of alternatives can always be arranged in a tentative rank order in other comparison areas, where assessments cannot be quantified – so long as there is some basis for judgement which allows one scheme to be rated, however hesitantly, as more desirable than, less desirable than, or roughly similar to any other.

Figure 66 develops this point by comparing the nine schemes A to I of Figure 22 in terms of their rankings on all four of the comparison areas which were originally introduced. The CAPITAL: and RESIDENTS: rankings are as earlier indicated in Figure 22; but the INCOME: and JOBS: rankings have been added on the basis of quick intuitive judgements about orders of preference within each of these two additional comparison areas.

On the basis of a set of rankings such as that in Figure 66, it may be possible to pick out one or more schemes which are *dominated* by particular others, in the sense that any dominated scheme is inferior to, or at least no better than, the other in each of the rankings in the different comparison areas. So, in South Side, there are four schemes – C, F, H and I – each of which is dominated by Scheme A in terms of this set of four comparison areas; and among them, Scheme F is dominated by Scheme B as well. So, it could be judged appropriate to exclude these four schemes from any shortlist selected as a basis for closer evaluation – accepting the risk that the excluded schemes might score quite highly in other comparison areas not considered at this stage, and also the risk that the rankings might change if major areas of uncertainty were to be investigated and new information uncovered.

As an alternative means of displaying the same information, it can often be useful to rearrange a set of rankings by reference to the principle of *rank ordering,* as shown in the second listing of Figure 66. Here the set of alternatives is arranged in four different orders of preference, each based on their rank order in one of the four comparison areas; so schemes which rate highly in terms of two or more comparison areas will tend to rise towards the top in the corresponding columns. It can be seen in this instance that Scheme A – which comes top in two of the columns – rates quite well also in the other two columns, while Scheme E – the most attractive from the residents' viewpoint – scores well enough in terms of income and jobs but is the least favourable in terms of capital cost. So, the comparison of A with E could be a promising one to explore more closely from the point of view of exposing underlying value issues; thus these two alternatives might well be taken forward to a committee of elected representatives for debate, perhaps after further assessment of their relative consequences has been carried out.

Further inspection of Figure 66 might suggest also that Scheme B be carried forward for closer comparison with A and E, in view of its high ranking in terms of both the residents and capital assessments – despite its low ranking in each of the other two comparison areas. Conceivably, too, Scheme D could be carried forward as a possible compromise alternative, making a quite manageable working shortlist of four schemes in all – A, E, B and D – to be used as a basis for closer pair comparisons taking uncertainty more explicitly into account. And this in turn could provide a basis from which to switch into the work of the choosing mode.

Figure 66   Shortlisting across multiple comparison areas

South Side
example

RANKING OF 9 SCHEMES BY EACH OF 4 COMPARISON AREAS:

SCHEME	CAPITAL:	RESIDENTS:	INCOME:	JOBS:	dominated by:
A	2nd =	4th =	(1st)	(1st)	–
B	(1st)	2nd =	7th	8th	–
C	4th =	4th =	6th	6th	A
D	7th =	2nd =	4th	5th	–
E	9th	(1st)	2nd	4th	–
F	2nd =	7th	9th	9th	A, B
G	4th =	4th =	8th	7th	–
H	6th	8th =	5th	3rd	A
I	7th =	8th =	3rd	2nd	A

RANK ORDERINGS OF 9 SCHEMES BY DIFFERENT COMPARISON ARENS:

RANK	CAPITAL:	RESIDENTS:	INCOME:	JOBS:	
1st	(B)	(E)	(A)	(A)	
2nd	(A) [F]	(B) D	(E)	[I]	
3rd			[I]	[H]	
4th			D	(E)	dominated schemes included in brackets
5th	[C] G	(A)[C] G	[H]	D	
6th	[H]		[C]	[C]	
7th	D [I]	[F]	G	G	
8th		[H]	(B)	(B)	
9th	(E)	[I]	[F]	[F]	

suggested working shortlist: A, E, B : possibly also D ?

Comparing

SKILLS

The ranking of alternatives taking several comparison areas separately offers a simple but useful aid to comparison where the set is neither too large to be readily handled in this way - in which case constraints can be introduced - nor so small as to make this step unnecessary. The setting aside of dominated schemes and the picking out of those ranking highly on several comparison areas can then aid the shortlisting process.

Further extensions in comparing methods

In Chapter 10 there will be found a brief discussion of the use of computer software to support the work of the comparing mode, and examples of three of the main window layouts used to support this mode in STRAD 2 for Windows will be presented in Figure 92. In the design of this software, the opportunity has been taken to make significant extensions in the methods of comparison presented in this chapter, although these remain based on the four basic concepts of the comparison area, the relative assessment, the advantage comparison and the working shortlist.

These extensions are possible because, provided assessments of option differences have been entered for all combinations of decision areas and comparison areas where these differences are judged to be significant, the computer can aggregate this information rapidly. The user can then introduce any adjustments which may be judged necessary to take account of expected effects of combining options from linked decision areas in particular ways.

The computer can carry out this process of aggregating differences not only across decision areas but also across comparison areas, provided some assumptions have been entered about their relative weightings or trade-off rates. A particular feature of the STRAD software is the way it enables intuitive assumptions of these weighting factors to be entered at an early stage of the comparing work, and subsequently adjusted as and when required.

Summary: process judgements in the comparing mode

This chapter has discussed various choices of method and emphasis that are continually encountered in practice when working in the comparing mode. They are choices which involve repeated judgements about the balance between simplification and elaboration in evaluation method; a balance which, as argued at the beginning of the chapter, is more usefully conceived in *dynamic* than in static terms. To maintain an appropriate balance through time can involve alternating between rough and ready comparisons among many alternatives, and closer comparisons of a selected few; however, this balance is one that has to be judged not only in the light of the application of broad guidelines such as those offered in this chapter, but also in the light of political and administrative considerations which can vary from context to context. These will include the perceived importance of different decisions; the range of interests affected; and the nature of their representation, direct or indirect, in the processes by which comparisons and choices are to be made.

Underlying many of the evaluative choices to be made are questions of response to uncertainty – feelings of uncertainty being, in practice, inseparable from the necessary processes of conjecture about what the consequences of alternative courses of action might be. The concepts of relative assessment and of advantage comparison developed in this chapter have provided a way of com-

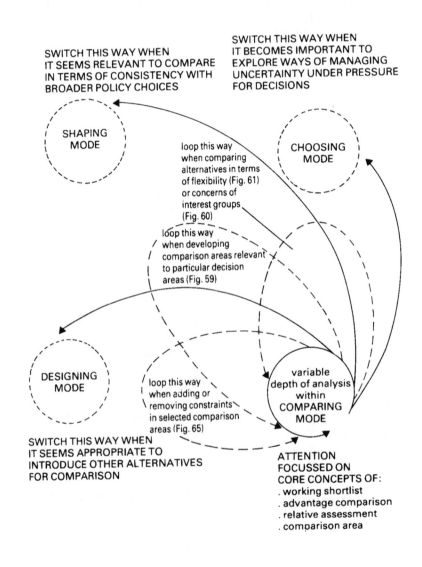

Figure 67   Process choices when working in the comparing mode

SWITCH THIS WAY WHEN
IT SEEMS RELEVANT TO COMPARE
IN TERMS OF CONSISTENCY WITH
BROADER POLICY CHOICES

SWITCH THIS WAY WHEN
IT BECOMES IMPORTANT TO
EXPLORE WAYS OF MANAGING
UNCERTAINTY UNDER PRESSURE
FOR DECISIONS

SHAPING
MODE

CHOOSING
MODE

loop this way
when comparing
alternatives in terms
of flexibility (Fig. 61)
or concerns of
interest groups
(Fig. 60)

loop this way
when developing
comparison areas relevant
to particular decision
areas (Fig. 59)

DESIGNING
MODE

loop this way
when adding or
removing constraints
in selected comparison
areas (Fig. 65)

variable
depth of analysis
within
COMPARING
MODE

SWITCH THIS WAY WHEN
IT SEEMS APPROPRIATE TO
INTRODUCE OTHER ALTERNATIVES
FOR COMPARISON

ATTENTION
FOCUSSED ON
CORE CONCEPTS OF:
. working shortlist
. advantage comparison
. relative assessment
. comparison area

Comparing

SUMMARY

ing to grips with these feelings of uncertainty, at least so far as their influence on comparative judgements is concerned. But the closer analysis of perceived areas of uncertainty, and the consideration of what might be done about them, is a matter that will be deferred for discussion in Chapter 8, as it is more germane to the work of the choosing than the comparing mode.

Figure 67 summarises the points made in this chapter, in terms of the various types of looping and switching judgements which centre on the comparing mode. Within the comparing mode itself, the idea of dynamic comparison, involving alternation between crude sifting of many alternatives and closer evaluations of a selected few, offers a key to the process judgements that have to be made. Considering first the brief loops that can be made out of the comparing mode towards other modes, Figure 57 indicates a loop in the direction of the *choosing mode* in situations where some rough and ready assessment of flexibility of future choice seems important; a loop in the direction of the *shaping mode* when developing a set of comparison areas relevant to a particular problem focus; and a loop in the direction of the *designing mode* whenever, for current working purposes, it is felt useful to reduce the range of alternatives by imposing additional constraints – or, for that matter, to extend the range by removing constraints previously assumed.

Turning to the question of less transitory switching into other modes, the normal progression in a conventional sequential process of decision-making would be from the comparing into the *choosing mode* – not necessarily to make a definitive choice among the alternatives that have been compared, but at least in order to make incremental progress in that direction. However, where a process is guided by the strategic choice philosophy, other directions of progress are possible. A move into the *shaping mode* will often be appropriate where the balance of advantage between alternatives across different comparison areas seems so problematic that choices of policy orientation should be brought more explicitly into the problem focus itself. At a more technical level, a switch back into the *designing mode* makes sense whenever it seems that a reformulation of options and option bars could lead to a clearer expression of the set of alternative to be compared.

Illustrations from practice

There now follows a set of three *illustrations from practice* illustrating some further practical points about the work of the comparing mode.

The first of these, from a planning exercise for North Holland, illustrates the merging of contributions from different members of a group in the building up of an initial set of comparison areas, and the collation of opinions about their relative importance. The second illustration, from north east Brazil, shows a variant of the advantage comparison method in which a list of uncertainty areas is built up as difficulties are encountered in arriving at group judgements. The third illustration is from an application in which ranking over several comparison areas was used in the formation of a working shortlist.

Figure 68 Illustration from practice – comparing 1

Comparing

PRACTICE

Theme: Developing key comparison areas for exploring the differences between decision schemes.

Problem: A provincial development plan for the disposal of household waste.

Context: Inter-organisational planning team, Province of Noord Holland, The Netherlands, 1986.

Commentary on Figure 68

These flip charts were drawn up during the final day of the first of a series of four workshops, held to bring together the thinking of planners from the province of Noord Holland, the central Government and the Municipality of Amsterdam on the problem of disposal of solid waste. The workshops were held in Heemstede, the Netherlands during January and February 1986, with Allen Hickling acting as process consultant to a team of two facilitators from the Directorate General for the Environment.

A number of alternative decision schemes had already been formulated, and these were set out in a list (3). A set of comparison areas ('criteria') was then composed in order to differentiate among these. The first step in this procedure involved the use of cards on which participants were encouraged to write their suggestions. All these were stuck up on the wall and then sorted according to three categories: physical ('fysiek'); social ('soc. maatsch.'); and economic ('fin. econ.'). Some cards naturally fell between categories, and were therefore positioned so as to overlap sector boundaries; others were found to be duplicates ('dubbellen').

From this, a straightforward list was drawn up, in no particular order, defining each criterion more clearly. Stickers were issued to the participants, who were asked to place them next to the comparison areas which they thought most significant in relation to the range of alternatives under consideration. The area of greatest concern emerged as practical feasibility ('realiseerbaarheid'), followed by environmental damage ('milieubelasting'), cost of disposal to local citizens ('verwijderingskosten, burger'), and flexibility of waste disposal method ('flexibiliteit techn. verwerking').

Assessments were then made by consensus in the group using very simple scales. A scale of + and − signs was used for the environment; the more plus signs the better. The Dutch, symbol for Guilders (f) was used for cost; the more symbols, the higher the cost. Spots were used for flexibility; the more spots, the more flexible. The note by the side headed 'PM' is merely an elaborated definition, describing the system of separating the waste at source.

This work in the comparing mode was not taken further on that day, because it was felt to be more important to explore further the uncertainties and assumptions which had been thrown up; these were listed elsewhere on the wall. As is quite usual with work carried out in the early stages of a strategic choice workshop, this particular part of the analysis was not resumed later. By the time the group was ready to move back to work in the comparing mode, the formulation of the alternatives and comparison areas had changed again, reflecting the further understanding of the problem that had been gained in the meantime.

Figure 69　Illustration from practice – comparing 2

1

2

Comparing

PRACTICE

Theme: Generating a list of uncertainty areas during an
advantage comparison of short-listed decision schemes.

Problem: Policy formulation in a comprehensive development plan
for an offshore island

Context: Five-Day workshop with a local inter-disciplinary planning
team, Recife, Brazil, 1984.

Commentary on Figure 69

These two photographs were taken in Recife, Brazil, during the course of the workshop already described in Figure 44, concerned with policies for the off-shore island of Itamaracá.

At the moment when the first photograph was taken, attention had become focused on a comparison between two sharply contrasted decision schemes, numbered 2 and 5, which had been picked out of a set of six feasible combinations of options from three linked decision areas. These covered respectively the choice of economic base for the island; the area chosen for urbanisation; and the access route to the undeveloped north. Scheme 2 involved retention of a traditional economic base, centred on farming and sea fishing, with a brake on any urban development beyond existing commitments; scheme 5 involved an emphasis on tourist development with additional allocation of land.

Initially, five comparison areas were chosen, concerned with fulfilment of metropolitan aims; with levels of income for the islanders ('renda'); with preservation of their way of life ('vida'); with conservation of the natural environment ('ambiente'); and with demands on a limited water supply ('agua'). A sixth comparison area was added later, concerned with internal transport for the islanders; it is interesting (Figure 44) that some of these comparison areas had earlier been viewed as decision areas.

In the top photograph, a member of the group has just filled in the top row of an advantage comparison chart, using a nine-point scale labelled (e c s m n m s c e). This is essentially similar to that introduced in Figure 21 – the words extreme, considerable, significant, marginal and negligible all having close equivalents in Portuguese. On the first row in the photograph, excluded parts of the scale have been blocked out. So there was thought to be no possibility that the balance of advantage on the metropolitan benefit comparison area could be in favour of scheme 2 to any degree, or as much as considerable or extreme in favour of scheme 5. For the group to arrive at this judgement, they had to confront many areas of uncertainty; and a tentative list of uncertainty areas is being started up on another chart underneath. The three uncertainty areas encountered in debating metropolitan benefit are to do with which groups might benefit; with the actions of another agency; and with assessing how far investors would be attracted.

The second photograph shows the same two wall charts at a later moment when all rows of the advantage comparison table had been completed and the list of uncertainty areas extended accordingly. The various uncertainty areas have now been classified, the Portuguese equivalents of UE, UV and UR being IA, IV and IR respectively. Also appearing in the second photograph is a second advantage comparison chart, in which schemes 2 and 3 are compared. In this case, the process was carried out initially by each individual completing a smaller version of the chart. One member then collated the results and presented them to the group in the form of the mode and range of the frequency distribution for each row, as shown here.

Figure 70   Illustration from practice – comparing 3

1

2

3

4

Comparing	Theme:	Comparison of selected decision schemes in order to identify important uncertainty areas.
	Problem:	Exploration of strategies for increasing applications of the Strategic Choice Approach in Japan.
PRACTICE	Context:	A demonstration workshop arranged in Tokyo by a committee of the Japan Society of Civil Engineers.

Commentary on Figure 70

These pictures are taken from a half-day demonstration workshop held in Tokyo in 1991, when John Friend was invited to visit Japan to speak at a symposium arranged by the Japan Society of Civil Engineers in order to launch a Japanese translation of *Planning Under Pressure* (Friend and Hickling, 1991). The topic selected for the workshop was the choice of strategy for encouraging wider dissemination and application of the strategic choice approach within Japan.

The participants were mainly civil engineers with a special interest in transport and infrastructure planning, and students specialising in this field – some of them from other Asian countries. A focus of three significant decision areas was chosen: domain of application; location of seminars/workshops; and method of training facilitators. Options were developed within each, and a set of ten feasible decision schemes was developed. As time was limited, each participant was given two stickers with which to indicate particular schemes to be examined more closely (1).

Using the resulting priority judgements as a guide, two contrasting schemes were then selected for pair comparison (2). Four comparison areas were used: success in application; number of users; cost; and influence on decision systems. Many uncertainties arose in discussion while these assessments were being made; these were listed on another flip chart and classified in terms of the UE, UV and UR categories (3). The participants were then again invited to place stickers on those uncertainty areas that they considered to be most significant (4). This led into a discussion of possible exploratory options for addressing the most prominent uncertainty areas; finally, a commitment package was constructed, including specific proposals for dealing with some of them.

In a quick evaluation exercise at the end of the afternoon, most of the participants rated the level of progress on the problem as slightly higher than expected, and the experience they had gained of the workshop process as considerably higher than expected.

The participants in this workshop were selected because they had some fluency in English. However the reliance on John Friend as facilitator, without any familiarity with the Japanese language, meant that some of the participants could make only limited contributions to the process. When he made a second visit to Japan the following year, two further workshops were conducted, in both of which he worked with Japanese co-facilitators – so the discussion was bilingual and a fuller level of participation was achieved.

The first of these subsequent workshops, in Tokyo, addressed issues associated with the design of a problematic section of the city's new outer ring road, with participation from some of the engineering consultants and municipal officials currently involved in the project. The second workshop, in Sapporo, addressed issues relating to the future of the small local airport linking the city with other urban centres on the island of Hokkaido.

8 Skills in choosing

Introduction

The work of the choosing mode calls for quite different kinds of judgements to the work of the comparing mode. In essence, they are judgements to do with the management of uncertainty and the development of commitment through time; for this is the mode in which the time dimension comes to the fore, and the pressures for urgent action have to be balanced against any concerns that the decisions faced may be too difficult to address before further explorations have been carried out.

The pressure for a switch towards the choosing mode can frequently be observed in the course of a conventional committee decision process. Typically, some participants start to become impatient, look at their watches and say 'isn't it time we reached a decision and moved on to the next business?', or 'isn't it time we brought the meeting to an end?' In practice, however, the issues involved in making progress through time become most complex and challenging where the problem under consideration is itself complex in structure, embracing many interrelated elements to which different urgencies and uncertainties apply.

Even though the challenges of making progress through time are readily recognisable from personal experience, they have received much less attention in the literature of planning and management methods than the more technical challenges of evaluation. This may be because judgements to do with choosing through time are much less easy to separate from the particular organisational or political context in which they arise than are judgements to do with comparison of specific alternatives, which scholars have generally been able to treat in a more detached, analytical way.

So in practice, the shift from the comparing to the choosing mode means a shift from the technical domain towards the political arena. But one political arena can differ sharply from another, in terms of the configurations of conflict, competition, consensus and coalition which influence the ways in which decisions are made; and such differences can reflect not only variations in the ways in which the participants themselves have shaped their own internal working relationships through time, but also deeper, underlying differences in their accountability to others with a stake in the decisions to be made. Even where progress is being sought towards action commitments by a set of participants who come together repeatedly in the same group setting – as has been supposed to be the case with the South Side Working Party – the members may differ from each other in terms of their external accountability. Indeed, in practice, the wish to include representation of all the most relevant departments, agencies or interest groups is often one of the explicit principles on which involvement in a decision process is designed.

So, in addressing complex issues, the working group in which all members share exactly the same accountability tends to be more the exception than the rule. Not only problems but also personal responsibilities may be perceived differently by different members of a group; and this in turn means that any guidance on the work of the choosing mode cannot always be addressed to all members of a working group as if they formed a single coherent team. There is no shortage of useful advice that can be offered in this chapter, at a generalised level, building on the four core concepts of the *uncertainty area,* the *exploratory option,* the *action scheme* and the *commitment package.* But readers should not be surprised when questions of whose uncertainty, whose exploration, whose action and whose commitment keep breaking through. Yet even in contexts where it is unrealistic to expect that views about these matters will be freely shared, there remains the possibility that individuals will be able to make good use of the concepts and methods offered here as a guide to their own personal contributions to a decision process.

Building a working list of uncertainty areas

The concept of the uncertainty area can be used to represent any area where alternative *assumptions* can be made about matters which are of some importance to decision-making. Such assumptions may relate to various aspects of the *working environment* within which people are trying to make decisions; they may relate to aspects of the *policy values* to which they are expected to pay heed; or they may relate to other *related decisions* where commitments have not, as yet, been made. The labels UE, UV and UR, which were introduced in Chapter 1 to differentiate these three types of uncertainty, serve not only as a means of classifying particular uncertainty areas as they are identified, but also as a useful reminder of the broad scope of the uncertainty area concept. Such a reminder can be especially appropriate to participants of an analytical bent, who are often predisposed to view the management of uncertainty primarily in terms of prediction or survey exercises using established statistical techniques.

In Chapter 3, the concept of the uncertainty area was first illustrated at a point in the South Side story where the focus of comparison had been narrowed down to a particular pair of alternative schemes, A and B, for which the overall balance of advantage across comparison areas was far from clear cut. However, it is only to be expected that people will experience personal feelings of uncertainty at many moments in a decision-making process, and that these feelings will change continually as they are exposed to what other participants have to say. People may feel uncertain as to where the boundaries of their problem should be drawn; they may feel uncertain as to whether or not particular decision areas should be seen as interconnected; they may feel uncertain as to whether particular options or combinations of options should be considered feasible; and they may feel uncertain as to the terms in which particular comparison areas should be formulated. Then, when it comes to comparing specific alternatives, they are bound to experience feelings of uncertainty both in attempting to assess their consequences within particular comparison areas and in judging where the overall balance of advantage lies; and it is at such moments that it becomes most important to find ways of viewing all areas of uncertainty together as sources of difficulty in choosing – some of which may be more significant than others – using the methods which will be discussed in this chapter.

Because feelings of uncertainty may surface at virtually any moment in a process of strategic choice, it is often useful in group work to set aside a sheet of paper on the wall where a cumulative list of uncertainty areas can be developed, recognising that such a list can always be restructured, and the items within it reformulated, at some later time. An example of a relatively unstructured list built up gradually in this way is presented in Figure 71. This illustration follows broadly the development of the South Side Story as recounted in earlier chapters, so the listing of uncertainty areas follows the broad sequence of shaping, designing and comparing in a more or less linear way – after starting by registering one uncertainty area, to do with air pollution, that is in this case supposed to have been so clearly recognised among the participants that it could be placed on record even before the group activity of shaping problems began. In practice, however, the more work is carried out within a group, the more the group is likely to switch freely between one mode and another; so the longer a list of uncertainty areas becomes, the more mixed it will tend to become in the modes of activity from which successive uncertainty areas are drawn.

In a group process, the recording of each uncertainty area on the list implies a working assumption that the feeling of uncertainty it contains is shared among different members of the group. Sometimes, of course, one member may express a feeling of uncertainty which is promptly dissolved because of some piece of information which another member of the group can supply from a position of greater knowledge or authority in some particular field. Sometimes, too, there may be areas of uncertainty which remain largely *latent* until exposed within the group. For example, one member of the South Side Working Party may feel quite confident in assuming that the football ground will be available for redevelopment, only to discover in discussion that another participant is equally confident that it will not; and they may then discover that neither is in a position to refute the other's assumption on the grounds of superior knowledge. Whereas neither participant had feelings of uncertainty on this point before the group interaction started, both share a feeling of uncertainty after some communication has taken place; so a new uncertainty area is recorded, and the decision process has become the more realistic as a result.

Because a working list of uncertainty areas may be subject to considerable

Figure 71   Building up a working list of uncertainty areas

South Side
e x a m p l e

UNCERTAINTY AREA (tentative description)	TYPE	note on how/why this uncertainty first encountered
? RATE OF EXPECTED REDUCTION OF LOCAL AIR POLLUTION	UE(UR?)	preliminary discussion of problem
? TIMING OF CONSTRUCTION OF NEW ROAD	UR	early work on shaping of decision graph and selection of problem focus
? CUTBACKS IN MUNICIPAL EXPENDITURE	UR	
? POLICY VALUE OF JOB CREATION	UV(UR?)	
? FEASIBILITY OF OTHER ROAD LINE OPTIONS	UE	work in the designing mode
? AVAILABILITY OF FOOTBALL GROUND SITE	UE	
? FEASIBILITY OF COMBINING HOUSING ON CENTRAL SITE WITH SHOPS AT KING SQUARE	UE	
? SERVICING COST PER HA. ON CENTRAL SITE	UE	assessment of alternatives within particular comparison areas
? ATTRACTIVENESS OF CENTRAL SITE TO EMPLOYMENT-INTENSIVE INDUSTRIES	UE	
? STEEL CORPORATION DECISION ON FUTURE OF STEELWORKS SITE	UR	advantage comparison schemes A vs B
? POLICY VALUE OF RESPONSIVENESS TO RESIDENTS' CONCERNS	UV	
? EASTWELL DISTRICT SHOPPING COMPLEX –SCALE AND TIMING	UR	advantage comparison schemes B vs E
? POLICY VALUE OF MEETING TRADERS' DEMANDS	UV	

Choosing

SKILLS

It is useful to build up a rough-and-ready listing of uncertainty areas progressively in interactive working, as new areas of uncertainty can surface when working in any mode. The use of the UE/UV/UR typology helps in drawing attention to any under-represented types as well as borderline cases. Notes on origination are here included for illustrative purposes and would be omitted in practice.

restructuring before it is put to operational use, it is usually not worth while assigning brief labels to the uncertainty areas at the time they are first recorded, in the manner that was illustrated in Figure 23. It can, however, be helpful to register from the outset whether each new uncertainty area seems to be of type UE, UV or UR, even if there remains some doubt over which classification is most appropriate. For the attempt to classify uncertainty areas in this way can provide a valuable check against any tendency to bias towards or against any one of the three basic types – a bias towards concern with uncertainties of type UE being a common experience among participants of a more analytical, apolitical cast of mind. Often there is a tendency in an initial list to include comparatively few uncertainty areas of type UR – most of them referring to decisions over which the participants feel they have relatively little control. This is natural enough at a stage of the process before a clear problem focus has emerged, because the tendency will have been to include most of the significant areas of choice within the decision graph itself. However, as soon as particular decision areas begin to be excluded from the problem focus, they become potential candidates for the list of uncertainty areas of type UR.

Finally, it is often helpful, as in Figure 71, to include brief notes against all the various uncertainty areas on the list, referring to the mode or moment in the process where each of them first surfaced. The value of this can be appreciated by noticing that some of the marginal notes recorded against particular uncertainty areas on Figure 71 – though not all of them can help in making reference back to earlier chapters which covered other stages in the development of the South Side story.

Putting uncertainty areas into a clearer decision perspective

Each uncertainty area on a working list, such as that of Figure 71, will have been recorded because at some moment in the process it appeared to have at least some relevance to the decision problems being addressed. However, the longer a list grows, the more it will usually become apparent that some of the uncertainty areas are more relevant than others – and that some of the less prominent ones might perhaps be set aside, or amalgamated with others to which they may seem closely related. So there will always be opportunities for the use of judgement and creativity in reformulating particular uncertainty areas, and in restructuring the overall list: opportunities of a similar kind to those already addressed in Chapter 5 in relation to the reformulation of decision areas.

Although a long and unstructured list of uncertainty areas can be tidied up at any time, where obvious opportunities for so doing can be seen, it is in practice usually worth saving any serious efforts towards restructuring until a moment arrives when there are pressures to explore preferences within a quite restricted working shortlist – perhaps a set of three or four promising schemes or, in many cases, only two promising alternatives – within which it is difficult to see where the overall balance of advantage lies.

Figure 72 Placing uncertainty areas in a decision perspective

South Side
e x a m p l e

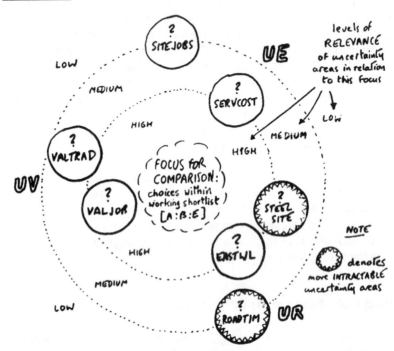

FULLER DESCRIPTIONS OF UNCERTAINTY AREAS in descending order of relevance

? VALJOB	? policy value of job creation	UV
? EASTWL	? Eastwell District shopping complex: scale and timing	UR
? SERVCOST	? servicing cost per ha. for development on central site	UE
? STEELSITE	? steel corporation decision on future use of steelworks site	UR (UE?)
? VALTRAD	? policy value of meeting traders' demands	UV
? SITEJOBS	? attractiveness of central site to employment-intensive firms	UE
? ROADTIM	? timing of construction of new road	UR

Choosing

S K I L L S

This kind of radial uncertainty graph offers a useful way of putting the more important uncertainty areas into a decision perspective, and bringing together judgements about type, relevance and tractability. It is usual to start by plotting the more clearly-understood uncertainty areas, and position others with reference to these, reassessing the first few when this process is complete.

The argument for leaving more detailed formulation and investigation of uncertainty areas until such a moment stems from the observation that in practice the relative prominence of different uncertainty areas can change quite dramatically as the decision perspective shifts. For example, some of the uncertainty areas listed in Chapter 3 (Figure 23) as relevant to the choice between Schemes A and B could well be overshadowed by others if some third scheme – such as Scheme E – were brought into the comparison as well. One way of picking out those uncertainty areas which are most relevant to a particular decision perspective is simply to use asterisks or some other symbol to pick out those in a longer list which are agreed to be most important in that particular light. However, Figure 72 illustrates one alternative form of presentation, which is sometimes found useful because it reflects the emphasis on creative use of graphics in communications which is characteristic of the strategic choice approach.

Figure 72 is an example of an *uncertainty graph* in which the more relevant uncertainty areas are represented by labelled circles, using rather similar conventions to those of the decision graph. But there is an important difference, in that the positioning of uncertainty areas on the uncertainty graph is judged in relation to a particular decision perspective that has been selected in advance. In the centre of the graph is indicated the current focus of comparison in this case the set of three schemes, A, B and E, which was selected in Figure 22. Different directions of movement outwards from this central focus then correspond to the three basic categories of uncertainty, UE, UV and UR, occupying broadly the same sectors of the graph as in the general introductory diagram of Figure 3. However, the graph leaves the boundaries between the three sectors undefined, so that any borderline cases can be plotted in intermediate positions. In addition, the more *relevant* uncertainty areas are positioned closest to the centre of the graph; these being the ones which are judged to bear most closely on the difficulty experienced in making choices among the particular alternatives currently in view. As an aid to this aspect of positioning, two or three concentric rings can be drawn around the centre of the graph. When working with wall charts and coloured pens, these rings are best drawn in an unobtrusive colour, such as yellow, so that they do not get in the way of the other, more specific, information which the graph is intended to convey.

Working from an unstructured list such as that of Figure 71, it is usually best to begin by scanning it to pick out the most relevant uncertainty areas first. These can then be positioned within the innermost ring, working methodically outwards to add others of lesser relevance. Another approach is to begin by placing on the graph those uncertainty areas that are best understood and use these as points of reference in positioning others. It is not usually necessary to overload an uncertainty graph by attempting to locate within it *all* uncertainty areas, however insignificant relative to others; and it is rarely in practice worth going beyond a set of eight or nine uncertainty areas which are judged to be of particular relevance in relation to the current focus of comparison. Although the classification of uncertainty areas as UE, UV or UR may have been noted on the original working list, the act of plotting them on the uncertainty graph can provide a useful opportunity for second thoughts and for further debate on any doubtful cases.

Usually, some at least of the more relevant uncertainty areas will have come to the fore in the comparing of particular schemes – for example, the three uncertainty areas ?VALJOB, ?SITEJOBS and ?STEELSITE all emerged from the original comparison of Schemes A and B in Chapter 3 (Figure 23). However, other uncertainty areas may have surfaced while comparing other pairs of alternatives, or even in the work of the shaping and designing modes – for instance one or two of them might reflect doubts as to whether particular options should be considered feasible or whether particular options bars should be assumed.

Various additional kinds of information can be added to the basic information conveyed by an uncertainty graph about the type and relevance of different uncertainty areas. But too much elaboration can confuse rather than inform; so the only additional information introduced in Figure 72 is the use of a serrated ring to pick out particular uncertainty areas which are judged to be more *intractable* than others. The message is that there is thought to be very little that could be done to reduce the current state of doubt in each such uncertainty area, whereas in the case of other uncertainty areas it is possible to conceive of at least some form of exploratory action whereby current feelings of uncertainty might be reduced. In the case of these more tractable uncertainty areas, any decision to carry out this exploratory action will then have the intended effect of pushing that uncertainty area some distance further outwards from the centre of the graph; however, in the case of a more intractable uncertainty area, this possibility either does not exist, or is assumed to be realisable only at an unacceptable cost.

Restructuring composite uncertainty areas

Once attention has been focused on a few of the most relevant uncertainty areas – whether through use of an uncertainty graph or simply through picking out the most important uncertainty areas on a list – it is only to be expected that doubts will begin to arise as to whether they have been clearly enough formulated. In some cases, closer investigation will suggest that a particular uncertainty area is *composite* in form, and could with advantage be broken down into two or more separate elements for which different kinds of exploratory action would be appropriate. Some of these elements might then be found to be more relevant than others to the present focus of comparison; furthermore, the elements might occupy quite different parts of the uncertainty graph in terms of the UE/UV/UR classification. Therefore, the reformulation of composite uncertainty areas in terms of their more significant elements can sometimes lead to quite a radical restructuring of the content of the uncertainty graph, and a reappraisal of the picture of opportunities for managing uncertainty which it conveys.

It is possible to explore such possibilities for restructuring uncertainty areas by working directly from the uncertainty graph. But the graph itself can become overloaded and confused if too much information of this kind is added. Figure 73 illustrates a way in which the elements of composite uncertainty areas can be explored on a separate sheet, with a view to possibly modifying the graph at a later stage. The first example of a composite uncertainty area relates to the policy value of job creation; this is an uncertainty area occupying quite a central position on the graph of Figure 72, which was classified as of type UV. In Figure 73, this value uncertainty is broken down into two different value elements, one of them relating to the general priority given by the municipal council to job creation as against other policy aims; and the other relating to the more specific question of whether there is to be discrimination in favour of economically deprived neighbourhoods, such as South Side, in the attraction of new jobs to different parts of the municipal area. The meaning of each element is made more explicit in Figure 73 by spelling out, in parenthesis, a set of two or more alternative assumptions which can be regarded as representative of the current range of doubt. Such a set of alternative assumptions is exactly analogous to the set of options used to represent the range of choice within a decision area; indeed, within an uncertainty area, similar problems of how best to represent a complex or open-ended range of possibilities may sometimes have to be faced.

In this instance, it is possible that the participants will be experiencing doubts over whether the general priority attached by members of the municipal council to job creation has shifted upwards or downwards since its last written policy statement on this issue was agreed. But it may be judged that this element of uncertainty is not so important as the element of uncertainty relating to positive discrimination in favour of particular localities, about which there might recently have been much political controversy. Therefore, Figure 73 shows the latter element rated as of medium-to-high relevance and so worth subjecting to further scrutiny straight away; while the former – rated as of only low-to-medium relevance – can perhaps be set aside for the time being. The latter element is assigned a brief label – ?JOBDISC – with a view to this replacing the composite uncertainty area ?VALJOB on the uncertainty graph. As a further step in analysing this more carefully defined uncertainty area, a note is made of the kinds of exploratory option which could be considered to reduce its relevance further. In this example, it is indicated that two alternative levels of policy soundings might be considered as possible exploratory options – the first of them more formal and the second comparatively quick and informal.

Turning to the second of the uncertainty areas in Figure 73 – labelled ?EASTWL – its original description in terms of 'scale and timing' of the proposed Eastwell shopping complex indicates that it also is composite in form. It is supposed here that further discussion of its content leads to the judgement that it is uncertainty over scale which is much the more prominent element. In the case of ?SERVCOST, it is supposed in Figure 73 that the analysis of elements can be taken further with the help of some more explicit *sensitivity analysis*, of

Figure 73 Reformulating composite uncertainty areas

South Side
example

UNCERTAINTY AREA - elements	TYPE	RELEVANCE to [A:B:E] focus	PROPOSED RESPONSE - exploratory options
? VALJOB ? policy value of job creation	UV	<u>HIGH</u>	EXAMINE ELEMENTS
┌ ? value of job creation v. │ other policy aims │ [as stated; higher; lower]	UV	LOW/MID	• examine no further ┐
│ ? whether to discriminate in │ favour of low income areas └ in creating jobs [yes; no]	UV	<u>MID/HIGH</u>	• label as ? JOBDISC - refer to policy committee — consult leaders ┘
? EASTWL ? Eastwell shopping complex scale/timing	UR	<u>MID/HIGH</u>	EXAMINE ELEMENTS
┌ ? scale of Eastwell shopping │ [as in plan; larger; smaller]	UR	<u>MID/HIGH</u>	• label as ? EASTWLSC - full analysis - brief liaison
│ ? timing of Eastwell shopping └ development [sooner; later]	UR/UE	LOW	• examine no further ┘
? SERVCOST ? cost of servicing central site	UE	<u>MID/HIGH</u>	<u>EXAMINE ELEMENTS</u>
┌ ? additional buffer zone in ha. │ if HOUS [3; 5; 7] *	UE	VERY LOW	• examine no further
│ ? unit servicing cost in k/ha │ if IND [12; 15; 18] *	UE/UV	<u>MID</u>	EXAMINE ELEMENTS FURTHER
│ ┌ ? geological/soil factors	UE	LOW/MID	• examine no further ┐
└ └ ? policy on range of services	UV	MID	• intractable: no action ┘

* SENSITIVITY ANALYSIS : refer to figure 62 for basic calculations

- additional buffer zone in ha [3; 5; 7] → │ cost of site servicing │ → [266; 250; 234]   ± 6%
- unit servicing cost in k/ha [12; 15; 18] → │ difference IND + HOU │ → [160; 250; 340]   ± 36%

Choosing

S K I L L S

The splitting down of composite uncertainty areas into more specific elements is often carried out directly on the uncertainty graph, reassessing type and relevance in the process. Judgements about the relevance of different elements can be seen as a type of informal sensitivity analysis, and the more explicit form of sensitivity analysis illustrated here is used comparatively rarely.

a kind that only becomes possible in circumstances where assessments can be made on the basis of well-defined sequences of calculations or logical steps.

The particular procedure of sensitivity analysis used in Figure 73 can be appreciated more fully by referring back to Figure 62. This indicated a sequence of operations involved in estimating the costs of providing site services for either industrial or housing development. Some of these steps involved calculations of a straightforward arithmetical kind, but others depended on expert judgements – and the logical structure of these will often be much less transparent.

In the particular example of sensitivity analysis included in Figure 73, it has been supposed that it is the cost of servicing the site for industrial use rather than housing use which is the source of most of the uncertainty; and the relative contributions to this uncertainty of two contributory elements are explored. The difference in usable site area for the two alternative uses was estimated as 0.5 hectares (Figure 62) – the difference between 2.5 hectares for housing and 3.0 hectares for industry. In Figure 73 it is supposed that the range of uncertainty over this estimate has been assessed, through a process of surprise limit analysis, as extending from a minimum of 0.3 hectares to a maximum of 0.7 hectares. In the same way, a range from 10k/ha to 20k/ha has been assessed for the cost per hectare of servicing the site for industry (see Figure 63); the equivalent cost of servicing for housing being taken as a more predictable 8k/ha.

Repeating the sequence of calculations in Figure 62 with the minimum and maximum figures substituted for the original estimates, first for the loss of site area and then for the servicing cost per hectare, Figure 73 shows that the former element causes very little variation in the estimated servicing cost for the site, while the latter element contributes considerably more.[1]

In pursuing this example further, it will be noted (from Figure 62) that this estimated site servicing cost per hectare can itself be broken down into four more specific elements of assumption – some expressed in numerical form and others not. So the process of breaking down elements of uncertainty can, in this case, be extended further. In Figure 73 this point is illustrated by indicating the two more important sub-elements of the uncertainty over industrial site servicing cost – the more significant of them in this case being of an intractable policy nature. This illustrates the general point that analysis of elements within an uncertainty area can lead to a revision of views about its classification within the UE/UV/UR framework.

Assessing exploratory options within critical uncertainty areas

Once attention has been focused on a few crucial uncertainty areas, attention can be turned to the question of what might be done about them. This involves

1 This is a contrast which can be quantified if statistical methods are used to calculate – on conventional assumptions of independence and normal distributional form – that the latter element explains some 97% of the combined variance.

Figure 74   Comparing alternative responses to uncertainty

South Side example

UNCERTAINTY AREA	EXPLORATORY OPTION	COMPARISON AREA	RELATIVE ASSESSMENT
?EASTWLSC (Scale of Eastwell shopping complex - as in plan - larger - smaller)	- ANALYSIS (systematic analysis of alternative shopping configurations for Eastern sector of municipal area)	CONFIDENCE : RESOURCES : DELAY :	more confidence in judging balance of advantage E:B extensive survey & analysis work (c. 100 planner days) 4 months
	- LIAISON (brief exploratory discussions with leading staff of shops planning team)	CONFIDENCE : RESOURCES : DELAY :	somewhat more confidence in judging advantage E:B a few hours discussion 1-2 weeks to arrange meeting

ADVANTAGE COMPARISON [LIAISON vs ANALYSIS]

examining more closely any exploratory options that are seen as realistic – whether they have already been identified or whether they only come to mind at this stage – and weighing up what the consequences of following these exploratory options might be.

In Chapter 3, one approach was illustrated (Figure 24) by which the implications of following any particular exploratory option could be compared with the consequences of not pursuing it. In this, the three comparison areas of *confidence, resources* and *decision delay* were used to represent the three most important dimensions of evaluation that normally arise when making judgements about how uncertainty should be managed. In practice, it is only rarely that it is worthwhile evaluating exploratory options in this explicit way. But the *principles* involved are crucial to the management of uncertainty in strategic choice; so Figure 74 illustrates how the comparison of exploratory options can be taken a step further in relation to any especially critical uncertainty areas where this deeper level of analysis may be justified.

Because the proposed scale of the Eastwell district shopping complex has emerged as an especially relevant uncertainty area (Figure 74), the implications of taking different exploratory actions in response are reviewed in Figure 74. The first exploratory option to be considered is that of undertaking a full and systematic analysis of alternative combinations of district and more local shopping centres in the broader eastern sector of the municipality that includes both Eastwell and South Side. But, in addition, a more modest exploratory option is also considered, which might go at least some way towards reducing the level of doubt within this same uncertainty area; this is the option of engaging in some informal liaison with leading members of a specialist team of planners which the municipality has set up to look at shopping provision within its overall administrative area. This second option may mean relying on the specialist team's own expert judgement of the consequences of adopting different shopping patterns, rather than on any more rigorous methods of survey and analysis. Nevertheless, it could be well worth considering as a more modest – but possibly more effective – way of reducing the level of doubt in this same uncertainty area.

Figure 74 records the judgement that the first exploratory option – labelled ANALYSIS – is expected to lead to more confidence in judging the overall balance of advantage between Schemes E and B – this pair comparison being a more appropriate one to consider than A:B within the working shortlist (A:B:E) because A and B do not differ in terms of options within the SHOP LOC'N? decision area. But the more modest LIAISON option is also judged likely to lead to 'somewhat' more confidence in relation to the same pair comparison – and to do so at considerably less cost in terms of both demands on resources and decision delay. The call on resources for the ANALYSIS option is here assessed in terms of a rough estimate of the number of planner days required – although of course it could have other dimensions such as the use of computer time and the cost of origination of data, possibly involving the recruitment of interviewers through agency or other channels.

To weigh up whether it is likely to be worth pursuing the full ANALYSIS option as against the more modest LIAISON option, it becomes essential to take the urgencies and resource pressures of the current decision situation into account. In practice, this will usually be done intuitively. But intuitive appreciations of urgency may differ from one participant to another; so it can sometimes be a useful aid to communication, in the case of especially critical uncertainty areas, to introduce an advantage comparison framework as an aid to this kind of judgement. This possibility is demonstrated in the lower part of Figure 74.

In this case, the advantage comparison indicates a view that the additional gain in confidence from adopting the ANALYSIS rather than the simpler LIAISON response to the uncertainty about the scale of the Eastwell shopping centre should be placed in the marginal-to-significant range. Yet Figure 74 shows that this benefit is likely to be outweighed by the considerable additional investment of resources required, along with the even more serious implications – in this particular decision situation – of a four-month delay before the decision in question can be made. This example merely makes explicit the kind of judgements that are being made all the time in an intuitive way, when people have to decide how far to invest in any kind of exploratory action to improve the confidence with which important choices can be made.

This particular example concerns an uncertainty area of type UR; but the judgement of whether or not to invest in exploratory action can be expressed in a similar way whether an uncertainty area of type UE, UV or UR is involved – as was indeed demonstrated earlier in Chapter 3 (Figure 24). Quick and informed judgements of this kind can be debated with reference to the comparative information about the relevance of different uncertainty areas which is contained in an uncertainty graph such as that of Figure 72. As a general rule, it is rarely worth making major investments in exploratory action directed towards uncertainty areas of lower relevance, so long as uncertainty areas of higher relevance remain.

Relating exploratory actions to the timing of decisions

As was discussed in Chapter 3, the consideration of what to do about particular uncertainty areas can bring concerns about the *timing* of choices in different decision areas directly to the fore. For any exploratory action invariably takes some time to carry through – whether this be measured in minutes, hours, days, weeks, months or even years – and can thus imply delays of a more or less serious extent in the taking of those decisions they are designed to inform.

The opportunities for taking immediate actions in some decision areas while deferring choice in others were approached in Chapter 3 through the core concept of the *action scheme,* chosen to cover some but not necessarily all of the decision areas within a problem focus. An example was then presented (Figure 25) of how action schemes could be compared in terms of the relative *flexibility* of choice left open; and various possible approaches to the comparison of flexibility were discussed further in Chapter 7.

There are, therefore, two types of timing judgement which have to be considered in practice. On the one hand there is the judgement of how far to invest in pursuing exploratory actions which imply delays in at least some decision areas; on the other hand there is the judgement of how far to make commitments to action in some decision areas in advance of others. This means that any consideration of the time dimension can make the structure of interconnected choices for the participants more subtle and complex; indeed, this is a reality that has to be faced whether or not the concepts and methods of strategic choice are being applied in an explicit way.

In dealing with these choices, a useful guideline is to focus first on any decision areas where considerations of *both* urgency and uncertainty arise. This is illustrated in Figure 75, *which* takes as its point of departure the set of nine possible decision schemes first developed in Chapter 2 (Figure 17) for the four decision areas in the original South Side problem focus. In Figure 75, these schemes are arranged (as in Figure 25) with the two more urgent decision areas – ROAD LINE? and DIST LIFE? – brought to the fore; then, focusing more closely on the comparison of schemes within the more limited working shortlist of A, B and E, Figure 75 identifies the points of greatest *difficulty* in the decision process, by means of question marks positioned at the relevant branching points of the tree.

It can now be seen that the DIST LIFE? decision area is the more urgent of the two decision areas in which there are differences between the shortlisted Schemes A, B and E; and it has already been discovered (Figure 74) that the ?EASTWLSC uncertainty area has an important bearing on the choice of routes at this branch point of the tree. So it could be especially important to explore how to deal with this particular uncertainty area if the urgencies of the problem situation are to be addressed. So, in the second picture of Figure 75, the first part of the option tree is shown expanded to introduce, as additional branching points, a choice of two exploratory options within the ?EASTWLSC uncertainty area. The first is the 'null option' of taking no exploratory action at all, and the second is the quick option of a brief liaison exercise with the shops planning team – it being here supposed that the more costly and time-consuming option of fuller analysis has been ruled out after the kind of advantage comparison exercise illustrated earlier (Figure 74).

In Figure 75, the assumption is made that the DIST LIFE? decision should definitely be *deferred* if the exploratory liaison option is to be followed through. It is also supposed there may possibly be an argument for deferring choice of DIST LIFE?, as an alternative to early commitment to any specific option, if it is decided to take the 'no explorations' route; for such a deferment could make sense if there were any likelihood that some event might occur which could clarify the choice within DIST LIFE? without any specific exploratory action being taken. For example, it might be known that there was a meeting of a South Side community forum scheduled in a week's time to debate this very issue.

Figure 75   Weighing uncertainty against urgency in decision-making

South Side example

[?] indicates a critical branching point for comparisons within working shortlist [A:B:E]. Uncertainty area ?EASTWLSC identified as critical to urgent choice of action scheme I v. III so examine [explore/not]

IMMEDIATE DECISIONS			DECISION SCHEMES OPEN	ASSESSMENTS* FLEXIBILITY	RESIDENTS
ROAD LINE?	?EASTWLSC	DIST. LIFE?			
NORTH ···	NO EXPLORATORY ACTION	COMMIT 10 YR	Ⓐ Ⓑ C	fff	RRR
		COMMIT 20 YR	D F	f	RR
		COMMIT 40 YR	Ⓔ G	ff	RR
		DEFER CHOICE	ⒶⒷ C D F Ⓔ G	ffff	R
	LIAISON	DEFER CHOICE	ⒶⒷ C D F Ⓔ G	ffff	R

* KEY TO ASSESSMENTS:
flexibility index f: minimum ffff : maximum
residents' satisfaction R: minimum RRR : maximum

The introduction of an option to defer choice within the DIST LIFE? decision area has the effect of subtly altering the *meaning* of that decision area; for it now represents a choice as to what should be done *now* about the life of the district, rather than what should be done in any more timeless sense. However, the main point about the expanded option tree in Figure 75 is that it displays five possible combinations of current choices and exploratory options that can be compared with each other as a basis for incremental progress; and these five paths can quickly be compared in terms of how many of the nine decision schemes remain available in each case. In Figure 75, the schemes remaining open are listed for each path, drawing attention in particular to the availability of the three shortlisted Schemes A, B and E.

In general, this analysis indicates that those courses of action involving immediate commitment in the DIST LIFE? decision area carry a risk of subsequent *regret,* through the foreclosing of particular decision schemes which might have been found to be advantageous had the explorations been followed through. For example, commitment now to a 40-year life for South Side might lead to regret if the work of the specialist shops planning team were to result in a proposal for a particular sector-wide shopping pattern which made it uneconomic to develop a new South Side local shopping centre on the King Square site; while commitment now to a 10-year life might lead to regret if geological difficulties on the central site were later found to be so severe that no uses other than open space could realistically be considered there.

In general, the choice of whether to opt for commitment or deferment in an urgent decision area involves some process, however intuitive, of weighing the risks of early commitment against the negative consequences of delay – including any political or professional penalties that might be incurred. In the particular circumstances of Figure 75, the deferment being considered is only a couple of weeks, so might well be considered worth while; unless, perhaps, there were an imminent meeting of the municipal council, or a closely fought local election, to introduce an added note of urgency over the commitment to district life, even within this otherwise insignificant time scale.

Accommodating uncertainty by preparing for alternative contingencies

Various approaches have now been discussed to the comparison of alternative courses of immediate action, in terms of the flexibility of future choice which they allow. At the simplest level, an intuitive judgement can be made that one alternative is likely to leave open more opportunities for future choice than another, without any analysis of what these opportunities are.[2] At another level, the patterns of future choice left open can be analysed and presented for visual

2 This was the kind of approach adopted when 'flexibility' was introduced as an additional comparison area in Figure 64.

South Side example

Choosing

SKILLS

Uncertainty areas in which the choice of assumptions can have a critical effect on the choice of path through a tree may become an important focus for contingency planning. This consideration is usually introduced only when attention is turned to the design of a commitment package, but the extension of the tree to show contingencies as extra branching points can be a useful aid to communication.

comparison, or the comparison can be simplified by introducing some form of robustness index (Figure 25).

However, it is possible to go further in circumstances where there has been some analysis of the relative importance of different uncertainty areas, and where some attempt has been made to represent the more important of these in terms of the range of alternative assumptions that could be held. Where this is so, then it is possible to bring those alternative assumptions more directly into the comparison of current actions, and to explore how far some such actions could have advantages over others in their capacity to respond to particular eventualities that could arise. One way of taking the analysis in this direction is illustrated in Figure 76. In Figure 76, two alternative action schemes for South Side are compared, each of which involves commitment to the northern road line and also to a particular option in the DIST LIFE? decision area. Referring to Figure 75, each such course implies that no exploratory action is being taken in relation to the important ?EASTWLSC uncertainty area. So the feelings of uncertainty over the scale of the proposed Eastwell shopping complex remains unchanged; and this uncertainty area has already been represented in terms of a choice of three possible assumptions labelled SMALLER, AS IN PLAN, and LARGER (Figure 73).

According to which of these assumptions is held, either *the feasibility* or the relative *attractiveness* of different courses of future action may be affected. In Figure 76, the judgement is made that the uncertainty about the scale for the Eastwell shopping complex is of such direct relevance to the choice of shopping location for South Side, that the King Square development must be ruled out on grounds of economic viability if the Eastwell complex is to be significantly larger than proposed in the current plan. Turning to the second of the action schemes in Figure 76 – Action Scheme III – this appears to allow no alternative to the King Square site; but it does afford protection against another contingency – the perhaps remote contingency of abnormal geological conditions being discovered on the central site, precluding the possibility of any use except that of open space.

However, another point in favour of Action Scheme I is that it leaves open the option of industrial use on the central site; provided geological conditions make this option feasible, Figure 76 shows that its attractiveness as a means of creating alternative local jobs could be enhanced should the contingency of early closure of the steelworks arise. So, the consideration of flexibility to accommodate different kinds of uncertainty can become more complex, the more contingencies are explored. Sometimes this kind of analysis can lead towards a searching re-examination of earlier assumptions. For example, the assumption that there is no possibility of using the central site for open space if a 10-year district life were chosen might now seem a rather unnecessary constraint. Referring back to the structure of the problem as reflected in the option graph (Figure 16), the reasoning behind this particular option bar could well now be challenged. The result could be an agreement that the option bar was no longer necessary, so removing an apparent advantage towards Action Scheme III on grounds of capacity to accommodate geological uncertainty.

Once the possibility is considered of introducing some of the more crucial uncertainty areas into the structure of possible paths through the problem situation, as illustrated in Figure 76, then it becomes possible to move in a number of different directions of further analysis, depending on whether these crucial uncertainty areas are of type UE, UV or UR. In the case of a UE-type uncertainty area – such as that over geological conditions in South Side – it may be important to ask whether the contingencies reflected in the alternative assumptions are of high or low probability: and questions then arise of how far it is worth safeguarding or insuring against specific *risks*. If these questions are of sufficient importance, then the analysis can be taken in the direction of the classical form of *decision analysis* in which numerical probabilities are assigned to different contingencies treated as alternate branching points in a decision tree.[3]

Any important uncertainty areas of type UV can, if desired, be absorbed into the analysis of decision areas expressed at a broader *policy* level – and such a step will open up the possibility of introducing the methods already illustrated for analysing relationships between *levels* of choice (Figure 54). Again, any crucial uncertainty areas of type UR can be absorbed into the problem structure as additional decision areas, thus in effect extending the problem focus. However, where these new decision areas relate to choices which are entirely or partially under the control of other parties – and, where there are elements of conflict or competition in relationships with those other parties – then the decision situation may have to be considered as more like one of a *game* in which moves, counter-moves and points of potential stability might have to be explored: 'If they did this, we could retaliate by doing that'. This points to another direction of analysis, based on the ideas about the management of conflict and collaboration discussed by authors such as Howard (1989) and Bennett, Cropper and Huxham (1989).

Moving towards the design of possible commitment packages

This chapter has, so far, covered various kinds of judgement which are relevant to the design of a commitment package, conceived as a proposed incremental step towards commitment through time. The four basic sections of a commitment package were first illustrated in Figure 26: a set of immediate decisions covering both *actions* and *explorations* to reduce uncertainty; then a set of proposed arrangements for *deferred choices* and *contingency planning* within a future decision space. In any setting where decisions call for formal commitment of organisational resources, there will be moments when it is important to give careful attention to the design of *alternative* commitment packages. Yet it is important to emphasise that at other times, when there is a desire to move

---

3 See, for example, Raiffa, 1968.

ahead informally, or to respond to particular urgencies of the moment, a commitment package may be much more skeletal in its content, and will not necessarily be recorded in written form.

In practice, important points of judgement can arise not only in developing the content of a commitment package, but also in judging the *format* in which it should be presented. This applies in particular to the rows as opposed to the columns of the framework. In the simple example presented in Chapter 3 (Figure 26), the problem structure was brought out by designating a separate row for each decision area. This presented no difficulty in that particular case, because each of the exploratory actions proposed to address uncertainty could be directly linked to a particular area of deferred choice. In practice, however, the number of decision areas to be brought together within the compass of a commitment package can sometimes be larger, and the relationships between explorations and deferred choices less straightforward. In these circumstances, it can be more practicable to group two or more decision areas together in the same row, perhaps relating to some designated sphere of responsibility. This way of presenting a commitment package is illustrated in Figure 77.

This example of a commitment package presents one coherent set of proposals which is, in effect, an expanded version of the first of the two alternative action schemes compared in Figure 76. The rows of the framework are organised into three broad spheres of responsibility, concerned respectively with local South Side matters, with transport issues and with economic development in the municipality as a whole. Only the first of these is within the direct sphere of responsibility of the South Side Working Party; and even then there may be procedures of formal authorisation or endorsement of proposals to be followed, requiring some consideration of contingency planning if any recommendations should be rejected or opposed. In the transport and economic development spheres, all the working party may be able to do is to make representations to other parties, and to use whatever influence or leverage they can exert to follow those representations through – perhaps again with some thought to possible contingency actions should the proposed representations or negotiations fail.

In Figure 77, asterisks are used to indicate the principal set of interconnected decision areas around which the commitment package has been built, as a reminder that it may be difficult to consider changing course in any one of these without considering what implications there might be for the others. However, there may be more scope for considering variations in other elements of the package; and the number of elements shown in this particular illustration, though quite large, is only a limited selection from those that could have been included if all the decision areas and uncertainty areas discussed in the course of the last few chapters were to be included. For example, extra spheres of housing or financial responsibility could have been included to reflect these other organisational interests in the South Side problem (Figure 41). Various other decision areas from this wider decision graph might then have been considered, in the shaping of either proposed actions or deferred choices. Further kinds of technical exploration could also have been suggested. For example, explora-

Figure 77 Building an appropriate commitment package

South Side example

COMMITMENT PACKAGE IA
- based on SHORT-TERM PUBLIC investment policy

	IMMEDIATE DECISIONS		FUTURE DECISION SPACE	
	ACTIONS	EXPLORATIONS	DEFERRED CHOICES	CONTINGENCY PLANNING
SOUTH SIDE local planning	DISTRICT LIFE * - commitment now to 10 YEAR LIFE			IF a major developer can be attracted THEN consider extended life 1
	SHOP LOCATION * - no action	- leads to arrange discussions with local traders	IN 6 MONTHS - decide Main St. OR King Square	IF scale of Eastcall complex increased, THEN reject King Sq. 2
	CENTRAL SITE * - no action	- commission quick geological survey	IN 6 MONTHS - decide industry OR housing IF main Street shops stay (c2)	3
	WEST STREET - no action	- initiate design and costing studies	IN 12 MONTHS - decide whether to improve West St.	4
TRANSPORT	ROAD LINE * - recommend NORTH route through South Side			IF north route rejected, THEN appeal 5
	MAIN STREET - no action		WHEN road is in firm programme, THEN consider closing street	IF new road not to be built in next 5 years, THEN extend parking 6
ECONOMIC DEVELOPMENT		ask M.E.O. to approach steel corporation to discuss joint jobs initiative		7

A   B   C   D

* identifies main set of interconnected decisions

SUMMARY OF COMPARISON with alternative package III A [LONG-TERM PUBLIC INVESTMENT]

[CAPITAL: IA to cost 100k - 300k LESS than III A
  INCOME: IA likely to generate marginally LESS income
  RESIDENTS: IA offers BETTER outlook
  JOBS: LITTLE DIFFERENCE if B7 successful
  FLEXIBILITY: IA preserves options in shop location

Choosing

SKILLS

The basic framework of a commitment package offers a framework for discussion in considering how to act which can be extended in a number of different ways, according to context. When working with large sheets of paper it is useful to add marginal notes against immediate decisions specifying agreed organisational responsibilities, resource commitments and deadlines.

tions could have been proposed into the feasibility of doubtful options, such as the possibility (examined in Figure 48) of combining some industrial with some housing development of the central site. Further explorations into policy values might also perhaps have been recommended: for example, into the issue of discrimination in job creation in favour of low income neighbourhoods.

So, however broad in scope it might appear, any commitment package is designed to be *selective* rather than comprehensive in its content, reflecting the various resource constraints, urgencies and priorities of the specific decision setting within which it is shaped. For it is intended as an incremental step in a continuing process of commitment, not as a conclusive response to the full range of problems that has been identified. Even so, there are many additional subtleties that can be introduced informally into a decision process while a commitment package is being designed, extending its scope beyond that of the analysis as so far pursued. For example, Figure 77 introduces for the first time the possibility that the uncertainty about the steelworks closure might not be so immune to municipal influence as earlier assumed, once the idea of a joint initiative to attract small business enterprises to the site has been conceived.

So, within the commitment package framework, a considerable amount of richness and complexity can be encompassed, even where a conscious effort is made to present its content in a form which is intelligible to people who may not have been involved in the analytical work which has gone into its presentation. Cross-referencing between elements in the package itself can be indicated by discreet annotations; in Figure 77, for example, row and column codes are used – sparingly – for cross-reference both within the commitment package and also in the brief statement of comparative information which appears below. The intention is that the format selected for the commitment package should offer a basis for structured debate about choices and assumptions; for closer comparison of alternatives, either within particular elements or on a broader scale; for modification to reflect new insights or representations; and – when the moment is ripe – for progress through commitment to decisive actions.

Helping decision-takers to choose

Even a carefully-organised and selective commitment package such as that of Figure 77 can present an overload of information for those decision-takers who may be called upon to authorise decisive actions. This problem of potential overload is of course not specific to the strategic choice approach; it applies equally to any form of decision technology, wherever actions have to be endorsed by busy people with multiple roles and responsibilities, who may not have the time to keep themselves closely acquainted with the progress of any analytical work.

However, if decision-takers are to exercise their right to choose *responsibly* in other than a token ritualistic way, it can sometimes be important that they be presented with more than one commitment package from which to choose.

Figure 78 Helping decision-takers to make progress

South Side
e x a m p l e

DOCUMENT 7 : Interim Report of South Side Working Party

ALTERNATIVES

The two most urgent decisions in South Side concern the alignment of the new arterial ROAD through the area and its continued LIFE as a residential neighbourhood. It is now clear that the balance of advantage lies with the northern road line; but the commitment to continued life of the district could range from the 10 years already pledged to a significantly longer horizon of around 40 years.   The following alternatives have been examined in depth:

–a SHORTER TERM INVESTMENT HORIZON (committed life 10 years) would allow options of either consolidating the local shopping centre on Main Street or moving it to King Square. In either case the now vacant central site could be developed for housing – but industrial development would be an alternative were the shops to remain on Main Street;

–a LONGER TERM INVESTMENT HORIZON (committed life 40 years) would mean relocating the local shops in King Square, with the central site used for either housing or open space.

THE SHORTER TERM HORIZON offers advantages in terms of flexibility and response to the concerns expressed by residents, as well as in terms of nett expenditure by this authority. The following RECOMMENDATIONS are therefore put forward at this stage:

RECOMMENDED IMMEDIATE ACTIONS

(1) A case be formally submitted to the Transport Authority for adoption of the NORTHERN ROAD LINE (see accompanying map);

(2) A renewal of the pledge to residents of a 10-YEAR period before further housing demolition, with public investment in environmental improvements geared accordingly.

LATER DECISIONS

(3) A decision on the location of the LOCAL SHOPPING CENTRE be taken in 6 MONTHS, after consultation with local traders and consideration of the impending proposals of the shops planning team on the scale of the new Eastwell shopping complex;

(4) The use of the now vacant CENTRAL SITE also to be decided in six months, in conjunction with (3) above.

CONTINGENCY PLANNING

It is just possible that the recommendation of the northern road line will be rejected by the Transport Authority; in which case a formal APPEAL is recommended, backed by evidence from the working party's analysis to date.

It is also possible that a major private developer may be attracted to South Side at some time; in which case, an EXTENSION to the life of the district can be considered.

FURTHER EXPLORATIONS

Because there still remain some important areas of uncertainty affecting future decisions in South Side, the working party proposes to continue carrying through a programme of explorations and consultations with other bodies. Priorities for further work will be outlined verbally at the meeting.

Choosing

S K I L L S

With ingenuity, it is often possible to present action proposals to decision-takers in forms which do not appear to deviate significantly from familiar forms of report, yet which reflect the underlying structure of a strategic choice analysis, as in this illustration. Use of diagrams should be viewed with caution and contingency plans may not be indicated explicitly where sensitive negotiations may arise.

Judgements must then be made about how many alternative packages should be presented, how much back-up information should be offered in support; and what the balance should be between different forms of communication – text, graphics, numerical tabulations, verbal presentation – as opposed to documents circulated in advance. These are judgements which will depend on the particular decision context, and the way in which its opportunities and constraints are understood by those who carry the responsibility of presenting proposals to decision-takers.

Figure 78 gives one example of the way in which the members of the South Side Working Party might decide to present their initial recommendations to the policy committee to which they report. It is here assumed that the latter group, with many pressures on its agenda, is accustomed to acting mainly on the basis of written documentation of a condensed summary form – backed up, if need be, by fuller information introduced in the course of discussion.

Figure 78 therefore takes the form of a one-page summary report, presented in fairly conventional written form, offering guidelines which can be followed, questioned or challenged at the discretion of the decision takers – in this case, the members of the municipal policy committee meeting as a group with the authority to commit resources to whatever course of action they may agree. To keep the report brief and readable, it is restricted in its focus to two main alternatives expressed in terms of contrasting policy orientations – one of these being a condensed version of the commitment package of Figure 77, and the other a contrasting package based on a 40-year horizon for the life of South Side as a residential area. In the interests of brevity, all but the most crucial characteristics of the two packages are omitted from the report; for the main aim of the report is to indicate what are the main differences in *structure* between the two.

It is likely that the main structural assumptions behind the alternative proposals will have been put to quite stringent testing well before this reporting stage; but it is important that they should be checked again carefully before the report is finally submitted. For example, if there were any serious residual doubts as to whether the 40 year life might, after all, allow the Main Street shopping centre to be retained, or whether industry on the central site might, in some circumstances, be compatible with the King Square shopping location, then the whole structure and emphasis of the report could be subject to challenge. The proposals might then either have to be redesigned in their entirety – or at least revised to allow this element of uncertainty to be acknowledged and an appropriate response prepared.

In any case, it will be only prudent that the working party members should prepare themselves carefully for the sorts of debate that could conceivably develop at the meeting, on the basis of their prior knowledge of the responsibilities of committee members, their interests, their power relationships and the idiosyncrasies or prejudices of particular members. As a first step, they could be well advised to prepare more detailed descriptions of each of the alternative commitment packages – perhaps using wall charts or other visual aids to present a broad picture of actions, explorations and future choices of the kind illustrated in Figure 77. They might also agree to come to the meeting armed with this kind of picture not only for the two contrasting packages highlighted in the report, but also for a 'compromise' 20-year package, to demonstrate how marginal the differences were between this and the 40-year alternative. Indeed, they might agree that it was a good move to prepare a further commitment package based on the southern road line, to indicate how limited a future it offers to South Side and what a strong case the Council has in recommending the northern alternative to the transportation authority.

Knowing the political inclinations of the committee members – which might cover quite a broad spectrum – the working party members might also feel it was important to prepare carefully the case for an emphasis on public rather than private development, in terms of the constraints presented by the local situation in South Side. They might, however, anticipate that the first contingency planning element of the package in Figure 77 offers a possible basis for helping the committee to converge on an agreed compromise view. They might also anticipate some surprise from committee members that this package is thought to offer local residents better short-term economic prospects than one based on a longer-term investment horizon. The explanation could be that a longer-term commitment to the future of South Side was expected to lead to rising house prices followed by gradual disintegration of the existing deep-rooted community structure; so they might have to be prepared for some challenging debate in the committee about the subtle issues of policy values this could raise.

The example of a commitment package given in Figure 77 is of a form which assumes that the decision-takers to whom it is addressed have significant influence not only in the sphere of responsibility of the Working Party itself, but also in their relationships with others. But this may not always be the case; and a decision situation involving negotiation between two or more autonomous or semi-autonomous parties may call for a different approach – especially if the parties are potentially in conflict, in which case it might not be thought tactically wise that all elements of the commitment package should be declared. For example, if the Working Party did not feel that the Council was in a powerful enough position to ensure that its recommendation of the northern road line would be accepted by the transportation authority, then it might have to re-think the whole commitment package in terms of a more subtle negotiating stance. To take another example, it might be thought more tactful – and more likely to yield results – if the idea of a joint small business initiative on the steelworks site were seeded informally in the mind of the Municipal Enterprise Officer, rather than suddenly presented to him in a background document during a formal committee meeting. So, the overt content of written proposals and background documents can be as much a matter of choice as any other aspect of the decision-making process.

To round off this particular episode in the South Side story, it will be supposed that some particular commitment package is accepted by the committee as a basis for action – whether this be Package IA as presented in Figure 77; or some variant of it which has attracted support in the course of discussions; or possibly some quite different package, perhaps embodying a higher level of commitment; or perhaps a lower level. For it is the committee that has the final responsibility and authority to decide.

Whatever the outcome of the meeting, the use of strategic choice concepts and methods does not mean that the problems of the South Side community are now 'solved' in any final or comprehensive way, any more than it is ever realistic to expect in a case as complex as this. But progress has been made; and it is progress both in the direction of action and of learning. For both the decision-takers and their advisers should have gained valuable insights into not only the problem but also the process; insights which will help to lay foundations for more confident decisions when further chapters come to be written in the continuing South Side story.

In Chapter 10, an illustration will be presented of the way in which the format of the commitment package has been adapted in the design of computer software to support the strategic choice approach. While the basic grid format of Figures 26 and 77 is closely followed in the design of the software, the phrase *progress package* is adopted in this context as a generic description as opposed to the phrase *commitment package.*

The aim of this is to encourage users to develop alternative packages, which can be stored in different data files, before proceeding to the further step of *adopting* a preferred progress package as an agreed basis for action. The STRAD software offers options of adopting any progress package either as a basis for *commitment,* in a situation where those generating the package have sufficient authority to do so, or as a basis for *recommendation* to others, or as a *strategic option* to be compared with other strategic options by those who carry the primary responsibility to decide.

Process judgements in the choosing mode

Of course, not every moment of commitment in a continuous planning process need be approached as formally or with as much preparation as this last episode in the South Side story might suggest. Sometimes, a commitment package might contain no more than a single action commitment on some aspect of the problem under consideration; and this action may fall within the personal sphere of responsibility of a single decision-maker. Perhaps this action may be accompanied by a decision to embark on some form of exploratory action to provide a clearer basis for other choices that have been deferred. Perhaps too – though not of necessity – that small step in the process will include some agreed arrangements for the making of those other choices at a later time.

But the latest episode of the South Side story does illustrate some of the subtle considerations of dialogue between advisers and decision-takers that can arise whenever a more formal moment of commitment arrives. And the story has at least touched on some of the complexities that can arise where there is more than one authoritative decision-taking body, and where different parties

Figure 79 Process choices when working in the choosing mode

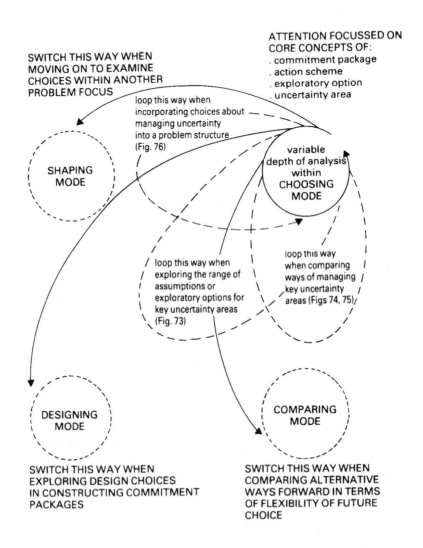

ATTENTION FOCUSSED ON
CORE CONCEPTS OF:
. commitment package
. action scheme
. exploratory option
. uncertainty area

SWITCH THIS WAY WHEN
MOVING ON TO EXAMINE
CHOICES WITHIN ANOTHER
PROBLEM FOCUS

loop this way when
incorporating choices about
managing uncertainty
into a problem structure
(Fig. 76)

variable
depth of analysis
within
CHOOSING
MODE

SHAPING
MODE

loop this way when
exploring the range of
assumptions or
exploratory options for
key uncertainty areas
(Fig. 73)

loop this way
when comparing
ways of managing
key uncertainty
areas (Figs 74, 75)

DESIGNING
MODE

COMPARING
MODE

SWITCH THIS WAY WHEN
EXPLORING DESIGN CHOICES
IN CONSTRUCTING COMMITMENT
PACKAGES

SWITCH THIS WAY WHEN
COMPARING ALTERNATIVE
WAYS FORWARD IN TERMS
OF FLEXIBILITY OF FUTURE
CHOICE

Choosing

SUMMARY

may be continually pulling in conflicting directions. In these circumstances, progress may well depend on quite complex negotiations across organisational boundaries – raising issues which will be discussed further in the next two chapters.

This chapter has shown how the work of the choosing mode can draw on prior work in any or all of the other modes – shaping, designing and comparing – sometimes in a very subtle way. Also, as summarised in Figure 79, the work of the choosing mode itself presents many opportunities either for looping briefly in the direction of these other modes, or for switching more deliberately to work for some time in a different mode, if it is judged that the moment for making commitments has not yet arrived. In particular, once a commitment package is adopted as a basis for immediate decision, there will remain the deferred choices to be dealt with at some later time. When this time arrives, all the various opportunities for shaping, designing, comparing and choosing will arise once again – perhaps in different forms, influenced by events and reappraisals over the intervening period. For the process of strategic choice is above all a continuing one which cannot be isolated from the processes of change within the wider environment in which it is set.

The content of Figure 79 will not be discussed in detail, as was the content of the equivalent figures at the end of the last three chapters. Rather, it is left as an exercise for the reader to reflect on the various switching and looping opportunities which it indicates. Indeed, the reader is encouraged to reflect on these not only in relation to the development of the South Side story in earlier actions, but also in relation to personal experience in choosing strategically in his or her own working life.

Illustrations from practice

This chapter again concludes with a set of three *illustrations from practice* selected to illustrate further points about the work of the choosing mode.

The first illustration shows how uncertainty areas can be mapped and sorted quickly and informally in a group setting. The second illustration presents three different examples of the use of 'action forms' in giving practical expression to the commitment package concept. The third illustration shows the use of a commitment package framework in presenting the proposals from a national policy development project, showing the wide range of actions and explorations involved in putting them into effect.

Figure 80   Illustration from practice – choosing 1

<table>
<tr><td>Choosing</td><td>Theme:</td><td>Putting uncertainty areas into perspective through the use of an uncertainty graph.</td></tr>
<tr><td></td><td>Project:</td><td>Development of an integrated policy framework for the management of solid waste.</td></tr>
<tr><td>PRACTICE</td><td>Context:</td><td>Workshops with an inter-organisational project team, Province of Limburg, The Netherlands, 1986.</td></tr>
</table>

Commentary on Figure 80

These charts record work done by a project group at the end of the first day of a series of three two-day workshops, designed to get a more substantial planning project under way. The group consisted mainly of Provincial Government employees, and was charged with preparing a policy plan to integrate the management of different kinds of solid waste.

In the first instance, uncertainty areas were listed as they occurred to members of the group, drawing on their everyday experience and on understanding gained through earlier analysis (2). They ranged from the quite specific (quantity, type and source of solid waste) to the relatively general (basis for recycling policy). When this process slowed, the analysis proper was started, although the list was left open for additions if there were any.

Firstly, each uncertainty area was classified according to type, as can be seen down the left hand side of the list ('OG' = UE in Dutch, 'OW' = UV, 'OR' = UR). As usually happens, a number of the uncertainty areas were seen as falling between categories and so given dual classifications.

The second stage of the analysis then identified views about the difficulty or otherwise of reducing uncertainty in the various areas. A distinction between 'diamonds' (hard to reduce) and 'jellies' (easy to reduce) was adopted as a starting point. As might be expected, this quickly developed into a more subtle range which is shown just below the uncertainty graph (3).

The third stage of the analysis involved assessment of relevance to the plan. For this, use was made of stickers. Each member of the group was given four stickers and asked to place them next to the four uncertainty areas which they considered most relevant to the policy plan. The results appear down the left hand side of the list. The three boxed uncertainty areas emerged as more relevant than the others. They included the uncertainty over support for a policy of recycling; over level of commitment to making the plan work; and over possibilities for combining with other fields of policy.

All this information was then transferred to the uncertainty graph (3), which has as its centre the focus: 'Beleidskeuzen in PAP II' (policy choices in the second Provincial Waste Management Plan). This was further analysed in line with principles outlined by means of a simplified 2 x 2 taxonomy (1). As a result the decision was taken to reduce uncertainty area number 6 about the level of support for a policy of recycling. However, because the project was still at an early stage, it was possible to give some more thought to ways of tackling the other central uncertainties which seemed more difficult to reduce. Had the process been nearer the end, they would probably have been tackled by making assumptions, perhaps backed up by some contingency planning.

Figure 81   Illustration from practice – choosing 2

1

FACILITATION WORKSHEET : Action Planning 2

The Strategic Choice Approach

A·H·A

© 1993 Allen Hickling and Associates

Example **ACTION FORM**

STRATEGIC OPTION *Encouragement of prevention*	MEASURE 1 *Essential Requirements* 4. *Improvement of Road surface*

DESCRIPTION OF ACTION
Carry out tests to evaluate on tyre wear, the effect of various surface pavement types (including mixes with Rubber binder or Rubber aggregates).

RESPONSIBILITIES		
IRF could co-ordinate the action managed by road industry with other partners.	X	European Commission
		Member States
	*	Producers
		Industry
	X	IRF ....
		....
		Users
		General Public

FUNDING (WHO, HOW, etc) *EEC*	COST/BUDGET *to be determined after study*

PLANNING (UNCERTAINTIES, CONDITIONS, etc)
start by 1994, to end by 1997

Time Scale:

CRUCIAL ASSUMPTIONS / 'CRITICAL SUCCESS FACTORS'
- good control of parameters (climate; geometry of roads; type of pavements).
- choice of vehicles

GENERAL NOTES
Paragraphs 'd' and 'g' of measure 4 seem to be non-funded assumptions. We recommend to delete them.

AHina | \AHA\PAPERS\CHKLSTS\WORKSHT7 : 2 | 9-30220

Y. Meunier

2

4.1

Problēma	Risinājums
Atkritumu ietekme uz vidi	

Rīcība
MK noteikumi par rūpniecisko atkritumu šķirošanu

Atbildīgie *
Darba grupa, kuras sastāvā varētu būt VARAM, Ekonomikas ministrijas, rūpniecības uzņēmumu, u.c. ieinteresēto institūciju pārstāvji

Iespējamie finansēšanas avoti | Aptuvenas izmaksas (Ls)
valsts budžets; ārvalstu donori | ~ 1500

Laika grafiks
1.5 gadi

1995   1996   1997   1998   1999   2000   2001   2002

Sagaidāmie rezultāti | Blakusiedarbība
Izstrādāti MK noteikumi, uzņēmumos uzsākta atkritumu šķirošana (vismaz dažos, kur tas ir ekonomiski izdevīgi)

Piezīmes	Prioritāte
Šobrīd Latvijā nav pieredzes (vai arī tā ir nepietiekoši popularizēta) par rūpniecisko atkritumu šķirošanu, tās tehnoloģiskajiem un ekonomiskajiem rādītājiem	IG
	Datums

* Aizimlt, kur nepieciešams
• Izpildītājs   x Koordinators   o Nepieciešams atbalsts

3

Actieprogramma CO₂-technologie

Er zal een actieprogramma worden opgesteld voor de ontwikkeling en demonstratie van technologieen om, in een situatie van eventuele stringente CO_2-beperking, invoering hiervan te kunnen versnellen.

ACTOREN	Rijk (VROM/DGM)
	VROM/DGM/LE/KV/dr. L.A. Meyer
	VROM/DGM/LE/KV/dr. L.A. Meyer
	meerdere doelgroepen
	n.v.t.
	EZ; V&W (via WIEK en SKIE)
PLANNING	lopend
	strategienotitie (eind 1995)
	bijdrage aan de Vervolgnota Klimaatbeleid (eind 1995)
	input voor nader onderzoek in de tweede tranche van het NOP-MLK
KENMERKEN	klimaatverandering; milieutechnologie
	voorbereid zijn op eventuele stringente CO_2-beperking door ontwikkeling van technologie maar ook van andere opties te versnellen en de mogelijke resultaten naar voren te halen in de tijd
	er zal een actieprogramma worden opgesteld om in situatie van stringente CO_2-beperking invoering van maatregelen te kunnen versnellen. Deze maatregelen omvatten technologie, infrastructuur en gebruik van technologie
	kennisvermeerdering, beleidsformulering

Choosing

PRACTICE

Theme: The use of action forms in developing draft and final documents (Action Plan)

Project: 1 Action planning for European waste management: used tyres.
2 Preparation of the National Enviromental Action Plan for Latvia.
3 Work document for the Netherlands national enviromental policy plan.

Context: Various national and international multi-organisational project groups

Commentary on Figure 81

There are three projects illustrated here. The intention is to reflect different stages of the choosing process and the way concepts were adapted to the situation 'on the ground' for the specific client at the time. Each project will be described in turn, in an order which reflects different stages of development.

1 The first example shows an early attempt to enable a multi-organisational project group, set up in 1993 by DG11 of the European Commission, to produce an action plan as part of the Implementation Strategy for the 'Priority Waste Stream' of Used Tyres. This was towards the end of a 30-month project which had demonstrated all the problems of being the first in a series.

The Project Group had had difficulty in adapting to the new style of working, and there had been a long settling in period. The facilitation team were also on a steep learning curve, as they had previously only experienced this kind of working at national level – the increase in scale being not a little challenging.

All participants had been asked to fill in forms which would then form the basis of the proposed Action Plan element of a draft strategy. This work was done between strategic meetings and assembled later by a technical support team. As it happened little more work was done on these forms and they were submitted without the benefit of sustained analysis and comparison.

2 The second example is taken from the work of an inter-governmental project group set up in 1996 by the Ministry for the Environment and Regional Development in Latvia. It is the most recent and up until now the most successful application of the action form concept. While the language here is Latvian, the boxes and their content are similar to those in the first example.

At this early stage in developing an environmental strategy in Latvia, it was decided that this first attempt would be restricted to the Environment Ministry. Accordingly these forms were first filled out by the staff of the regional offices, then brought to an Action Gallery event (see page 314) in Riga, prior to being put through a process of integration to produce a first draft plan. This example shows a format adopted in that second stage of development just after the Action Gallery, after word-processing for presentation purposes. The final version which is to be properly co-ordinated and agreed should be published around October/November 1996 while this second edition is being finalised.

3 The third example is chosen to demonstrate how an action form can end up by being presented in a published Government document – in this case the so-called Work Document of the second National Environmental Policy Plan for The Netherlands. It is the work of a project group of the Netherlands Directorate-General for the Environment in 1994.

The document contains 125 actions grouped in each case according to the primary actors – described as 'target groups' in the plan (for example Agriculture; Industry; Central Government). It also shows the current status of all the actions agreed in the first National Environmental Policy Plan. Although the presentation here is more sophisticated, the various headings are similar to those used in any typical action form. The amount of information under each heading is limited according to the intended readership, but references are provided to enable more detailed information to be located.

Figure 82   Illustration from practice – choosing 3

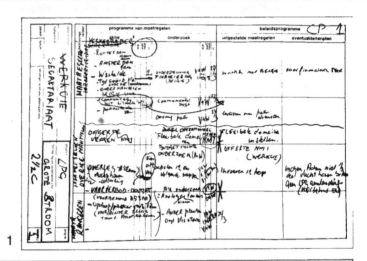

1

An excerpt of the commitment package for Dutch national LPG policy (1984)

Action set

Actions:
- traffic regulation: increase regulatory measures for LPG ships on the main national waterways;
- LPG inland tankships: adapt design and construction in order to effectively prohibit large LPG outflows;
- LPG railcars: large contingents should always be shipped in block trains: in case (for smaller contingents) of shunting some extra measures are specified;
- LPG road tankers: extra design adaptations are introduced to further decrease probabilities of LPG outflows;
- Stationary installations: specifications for zoning around such installations are given;
- Road transport routes: will basically be limited to the Dutch dangerous goods network. New stationary installations will be located in places compatible to this network.

Explorations:
- research into the safe domains around seaships will be done;
- the collision safety of seagoing tankers carrying pressurised LPG will be analysed;
- the possibilities of repressing fire around LPG inland tankers will be analysed;
- the further analysis with respect to effective and economic means of prohibiting Bleve's on LPG road tankers will be conducted.

Policy set

Delayed actions:
The result of the above mentioned analysis will be implemented in the relevant policy decisions and it will be introduced in national regulation and in international regulatory bodies.

Contingency plans:
- in case an LPG-terminal in Amsterdam is conceived then a refuge location for LPG tankers will be constructed;
- in case international regulatory bodies do not accommodate the proposed measures then the general character of such measures must be guaranteed along other lines;
- in case the analysis with respect to prohibiting Bleve in road tankers does not give satisfactory results then other means will be used to create an acceptable situation;
- in case measures with respect to LPG filling stations prove to be intractable due to local situations, then a decision will be made regarding other necessary measures or removal of the filling station.

2

Choosing PRACTICE	Theme:	Finalisation of a policy statement using a commitment package framework.
	Project:	National policy on the handling and distribution of liquid petroleum gas (LPG).
	Context:	A multi-disciplinary inter-ministry working party, Den Haag, The Netherlands, 1983–84.

Commentary on Figure 82

This illustration is taken from a published case study (van de Graaf, 1985; see also Hickling, 1989) of the application of strategic choice methods to the development of a new national policy in the Netherlands for the landing, transportation, storage and distribution of Liquid Petroleum Gas (LPG). The author of the paper is a civil servant in the Dutch Ministry of Economic Affairs who played a leading role in the project alongside representatives of other Ministries, with Allen Hickling and Arnold de Jong in the role of process consultants.

The situation was one in which the basic assumptions of the previously adopted policy had become eroded, because it had not proved possible to concentrate the landing of this economically attractive but hazardous hydrocarbon – of international importance as a fuel and feedstock – at a single installation at the mouth of the Rhine, with distribution by pipeline. For two years, the search for an alternative policy had exercised the attention of civil servants from the Ministry of Economic Affairs, the Ministry of Transport and Directorates of the Environment Ministry concerned with land-use planning and environmental protection. Progress had been blocked by the well-known tendency to defend departmental positions. The explicit use of a more interactive approach based on strategic choice methods allowed rapid progress towards an agreed set of policies. However, the participants found it useful to switch back from time to time to a more adversarial mode of working, so as to appreciate more clearly the policy and other constraints they would have to contend with outside the context of the working group.

The working document reproduced here (1) was one of several in a set which were needed to cover all aspects of the problem. The printed framework adopted here is one that can be used large (AI size) on the wall or small (A4 size) in a loose-leaf file. Notice the explicit accommodation of responsibility ('wie' – who), deadlines ('wanneer' – when), and budgets ('fl.' – guilders (money)). The decision-taker is listed on the left ('secretariaat'), as is the orientation ('grote stroom'). Otherwise it is a standard commitment package framework.

The condensed extract from the final recommendations (2) is presented using the four headings of the commitment package framework – as was the actual set of proposals. These were formally adopted in February 1985 by the second chamber of the Dutch national parliament.

It will be noticed that the explorations are primarily of a technical and economic nature, reflecting concern with uncertainty areas of the UE type. However, the significance of uncertainty areas of type UR is clearly indicated in some of the proposals listed under the contingency plan heading – the other decision-makers identified ranging from international regulatory bodies to local agencies concerned with the siting and safety of filling stations. Uncertainties of type UV in the form of the conflicts between economy, safety and other criteria were accommodated in the design of the inter-Ministry working process.

9 Practicalities

Taking stock

The last four chapters have completed a second and fuller cycle around the four basic modes of planning seen as a process of strategic choice. In contrast to the briefer, introductory tour made in Chapters 2 and 3, the emphasis has been on *appropriate* ways of drawing on the core concepts and basic methods of the strategic choice approach, in adapting to different working situations. Although certain elaborations of these concepts and methods have been introduced, it is important to stress again that moves towards elaboration should not necessarily be seen as moves towards 'better' use of the strategic choice approach. Simplification is usually a virtue when working under pressure; and in striking a balance between simplification and elaboration the most useful working rule is to favour simplification except where there are convincing arguments to the contrary.

At various points in Chapters 5 to 8 consideration was given to some of the *organisational* aspects of the strategic choice approach; to the switching of the *process* between modes; and to the forms that the more visible *products* might take. Also, those aspects of *technology* concerned with effective interaction and facilitation in a group setting were considered more closely than in the earlier introductory tour of core concepts and methods. But the exposition of the last four chapters has still followed the structure of the four modes in a sequential way. It has to be recognised that, the more effective a working group becomes, the more the process will tend to move freely and adaptively between modes through a succession of rapid switching and looping judgements. So the offering of operational advice on the management of the strategic choice approach cannot be organised according to the structure of the four modes alone. There is another level of practical advice which relates generally to the management of the approach as a whole. It is this kind of advice with which the present chapter is concerned.

The starting point for the advice to be offered here will be the general picture of the *orientations* of strategic choice presented at the end of Chapter 4 (Figure 34). That diagram used the framework of technology, organisation, process and product to compare the strategic choice approach with more conventional approaches that could be regarded as quite appropriate in dealing with simpler problems. In successive columns, contrasts were drawn first at the level of general orientations, then at the level of operational guidelines, then at the levels of emphases in management choice and in evaluation. This chapter will interpret these last two aspects in still more concrete terms, reflecting the body of experience in *application* of strategic choice ideas that has been built up through working with many different people on a wide range of practical problems over a considerable period of years. First, this body of practical experience will be briefly reviewed. Then, the main lessons to be drawn from it will be presented; first in terms of the emphases on *selectivity* and *adaptiveness* which distinguish the overall approach, and then in terms of the four headings of Technology, Organisation, Process and Product, considered each in turn.

The base of experience

The advice that will be offered in this chapter is rooted primarily in the experiences of the authors, working with many other people in many different project settings, and the picture that has gradually developed through this experience of what constitutes 'good practice' in working with the strategic choice approach. This view of the current state of the art is one which is unlikely to stand still in the years ahead, as further experience accumulates. For the range of applications to different fields of decision-making seems likely to extend and, with it, both the variety of people and organisations involved, and the range of further adaptations made.

However, our current view of good practice is one which already has quite a broad base in terms of the range of planners, managers, specialists and lay policy-makers who have become exposed to the approach and played some part in its development. The people with whom we ourselves have worked have come from several different countries and decision-making cultures; and the types of working relationship through which we have collaborated with them have also been diverse. So, it will be a useful prelude to the advice of this chapter to indicate briefly what the range of these working relationships has been and, broadly, what has been learned through each type of experience. For this purpose, three broad headings will suffice – sponsored experiments, training events and consultancy projects. Each type of experience has complemented and reinforced the others: but the order in which they will be introduced here corresponds broadly to the historical sequence in which they first emerged.

Much of the early development work on the strategic choice approach took place through the medium of *sponsored experiments,* in which an organisation interested in the possibility of promoting new methods of planning and decision-making has been prepared to invest in a programme of one or more experimental applications of the strategic choice approach to 'on line' problems within its general area of concern. Leading examples included the initial LOGIMP experiment of 1970; the structure plan project of the mid-seventies; the Netherlands project on environmental policy plans in the early eighties; and successive projects in the states of Sao Paulo and Pernambuco in Brazil. References to some of these experiences will be found in the Guide to further reading at the end of the book. Each exercise was sponsored not so much to help with specific decision problems, as to test the relevance of the strategic choice approach to a wider class of problems; yet success in helping with specific cases was quite central to this testing process. In each of the first three projects mentioned, between two and six 'live' planning problems were pursued in parallel, with the authors and other colleagues or associates acting as advisers to the local teams responsible for producing recommendations on these selected problems. The different teams would all meet together from time to time, to exchange experiences, review difficulties and provide mutual support – with representatives of the central sponsoring body maintaining oversight of the programme as a whole.

The overall style of working in these sponsored experiments has been one of *action research,* designed through negotiation with the dual aims of discovery and practical service to users in view. In contrast to more classical action research studies (Clark, 1976), there was the added dimension that the action research team was engaged in collaboration with people not just from a single organisational context, but from a set of two or more local 'host' organisations together with a central sponsoring body, each with its own expectations of what the collaboration should achieve.

Inevitably, each sponsored experiment has involved elements of training in the strategic choice approach – partly in the form of 'on the job' training for the members of the local teams, and partly in the form of introductory lectures on philosophy and method. In addition, however, from 1971 onwards, free-standing *training events* have been arranged under the auspices of a wide range of other organisations, in various parts of the world. The duration of such an event has generally been short – ranging from as little as half a day to two weeks at the most – because those participating have generally been not full time students but decision-makers and planners with many other pressures on their time. The design formula for all but the shortest half-day events – a two- or three-day duration being most typical – has been for lectures to be interspersed with work in small groups on a realistic problem exercise. The aim is to move progressively through the shaping, designing, comparing and choosing modes, as in this book, with as much attention as practicable within the time available to the various opportunities for recycling that can be explored as understanding grows and circumstances change. The experiences of both sponsored experiments and consultancy projects have provided a rich source of case material for use in these training events, allowing the various facets of planning under pressure to be realistically reproduced. At the same time, the wide variety of management contexts and positions represented by those participating in the various training events has considerably enriched the process of feedback from practice through which strategic choice ideas and methods have gradually evolved.

Involvement in direct *consultancy projects,* where the primary aim has been to help with a specific planning or decision problem rather than to explore the relevance of the approach to some class of problems, has achieved momentum as the experiential foundations of strategic choice have become more secure. In almost all cases where we or others associated with us have been involved as consultants, arrangements for direct collaboration with people from client organisations have been treated as an important part of the project design, and opportunities for interactive working have been stressed.

The scale of such projects has varied from substantial engagements with national governments on national policy issues, to briefer assignments for commercial, public and voluntary organisations. Sometimes, too, brief exercises in mutual consultancy have been designed within short-term training events. Typically, an hour or two has been allowed for participants to talk about instances of specific problems which are currently concerning them in their own management situations.

While the various training and consultancy experiences have provided opportunities to experiment with many different styles in managing the process of strategic choice, the advice that follows is based primarily on one 'prototypical' style that has proved successful in many different settings and has been widely used both in sponsored experiments and in consultancy projects. It is a style that reflects the basic orientations and operational guidelines of Chapter 4, in that it is built around a programme of interactive group sessions of limited duration in the kind of working environment illustrated in the upper picture of Figure 30.

Within the group, the methods of strategic choice are used as an 'open technology', starting from some initial state of knowledge or uncertainty about the problem among the participants, that will gradually be revealed. The agenda is treated as flexible within the time constraints of the working session or sequence of sessions that has been arranged. Little or no backroom preparation is expected for the first session – though priorities for backroom work can build up as a shared view of issues and uncertainties develops within the group. Typically, a working session will cover two or three hours either in a morning or an afternoon, with the same kinds of pressures on time as in the more traditional committee setting depicted in Figure 6 – but with the important exception that there is no expectation of working through a preconceived agenda from start to finish as the session proceeds.

Selectivity and adaptiveness: The toolbox analogy

It is most important that the strategic choice approach is not seen as a mere technique. The straightforward application of techniques, with some well-defined rules as to how and when they should be applied, has all the attraction of simplicity and is easily taught in a classroom setting. But such an approach has severe limitations, unless the problems being addressed are 'bent' to fit it – something which in practice happens rather more often than it should. The strategic choice approach has been developed in a way designed specifically to avoid this difficulty. This means that there is no one right way to use the approach. There can be no 'correct' sequence in which to do things, and no prescribed combinations to adopt – whether these be viewed in terms of technology, organisation, process or product. It is all a matter of judgement as to what is appropriate to the circumstances at that particular time. Every problem is different. Each must be tackled on its merits.

Use of the strategic choice approach has been likened to the use of a toolbox. The analogy is extremely apt so long as it is remembered that in strategic choice the tools are many and varied – including a wide range of concepts, modes, frameworks, techniques, activities and media.

Imagine taking a toolbox to mend a car engine. Having opened the bonnet and looked at the engine, it is likely that a start has to be made by undoing a nut. Reaching into the toolbox, one selects a spanner, takes it out and tries it on the nut. The first time, almost invariably, it does not fit. So one puts it back and tries another. It may be that the nut is still stubborn, in which case one dips down into the toolbox and chooses another spanner, using now the two in combination. It may be that this combination fails too. If so, they can be put back and another combination tried; or perhaps some penetrating oil is used in addition, thus using three items in combination; and so on, until it works.

As progress is made through the job in hand, different situations will emerge requiring different combinations of tools – and so on, until the job is finished. Also, the next time it is necessary to do the same job, it will probably be appropriate to use different tools, in different combinations and sequences. Imagine that the same car engine requires the same maintenance three months later. It may now be easier to shift that nut, which was once so difficult that several spanners had to be used to shift it; perhaps because it was greased before being tightened. This time, the tools needed may be different again. Perhaps a pair of pliers will be enough to get it undone – or it may be found to be only finger-tight in any case. Meanwhile, however, other things might have changed; a bolt might have become rusted in, or broken off, or weakened in some way. So yet more different tools, sequences and combinations might have to be tried.

This analogy illustrates well the two key ideas which govern all the operational advice offered in the sections which follow. The first is the idea of **selectivity**. This follows inevitably from the wide variety of choice available in the use of the strategic choice approach. Indeed, it is clearly implied in the tool-box analogy; there are many tools which obviously cannot all be used on a specific task, even if they were all appropriate – which is most unlikely. Even more inconceivable is the idea that they could all be used at the same time. Thus it is necessary to be selective; to choose carefully what to do and what not to do – and how, with whom and when.

The second idea is that of **adaptiveness**. This follows from the feelings of uncertainty which are endemic to working with complex issues – uncertainty about what the problem is (and is not); what the alternative ways of dealing with it may be; how they rate one against the other; and, indeed, what to do about it. The idea that one can always, unerringly, select a good way of working in such a context is plainly unrealistic. It may serve some purpose to try to predict the course that the analysis should take; but to believe that it will be sensible to maintain that course whatever happens in the process is similarly far-fetched. So, there can be only one way of working; and that, paradoxically, is to be ready to work in many ways – in fact, to work adaptively via the explicit acceptance of the learning process, part of which is learning how to conduct that process. One's capacity to think about what to do; what not to do; how, when and in which context, is bound to evolve as one's understanding develops. It is only sensible, as long as time allows, to give that evolutionary process full rein.

Therefore, every opportunity has to be taken to promote that evolution – to keep the learning process going in a smooth and adaptive way. Referring back to the description of the toolbox analogy, there was an important moment when the first spanner selected proved to be the wrong one. This was not bad or inefficient – it was a vital step in the learning process. Being mistaken in this way is important because so much is learnt from it. Thus the second spanner was more likely to be right because the choice of it was so much better informed than the first. This is a classic example of learning from one's mistakes – a phenomenon well known in all cultures of the world, old and new. It leads to the idea of *learning by doing*. The only way to make mistakes is by doing something – so it follows that the more one does, the more mistakes will be made, and the more one will learn.

But this does not mean that selectivity is unimportant. Selections have to be made all the time, in order to keep the process going, and there are times when making a mistake can be costly. So it means that care must be taken in that selection; yet that too much time must not be wasted on it. Going back to the toolbox analogy again, a lot of thought could be given to the choice of which tool to use at any time. It is easy to hesitate when there are so many alternatives – not only which size of spanner to use, but also which sort of spanner, and, indeed, whether a spanner was an appropriate tool in the first place. The important thing is not to agonise too long over the choice of which to use; but to try one, drawing as much as possible on past experience, with an open mind and in a spirit of learning. As a rough-and ready rule, it is worth bearing in mind that the time spent thinking about it should not exceed the time it would take just to try one out.

Naturally, experience is a vital help in selectivity. This in itself can lead to the idea of each user having his or her own individual *repertoire*. This is the sub-set of all the available tools which that person tends to use more freely and frequently than others – a form of behaviour which is systematically reinforced because it is the most frequently used tools that tend to stay at the top of the toolbox, thus being the first for consideration the next time. Tools from lower in the toolbox only get used when the earlier ones do not work so well, or when the specific task is very well defined. Different people's personal repertoires are likely to have a number of tools in common, and these may be expected to be those with the more general application; the equivalent of hammers, pliers and screwdrivers, though even these may be of various sizes and types. For users of strategic choice, among these common tools would probably be the basic concepts of AIDA; though even here such core concepts as the option bar and the decision scheme can be represented and used in different ways, as earlier chapters have shown.

So, even the experienced consultant or practitioner in strategic choice will have a personal repertoire, which will be similar but probably by no means identical as between individuals. There will be differences in their personal styles as well as in their work experiences in collaborative settings. The two authors, for example, recognise some clear personal differences in the emphases they give to particular concepts and methods in their respective repertoires.

Most people already have personal toolboxes of their own and, indeed, their own repertoires with which they are likely to feel quite comfortable. What is more, they are probably loath to abandon these just to take up what could seem to be a self-contained box of tools for strategic choice, such as that presented here. In most cases, this is not necessary. The strategic choice approach is intended to be open and flexible – and most of its tools can be used in combination with other ways of doing things. Indeed, mention has already been made of certain other tools of evaluation and design at particular points in the preceding chapters. There is also some development work under way which is likely to clarify the relationships between the tools offered here and others. Further discussion of these relationships will be found in Chapters 11 and 12.

Choosing tools under pressure

The most distinctive and significant feature of the strategic choice approach is that is has been developed directly out of practice, working with planners and decision-makers who are usually working under pressure. Consequently, it is under these conditions that strategic choice is most useful, and it is generally where deeper and more lengthy analysis is relevant that some of the other approaches come into their own.

In developing the strategic choice approach, it has been found helpful to distinguish between contrasting ways of handling work under pressure – especially pressure caused by the shortage of time. These are what is often called the *quick and dirty* way, and what may be called the *fast and effective* way. Taking up the toolbox analogy again, they can both be likened to types of screwdriver. The quick and dirty way can be likened to the 'Brummigem' screwdriver, whereas the fast and effective way can be likened to the 'Yankee' screwdriver. The 'Brummigem' (which is a corruption of the name Birmingham) is, in fact, a heavy hammer. Although designed for other tasks, such as banging in nails, it can be a very quick way of driving in screws. Of course, there tends to be a loss of effectiveness in the result, although the appearance may sometimes be satisfactory. The 'Yankee' (actually a trade mark) is a specially designed 'plunge'-type screwdriver which, by means of a helical thread inside the handle, turns the screw automatically as the tool is pushed on. It is very fast and, indeed, can be very effective. But the trouble is that it is not suitable for all situations and, unlike the 'Brummigem', it cannot be easily used for anything else.

Thus, it can be seen that there is no clear-cut recipe for the use in practice of the strategic choice approach. Selectivity and adaptiveness are both essential and, by definition, require that choices be made. And, as was implied in the toolbox analogy, these choices mean balancing ideas about effectiveness against ideas about the expenditure of effort, time and resources – whether the balance is struck in a conscious or subconscious way. Here it is worth mentioning the *Sutton Principle*, which many users of strategic choice have found helpful as a simple, light-hearted way of reminding themselves of the issues involved.

The Sutton Principle is named after Willie Sutton, who was an infamous American bank robber.[1] One day, when he eventually became available for interview, Willie Sutton was asked why he robbed banks. To this he came back with the now immortal reply: 'Because that is where the money is!' His reasoning was very simple. Given a limited amount of time and effort (in Willie's case his own), these resources should be directed where the rewards are likely to be greatest.

Without examining Willie Sutton's logic too deeply, two important lessons can be drawn. The first is that if one cannot deal with everything adequately then, rather than deal with all things inadequately, it is better to deal adequately with some things only. The second is that, in choosing which things to do, the process should always be steered in the direction where it is believed the greatest progress can be made. So it is also with deciding how to select tools from a toolbox – always remembering that in the strategic choice approach the toolbox includes modes, concepts, frameworks, media of communication and ways of working, as well as analytical techniques. The costs are generally the demands which the use of each tool places on the available *resources*; and, in the management of a process of strategic choice, the resources in question tend to take many forms. They include elapsed time; the skills and experience of relevant people; access to relevant information; and access to the capacity to process such information by electronic or other means. The effectiveness of alternative ways of proceeding has to be weighed against the demands they make on resources of all these kinds and, as such resources tend to be limited, they can become constraining, limiting the range of choice. Or sometimes, of course, they can be bought in from elsewhere.

Money has not been mentioned yet as a resource because it is rare for the selection of a tool from the toolbox to carry a direct financial cost. Where such costs do arise is in trying to make up for shortfalls in resource supply. This means giving consideration to improvement, support or, in some cases, replacement of the resources already available, in such forms as:

- more and/or more effective people (e.g. training and consultants);
- more and/or more relevant information (e.g. surveys and research);
- better and/or faster technological support (e.g. computers and software).

1 This principle was first enunciated as the 'Sutton Effect' by Robert E. Machol in one of a series of brief, tongue-in-cheek articles on Principles of Operations Research (Machol, 1976).

However, this is always assuming that there is enough calendar-type time available – and this is often the most inflexible constraint of all.

The effectiveness side of the resource-effectiveness balance is difficult to judge in advance because it is so intangible and uncertain. It is concerned essentially with the *potential* of the tool; in particular, the potential progress it might generate in terms of those broad and comparatively subtle dimensions of evaluation which were indicated in the final column of Figure 34. Progress in the directions of sharing, synergy, understanding and confidence can be difficult enough to assess in retrospect, let alone to judge with any clarity in advance.

So far, this chapter has discussed the practicalities of working with the strategic choice toolbox in rather general terms. The aim has been to explain more fully the broad management emphasis on selectivity and adaptiveness which appeared in the top row of Figure 34, and also to develop further the idea of effectiveness as an evaluative principle. To move to a more concrete level in this discussion of the practicalities of strategic choice, it will be necessary now to consider the overall approach in terms of the four components: technology, organisation, process and product.

Technology: managing the open technology in practice

In Chapter 4, it was argued that the technology of strategic choice was designed above all as an *open technology;* as a means of assisting and encouraging effective communication and interaction within a working group and not just as an aid to backroom analysis by experts. It is because of this emphasis on sharing between participants with diverse perspectives to contribute that the technology of strategic choice can be considered an *appropriate* technology for group working on issues the very shape of which may be both complex and confused.

The emphasis on an open technology was interpreted in Chapter 4 into an operational guideline of a *focus on decisions.* This guideline finds more specific expression in the set of core concepts to do with decision areas, decision options, decision schemes and the various other linked concepts which were introduced in relation to the work of the comparing and the choosing modes. In addition, an impression was presented of the kind of interactive work setting in which the spirit of an open, decision-centred technology can be achieved in practice (Figure 30). It was argued that choices about the use of rooms, furniture and equipment were just as much a part of the management of the strategic choice technology as were matters to do with the application of specific concepts and techniques. So there are various practical matters to do with these *physical* aspects of technological choice to be discussed in this section; after which, some further points will be made about the kinds of *social* technology that can be helpful in stimulating productive forms of interaction within a working group.

Some of the advice to be offered on effective use of walls, paper and pens may seem quite trivial and mundane. However, long experience in using the strategic choice approach with groups does indicate that the quality of group communication and interaction can be quite severely impaired by failure to pay heed to such considerations, especially in the early stages of group working, when patterns for future interaction are being set. It is important, firstly, to choose a room which is not so small in relation to the number of participants that their freedom of movement is restricted, constraining them to sit in fixed positions in relation to each other, as they would in the familiar committee setting. For the same reason, it is important to avoid creating a situation in which a table becomes the centrepiece. Indeed, a first step in preparing a room is usually to push any tables to one side, where they can still be used as required, for documents, refreshments, materials or note-taking, but do not create barriers between the participants as they move around. It is a matter of comfort and convenience to provide enough chairs for participants to be able to sit down whenever they desire. However, they are likely to spend much of their time standing and moving around when the process of interactive working is in full swing; and at such times the focus of attention will normally be on the ever-changing pictures of decisions and their relationships which are building up around the walls.

Fixtures such as blackboards or whiteboards do not allow this to happen. This is simply because the information they contain has to be eradicated once they are full; this is not consistent with effective working in a cyclic process, which requires the ability, at any moment, to go back to a previous point and to pick up where one left off. Nor do 'flip chart' boards on easels by themselves serve the purpose, because of their limited surface area.

It is important in strategic choice to display as much of the work as possible at any one time, thus encouraging instantaneous, ad hoc *looping* to take place. Participants should be able to compare the focus of the moment with previous work, skipping backwards and forwards through the process as freely as possible.

So, *walls* are important; and the interactive process can be impeded quite seriously if people are working in a room where the wall space is broken up by too many windows, or projecting panels, paintings or shelves; where access to the available wall space is restricted by too much furniture; or where the walls are uneven or richly decorated in a style which is designed to impress. This means that conventional boardrooms or council chambers do not make an ideal environment for this kind of interactive working; for tensions can often arise with other people who wish to preserve such rooms as settings for more orthodox meetings. Such tensions can usually be avoided by choosing to work in a more sparsely furnished and plainly decorated space. To work effectively on walls, plentiful supplies of *paper* of generous dimension are required. Continuous rolls of paper have sometimes been used; but pads of flip chart sheets of international A1 size have been found to be more flexible when it comes to rearranging and consolidating information as the work proceeds.

The more sheets of paper accumulate around the walls of the room, the more important the practicalities of *paper management* become. Sheets of paper can be affixed to the walls either by masking tape or by a re-usable putty-like substance such as 'Blu-tack'; pins only provide an acceptable substitute where walls are covered with cork or some similar soft surface. Blu-tack has been found to provide high flexibility in removing and repositioning sheets of paper quickly and, if properly handled, leaves no permanent marks on most types of surface. It is generally quite sufficient to fix each sheet by the top two corners only, placing the Blu-tack a centimetre or two in from the corner; each new sheet should be positioned with its upper edge a little above head height, for purposes of writing and of visibility. As wall space at this level becomes more scarce, sheets recording past work can either be moved down to a lower level or overlaid by others. However, in doing so, it is important to avoid hanging paper on paper – for the additional weight is then likely to pull the original paper away from the wall, usually to the distraction of all concerned.

It is not always possible to keep the papers on the wall neatly arranged – evenly spaced and vertical. However, well ordered walls can help a group overcome the strangeness of working in this way and give a sense of organised purpose. Architectural features, such as joints in walls, door frames and even wallpaper patterns can be used for guidance – not only with hanging the papers but also with setting up lines, grids and matrices on them. Paper over-printed with a feint grid is also helpful in this respect. Large sheets of paper with pre-drawn frameworks, such as:

- compatibility and consistency matrices;
- concentric circles for uncertainty graphs;
- advantage comparison charts;
- commitment package frameworks;

not only make the work look more organised; they also promote faster, more effective working. They can be copied quite easily by the same processes that architects and engineers use. In this way, one can have a large enough supply not to have to worry about running out.

The paper used need not be of high quality, so long as it is not too porous when put to the test of being written on with coloured marker pens. The *pens* themselves should be sufficient in number for participants not to have to compete with each other when they feel moved to add something to the 'maps' of problems that are building up around the walls; and they should be sufficiently varied in hue to allow colour differentiation to be used freely as an aid to communication.

Experience has shown that some brands of marker pens are much more reliable than others in terms of ink flow. Those using water-based coloured ink have been found to provide the best service; and those with a wedge-shaped felt tip, three to five millimetres wide, allow a variety of line thicknesses, and clear visibility in most interactive environments. Many experiences in group working have been impoverished by reliance on pens which can only make thin, pale lines; which squeak in a jarring way; or which are prone to dry up at important moments. However, this is not to say that pale colours are never useful. In particular, a barely visible yellow makes a good colour with which to pre-enter frameworks for guidance in adding more substantive information; for example, it can be used to draw up the rows and columns of a grid or matrix, or the concentric rings of an uncertainty graph. In drawing up an option graph for a selected problem focus, one useful 'trick' is first to draw a faint yellow ring intersecting each of the decision areas, then to space out the options within each decision area at intervals around this ring.

There are also more general points of calligraphy and style which regular users of flip charts have tried to cultivate – points about holding the pen, about drawing freehand lines and circles, about positioning of information on a new sheet of paper in a way that anticipates the further information that is still to come. Practice and discussion can lead to gradual improvements in these directions; but it is important above all that concern with the quality of the graphics should not be so pervasive that participants who feel they have few graphic skills should feel inhibited from taking part.

It is not to be regarded as a sign of failure to make mistakes, or to revise earlier views; it is a vital part of the learning process. So it is important to make corrections quickly and move on, rather than go to pains to erase any signs that a change has been made. Trivial mistakes can be covered up by self-adhesive labels; but less trivial changes or corrections are better left as part of the record on the wall, in so far as they represent a significant step in the learning process which people may wish later to recall. A decision graph or similar picture which has become too untidy and confused can always be re-drawn and the new version placed over or alongside the old, treating the original as a secondary record only. Every now and again, too, it may be sensible for the participants to pause and rearrange the total set of flip charts around the walls, perhaps grouping together those to which they expect to refer most frequently in the course of subsequent work.

Turning to what has been called the *social* technology of strategic choice, there are further management choices which arise when working with a group of participants in which there is little or no prior experience of this style of interactive work. It is appropriate for the person or persons acting in a facilitating role to take the lead in the use of pen and paper in the early stages, if only to demonstrate the general method of working and set a style for others to follow. Yet, in training courses which include small group exercises, it is usually found that most people start working on the walls spontaneously enough, provided they have had at least a brief demonstration of the art of paper management beforehand.

How quickly and energetically moves are made to open up the process of writing on the walls to wider participation is a matter which has to be judged according to the situation and the sense of how well a group momentum is developing without active steps to promote it. Sometimes it will be easy to encourage people to start using the walls, paper and pens in an interactive way;

sometimes, they will be more inclined at first to sit and talk and leave any writing to the facilitator, unless they are explicitly offered a pen and encouraged to use it. In a brief exercise with inexperienced users with only an hour or two to run, it may be acceptable that the facilitator continues to play the main recording role, concentrating on capturing what other people have to say; but the longer the time available, the more feasible it becomes to build up pictures around the walls in which the draughtsmanship of many participants has been merged, so that the sense of common ownership can take on a visible reality of its own.

Mention has been made in earlier chapters of the advantages of punctuating interactive group working with brief opportunities for individuals to work on their own. It can help to ask participants to write down their own ideas about relevant decision areas, uncertainty areas or other elements in their own words, using cards or small sheets of paper. These individual contributions can then be compared and merged in such a way that each participant feels he or she has participated directly in building up the shared pictures that are taking shape around the walls. The use of floor or table space to sort and re-group the various individual contributions can itself help to build up a spirit of interactive working.[2]

There is a related technique, which can be especially helpful in bringing invisible products to a conscious level. It involves the use of small circular coloured stickers (about 2cm diameter), for the structuring of informal interactive evaluation. For example, if it is thought a good idea to review the growth of joint commitment in the grouping, each participant can be asked to place one sticker on a scale from very good to very bad which has been drawn on the paper. And much the same sort of process can be used for identifying the most important items in a list – such as comparison areas or uncertainty areas. The resulting pattern is then used as the basis of a creative discussion of the subject, often leading to consensus in the group.

It can pay to introduce brief opportunities for individual working from an early stage in a group process, with further such opportunities whenever the momentum of interaction appears to be flagging or dominated by a sub-group. In order to be ready when such opportunities occur, it is recommended that a supply of cards and stickers be on hand at all times – in addition to the pens and the paper. All these techniques can be adopted – without them sheets of paper can always be cut or torn into smaller pieces and marked with coloured blobs but cards and stickers in several sizes, shapes and colours give the process an air of professionalism which can be reassuring to some participants.

---

2 Working on paper on the wall is not exclusively a strategic choice style. There are others who adopt a similar style of working (Doyle and Straus, 1976); but very few have a structured approach to the use of the papers themselves. One such approach, which has much to offer, originated in Germany in the early seventies. It is called 'Metaplan', and is based on the use of shaped coloured cards (oval, circular, rectangular) on which the participants write, before pinning them onto special screens (Schnelle, 1973). There are some close parallels with the use of cards in strategic choice group processes, which started about the same time.

Figure 83   Management check-list: Technology

PHYSICAL SPACE for interactive working
- ● check provision in advance [with hosts] for main group and any subgroups
- ○ Large enough ROOM to accommodate participants
- ○ enough uncluttered WALL SPACE (ideally to take about 20 A1 flip charts at two levels)
- ○ lack of OBSTRUCTIONS to free movement [e.g. central tables]
- ○ enough CHAIRS [moveable]
- ○ one or more SIDE TABLES for documents, refreshments

TECHNICAL RESOURCES – materials
- ● check supplies before session
- ○ PAPER – ample supply of large sheets for wall work (ideally about 50 A1 flip charts)
  – smaller sheets (e.g. A4/A5) for individual use/records cards/coloured stickers for use individual contributions
- ○ PENS – ample supply of marker pens in varied colours (preferably wedge tip, water base)
- ○ ADHESIVE – non-marking/removable (e.g. Blu-Tack, masking tape)
- ○ CAMERA (& film) for recording
- ○ RECORDS/DOCUMENTS as required: including records from earlier sessions (see figure 87)

continuous management of interaction and communications in this session

TECHNICAL RESOURCES – personal
- ● check one or more participants can bring
- ○ knowledge of relevant working methods/concepts (e.g. chapters 1, 2, 3)
- ○ skills in applying these selectively and adaptively (e.g. chapters 5, 6, 7, 8)
- ○ process management skills (see Figure 86)
- ○ substantive knowledge in this problem area and related fields

SUPPORTING SERVICES
- ● check access in advance
- ○ TELEPHONE – ideally just outside room
- ○ COMPUTER HARDWARE/SOFTWARE [not essential]
- ○ REFRESHMENTS – preferably continuous supply of coffee, tea, juice to avoid interuptions between meal breaks
- ○ ROOM CLEANING etc. – staff alerted not to remove/throw away work in progress

Technology

A-TOPP

PRACTICALITIES

In Figure 83, all these practical points about the management of the technology of strategic choice are drawn together, in a form intended for quick reference, both when preparing for an interactive group session and while reviewing progress subsequently. The key distinctions made are between choice of the physical *setting* which usually has to be negotiated in advance; the provision of adequate *supplies* both for interactive participation and individual working, not forgetting refreshments; and, finally, the requisite *techniques* and *skills* to allow these resources to be used to good effect once the group process is under way.

Organisation: managing interactive participation in practice

It is neither practicable nor useful to attempt to draw a firm line to define where the management of technology ends and the management of organisation begins. There are some further points to be made about ways of managing the *dynamics* of a working group, and about opportunities for forming sub-groups and subsequently bringing them together. These points will be touched on briefly here, leaving some deeper points about the understanding of group dynamics to be opened up in later chapters. However, it is most important to recognise that any working group has to be seen as embedded in a wider organisational environment in which many other people may have a part to play. So important practical questions have to be asked about what levels and forms of participation and of interaction will be appropriate for other people beyond the confines of the present working group; and these questions too will be dealt with in this section.

It is quite easy to think of good reasons for involving many and various people interactively in the process of decision-making. But it is not so easy to make a case for the meetings that this entails. It is regularly argued that meetings are a waste of time; that there are too many of them; and that the decisions made as a result cannot be proven to be better. This is entirely justified and will continue to be so, as long as meetings are organised in the conventional manner. Therefore, in using the strategic choice approach, changes have to be made. Already, in the last section, ways in which the conduct of meetings can be changed have been dealt with at some length. In this section the concern shifts to questions about how the meetings should be set up, especially with reference to who should meet with whom.

The form of association will vary from person to person and from time to time. Of all the people who might be involved, only some may wish to be; others may be content to be consulted occasionally, in a reactive rather than an interactive way. It has to be remembered that interactive working, for all its advantages, is demanding in terms of time and energy; and people in practice must always find ways of distributing their personal resources of time and energy effectively, depending on the overall range of responsibilities they carry.

The general picture of three kinds of uncertainty was used in Chapter 4 (Figure 31) to indicate some of the main ways of initiating connections with other

**Figure 84   Organisational responsibilities in
               strategic choice**

HEAVIER BOUNDARY LINES indicate
direct responsibilities in this field of decision
BROKEN BOUNDARY LINES indicate
less continuous involvement

UE

WORKING GROUP

assigned to
work on this
problem

RESPONSIBLE
GROUP

(steering)

regular   occasional
participants   participants

UV

ACCOUNTABLE
GROUP(S)

CORE
GROUP

decision
taking

REFERENCE
GROUPING(S)
[pre-coordination]

STAKEHOLDERS
[what involvement?]

REPRESENTATIVE
GROUPING(S)
[consultation]

technical

political

internal
external

internal

external

technical

political

UR

Organisation

A-TOPP

PRACTICALITIES

people, whenever it was found difficult to deal with a current decision problem in the present working context – whether it be that of individual work or an interactive working group. However, there are various types of relationships which can be distinguished, with different implications for the grouping and linking decisions that have to be made. They reflect different roles people can play in relation to an overall decision *process,* as contrasted to the roles they might play in relation to the work of a particular *group.*

It is helpful to think of people in seven prototypical *roles* in relation to the decision-making process:

- those who are charged with *working* on the project in the sense of performing all the technical tasks involved in shaping, designing, comparing and choosing (as described in Chapters 5 to 8);
- those who undertake the continuous *process management* of the project, looking after the day-to-day co-ordination of all the various activities and groupings;
- those who are *accountable* for the decisions to be taken in a broadly political way;
- those who are directly *responsible* for guiding the conduct of the decision-making process, at a managerial or senior professional level;
- those to whom periodic *reference* should be made because they have roles in other fields of decision-making which are instrumental in this case;
- those who fill a *representative* role in relation to specific interests which may be affected by the decisions;
- those who are *stakeholders* in the sense that they will be directly impacted by the decisions.

It is important to recognise that in any given decision process the exact way in which people in such roles should participate is a design question in its own right. This means that some of the roles – though not necessarily all of them – will be played by groups or semi-formal *groupings.* There will often be overlapping memberships and/or vacancies; and, in some cases, sub-divisions may be recognised. For example, it is common, in public agencies, to distinguish between internal and inter-agency reference groups.

Nevertheless, in discussing these roles and relationships, it is useful to take as a reference point the task of a particular **working group** – a group which, in the prototypical decision setting being considered in this chapter, may be constituted as a more or less formal *project group* charged, like the South Side Working Party, with working on an issue of some importance over a period of several months. However, most of the points to be made here are also relevant to briefer, more informal exercises.

The typical relationships between these groupings, one to the other and all to the working group, are illustrated in Figure 84. Broad distinctions are superimposed between those groupings which have a role to play in the technical domain and those with a role more in the political arena. In addition, a distinction is drawn between groupings which are internal and those which are external to the main locus of responsibility for the decisions being addressed.

There are advantages to be gained by keeping the working group as compact as possible without losing the representation of important interests, especially with respect to the ease of calling the group together often at short notice. Therefore it has been found helpful to consider two sorts of participant:

- *Regular Participant*: responsible for regular substantive input, and team member functions;
- *Ad Hoc Participant*: responsible for a specific area of specialised substantive input, and general team functions when present.

In the typical project situation, the role of maintaining continuity is usually handled by a small subset of all the people who form the main working group. The task of this process management grouping, or **core group**, is to promote the effectiveness of the wider process in which members of all other groupings shown in Figure 84 may at different times be involved. It is a small group – generally two or three people – because it must have the capacity for extremely flexible behaviour, especially in its arrangements for meetings. It normally embraces the four specific intra-group roles:

- *Leader:* responsible for the substantive work, controlling the quality and quantity of the analysis and information input;
- *Co-ordinator:* responsible for process rather than substance, making sure that the right people are at the right place at the right time;
- *Facilitator:* responsible for internal group relations, guiding interactive sessions and helping with grouping and linking;
- *Recorder:* responsible for the visible results, co-ordinating the continuous output from the process and its distribution in appropriate forms.

Process management is sometimes seen as a function which can ultimately be handled by one person. When this occurs, that person is often described as the *project manager.* Unfortunately, neat as this arrangement may seem, all four roles are very difficult to play together in particular – the facilitator role sits uncomfortably with the other three. Also, it is often the case that the co-ordinator and facilitator have little direct knowledge of the specific problems being addressed. In such a case it is important to recognise the vital contribution which the leader can make. Thus, there are distinct advantages when such a project management function is given over to a small group. While any one person can take on any one role, there is a limited number of combinations of roles which any one person can play. These are the combinations of:

- leader and recorder (product manager);
- co-ordinator and recorder (secretariat);
- co-ordinator and facilitator (process manager).

Another issue which can arise in the choice of core group membership concerns the introduction of external consultants. While a capable process consultant should be able to take on any of these functions or roles, there are some to which they are better suited than others. For example, in many cases the facilitator role can be better performed by someone from outside the immediate organisational framework. Basically, there are two reasons, in addition to the extra manpower, why help of this sort can be useful. The first is that strategic choice skills may be lacking and need to be developed in the team; and the second, where several organisations are involved, is that an independent view may be required. In either case, it is important that the external consultant is given a *counterpart* from within the client group, to provide the detailed knowledge and experience of the problems, the people involved and the culture within which they work.

Next to be described will be the set of people who are formally **accountable** for the decisions with which the working group is primarily concerned. These can be thought of as the *decision-takers* in relation to a wider, more diffuse set of *decision-makers*, if the distinction is made between decision-making as a continuous process and decision-taking as something that happens at comparatively rare moments when formal authorisation of actions or policies is required. In the classical management hierarchy, decisions are taken at most levels throughout the process; but there is often a level of importance at which authorisation by some accountable group, such as a Board or Council, is required. In the public sector as opposed to commercial organisations, the stakeholders are usually more diffuse, so the principle of group accountability is rather more widespread. Sometimes, accountability is vested in joint organisations – joint committees or 'standing conferences'. In general, the more complex the problem, the more complex will be the politics of accountability; so a working group may have to relate to more than one accountable grouping in some cases.

There have been a few applications of the strategic choice approach where decision-takers in such accountable roles have become involved in interactive working with members of a working group.[2] This can bring powerful benefits both in terms of the level of awareness with which formal decisions are taken

---

2 Members of the accountable grouping tend to find such a role shift easiest through involvement in the responsible grouping, and there is extensive experience of this. However, there have been some examples of the direct involvement of local politicians in the working group. This occurred during preparation of the Structure Plan for the County of Hereford and Worcester in England, and also in the preparation of local environmental policy plans in the Netherlands.

and in terms of the direct input of political considerations into the work of the working group. However, it has to be recognised that senior decision-takers – whether appointed or elected – are often subject to multiple and severe pressures on their time. Their inputs can be particularly significant in the work of the shaping and choosing modes and, given limited opportunities to involve them in interactive working, it is important that their involvement should be focused in these areas.

Often, a link between a working group and a set of accountable decision-takers is made by means of a project *steering group*. Meeting more or less regularly, guidance is provided on the directions and priorities of the work, progress is reviewed and any difficulties discussed, especially so far as the handling of external relationships is concerned. In multi-accountable decision settings, such a **responsible** grouping will often have been deliberately designed to bring together representatives of different organisations or departments involved in sponsorship of the project work. The membership can be relatively small; leading members of the project group may be directly involved either as members or in a reporting capacity; and there should be opportunities between scheduled meetings to work through informal links with individual members.

So, a great deal of informal *negotiation* about difficult or contentious matters can take place through the channels offered by the responsible grouping, both during and between meetings; and there will be opportunities here to use various aspects of the strategic choice approach. It is also through this set of relationships that members of the working group can retain the sanction of their departmental heads to continue acting on their behalf; and that changes in the membership of the working group can be discussed and approved. So the responsible grouping offers a channel through which the highly cyclic, adaptive work process of the working group can be adjusted to the more formally structured procedures and political realities of the wider organisational environment. It is, therefore, important to allow the time and resources for this element of the wider participative process to work in an effective way.

What is referred to in the prototypical working context as a **reference** grouping consists of delegates or representatives of all those other organisations whose co-operation will be important if proposals arising from the work of the project group are to be put into effect. Where the project group's task is to produce a relatively generalised 'plan' or set of policies, the application of which depends on actions of many other agencies, it is important that there should not only be co-ordination during some eventual 'implementation' stage. A realistic framework for *pre-coordination* is also recommended, by which these other organisations or departments can have the opportunity to participate at an appropriate level throughout.

Even in comparatively simple contexts of inter-agency or inter-departmental working, an element of pre-coordination can be important so that duplication, omission or contradiction in the provision of services can be anticipated and avoided. However, when working on broader problems of strategic choice, pre-coordination can involve more complex issues of adjustment of values and perceptions. In larger-scale exercises of policy planning it is sometimes appropriate to invite representatives of all related agencies to participate in occasional seminars. In these some of the spirit of interactive working can be generated – even though given time pressures it might not be feasible to introduce the strategic choice methods in an explicit way.

There are two further types of grouping which it is important not to overlook; both fall into the external political arena. They are the **representative** grouping through which the political interests of specific sections of the population, such as car owners, conservationists or small businesses, are protected and promoted; and the wider **stakeholder** grouping of those directly impacted by the decisions, such as residents, consumers, or employees. They involve those who are concerned directly from time to time through exercises in direct public or employee participation.

Conventional attempts at a more general sort of participation, involving 'the public at large', tend to end up being conducted with members of these groupings. Unfortunately, because such exercises are aimed at a broader audience, they most often take the form of seeking reactions to well-formulated proposals, which it is too late to influence in any fundamental way. A more sensitive appraisal of which people in which roles are being addressed – and are willing and able to contribute – is the key to selective design of participative frameworks in which a high level of creative feed-back can be realised.

So the way in which all these types of relationships evolve through time forms part of the broad concern with *management of organisation* in a process of strategic choice. This applies not only in the prototypical project group situation that has been discussed here but also in other more modest working situations. Sometimes, in such cases, it can be more realistic to relate to those in other roles through more familiar patterns of bilateral contact and negotiation. So this is where patterns of *linking* through personal networks can play an important part in supplementing any *grouping* arrangements of a more formal kind. The extent to which strategic choice ideas can be used to guide such interactions will depend on the judgement of the user and the extent to which support has already been established.

The larger a working group, the more difficult it becomes to sustain a spirit of interactive participation through time. To make progress in such circumstances, it is useful at times to suggest that the group breaks into smaller subgroups to pursue complementary aspects of the overall task. There are many possible grounds on which such a sub-division of work can be made. Conventionally, work is sub-divided by disciplines, professions or organisational units; but, once some shaping of problems and their implications has been recorded on the walls of the room, other possibilities become available. The conceptual frameworks of strategic choice provide a rich source of logical ways for defining sub-groups. The four different modes of work taken individually, or in looped pairs, provide one useful division. And there are many other possibilities such as different problem foci, separate working shortlists, or commitment packages based on alternative orientations. Some such tasks for sub-groups may require considerable time, and so should be scheduled to be done in the periods between the main interactive sessions of the working group. However, there are many ways in which strategic choice structures can be used to identify briefer tasks for sub-groups within a working session. Examples of such tasks include designing options within decision areas separately; assessing alternatives by individual comparison areas; and exploring different areas of uncertainty. Such divisions of labour can be most helpful, but it is important:

- to use the structure of the analysis as the basis of the division;
- to set, and keep to, a strict time limit;
- to allow plenty of time for the sharing of results afterwards;
- to use the structure of the analysis to integrate the various contributions.

Of course, in suggesting which people might be assigned to which sub-groups, the skilled facilitator should be able to take into account which participants work well – or not so well – with each other, and which individuals can be looked to in order to provide stimulus and leadership for the more reticent members of the group.

Then, if it is intended that there should be not just one working session but a series of sessions – whether concentrated within a few successive days or spread out over a longer period – it is likely that the composition of the group will alter at least a little from session to session, whether by design or because of restricted availability on the part of some participants. Such changes can, of course, affect the momentum and patterns of interaction within the group. This means that there is a balance to be struck between a desire for continuity of membership, with the advantage that everyone is working from the same basis of shared group experience; and a desire to keep the membership open, so that new participants can join and others drop away.

This desire to keep the group boundaries permeable can be especially important where ideas about the shape of the problem are initially unclear. Where this is so, the focus of attention may shift in unexpected ways, suggesting that others should be involved who were not seen as relevant earlier on. But it is important to keep in mind the point that extending the boundaries of a working group is not the only way of extending the processes of communication and interaction: and this is where a whole range of possible ways of *grouping and linking* can be considered. For any complex problem which impinges on many different organisational interests, it is only to be expected that participation also becomes a complex matter, with many people becoming associated with the process in one way or another.

Thus, the whole task of *managing the organisation* for strategic choice can be seen as a process of dynamic grouping and linking, in which there are many variables. It is not only a question of which people in which decision-making roles should be active, but of how frequently; in which combinations; and in what relationship they should be to each other and the current decision situation. A summary of the considerations which arise in these areas of choice is put forward in Figure 85. This is intended as a guide for those faced with the task in practice – probably in the core group role. The key emphasis in evaluation of such organisational choices will be not so much on efficiency and control, as in a classical hierarchical structure as on the creation of *synergy* which can be realised through the orientation towards interactive participation.

Process: managing the learning process in practice

In the *process* aspect of the A-TOPP framework, the practical choices which people face are primarily to do with the effective use of time. Choices about the use of time have to be faced continuously during an interactive working session; and these have already been described at the end of Chapters 5, 6, 7 and 8, in terms of the various switching and looping judgements that have to be made in moving from one mode of work to another. This section will offer some further practical advice on how this switching and looping process can be managed within an interactive working session.

However, in a longer-term project, where there can be a commitment to a series of such working sessions over the project period, there are also important choices to be considered about the management of time in the intervals between one working session and another. During these periods, there will usually be backroom and investigative work to be done by at least some of the participants, individually or in sub-groups, and there will often also be various activities of a consultative or co-ordinative nature involving other people.

There are two interrelated tasks which are often overlooked, but which are of crucial significance – especially in situations where there are conflicting interests. These are the need for participants to:

- report progress made in the working group to their home organisation;
- and gather feedback as input to the group process in return.

If these activities are neglected, or given too little time, the results can be, at worst, that the work loses all credibility; or, at best, that there is a withdrawal of the backing that is necessary if the recommendations are going to be carried out.

Some of these tasks may have emerged directly from the activities of the working group, as ways of dealing with important areas of uncertainty; while some of them may have been explicitly recorded in the format of a commitment package. But of course, not everything that happens between sessions

Figure 85   Management check-list: organisation

WORKING GROUP
FORM? recognised project group/
working party
WHO? professionals, middle
managers
TASK? progress in working on
THIS problem
WHEN? series of sessions fixed on
calendar, BUT flexible scheduling
STYLE? intensive interaction during
sessions, reactive at other times

RESPONSIBLE GROUP
FORM? steering committee/group
WHO? senior managers
committee representatives
TASK? sanctioning, policy
guidance, link to accountable group
WHEN? linking work group session to
agenda cycles; + brief ad hoc
STYLE? keep mainly reactive, BUT
informal links to other groups

CORE
GROUP
process
management
see figure 86

ACCOUNTABLE GROUP(S)
FORM? Board, Council, Committee
WHO? Directors, elected politicians
TASK? decision-taking, shaping
of policies and priorities
WHEN? normally use regular
scheduled meetings + occasional
brief/ad hoc/exploratory
STYLE? maintain formality except
in exploratory meetings

REFERENCE GROUPING(S)
FORM? liaison committee, group(s), network
WHO? professionals, middle managers
TASK? coordination of activities, feasibility
testing, reduction of uncertainty (UR)
WHEN? from start of a project: occasional
formal but continuous informal
STYLE? interactive and reactive – regular
bilateral or subgroup contacts

STAKEHOLDERS
open meetings?
opinion/attitude

REPRESENTATIVE GROUPING(S)
FORM? consultation meetings/conferences
WHO? appointed office holders/delegates
TASK? sounding board; policy/priority
inputs, value judgments
WHEN? occasional: starting early in
project
STYLE? as interactive as possible:
consider small groups

involvement in four
modes (Figure 8):
● intensive
◑ intermittent
○ occasional

Organisation
A-TOPP
PRACTICALITIES

flows from the work done in this interactive setting. All participants will have competing claims on their time between sessions, some more than others. They may have to respond to unexpected events of quite separate origins: some of them may be involved in more than one interactive process or have pressing outside deadlines to meet. So there is a fine balance to be struck between adapting to these pressures and maintaining the momentum of progress in the agreed common task.

The core-group task embraces all the mundane jobs associated with organising meetings: tasks which range from the time-consuming job of getting people together at the same time and in the same place, to the provision of appropriate spaces to work in and adequate sustenance for the participants. However, in addition, it involves proper preparation for and steering of the interactive working sessions themselves; and it can take continual effort to keep those not involved in these sessions in touch with what is going on.

One of the greatest cultural difficulties encountered when introducing the strategic choice approach to organisations is that most of these tasks are not conventionally considered to be 'real work'; or at most they are considered as simple administrative tasks which can be delegated to clerical staff to be dealt with in a routine way. Some aspects of the arrangement of meetings can, of course, be dealt with as a matter of routine; but experience has repeatedly shown that the time involved between meetings on the part of those who carry the main core group responsibilities should not be underestimated. Many negotiations about involvement in meetings and related matters have to be handled informally on the basis of the rapport which is developing through interactive working; and a failure to allow time for this can soon begin to erode the quality of the process as a whole.

Even where there are several members of the working group who are committed to the project for much or all of their working time, some element of advance scheduling of meetings is essential. For example, the same day of the week can be scheduled for a number of weeks in advance, with the understanding that members of the working group will normally meet for two and a half to three hours in the morning and a similar period in the afternoon. Where possible, some flexibility should be built in by an understanding that, if necessary, the afternoon and/or evening before a session might also be used or perhaps the morning of the next day. In some cases it may be necessary to use two or more days together; while, in other cases, less time may be necessary, allowing sessions to be cancelled. At intervals, other types of meetings may be fitted into this kind of schedule. In particular, allowance can be made for meetings of the responsible grouping, which involves senior managers in a steering capacity, and of the reference grouping through which working liaison is maintained with other departments and agencies. This *flexible scheduling* approach means arranging in advance a series of meetings, in which there are some basic and fairly firm expectations about time commitment and participation in meetings, with the understanding that either may be extended or curtailed should circumstances require.

Between sessions, the core group should arrange to meet every few days, although such meetings need not be very lengthy. The periods immediately before group sessions, and also immediately after, are also important times to exchange notes on progress and ideas on how the dynamics of group interaction can be maintained in the current situation. Laying out the room, setting targets for the day, monitoring progress towards them, analysing the results, recording wall charts; these are among the vitally important activities which the core group must undertake during such sessions. Without them, progress and direction can quickly become lost. It is better than nothing to get together in the main working room a few minutes in advance of the others – but that is really not enough. On the other hand, it should not be necessary to organise such meetings formally – they should happen spontaneously – but it is important that they should not be so squeezed out by other pressures. It is also important that the core group meetings should not be seen as secretive. If other members of the working group happen to come into the room while the core group is discussing process management issues, it is important that they should not feel excluded from the discussions but should be explicitly brought in.

It is not recommended that a half-day working session be formally broken, for instance to go to another room for coffee or tea at some appointed time. For the loss of momentum can be serious and it is much preferable that coffee, tea or other light refreshments be available in the working room itself. Lunch breaks, on the other hand, are more essential; they can be important not only as respite for the participants and as consultation time for core group members, but also for other informal purposes. In particular, process consultants working for the first time on a problem, in an organisation of which they have little or no inside knowledge, will often find themselves being briefed during the lunch hour on aspects of the internal political background which are well enough known to most of the participants yet cannot be openly discussed during the course of a working group session. Also, of course, social interactions in the evenings and weekends can play an important part in the cultural acclimatisation of all concerned, especially those who come from a distance to an unfamiliar organisational setting.

The facilitator role is of particular importance because it is concerned with the *group process*. The role is one with many parts and is sometimes handled flexibly between two or more people who are experienced in process management. This sort of *team facilitating* can be most effective, with the active facilitator role changing hands from time to time. It allows the benefits of active facilitating to be combined with simultaneous reflection on it, which improves the effectiveness of the review process. In many cases, it can enable process issues to be discussed openly between members of the group, with the input of two or more independent views of what is happening at any one time.

The facilitator has always to be ready to aid communication between the participants, especially where they may have difficulty in sharing their different perceptions, concepts, assumptions and priorities. The task is to prevent progress being blocked whenever possible, and to unblock it when it is. It means keeping all the participants feeling involved by creating opportunities for all to make their contributions effectively. It includes active guidance of the interactive work of the group and, in particular, guidance of the judgements associated with switching and looping between modes of work. In making switching and looping judgements, the main evaluative emphasis is on seeking always to move in directions where the growth of *understanding* is expected to be greatest in relation to the time and energies of the participants. It is not, of course, easy for anyone, however skilled, to make judgements in advance as to whether more will be learned by a shift of mode in one direction rather than another. These are, essentially, judgements about where the rate of *potential learning* is likely to be greatest; and here the idea of the *learning curve* is of value.

When starting work in any mode, there is usually an initial period of quick learning, the duration of which will depend on how much is already known – and shared among the participants – at that time. When little is known about a problem, it can be some time before the rate of learning – the learning curve – begins to level off. But where there is an established base of understanding, a 'tailing off' effect in learning is soon experienced, so more rapid switching and looping are to be expected. A group which starts with little experience in strategic choice is likely to be dependent on a process manager or facilitator for judgements of this kind; but as a group becomes accustomed to this way of working, so the breadth of participation in active process management can increase. What is important is that people should be conscious of the mode in which they are currently working, and of the opportunities for switching and looping which exist at any particular moment. For this reason, it is a useful guideline that any group which includes members who have never worked with strategic choice before should have at least some experience of work in each mode during the course of the first working day. A flip chart showing the four modes (as in Figure 8) can be posted on the wall as a point of reference to which such people can refer; and occasional reference to the 'Sutton Principle' will help people to be conscious at any time of the opportunities to switch to the mode where they think the greatest rewards will be found.

But switching judgements can be difficult, especially if there is a sense of leaving work *unfinished* when moving into another mode. Part way through a lengthy analysis, the feeling often develops that there is little more to be learned by going on – so the learning curve is now becoming flatter, but nonetheless there is resistance to a switch because the analysis is incomplete. At this stage, a relaxed approach is recommended and the switch should be made. The analysis can always be completed later if, in coming back to it through the cyclic process, that seems a helpful thing to do.

A somewhat different form of this is experienced when people find themselves labouring to define some aspect of the problem, often in terms of a decision area, comparison area or uncertainty area the meaning of which is ambiguous, or the wording of which is difficult to agree. In such situations, the device of *temporary labelling* has been found very helpful in maintaining the pace of learning. The idea is that a name is given to whatever is unfinished; it is

Figure 86 Management check-list: process

ADVANCE AGREEMENT ON SCHEDULE OF MEETINGS FOR WORKING
GROUP AND ASSOCIATED GROUPINGS (RESPONSIBLE, REFERENCE . . .)
WITH UNDERSTANDINGS ABOUT FLEXIBILITY TO EXTEND/CURTAIL . . .

SET OF PROCESS MANAGEMENT
ROLES represented in core group

T
I
M
E

- prior arrangements for next session
  [place/time/involvement]

PRIOR MEETING
OF CORE GROUP
- informal
- 10–30 minutes

- targets for this working group session?
- roles for this working group session?

WORKING GROUP
SESSION
- pre-scheduled
  BUT some
  flexibility
  over duration/
  involvement
- typically half day
  OR full day with
  lunch break

FACILITATOR ROLE
RECORDER ROLE
LEADER ROLE

- starting points?
- switching/looping into
  other modes?
  [see Figures 43, 55, 67, 79]
- tasks for individual/
  subgroup working?
- rearrangement/consolidation
  of flip chart records?
- agreement on individual and
  subgroup tasks before next session?

PROGRESS MEETING
OF CORE GROUP
- informal
- 30 + minutes

- recording/interpreting of products?
- review of process
- changes to membership of group?
- communications to others?

COORDINATOR ROLE

- activities as agreed
  – backroom investigations (UE)
  – policy soundings (UV)
  – liaison/negotiations (UR)
- responses to external events
- prior arrangements for next
  session and/or associated
  meetings of other
  groups

INDIVIDUAL MEMBERS
OF WORKING GROUP
REPORTING BACK TO
BASE
ORGANISATIONS
AND NEGOTIATING
SANCTION FOR
CONTINUED INVOLVE-
MENT IN THIS
PROCESS

NEXT PRIOR MEETING
OF CORE GROUP

NEXT MEETING OF WORKING GROUP (or RESPONSIBLE GROUP or . . .)

Process

A-TOPP

PRACTICALITIES

put on one side; and then it can be picked up later if it is still relevant. This device has become known as the 'Rhubarb Principle',[3] and around it has developed the informal shorthand of putting unfinished work 'in the rhubarb sack'. In practice, the rhubarb sack is usually an open-ended list of unresolved items built up on a separate flip chart on the wall. This is then used during review, and as input to agenda building exercises for future sessions.

To summarise at this point, process management choices are vital to effective progress, though not often recognised adequately in conventional practice. It is important that they be made explicit wherever possible, and that adequate time be allowed for them. As an aid to this, a summary of relevant process issues is presented in Figure 86. Some of the most important aspects of process management to be considered are those associated with judgements about switching and looping within and between group sessions, combined with the passage of time. In evaluating the use of time through process choice, it is important to be guided by considerations of growth of understanding rather than just good time-keeping or productivity in terms of substantive plans; and these are judgements to which all members of a group can contribute, once they have become conscious of the considerations which arise.

Product: Managing incremental progress in practice

In a process of strategic choice, there are both invisible and visible products. Various forms can be identified (Figure 33), taking the substance-process dimension as well as the visible-invisible into account. The management emphasis is placed on the *recording and interpreting* of these products as well as the act of producing them (Figure 34).

In any interactive working session, visible products will be continuously building up on flip charts around the walls of the room – apart from any notes that may have been made by individuals. At the end of a session, the choice arises as to what should be done about these products. At one extreme, they can be thrown away, while at the other extreme, they can be left intact as a starting point for the next session, provided the space is not required for other purposes. But there is a range of other more practicable possibilities in between; and this is where the task of *recording* becomes important.

Flip charts can, of course, be saved at the end of a session; and where this is the intention it is useful that somebody charged with the recorder role should number them in the sequence they were first written on – and add a date – at the end of the session. But flip charts are bulky, and to save too many can be to create both a storage problem and potential information overload, with severe

3 This name arose during early work on the formulation of policy choices for the Avon County Structure Plan, where the working group was struggling with the definition of a decision area about the quality of life. The impasse was resolved by one member suggesting that they label this decision area 'rhubarb' for the time being and pressed on to something else.

difficulties of access and retrieval.

One of the most useful and simplest means of recording is simply to *photograph* the set of flip charts around the walls of the room at the end of a session – and possibly also at critical moments during the course of a session, especially at any moment when the information on the wall is being reorganised, breaking up a pattern of relatedness between flip charts which has become familiar to the participants and which they might later wish to recall. Colour prints are recommended to capture the way in which coloured pens have been used; but such niceties often have to be given up for the purposes of speed and effective sharing of information. For example, it is important that the information in the *photo-record* be easily retrievable, and that closely related parts of the work are kept together – a pile of separate prints does not do this. However, mounting sets of three or four prints together on A4 sheets of paper has been found to serve such purposes well, especially if they are suitably coded, dated, labelled and indexed (Figure 58). It is important that all members of a working group have a copy of the photo-record; and, unfortunately, it can be too time-consuming to make many such sets. Thus photocopying becomes essential, even though the added dimension of colour may be lost and care has to be taken with the use of particular colours – such as yellow and pale blue. If pictures are required for immediate use, a polaroid-type camera producing quick prints can be useful – even though the prints are small. It is sometimes found useful to take pictures of people working as well – both as a reminder to the participants of the process, and as an indication to others of the general style of working within the group.

Another way of recording is to write up the key aspects of visible progress in the form of a *loose-leaf* record in a ring-back or similar file, which can provide a more accessible set of reference points for the participants when they reconvene for another working session. This can of course be supplemented by photographs of the flip charts in groups on the wall – in which case, some or all of the charts themselves can be scrapped, or the reverse sides written on again where the paper is of sufficient quality.

Any act of recording – even one of mere photographic recording – involves some element of *interpretation* of information into another form – usually a more condensed form appropriate for later use. If the intended use is reference by the same working group at a later meeting, the extent of the interpretation may be quite small, because those concerned have become used to the language of strategic choice – the graphical conventions, the vocabulary, the abbreviated labels by which they have learned to communicate with each other. But it is important to remember that this sort of recording can easily become, in effect, another cycle in the process. In some cases this may not be too serious; in others it can be interpreted by other participants as an attempt by the recorder to manipulate the results. It is hardly necessary to point out that this could have very negative effects on the group process. Where there is a danger of this, and when there is time enough, it is better to make recording the explicit subject of another group session – perhaps using a photo-record as a starting point. Another way, if time is short, is to allow the recorder to go ahead, but also to allow a reasonable amount of time for questioning and clarification at the start of the next group session. This can be usefully combined with circulation of the record in a reactive style between sessions.

It is only to be expected that the members of a working group will develop their own form of *jargon* – graphical as well as verbal. This can be extremely useful insofar as it helps them talk about problems rapidly and effectively among themselves. But such jargon, of course, can be of little value in communicating with others and, indeed, it can have the effect of confusing more than it informs. In practice, there is always a temptation for members of a working group to try to communicate with others in such terms, presenting decision graphs or lists of alternatives described in terms of brief labels which have acquired significance to them through the process of interaction within the group. But such information cannot have the same significance to others not so intimately involved. There is a danger that findings and supporting information presented in terms of apparently esoteric jargon will annoy and alienate rather than bring any sense of involvement to those only intermittently involved – such as members of accountable, reference and representative groupings (Figure 84). So, in reporting progress to others, and in providing a basis for interactive discussions with those who are only occasionally involved, some more substantial form of interpretation into plain language is required.

A general impression of the progressive build-up of visible products is presented in Figure 87. This shows the development of a loose-leaf record drawn from the flip charts relevant to each mode and, from that, the further development of documents suitable for use outside the group. The process of production is one of *incremental documentation*. In practice, the loose-leaf record builds up and evolves gradually, providing at any one time a statement of the latest findings and possible recommendations coming out of the work. Whenever it is necessary to produce a formal statement or recommendation, it is then a matter of taking the relevant leaves out of the loose-leaf system; assembling them in an appropriate order; and considering how to present the result. The remainder of the loose-leaf system provides the basis for any *reasoned justification* for the choice; a source of supplementary information; and a starting point for future cycles.

It is important in building up a loose-leaf record that it should reflect the products of work in all four process modes. It will, of course, be vital to record the content of a commitment package where the work of a session has culminated in a product of this form; but information on decision areas, decision graphs, problem foci, options, decision schemes, assessments, advantage comparisons, shortlists, uncertainty areas and exploratory options can be vital for future reference as well. On some major strategic choice projects, standard preprinted forms have been used to record some of these kinds of information, so that it can be retained in as organised and immediately accessible a form as possible. What is most important is that the decision-takers should be in a position to question and challenge the presented argument; and that their advis-

Figure 87   Recording and interpretation in strategic choice

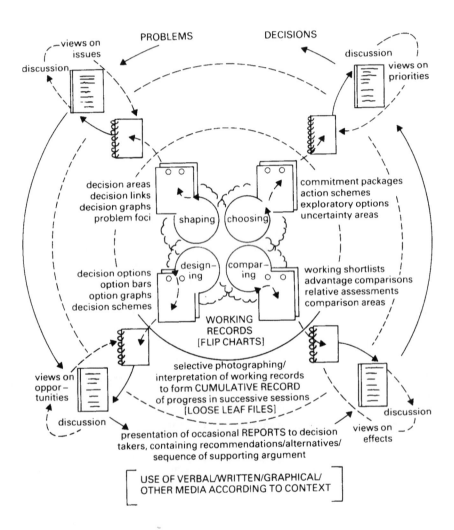

PROBLEMS   DECISIONS

views on issues   discussion   views on priorities

discussion

decision areas
decision links
decision graphs
problem foci

shaping   choosing

commitment packages
action schemes
exploratory options
uncertainty areas

design–ing   compar–ing

decision options
option bars
option graphs
decision schemes

working shortlists
advantage comparisons
relative assessments
comparison areas

WORKING
RECORDS
[FLIP CHARTS]

selective photographing/
interpretation of working records
to form CUMULATIVE RECORD
of progress in successive sessions
[LOOSE LEAF FILES]

views on
oppor–
tunities

discussion

discussion

views on
effects

presentation of occasional REPORTS to decision
takers, containing recommendations/alternatives/
sequence of supporting argument

USE OF VERBAL/WRITTEN/GRAPHICAL/
OTHER MEDIA ACCORDING TO CONTEXT

Product

A-TOP**P**

PRACTICALITIES

ers, when challenged, should be able to retrieve further information from the loose-leaf system wherein the fuller records of their work are stored. So the outer rings of Figure 87 are linked by loops which indicate a two-way flow of questions and responses. It is in this way that decision-takers, with many pressures on their time, can become interactively involved in the process – and can do so on their own terms, as it is they who set the questions on which the dialogue is based.

In taking a view of planning as a decision process in which uncertainties are managed continuously through time, it is vital to recognise the importance of process-related products. Nonetheless, it is the recommendations about the *substantive* problems which will be the focus of attention when the time comes for formal decision-taking. Even where they have been developed using a commitment package framework, these may differ little in visible form to recommendations made without the use of strategic choice methods.[4] But it has to be recognised that such recommendations may include many partial and interim actions, to complement those which are explicitly deferred or made contingent on future events.

Although what decision-takers are being asked to sanction may be primarily the products of work in the choosing mode, the provision of some supporting information on the work of the other modes is essential if they are to feel that:

- the advice they are offered is soundly based;
- their advisers have explored the shape of the problem in a realistic way;
- they have looked at a wide enough range of alternatives;
- they have taken all the most significant consequences into account;
- they have attempted to deal with uncertainties in an adequate way.

To demonstrate these things can mean a degree of *post-rationalisation* of the highly complex and adaptive processes of switching, looping and re-cycling through which members of the working group in reality arrived at the findings they present; processes which could seem quite chaotic if any attempt were made to present them realistically in full.

As suggested in Figure 87, it is possible in strategic choice, as in other ways of working, for a reconstructed argument to follow a linear course from shaping, through designing and comparing, to choosing – though there is no reason why one or two feedback loops in the process should not be presented as well, if they are sufficiently critical in their implications. However, in strategic choice, such a linear framework is not essential. Free of the constraint of a retrospec-

4 This was particularly evident in the English Structure Plan project. However, some of the participating teams made use of structured frameworks of 'policy management information', to interpret commitment package concepts into forms of presentation which indicated how policies might be adapted through time. Assumptions were clearly stated, together with contingencies which would warrant change, and constraints which would limit that change.

tive process-based logic, the reasoning can be based instead on the structure of the problem – with an increased emphasis on the *prospective* aspects of the continuous decision process.

Indeed, this kind of 'prospective process-based logic' is essential in strategic choice, where the decisions are structured over time. Future *procedures* form an important part of most commitment packages. Not only is there explicit provision for various forms of exploration to reduce uncertainty, but statements in the 'future decision space' are likely to be couched in terms of procedures to reach decisions, rather than definitive plans. Such recommendations are likely to be needed in order to:

- keep track of how proposed actions turn out, and review the need for adaptive planning;
- monitor the performance of assumptions so that critical misjudgements can be managed;
- provide for decision-making on a regular basis, as well as prepare for cases of emergency and/or unforeseen circumstances;
- allow for participation by individuals and relevant groupings with respect to expected and unexpected future decisions;
- maintain progress in implementation programmes related to time schedules and budgetary cycles.

In addition, documentation in relation to future processes is likely to include potential sources of information, as well as key individuals and organisations who are particularly relevant to the case in hand.

However, it is often difficult to define procedures exactly – and especially uncertain is the behaviour of the individual people who will ultimately enable them to work. Therefore, it can be very helpful to have developed a high level of understanding among the participants during the decision-making process, so that there is a foundation of shared perception, mutual respect and trust which can be built on in the future. This entails not only knowledge of others' ways of working, but also extended networks of communication within which these *invisible* products can be put to effective use.

Such products, which are continuously developing in a process of strategic choice, emerge from work in all modes and take shape in many ways. They take shape in the minds of individuals, as peoples' limited perceptions of problems, possibilities, implications and uncertainties gradually become replaced by richer perceptions through the sharing of views within an interactive group setting. Indeed, it can be said that invisible products build up in the 'hearts and souls' rather than just the minds of individuals, insofar as they come to share values as well as perceptions and to develop a sense of shared commitment to common directions of action or policy. These somewhat nebulous products can have an immediate value through the production of better integrated and more strongly supported decisions. But, in most cases, their full worth is experienced over time – paving the way for more effective working in the longer term future. However, they are likely to escape unnoticed unless explicit efforts are made to help participants:

- first of all to become conscious of them;
- and then to find ways of harnessing them.

Invisible products can be brought to a conscious level most effectively as they happen; and the facilitator will be trying to do this. Unfortunately, this is no easy task; so it becomes important also to try to capture the invisible products retrospectively. Most commonly in a strategic choice exercise, this is done at the end of sessions, through allowing opportunities for reflection at that time. A quick recognition of the visible work done during the session is followed by evaluation not only in terms of progress on the wall, but also in terms of the growth – or lack of it – in understanding, consensus and commitment. Peoples' ideas about matters of process as well as substance are likely to change; and these can also have profound implications for the quality of decision-making in the longer term. So these also can be usefully included in any end-of-session sharing of views.

Taking a more extended view, it is worthwhile to suspend business for slightly longer after a series of working sessions, so that participants have an opportunity to consider the cumulative growth of invisible products – increments of which may easily slip by without comment during more frequent evaluations. Longer, more formal surveys can be most effective at the end of a project.[5] Questionnaires can be focused on the *potential* of invisible products and ways in which participants intend to capitalise on them. Retrospective questions paired with prospective ones, addressing the same issue in different words, reveal changes in attitudes. These changes may have been perceived at an individual level but become much more powerful when they are seen as part of a group development. Naturally, as with any survey of this kind, feedback of the results to the respondents is essential.

But all of this emphasis on process-oriented products – visible and invisible – is to no avail if nothing happens as a result of the work. What is required also is a convergence of view towards a common understanding about what has to be done – or not done, as the case may be. For this sort of joint commitment, there must be a degree of sharing of perceptions about what the problems are; the solutions which are available; and their likely consequences. All of which can build up to a well co-ordinated set of feasible recommendations with the

5 Evaluative questionnaires were used for this at the end of the LOGIMP experiment (Friend Wedgwood-Oppenheim et al, 1970) and, more recently, in a number of environmental policy projects in the Netherlands. On two occasions, follow-up studies have been carried out by means of interviews with participants three or more years after the event, and the findings presented in internal papers.

Figure 88 Management check-list: Products

VISIBLE

recording and interpreting through
● photo-record?
● loose leaf documentation?
● reports?

documented commitment to:

● actions
– now
– deferred
– contingent
● policies
– espoused/recommended
– advocated to others
● follow through
– responsibilities
– resource budgets
– deadlines
● Supporting argumentation
– problems
– alternatives
– consequences
– uncertainties

documented commitment to:

● explorations
– investigations (UE)
– policy soundings (UV)
– liaison/negotiation (UR)
● procedures
– future policy management
– monitoring and review
– decision taking/making
– participation
● communications & contacts
– reference groups
– information sources
– representative bodies

SUBSTANCE

GROWTH OF PRODUCTS ?

PROCESS

conscious appreciation of:

● growth in shared perceptions
– problems
– alternatives
– consequences
– uncertainties
● growth in shared orientations
– joint commitment
– pre-coordination
● unresolved difficulties
– political
– technical

conscious appreciation of:

● other organisational cultures
– ways of working
– ways of negotiation
– ways of decision-making
– ways of communicating
● other personal styles
– ways of thinking
– concepts and beliefs
● constraints/pressures on others
● growth of shared ways of working

INVISIBLE

surfacing and sharing through
● monitoring of attitudes/opinions
● group feedback & discussion

Product

A-TOP**P**

PRACTICALITIES

backing of all concerned – especially given a framework for structuring them over time.

Where a working group has an inter-departmental or inter-organisational membership, there is a need for a framework which will enable the actions required of the various participants to be brought together. In the strategic choice approach, this can be achieved via a *mutual* commitment package. Each set of participants in a working group will have their own separate commitment packages, within their own spheres of responsibility which may be expressed in a variety of forms. Parts of each such commitment package can however be merged to form a composite statement of the way forward or – mutual commitment package. But how much should be expressed in this form will be a matter for negotiation, as there may be various political sensitivities to keep in mind.

In such a multi-organisational group, the range of uncertainties encountered in agreeing how to move forward at any time may include areas of recognised conflict, which cannot be resolved at that point. But a decision process, structured within a commitment package framework, provides opportunities for the management of such conflicts. It allows decisions over which there is conflict to be deferred, whilst others over which there is agreement can be put into action. In many cases, when the time comes for the deferred decision to be taken, the conflict will have dissolved. Options can become infeasible over time, while new ones, over which there is more agreement, can emerge. In any case, even if the conflicts have not disappeared, at least those involved will by then have a better chance of understanding their consequences. Another source of conflict arises from uncertainty over events which may – or may not – occur. The commitment package includes space for contingency planning which can be used to handle this sort of uncertainty. Provision can be made to reduce the impact of adverse circumstances and thus remove the fear which is causing the conflict.

Of course, there may be times when it will be necessary to recognise deep-seated conflicts of interest, reflected in divergent pressures from different members of the group. Such conflicts are not often such as to block the opportunities for progress in a group using strategic choice methods; but where this happens, resort may have to be made to other means of resolution, such as external arbitration or mediation. Sometimes, where there is not one accountable grouping but two or more, conflicting interests may have to be reconciled in an incremental way, through a process of gradual mutual adjustment over time.[6] Even here, the commitment package framework can still provide a dynamic structure to aid collaborative negotiation.

Figure 88 contains a summary of the range of products which might be considered – structured as in Figure 33, along the dimensions of substance/process and visible/invisible. Naturally, it is necessary to be selective in the choice of products as in the other aspects of strategic choice. The evaluative emphasis

6 See, for instance, the case of Droitwich Town Development – Friend, Power & Yewlett (1974) or Batty (1979).

which is most appropriate to the consideration of products is an emphasis on *confidence;* the gradual accumulation of confidence among participants that they are moving towards decisions which are soundly based, at least so far as a realistic appraisal of uncertainties and time and resource pressures allow. This is the emphasis which was contrasted with the more conventional emphases on accountability and completeness of products (Figure 34), important as these more tangible considerations remain. And the evaluation of growth in confidence is a matter not just for the working group itself, but for all those other participants who may be involved in other process roles.

Continuity and the individual

In the prototypical working situation where substantial human and other resources are being committed to a major planning task, the rate of progress towards a more *continuous* way of working becomes an important test of the extent to which the philosophy of strategic choice is becoming diffused; especially so where there remains the expectation that the main substantive product will take the form of a fully integrated 'master plan', delivered by some appointed deadline. This shift in the direction of continuity has been called the *continuisation* of a planning process (Hickling, 1982) and it becomes an important evaluative emphasis in process terms, to accompany the emphasis on growth of confidence in the more substantive products.

But the shift towards continuity has its limits, especially when combined with the emphasis on interactive working. People cannot work interactively all the time and, indeed, practical ways of managing the process and products are essentially to do with the management of those *discontinuities* that inevitably arise when people can only come together periodically and for limited lengths of time. Two expressions that are often heard from people involved in complex planning tasks are 'let's start from scratch ...' and 'at the end of the day ...'. In real life planning, there is no such thing as 'scratch' and people never do reach 'the end of the day' in that final sense. Yet successive working days will come to an end and new working days will begin – whether the new day is spent working on the same problem or on another. And these are the realities against which moves towards continuity of process and incremental products must be judged.

Inevitably, it is at the level of the individual that the *experience* of continuity finds its fullest expression. For individuals exist continuously, in states of consciousness punctuated by more or less regular periods of sleep. While conscious, they make choices of many kinds, some of them in a more or less programmed and automatic way. They make choices about eating, drinking, moving from place to place; about small-scale social interactions and economic transactions. Indeed, one of the first examples of a decision area quoted in Chapter 2 was of the choice facing an individual as to how to respond to an early morning alarm, as the first choice of all at the start of another decision-making day.

Some personal choices, of course, call for more deliberation – either through a process of *simple choice* (Figure 6), with work concentrated in the designing and comparing modes – or through a more subtle process of *strategic choice* such as that exercising the individual depicted earlier (in Figure 30) relaxing in an armchair and contemplating how some set of uncertainties should be managed – in which situation one possible response could be to rise out of the chair and to discuss it with someone else.

Choices for the individual arise over where to direct his or her attention at any moment; where to look; what to read; to whom to listen; and, indeed, how to use any of the various sensory mechanisms with which the body is equipped. These choices about *scanning* are continuously being made, more or less consciously, and are accompanied by choices in the realm of action, or *doing,* through the motor mechanisms of the body. So any complete model of individual decision-making must include some representation of these motor and sensory mechanisms which provide connections to the physical world outside. Indeed, various authors (Beer, 1966; Faludi, 1973) have built on this kind of cybernetic modelling in the attempt to develop more complete models of a planning process.

Following this line of argument, any complete representation of a process of strategic choice should include **scanning** and **doing** modes in addition to the four already considered in depth in this book. A more complete six-mode representation appears in Figure 89. The two additional modes are shown as embedded in a *world of operations* in contrast to the *technical domain* of designing and comparing, and the *political arena* in which the shaping and choosing work are done. So what has been called the process of simple choice (Figure 6) in effect by-passes the political arena – unless and until difficulties are encountered which mean moving in the direction of increasing complexity and, therefore, increasing interactions with others whose values and perceptions may conflict.

Of course, organisations as well as individuals have their 'worlds of operations' which tend to provide the strongest strands of continuity and predictability in their work. Individuals who are employed by organisations will spend parts of their conscious lives making choices within the framework of their employer's field of operations, and other parts of their lives making choices within more personal settings. Many of these choices will be simple, others more complex – possibly involving not just one technical domain or one political arena, but several, which may be inter-related in intricate ways. So the six-mode diagram of Figure 89 provides no more than a conceptual reference point in attempting to follow activities within a set of processes which may, in practice, have a very rich and complex texture – with threads of continuity provided by the scanning and doing activities of all the various individuals who may become involved.

The six-mode model of strategic choice will not be further developed here, but it can be used as a base from which to explore further what is involved in work in any of the four main process modes, with reference to the others. In particular, Hickling (1985) has developed a view of evaluation as a five-finger

Figure 89   Strategic choice as a continuous process

FIELD OF OPERATIONS

concerns   actions

observations

SCANNING   DOING   powers

perspectives   commitments

SHAPING   POLITICAL ARENA   CHOOSING

foci   priorities

DESIGNING   COMPARING

ideas

alternatives   discrimination   judgements.

TECHNICAL DOMAIN

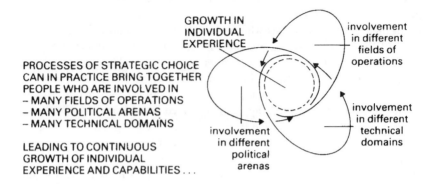

GROWTH IN INDIVIDUAL EXPERIENCE

involvement in different fields of operations

PROCESSES OF STRATEGIC CHOICE
CAN IN PRACTICE BRING TOGETHER
PEOPLE WHO ARE INVOLVED IN
– MANY FIELDS OF OPERATIONS
– MANY POLITICAL ARENAS
– MANY TECHNICAL DOMAINS

involvement in different technical domains

LEADING TO CONTINUOUS
GROWTH OF INDIVIDUAL
EXPERIENCE AND CAPABILITIES . . .

involvement in different political arenas

exercise, in which the comparing mode is treated as the palm of the hand, with the five 'fingers' of designing, shaping, scanning, doing and choosing being used in various sequences and combinations as the pianist consciously works to extend his or her skills.

Keeping it simple

The emphasis of this chapter has been on practical guidance in managing a process of choosing strategically through time. Attention has been given in turn to the four aspects of technology, organisation, process and product. These together comprise a coherent approach – or merely a 'way of working' if these aspects are developed in an informal rather than a conscious way. In the use of the strategic choice approach, these four aspects have provided a structure for the design and management of comparatively large-scale exercises. In some cases, governmental bodies have committed substantial human and other resources over a period of months to work on important national, regional or local problems. It is in such settings that deliberate attention has been paid to the finer points of technological choice (Figure 83); to the relationships of different groupings (Figures 84 and 85); to the scheduling arrangements for meetings (Figure, 86); and to the systematic documentation and interpretation of products (Figures 87 and 88).

Important as these practical points are, they cannot, of course, be taken into account so consciously in every application of the strategic choice approach. The most important guideline of all is to keep things simple wherever possible. Problems vary and pressures vary. If an opportunity suddenly emerges to draw on strategic choice ideas in the heat of working with a few other people on an urgent problem, the setting and materials may not be ideal; the working group may have to be treated as given; and the time constraints may be severe. So the immediate products might have to be simple and direct. But a consciousness that there *are* management choices involved in each of the four aspects of technology, organisation, process and product can provide a valuable background to the snap judgements that have to be made, even in such informal working situations – and a framework for reflection once the moment of creativity has passed.

10 The electronic resource

Why bring in the computer?

Should information technology have a significant role to play in the strategic choice approach? This has been a subject of sustained debate over many years. On the one hand, it is not hard to see that there are some aspects of the methods presented in earlier chapters which might be handled more quickly by computer methods. On the other hand, it can be argued that the idea of giving the computer a central role does not sit at all easily with the overall philosophy of planning presented here.

In support of this latter view, it can be maintained that the primary purpose of the strategic choice approach is to facilitate a flexible and creative interaction among the human participants in a collaborative planning process. If this is so, then it becomes questionable, to say the least, how far this aim can be reconciled with an intensive process of human-machine interaction of the kind which is demanded by any kind of computer-aided decision support system.

This kind of debate is by no means unique to the set of methods presented in this book. Significantly, there are sharp differences in the use of computers between the two other interactive approaches from the management sciences which are most frequently compared to the strategic choice approach: Checkland's Soft Systems Methodology (Checkland 1983, 1989) and Eden's Strategic Options Development Analysis (Eden 1981, 1989). While the use of computer methods is usually avoided in applications of Checkland's approach, it is actively encouraged by Eden and his associates – who have adapted the COPE software for group use and make effective use of it even with quite large groups, while maintaining that this is merely a useful means of supporting the methods in practice, rather than an essential element.

Designing Software for Strategic Choice

Computer software to support the process of strategic choice as a whole has been continuously under development since shortly after the first edition of this book was published in 1987. Indeed, software to support particular methods within the approach – specifically, the Analysis of Interconnected Decision Areas – has a history extending back as far as the early seventies.

At the time of writing, there has been sustained investment over a period of

Figure 90   Design of the STRAD software

Overall design

The overall window

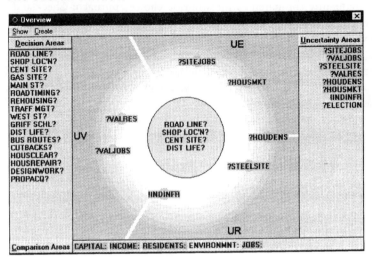

more than eight years in the development of a program for personal computers by the name of STRAD – short for *Strategic Adviser* – which is modelled directly on the methods presented in this book. The first commercial version of STRAD was published in 1991, for IBM-compatible computers running under the MS-DOS operating system. An extended version with much enhanced graphics capabilities, STRAD 2, was published in 1994 for personal computers running in version 3.1 or higher of the Microsoft Windows operating environment, and further development work is under way.

In order to demonstrate the state of progress at the time of writing, this chapter will present a few illustrations of typical displays based on STRAD 2.02, which is the latest version available at the time of going to press. Readers can obtain a more up-to-date picture of the latest state of progress by visiting the Stradspan site at the address *http://www.fdgroup.co.uk/neo/strad/* on the World Wide Web.

The upper picture of Figure 90 shows how the design of STRAD 2 reflects the model of four modes of strategic choice – shaping, designing, comparing and choosing – which was first presented in Figure 8. Surrounding this basic process diagram, Figure 90 shows a set of eight 'process windows', two of which are associated with each of the four modes. In broad terms, the first window of each pair is concerned with helping users to organise their inputs to that mode, while the second is more concerned with helping them to organise their outputs.

This diagram is designed to bring out the key point that the four interlinked modes of shaping, designing, comparing and choosing represent complementary aspects of the *human* process by which people work on complex problems, whether on their own or collectively, while the eight associated process windows represent 'windows of access' to the supporting *resources* which the STRAD program can bring them in their endeavours.

The illustrations that follow will be based on the South Side case that runs throughout this book, so as to facilitate comparisons with the freehand drawings that accompany earlier chapters. However, various other illustrative examples have been developed for use with the STRAD software. These cover such diverse areas of application as the management of consultancy projects; industrial marketing and relocation; development strategy for a small printing business; care of the mentally ill within the community; organisational change in a national corporation supplying networked services; rural development in a tropical country, and even the planning of a family holiday. These examples can be explored as demonstration project files using either the STRAD software itself or the demonstration disk which is available as indicated in the Points of Contact section at the end of the book.

In STRAD, all the information so far entered on the structure of the current problem situation is stored in a *project file*. Whenever this file is loaded, a summary of its current status is displayed in an *overview window*, the format of which is illustrated in the lower picture of Figure 90. Users then have the option of keeping this window permanently open in the background while work is

Figure 91 Shaping and designing in STRAD

Shaping

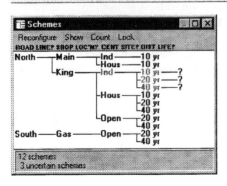

Designing

carried out in the various other process windows.

Around the periphery of the overview window appear lists of the short labels for all the decision areas, comparison areas and uncertainty areas which have so far been entered. Fuller details of any of these problem elements can be read through double-clicking on its label to call up an 'area detail window', the format of which differs from one type of area to another. This information can be edited, and new areas of any type can be added whenever desired. By clicking on the heading of each list, fuller descriptions of all the areas within it can be viewed.

In the centre of the overview window appear the labels of all those decision areas which are currently in focus, surrounded by the labels of all those uncertainty areas which have so far been classified in terms of the UE, UV and UR categories. This layout has been adapted from a format which has been found useful in a workshop situation, when presenting a summary picture of a problem situation on a single flipchart.

At any time, an *issue list form* can be called up via the *Show* menu of the overview window, as an overlay to its central section. This form enables users to list a succession of new issues in a brainstorming fashion, classifying them as decision areas, comparison areas or uncertainty areas as they go – or, where you find this difficult, temporarily storing them in an *issue bank*. The issue list form appears automatically in the overview window whenever the users are starting to build a new project file.

Shaping and designing with STRAD

Figure 91 brings together examples of the three other main window layouts, in addition to the overview window, which are included in STRAD 2 to support the work of the shaping and designing modes.

The first window in Figure 91 should be recognisable as an example of a decision graph; it is equivalent to that of Figure 42 in Chapter 5. This illustrates the layout of the *focus window* of STRAD, within which various operations corresponding to those discussed in Chapter 5 can be carried out. Decision areas can be dragged into or out of the list on the left of those excluded from the graph ('ex graph'), or they can be repositioned freely within the graph. Further dragging operations enable decision links to be inserted or removed. Colour distinctions are available to emphasise important or urgent decision areas; to distinguish uncertain from firm decision links; and to indicate differences in the 'ownership' of decision areas.

The program offers a choice of aids to the development of a new problem focus. For example, STRAD will highlight a recommended 'triad' of three interlinked decision areas as a starting point for choosing a new focus – its recommendation being based on a user-adjustable points system which enables criteria such as importance, urgency and number of links to be taken into account. However, such recommendations are always subject to the overriding

Figure 92 Comparing and choosing in STRAD

Assess window — Operations

Comparison Areas

Decision Areas	CAPITAL:	INCOME:	RESIDENTS:	JOBS:
ROAD LINE?				
SHOP LOC'N?				SIGNIFICANT
CENT SITE?				
DIST LIFE?				
ALL				

What level of impact would you expect the choice within the Decision Area 'SHOP LOC'N' (Options: Main/King/Gas) to have within the Comparison Area 'JOBS' ?

Comparing

Option Assessment

CENT SITE?   CAPITAL:

	‹Cheaper	Dearer›	
Ind		‹ ● ›	726
Hous		‹ ● ›	566
Open	‹●›		285
			x £10,000

Refresh	Sort	Calibrate	Undo	Close

Combined Scheme Assessment

CAPITAL: INCOME: RESIDENTS: JOBS:

ROAD LINE?	SHOP LOC'N?	CENT SITE?	DIST LIFE?	‹Less preferred More preferred›
North	Main	Ind	10 yr	‹ ● ›
		Hous	10 yr	‹ ● ›
	King	Ind	10 yr ?	‹ ● ›
			20 yr ?	‹ ● ›
			40 yr ?	‹ ● ›
		Hous	10 yr	‹ ● ›
			20 yr	‹ ● ›
			40 yr	‹ ● ›
		Open	20 yr	‹ ● ›
			40 yr	‹ ● ›
South	Gas	Open	20 yr	‹ ● ›
			40 yr	‹ ● ›

Refresh	Sort	Exclude	Tree/List	Close

Choosing

Progress — Adopt

	NOW		FUTURE	
Sector	DECISIONS: Actions	UNCERTAINTIES: Explorations	Decisions	Uncertainties
Transport	ROAD LINE! North! TRAFF MGT! one way!		MAIN ST? ROADTIMING? BUS ROUTES?	
Locational	SHOP LOC'N! Main!	!STEELSITE liaison!	CENT SITE? GAS SITE?	
Housing	PROPACQ! new rules!	!HOUSMKT analysis!	REHOUSING? HOUSCLEAR? HOUSREPAIR?	?HOUDENS
Finance	DIST LIFE! 10 yr!	!SITEJOBS expert!	WEST ST? CUTBACKS? DESIGNWORK?	
Education			GRIFF SCHL?	
Policy		!VALJOBS sounding! !UNDINFR Policy Cttee!		?VALRES ?ELECTION

judgement of the user. A strip at the foot of the window displays miniature pictures of all earlier stages in the focusing process, enabling any of these earlier graphs to be called up as a starting point for further work.

The second window of Figure 91 illustrates the layout of the *compatibility window*, which is used in STRAD to organise inputs to the designing mode. A grid format similar to that of Figure 15 is used in preference to the option graph format of Figure 16, as this representation is simpler to use in any situation where there are more than a few option bars. One of the option bars is here shown as uncertain (?) as in Figure 49. Reasons for inserting option bars can be registered in a list; and there are procedures to enable you to inspect, suspend or cancel any reason on the list to expand the set of feasible schemes. Below this list, an estimate of the total number of feasible decision schemes is presented, using the formula explained on Figure 52.

The final window in Figure 91 presents an example of the *schemes window*, through which the set of decision schemes resulting from any specified pattern of option bars can be rapidly displayed – normally in the form of a tree as in Figure 17, though an alternative list format is also available.

In this window, there are procedures for altering the sequence of decision areas in the tree; for calling up a count of the appearances of each option; and for selecting and 'locking' a preferred option in the first one or more decision areas in the tree, working from the left. This is normally only done after some assessment of the schemes has been carried out, and a working shortlist developed through the assessment procedures now to be described – thus giving effect to the principle of robustness discussed on page 71.

Comparing and choosing with STRAD

In Figure 92, a set of further illustrations of STRAD windows is presented, indicating some of the main procedures used to support the work of the comparing and choosing modes.

To support the work of the comparing mode, STRAD introduces a number of features which go some way beyond the relatively simple methods suggested in Chapters 3 and 7. For the computer makes it possible to carry out quickly various aggregating and sorting operations of a kind which are barely practicable in the workshop setting if a climate of interactive working is to be sustained.

The main *assess window*, illustrated at the top of Figure 92, provides access to other secondary assessment windows, two examples of which appear below. The main window displays a grid of all decision areas currently in focus against all comparison areas which are currently in use for assessment. Within this grid, users can enter their intuitive judgements about the relative levels of impact within particular comparison areas of the choices within each decision area, as a preliminary step before entering their assessments of differences between specific options. Having thus entered their initial judgements about the relative value weightings of comparison areas in an intuitive yet logically defensible way, they can then focus their attention on those cells of the grid where they expect to find the most significant differences. They can modify these judgements later if they wish, by means of an optional 'ALL' display at the foot of the grid covering all decision areas combined.

Coloured rectangles indicate those cells where option differences have already been assessed; open ones indicate those in which this is not yet done. The width of any cell is initially set at zero, as in the case of the cell for SHOP LOC'N in this example. However the cell width can be altered, by means of a mouse dragging operation, to show anything from a *marginal* to an *extreme* impact, in answer to the question posed in the space below the grid.

A double click on any cell opens up a secondary *option assessment window* for that cell, as shown in Figure 92. Each option is initially represented by a marker in the centre of the range. These markers can be moved to new positions to represent the user's assessment of option differences. Each option also has a pair of symmetrically-placed 'range markers', the distance between which can be increased to represent perceptions of uncertainty.

The scale used for assessment in any comparison area can be calibrated with reference to recognised units of measurement wherever these can be defined. However STRAD does not require you to make such a calibration in the case of less tangible comparison areas. For STRAD applies its own internal metric defined by the intuitive judgements entered in the main assess window – and there are procedures for automatic adjustment whenever the limits of the working range of the window are exceeded.

The option assessments from all the filled cells of the assess window can then be automatically combined – across decision areas, across comparison areas or both. The *combined scheme assessment* window of Figure 92 shows the outcome of this process. It displays a set of multi-criteria assessments for all the feasible decision schemes displayed in the tree of Figure 91, after aggregating all the option assessments entered so far. The formula applies the weightings to the comparison areas as they were last adjusted in the main assess window, applying a standard sum of squares rule as a means of estimating the combined range for each scheme.

Any of these scheme assessments can be adjusted at this stage to reflect any further knowledge about the effects of combining options from different decision areas in particular ways; and STRAD can quickly sort the schemes to display them in descending order of preference. Schemes near the top of the sorted list can then be selected to form a working shortlist. Information on the schemes excluded from this shortlist will then be carried back to the schemes window, as a basis for the selection of robust actions in the more urgent decision areas.

The set of shortlisted schemes can also provide a starting point for closer comparisons of pairs of promising alternatives using the *balance window*. This window is similar in its layout to the type of advantage comparison chart shown in Figures 21 and 64, and is therefore not reproduced here. Also not shown in Figure 92 is the format of the *uncertainty window*, which is designed to help in the judgements about alternative ways of managing uncertainty, using the types of procedure illustrated in Figures 24, 71, 72 and 73.

Figure 92 does, however, conclude with an illustration of the layout of the *progress window*. This displays the current state of progress towards decisions in the form of a commitment package grid, using a broadly similar format to those illustrated in Figures 26 and 77. In STRAD, the less definitive phrase *progress package* is adopted to describe any tentative package which may be developed. This enables any such package subsequently to be *adopted,* at the discretion of the user – either as an explicit *commitment,* or as a *recommendation* to others; or as a *strategic option* to be saved and compared with any alternative strategic options which might be developed.

Clicking operations enable fuller details of any elements of a progress package to be entered, edited or inspected – including details of any proposals for implementation (who, when, how) similar to those described in the commentary to Figure 82. Then there are various print procedures which enable the content of a progress package – or indeed of any other STRAD window display – to be printed out as hard copy which the user or users can take away as a record of what has been agreed at this stage in the process.

Uses for strategic choice software

As will be apparent from these illustrations, one effect of the use of software is that it enables the results of work using strategic choice methods to be presented in a neater form than the freehand diagrams accompanying earlier chapters, or the photographs of flipcharts from workshops which appear on the *illustrations from practice* pages. Of course, this greater elegance in presentation does not signify any superiority of computer methods in terms of the quality of the interactive process. It is therefore important to evaluate carefully the role of the software within the wider approach: in what circumstances can it bring added value, and in what circumstances is it likely to be unhelpful or even harmful in its impacts on the process?

Since the first production version of the STRAD software was released in 1991, there has been a steady accumulation of evidence that it is fulfilling its intended purpose in extending the range of situations in which the methods of strategic choice can be successfully applied. From the experience so far, it is possible to distinguish six broad types of ways in which the software can come to play a role in the wider process:

- as a form of **personal decision support** to the individual;
- as a means of structuring participatory planning in a **small group**;
- as an interactive **consulting tool**;
- as an **off-line resource** to a strategic choice workshop;
- as a means of keeping a **record** of the assumptions behind decisions;
- as an **interactive learning tool**.

Over the years since 1991, there has been enough feedback on uses of STRAD – and enough direct interaction with some users – to be able to report with some confidence on the experience so far under each of the above broad headings.

Decision support for individuals There has now been an encouraging number of reports from individual users of STRAD in industry and the public sector on their use of the software as a personal decision support tool. Also, demonstrations of the software to individuals have involved inviting the prospective user to focus on some current decision situation with which they are concerned; to structure their thoughts on key issues; and to start developing a preferred strategy for progress.

Such a situation comes close to that of consultant and client to be discussed below. It demonstrates how, once a user has developed an understanding of what the software can do, it can lead within an hour or two to progress of a kind which could have been hard to achieve over a much longer period without this kind of logical structuring process to guide their thinking.

Facilitating small meetings There have been several occasions when STRAD has been put to good effect in facilitating a small meeting of two, three or four people – or occasionally more – grouped around a desktop computer.

All that is required is that at least one of these people should be familiar enough with the software – and should have sufficient personal facilitation skill – to be able to drive the process forward, balancing the concern for steady progress against the concern to encourage each participant to contribute to the full. In such a group, it has been found quite possible to transfer the responsibility for keyboard and mouse input from one person to another from time to time, even if there is only one experienced STRAD user – recognising that this person may still have to give verbal guidance on the basic operations.

At this scale of the 'intimate group' clustered around a desktop computer, the evidence is that it is possible to achieve a creative synthesis between a process of group interaction and a process of interaction between human and machine. For it is not hard at this scale for people to switch their focus from the computer screen to the other participants in the group. This kind of switching does, however, become less natural in a larger group – especially if, to make the content of the screen more visible, it is projected onto a wall.

Computer-aided consultancy The situation of a consultant using STRAD interactively with an individual client – or with a small client group – is in most respects little different from that of the small computer-supported meeting as already described. The key difference is that – assuming that the consultant is acting as 'process driver' – he or she will be drawing inputs out of the others without also making any substantive inputs to the decision process.

The benefit of this style of consultancy, as compared to consultancy without computer support, is that the clients can see a continually evolving picture on the screen of the decision situation as built up from the various information inputs that they themselves have provided. This enables the clients to make adjustments and corrections at any time, and provides a foundation from which a firmer and more confident client–consultant relationship can be built.

Off-line support to a strategic choice workshop There has been much discussion of the possibility of using STRAD as an off-line resource in support of a strategic choice workshop facilitated using more conventional flipchart methods. Although experience so far is limited, one illustration from practice is presented in Figure 46. The function of the computer is then to provide analytical support at key points in the process where it becomes difficult to work entirely on the walls without losing the attention of participants. For example, when it is desired to develop the set of feasible schemes after introducing some assumed set of option bars, or when it is wished to rank a set of schemes in relation to a combination of several comparison areas, then the computer can perform the required calculations speedily with minimum disruption to the dynamics of the group.

What is required firstly is that someone in a recording role, with enough familiarity with the approach and specifically with the use of the software, should be continually building up a STRAD file of the project in a corner of the room while the workshop is in progress. Then, at an appropriate moment, the person in the computer recording role should be capable of taking over the work that has been done, analysing it, and presenting the outcomes in a way which is both understandable and useful to the working group. If the group is not too large, they can then gather for a few minutes around the computer screen; in a larger group, projection on a wall may be helpful at this point.

One cautionary comment is that the use of the computer in this supporting role does mean that the workshop facilitator cannot stray too far from orthodox strategic choice methods. This can be a constraint in those types of workshop situation which call for flexibility in the use of strategic choice conventions, and creativity in combining them with other methods.

Recording the assumptions behind decisions One use of STRAD which has attracted increasing interest lies in its use in providing a readily accessible record of the way in which important decisions are made, and thus in helping to develop a continuous process of *organisational learning*. Clearly, it is possible to use STRAD to keep a running record of the decision areas identified; the options that have been considered; the linkages perceived with other decisions; the criteria that have been applied; the uncertainties that have come to the fore; and the exploratory actions that have been agreed, in addition to the actual commitments to actions or to policies that emerged.

STRAD as an interactive learning tool Staff of several business, planning and policy schools have now started to make use of STRAD in courses designed to help students in exploring the realities of strategic decision-making in complex fields. On full-time undergraduate and postgraduate courses, this usually requires providing realistic case materials which they can use as a starting point for work in groups. With part-time mature students, however, the opportunity arises to ask them to work with live issues which are currently on their own various organisational agendas.

In either setting, the STRAD software is proving to be a stimulating means of introducing students to the general principles and the working methods of the strategic choice approach. At the same time, it is proving an effective means of giving less experienced students a feel for the realities of strategic-decision processes under conditions of uncertainty and pressure to commit.

Limits to use of the computer

In conclusion, it is important to re-emphasise the dangers of adopting a view that the use of computers will one day supersede the use of flipcharts and other low-technology tools for strategic decision support. The experience of neither of the authors lends support to such a view. Indeed, Chapter 11 will review a number of parallel innovations which focus on the interpersonal and interorganisational challenges of strategic decision-making, and on ways of tackling these which do not require any form of electronic support.

The opportunities for exploitation of the electronic resource will undoubtably continue to expand, as further technological advances come on stream and as experiences in application of strategic choice methods and other participatory approaches continue to accrue. One of the most intriguing opportunities concerns the use of computers to support strategic interaction and negotiation among people in remote locations. Further discussion of this opportunity will be deferred to Chapter 12.

11 Extensions in process management

Extensive participatory projects and the strategic choice approach

Since the first edition of this book went to press, opportunities have arisen to apply the general approach presented here to the management of ambitious projects on an increasingly large scale. Typically, these projects have involved people with many different allegiances and cultural backgrounds coming together to address important issues in which they have a shared concern. The theme of this chapter will be the challenge of adapting the strategic choice approach to *extensive projects* of this kind, and the further adaptations in technology, organisation, process and products which have evolved in response.

As mentioned in the preface to this edition, many of these extensive projects – though by no means all – have been concerned with issues of environmental policy in a national or an international setting. Some of them have brought together participants from many countries of western and eastern Europe, building on the success of the earlier projects in the Netherlands from which several of the illustrations from practice in earlier chapters are drawn.

The emphasis on environmental policy is no accident – for it is this field of policy which, more than any other, reflects the current convergence of two highly significant trends in the modern world of policy formulation, planning and decision-making. These are:

- *A growing appreciation of the complexity of the issues.* It is becoming more and more clear that the issues we are now facing are often of global significance on a time-scale involving generations far into the future – as expressed in the concept of sustainable development. Not only are the issues themselves more complex but, at the same time, they are being seen as increasingly interrelated – to the extent that what could once be seen as externalities have now to be handled as central concerns.
- *A growing emphasis on collaborative methods of working.* The wider the set of issues being addressed, the wider the range of interests and organisations that will consider themselves as having a stake in the process – and so the more widely it is now becoming recognised that collaborative as opposed to adversarial styles of working offer the only constructive opportunities for effective progress. There is a widespread understanding that it is only through

their involvement in the process that stakeholders will feel the sense of ownership of the results necessary for there to be a high level of commitment to their implementation.

While there is recognised to be still much scope for improvement, the proliferation of projects based on the ideas of consensus-building is increasingly apparent. This has been especially evident in projects where the aim has been to harmonise policies across international boundaries, for example within the European Union or the countries of eastern Europe which share a common history. Work in groups the membership of which crosses organisational and sectional boundaries, such as the so-called 'round tables', while relatively new in Britain, is well established in North America and Australasia.

These two trends have led to three types of changes in the political context within which extensive projects must be planned; and these in turn have called for adaptations in the strategic choice approach. The three main changes are:

- *Extended numbers of participants.* The wider the set of issues being addressed, the wider the range of interests and organisations that will expect to have a stake in the process – and so the larger the number of people with a claim to be involved. No longer is it sufficient to rely on one or two informal workshops, producing quick results. It has become important that any stakeholder who has the power to make things happen – or conversely to block things happening – should be an active participant.
- *Extended channels of communication.* The wider the issues, the more attenuated become the channels and procedures of communication which link the participants to their constituents. The more extensive the range of participating organisations, the more complex will become the required procedures of authorisation, resource commitment and control. In particular, those representing governmental organisations will have to assure those to whom they are accountable that they are undertaking a finite project with prescribed forms of outcome.
- *Extended time-frames.* An important consequence of this is that time-scales become extended if lasting progress towards agreement is to be secured. A process has to be designed which may often extend over one or two years, with successive meetings of many different types, managed together as a series with ample time allowed for maintaining the link between representatives and their constituents.

All these broad trends reflect a growth in the complexity of the organisational and political context within which the search for progress is set. Therefore, they require that greater attention be given to the design of the more political, as opposed to the more technical, aspects of the work. There have been the following consequences for the adaptation of the strategic choice approach:

- in the overall design of the process, considerably greater attention has had to be given to the *design of the work that has to be done in the political arena*, as presented in Figure 89, as against the technical domain;
- an increased emphasis is required on methods designed to *help participants to work with each other*, as much as with the complexities of the issues they are addressing;
- it becomes important to *simplify the analytical methods* used as far as possible, especially where there are differences of culture and mother tongue among the participants;
- concepts relating to the *management of uncertainty* may have to be *kept in the background* of the work rather than brought to the foreground, as they are sometimes seen as threatening to people in policy roles;
- it becomes necessary to *reinforce the skills involved in process management*, by introducing other third-party skills from such related fields as mediation and alternative dispute resolution;
- it becomes increasingly difficult for one person to handle effectively the extended facilitation role; so a requirement arises for the *formation of facilitation teams* – often calling for a planned investment in training in facilitation skills;
- it has become necessary to *reconcile the cyclic process with the linear principles of conventional project planning* and to agree a clear series of stages through which progress towards outcomes can be monitored;
- it becomes important to give more explicit attention to the challenge of actively *managing the process*, within an extended organisational context, throughout all phases of a project.

For all these reasons, the strategic choice toolbox as presented in earlier chapters has come to be supplemented, in the management of extensive projects, by various further concepts, processes, techniques and methods. Some of these have been borrowed from other toolboxes – with adaptations where appropriate – while others take the form of more direct extensions to the concepts and methods presented in earlier chapters.

The main purpose of this chapter is to introduce the extended principles of process management which have evolved as a result of a decade of experience in the management of extensive projects. A few more specific examples will also be given of the more specific adaptations that have been introduced in the technology and the organisation of the strategic choice approach, and in the strategies used to capture both the visible and the invisible products.

A twin track approach

The argument that any process of strategic choice involves a subtle interplay between relatively technical and relatively political types of work was first

Figure 93   Linking technical and political work

Conventional approach

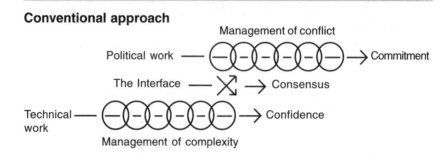

Management of conflict

Political work — Commitment

The Interface — Consensus

Technical work — Confidence

Management of complexity

Twin-track approach

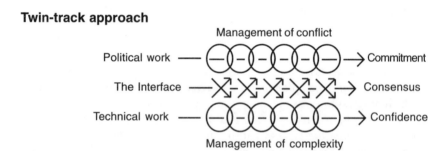

Management of conflict

Political work — Commitment

The Interface — Consensus

Technical work — Confidence

Management of complexity

The political – technical U-loop

PROBLEM INPUT   DECISION OUTPUT

Political work   scoping   committing
DIRECTION   APPROVAL
framing   packaging

The interface   INTERACTION   DOCUMENTATION

Technical work   generating   balancing
ANALYSIS
scheming   assessing

introduced in the discussion of the basic process diagram on page 24, and was developed further in Chapters 4 and 9. This line of argument culminated in the presentation of a general model – Figure 89 – indicating an intricate web of relationships linking a **technical domain**; a **political arena**; and a **field of operations**.

To reflect the increased complexity and significance of the political arena in the circumstances of an extensive project, an extended model of the process has now evolved, based on the concept of a *twin-track approach*. This model is based on a recognition of parallel and interdependent streams of work for the technical domain and for the political arena.

These streams have come to be known as the **technical** and the **socio-political** work streams. The phrase 'socio-political' has come to be used as a means of reassuring senior civil servants that their role is not being seen as intruding on that of elected politicians. This point can also be reflected by talking of a *policy stream* rather than a political stream – and this is the term that will be adopted in this chapter.

The two streams of work play complementary roles in the overall process:

- the work in the **technical stream** involves managing the complexity of the issues, so as to develop *confidence* in the quality of the results;
- the work in the **policy stream** involves managing the conflicting positions of those involved, so as to develop *commitment* to the results.

It is important for the participants to recognise that the distinction is one between types of work rather than between types of *roles*. Indeed, those in more technical roles often have a significant part to play in the policy as well as the technical work streams – and it is helpful to keep them aware of this reality. Likewise, those in policy roles may make contributions to the technical work streams, although pressures on their time will often limit the extent of these.

Most conventional planning projects begin with a series of technical stages leading to the production of a proposal of some sort – for example a draft plan. Professional norms often create an expectation that this be made as technically perfect as possible, before work begins in a series of political stages aimed at developing commitment to that proposal.

The first diagram of Figure 93 illustrates this relationship – recognising that, for a short while at least, the two types of work may run in parallel, and also that each stage may in practice involve work of a cyclic rather than a strictly linear nature.

It is at the interface between the two types of work that the all-important process of consensus-building takes place. Conventionally, however, the duration of this interface is so short that the opportunities for consensus-building become severely limited. If these opportunities are to be increased, it is important that both types of work should start as early as possible in the life of a project. This means extending the length of the interface as illustrated in the second diagram of Figure 93.

In an extensive project, this can be achieved through structuring the overall project timetable with reference to an agreed schedule of events, each with an emphasis on consensus-building at the policy-technical interface, and each usually involving a substantial number of people. The progress of the overall project can then be managed through commitments on the part of those involved in both work streams to the production of draft documents in preparation for future events.

The policy work and the technical work in combination can be viewed as covering the four modes of work which together form the basic process model of the strategic choice approach – *shaping* and *choosing* within the political arena, together with *designing* and *comparing* within the technical domain. To further clarify the nature of the work involved in each mode, it has been found helpful to subdivide these activities further, as follows:

POLICY: scoping   —   focusing   —   packaging — committing
                (s h a p i n g)   (c h o o s i n g)

TECHNICAL: generating — scheming   —   assessing   —   balancing
                (d e s i g n i n g)   (c o m p a r i n g)

Several of the terms introduced above reflect the terminology of specific strategic choice concepts introduced in earlier chapters – for example, the terminology of the problem focus, the decision scheme and the commitment package. Some correspondences will also be noticed with the terms used to describe the principal process windows of the STRAD software, as illustrated in Figure 90.

The fundamental relationship between the policy work and the technical work is illustrated in the third diagram of Figure 93. This model has become known as the *political–technical U-loop*. Recognising that each stage of policy work will rarely in practice follow a linear logic, each policy stage is shown as a *cycle,* involving inputs not only from previous cycles but also from what is described in Figure 89 as the *field of operations*. The outputs of each policy cycle will then provide inputs to later cycles, together with any agreed policies or actions directed towards the field of operations.

In the diagram, each technical cycle is seen as, in effect, an extension of the middle part of a political cycle. It begins with inputs from the first part of the political cycle, taking the form of agreed directions for the work – sometimes expressed as terms of reference. It ends with some form of recommendation or proposal, providing input to the latter part of the political cycle – often taking the form of a draft document.

What is essential is that the two streams of work should not be taken forward in isolation; rather, it is important that the interaction between them should be carefully structured. The principle of the political–technical U-loop as illustrated in Figure 93 offers an important conceptual reference point in doing this. However, if it is to provide practical guidance over the course of an extensive project, it has first to be adapted to the gradually changing nature of the work carried out at successive stages.

Applying the concepts to project planning

The design of any major project involves planning some progression of activities extending from its beginning to its intended end date, related in some way to the passage of time. The purpose of formalising this is to enable all those involved to keep track of what is going on at any time.

The following set of terms indicates the changing emphasis of both the policy work and the technical work over the course of any extensive project:

	policy work	*technical work*
1	initiation	structuring
2	orientation	generating
3	preferencing	evaluating
4	revision	composition
5	agreement	finalisation

In practice, it is usual for more than one kind of work to be in progress at any particular time, even though the primary emphasis will tend to shift gradually over the course of a project.

In order to reflect this shift, it has been found helpful to view the progression of a project in terms of a *succession of linked U-loops*, in which the nature of the work to be done at the policy–technical interface changes, as well as the nature of the work within each of the policy and technical streams. This progression is reflected in the first diagram of Figure 94.

In this diagram five sorts of activity are identified which, based on experience, are suited to inter-reactive work at the policy–technical interface. These are summarised in the acronym **ISCRA**:

I	Identifying the Issues
S	Setting the Structure
C	Confirming the Concept
R	Reviewing the Recommendations
A	Approving any Amendments

It will be noticed in Figure 94 that these five activities do not proceed strictly in step with the five sorts of work in the political arena and the technical do-

Figure 94　Phasing work in an extensive project

Principles of the ISCRA sequence
I – identify issues; **S** – set structure; **C** – confirm course; **R** – review recommendations; **A** – approve ammendments

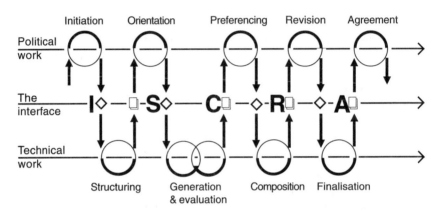

Interpreting ISCRA in practice

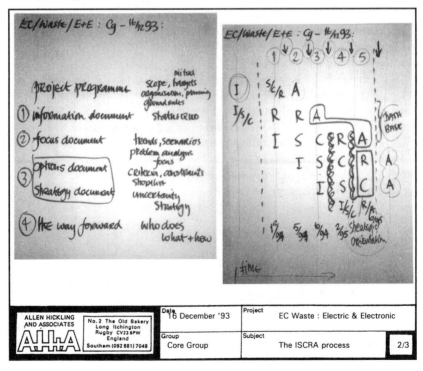

Date	Project
16 December '93	EC Waste : Electric & Electronic
Group Core Group	**Subject** The ISCRA process　2/3

main. In particular, the two closely intertwined technical cycles introduced in the discussion of the basic process diagram on page 24, *generating* and *evaluating*, are shown as appearing together between *Setting the Structure* and *Confirming the Concept*.

It will also be noticed that the primary inputs to the early stages (I and S) are shown as coming from the political arena, whereas the primary inputs to the later stages (C, R and A) are shown as coming from the technical domain. This change in emphasis recognises that, in an extensive project where there are many diverse interests at stake, value judgements are required in order to identify what are the key issues to be addressed, and thus give direction to the technical work. The contrast here is with more conventional models of project planning in which technical issues are regarded as dominant in the early stages.

However, this relationship does not extend throughout the process. Towards the end, those in more technical roles will tend to become more proactive, as it becomes necessary to draw the threads together and prepare documents for the approval of those who carry political accountability for the project.

The most important practical challenge can then be seen as one of designing, over the course of a project, the settings within which the work at the policy–technical interface is to be done. In an extensive project, it has become usual for much of this work to be carried out in the course of relatively large events which are sometimes called *strategic discussions*. These are designed to bring together a considerable number of people in both policy roles and relatively technical roles. Some of the work may, however, be done in smaller sub-group meetings of various kinds. At other times – especially at the beginning or end of a project – it will be appropriate for all the participants to come together for events of a more celebratory nature.

The number of full strategic discussions scheduled over the course of a project will depend on the project context. In a project designed to be completed in a few months there may be relatively few, whereas as many as seven or eight strategic discussions may be scheduled in the case of an international project extending over two years or more.

A strategic discussion is usually planned to extend over at least one full day and usually two days, in the course of which various more specific activities – sometimes called 'work bites' – will be scheduled, often in series but sometimes in parallel. Many of these work bites will involve interactive working, but others may involve a more reactive style of work. The overall nature of the work done in a strategic discussion can therefore be described as *inter-reactive* in nature.

As might be expected, the nature of the joint work carried out in such meetings is designed to be different from the nature of the work normally carried out in either the political arena or the technical domain. For there are only certain forms of consensus-building activity that such mixed groups can be expected to undertake. As is also to be expected, the nature of this work will change through time to reflect the changing emphases of the work within both the political arena and the technical domain.

In an extensive project involving many participants, it becomes a practical necessity that most of the primary inputs take the form of documents of some kind. At some stages, these may be relatively formal papers; at other times, they may be briefer and more informal. This will depend on the overall scale of the project as well as on the stage of progress that has so far been achieved.

The extended ISCRA model

In planning major projects, it has become common practice to apply the ISCRA model not just to the project as a whole, conceived as a unitary work programme, but to a set of interrelated streams of work, each associated with the production of a different type of documentary output. These streams are usually scheduled to begin at different stages of the project, then to run in parallel with phased completion dates, geared to an agreed schedule of strategic meetings.

A typical set of work streams is:

- **Project Programme:** initial focus & aims, organisation & planning;
- **Information:** the status quo and any actions already in train;
- **Focus:** the scope of the project; problems and opportunities;
- **Options:** alternative strategies, including any so far rejected;
- **Strategy:** reflecting the management of uncertainty;
- **Actions:** agreed actions, responsibilities, budgets and deadlines;
- **Policy Management:** ongoing processes of monitoring and adaptation.

This set of streams, which is designed to conform to relatively familiar models of strategic planning, is used as a framework for the phased drafting and revision of a series of documents – one for each of the streams. Each type of document is developed incrementally over the course of the project and becomes a self-contained report on that part of the work – ultimately forming one of the main sections of the overall project document.

In general terms, the ISCRA sequence of activities is then applied to each document in the following manner:

Time dimension   → → → → → → → → → → →

Documents

Project programme	I	S	C	R	A						
Information		I	S	C	R	A					
Focus			I	S	C	R	A				
Options				I	S	C	R	A			
Strategy					I	S	C	R	A		
Actions						I	S	C	R	A	
Policy management							I	S	C	R	A

It is important to reiterate that this 'model' is intended only as a framework for the design of a process specific to the requirements of each project – depending on such variables as the complexity of the issues, the number of stakeholders and the time available. It is common for documents to be combined and/or some of the steps brought together or extended in time. For example the Information and Focus documents together can be seen as the *database*; the Options and Strategy documents combine to form a *strategy*, and the Actions document and Policy Management programme provide the basic components for an *action plan*.

The lower section of Figure 94 presents one particular illustration of the way in which the generalised ISCRA model was used in practice to design a specific programme of strategic events, scheduled over the course of an extensive project – in this case, the co-ordination of the implementation of waste management policy concerning electrical and electronic equipment within the European Union.[1]

There are two important advantages in the application of the extended ISCRA model as a general framework for the design of extensive planning projects.

Firstly, it provides a practical means of reconciling the principle of cyclic continuity as discussed in Chapter 4 with the expectation of steady and sustained progress which is so vital to most of the participants – and their sponsors – in any project of this nature. For example, opportunities will still remain to review the focus of the project, and to reformulate the options, even when the project is well advanced, as the participants develop closer mutual understanding and as they adjust to any important changes in their working environment.

Secondly, the extended ISCRA model provides a framework for the design of sufficiently compact 'work bites' for the work even in relatively large strategic discussion meetings to be subdivided in such a way as to give each participant a series of meaningful parts to play, working for much of the time in relatively small sub-groups with defined types of outcome which have a recognisable role in the overall project design.

Within these broad principles of process management, many specific adaptations can be introduced in terms of the technology, the organisation and the products of the strategic choice approach, as discussed in the relevant sections of Chapter 9. The following sections will give a few of the more significant examples of the ways in which strategic choice methods have so far been extended and reinforced in the management of extensive projects.

---

1 It will be noticed here that a series of five strategic discussions was scheduled in all, with more than one stage of the extended ISCRA model compressed into one meeting in some cases. The annotations on the two flip charts reflect the way in which the basic ISCRA process was 'customised' through thinking developed in the course of discussion within the project management team.

Extensions to the project organisation

One significant extension to the principles of organisation as discussed in Chapter 9, and illustrated in Figure 84, concerns the overall management of a project.

In an extensive project, it is especially important that there should be a recognised *project leader* who carries continuous responsibility for the overall management of the project, yet who draws authority from an extended *project group* which includes representation of all the main interests involved. In a typical large environmental project, these will include various governmental bodies plus a range of organisations representing business and community interests.

This project group carries the ultimate responsibility not only for the conduct of the project work itself, but also for the production of a management programme or implementation document through which the work will be carried forward into the field of operations, to influence future decision-making after the project comes to an end.

In the formation of the project group, it can be important to go through explicit processes of *stakeholder analysis* – preferably extending beyond the kind of brief brainstorming exercise which is often considered adequate in a more limited project setting. Various methods of stakeholder analysis are available (GTZ 1991, Wilcox 1994) which not only enable lists of stakeholders to be identified, but also help in understanding the positions they might be expected to adopt, the factions or coalitions which might be expected to form, and the possible strategies through which they might be approached when invited to participate in the project work.

It is important too that an extended view be taken of what are referred to in Figure 84 as the *reference* and *representative groupings*. In an extensive project, it has been found useful to introduce an extended concept of a *reference network*, emphasising that the task of developing this falls on all those who become directly involved in the project work. For the reference network is intended to tap into the personal networks of all participants, who are encouraged to suggest the names of individuals whom they consider should be included in the first instance. From this basis the network can be allowed to grow freely, encouraging anyone who shows an interest to join.

Members of this wider network can then be kept in touch with the course of the project work through a periodic project newsletter, and encouraged to contribute by providing inputs of information or opinion through whatever channels are available. In some circumstances it may be appropriate to invite them to particular sessions of the project group – for example in the evening between the two days of a strategic discussion. The membership of this reference network will tend to expand over the course of a project as more and more people find out that the work is in progress – ultimately evolving into an implementation network focussed directly on the often complex processes of implementing the agreements reached.

Wherever it is important that the project group should have a larger membership – as is especially the case in international projects – it becomes essential that smaller, more flexible sub-groups be formed to carry out certain aspects of the project group's work at some stages of the process. There is no intention that these groups should take over the responsibilities of the project group – they are merely intended to enable it to work more effectively.

It is usual to view such groups as falling into one or other of two categories – *task groups*, which are primarily responsible for more technical aspects of the work, and in particular for preparing specific outcomes of this for handling within the project group; and *guidance groups*, which are responsible for policy aspects and can act as political sounding boards where necessary.

Whereas the task groups will tend to operate in a proactive style, developing proposals for consideration in the full project group, the guidance groups will tend to play a more reactive or responsive role, acting as a sounding board where necessary – typically, during the final stages in the preparation of specific documents.

In an extensive project, as in any other, continuous management through a relatively compact *core group* between one scheduled event and another is crucial. Typically this group will be enlarged to include at least one *process consultant*, whose role is to advise the core group on matters of organisation, communication, process management, network development and project methodology. These people will usually be centrally involved also in the strategic discussions and many of the sub-group meetings, acting as facilitators as and when required.

It is also important in some circumstances that the core group includes a *technical support team*, with expert knowledge of the substance of the issues. Its members are likely to be consultants, though this is not necessarily so; they will often have a role in assisting any *administrative staff* in compiling the documentation necessary to keep the process moving forward, based on the directions indicated by the project group.

Adaptations in working methods

As already mentioned, the working methods introduced to facilitate the work of participants in the strategic discussions and sub-group meetings may draw both on the strategic choice toolbox as discussed in earlier chapters, and on complementary methods from other sources – especially those which are addressed not so much to the complexities of the issues as to the challenge of helping people to work constructively with each other.

In the three sections that follow, three examples will be given of adaptations to the strategic choice toolbox which have proved effective at different stages of the ISCRA sequence: first identifying the issues in the early (I) stages; then agreeing preferred ways forward in the middle (S and C) stages; and finally developing commitment to action proposals in the later (R and A) stages.

These three sections will be followed by another section on the opportunities for *socio-technical design* which can be seized at any stage of the process to provide a firmer framework for collaborative working – especially in those projects where there may be linguistic as well as professional and cultural barriers to communication among the participants.

Methods for encouraging joint working in identifying issues

Chapter 5 has already described (on page 109) a general approach to the shaping of problems through building up a shared list of issues of concern – issues which may later become variously re-framed as decision areas, comparison areas or uncertainty areas – or in some cases as assumptions or constraints.

In an extensive project it is helpful to start building consensus in the group as early as possible in the process. An opportunity for this lies in the generation of a first shared list of issues, as this has been found to provide a non-threatening means of enabling participants of diverse backgrounds to begin working interactively together.

Here it is important that the facilitator should demonstrate both listening skills and questioning skills. For example, it is quite common for the participants to tend at first to formulate issues in the form of position statements; this can be seriously counter-productive in the search for consensus. Here the skilled facilitator can demonstrate ways in which these issues can be reformulated in terms of interests or needs.

Over time, this process can have the effect of making the contributions of different participants more consistent in their language – with some issues being re-framed in terms of broader goals or values, and others in terms of more concrete action possibilities or contingencies. Some examples of relevant questions, sometimes known as 'restructuring heuristics' (Shakun, 1995), are:

> So why should this be a problem?
> What might be the causes of that?
> Why might we want to do that?
> If that is a goal, how might we get there?

Time spent in this kind of discussion can be important in demonstrating to the participants how their own concerns, which may at first have been expressed in quite diverse ways and at diverse levels, can be gradually re-framed in terms of a shared framework of understanding. Once in this form, the issues can be analysed further by clustering similar ones together and, where there are many, establishing the priorities between them so that a collective approach can be taken in deciding where to begin.

Then, more specific concepts of problem-structuring – such as those of the decision area, the decision option, the comparison area and the uncertainty area from the strategic choice toolbox – can be introduced gradually and selectively, as a means of enabling people to build together on the inputs that they and the other participants have provided.

Facilitating extensions to the common ground

As the work of a project develops, consensus will gradually develop on the nature of the key choices ahead – in strategic choice language, the key decision areas – and on the range of realistic options available within each, although they may not be presented as such. An approach can then be introduced which has come to be known as *common grounding*. The purpose of this is first to identify and make visible any common ground which already exists among the various interests represented; then gradually to enlarge this – drawing on the experience of effective negotiators (Fisher and Ury, 1981) that this can be a more productive way of working towards agreement than focussing more directly on the differences between the parties.

This approach is illustrated in Figure 95 through photographs of a set of flip charts from a European Union project concerned with implementation of the European waste management policies for health care waste. The flip charts to the left show the options within some of the key decision areas, as identified part way through the project. The columns at the right show the preferred options as identified by five sub-groups which, at that stage, were formed to represent different, and relatively homogeneous, sets of interests.

As often happens in such circumstances, the participants were surprised to find the extent to which they already agreed: there were a few decision areas where there was complete agreement, as well as some options which none of the groups had selected. The process of developing common ground then continues by focussing on decision areas where there is a considerable measure of agreement, for example where there is only one sub-group out of line.

That sub-group is then asked 'In what way would this option, which the other sub-groups have selected, have to be modified to make it acceptable to you?'. Often, slight changes are all that is required. Each of the other sub-groups can then be asked the classic consensus-building question 'Could you live with that?' If the answer is positive, then the common ground is thereby extended.

Where there is difficulty, a decision area can be set aside until later, and another one explored. When only a few decision areas remain which require further work, the experience of working together successfully will often have had the effect of enabling options to be reformulated in a creative way so as to resolve the outstanding difficulties.

Where difficulties prove harder to resolve, one way of proceeding is to invite the participants to join one or other of two competing teams, each with its own appointed 'captain'. Each team is then set the challenge of considering: 'What are the needs of the other side?', and reformulating its preferred option as an *option for mutual gain*.

At this point, the principles of managing uncertainty covered in earlier chapters can become helpful; for they can help people to probe the conflicting as-

Figure 95 Building common ground

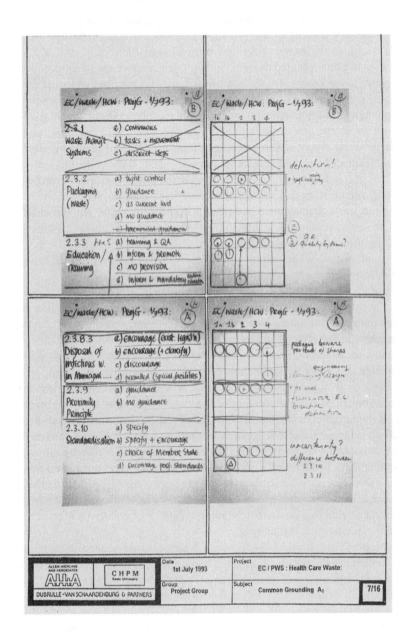

sumptions which often underlie apparent disagreements. Inter-group discussion can then help to reduce uncertainty both about the different values in operation, and about the future intentions of relevant parties – leading in many cases to agreement on appropriate exploratory actions or contingency plans.

Securing commitment to action proposals

At a stage when proposals for action start to be developed in some depth – often through the work of sub-groups charged with generating these within specific policy areas or from the point of view of a specific group of stakeholders – it becomes important to subject these to critical scrutiny – and to encourage constructive amendments or counter-suggestions by members of other sub-groups. At this stage it has been found helpful to use standardised *action forms* with a prescribed sequence of headings such as:

> Description of the action
> Responsibilities
> Funding and Cost/Budget
> Planning (uncertainties, conditions, etc.)
> Crucial assumptions/'Critical success factors'

Some illustrations of action forms have already appeared in Figure 81. A structure such as this offers a means of relatively easy access to what can be a considerable amount of detailed information, so that it can be shared among all the members of the wider project group – even in circumstances where conventionally it might be thought more appropriate to use such concepts explicitly only within the core group. It also provides a way of introducing the set of ideas about the management of uncertainty and the design of commitment packages which have been discussed in earlier chapters, thus releasing the potential for managing conflict which that allows.

One technique which can be used to bring the proposals of the different sub-groups together for display is to create what has become known as an *action gallery* – enabling members of other sub-groups to comment and add any further suggestions of their own. This process can take various forms – including that of the *carousel* discussed below – all based on the need to allow free interaction between the participants in order to achieve a high measure of pre-coordination as described in Chapter 9. The principle is that of an art gallery or antiques fair in which the action forms are displayed in groupings which may be defined in various ways – for example, according to those with primary responsibility for implementation, or according to the relevant issues.

Opportunities for socio-technical design

At all stages of a project, opportunities arise for exercising creativity not only in the methods by which people address the substance of the work, but also in the methods by which they are helped to work with each other. So the challenge can be conceived as one of *socio-technical design* (Trist and Murray, 1993).

The choices open can include devising completely new methods; adapting and combining established techniques; or making a myriad of spontaneous adjustments as particular challenges present themselves.

For example, one design, which has evolved directly in the course of the projects on which this chapter is based, involves a way of structuring interactions between members of different sub-groups which has become known as the *carousel* approach. This has shown itself to be effective both at the stage of introducing an action gallery, and in earlier stages where sub-groups have been assigned to differentiated but parallel tasks within the context of a strategic discussion event.

This approach involves first inviting the sub-groups to work on allotted tasks in different corners of a large room, or a suite of adjoining rooms, using flip charts as a means of recording their progress. Then a schedule is agreed whereby the members of each sub-group visit the territory of each other sub-group in rotation, inspecting the results of their work, commenting spontaneously on what they see, asking questions on anything which appears controversial or unclear, and adding their own ideas and opinions if they wish.

It is essential that one or two members of each 'home' sub-group should stay behind to answer questions, to make notes on the points raised and to report back to the other members of their own sub-group once they have completed their tour and returned to base.

In the second category of socio-technical choice, there are three well-established and reasonably well-known methods which have proved to be fully consistent with the strategic choice approach. Either in whole or in part, these form basic tools in the toolboxes of many facilitators. They are:

- **Metaplan** (Schnelle 1973) This is a complete approach in its own right, developed by the Quickborn Group in Germany in the early seventies; however two techniques within it have a general application and can be used independently. The first is a form of brain-writing in which the participants write their ideas on small pieces of paper prior to sticking them on the wall for further analysis – usually a form of clustering. The second is the use of small coloured sticky spots as a means of collecting opinions within a group – whether that is a matter of prioritisation in a list of items or an evaluation.

- **Brainstorming** (Rickards 1974, van Gundy 1981) This is probably the best known technique, although the word is often used with very little understanding of what it actually means. There are many derivative forms, and it is considered to be the forerunner of most idea-generation methods. Nevertheless, application of the rules of the classical form is still the best way of helping a group to be creative while also maintaining a sense of discipline.

- **Nominal Group Technique** (Moore 1987) There are two aspects of this technique (usually abbreviated to NGT), which have proved valuable in association with strategic choice methods. The first is the use of sub-groups working together in the same room, provided that their tasks are kept the same and quite simple. This allows intensive interactive working – even for very short periods of a minute or so, without the waste of time caused by the sub-groups having to change rooms frequently. The second is a simple sequence starting with the generation of ideas (for example issues, options, or uncertainties) in small groups, leading to the formation of a mutually understood joint list, then discussion of the relative importance of the items on the list – often using the sticky spots technique from Metaplan.

It is in the third area of socio-technical choice – that of spontaneous adjustments – that combinations and variations of these techniques are often devised. There are many choices to be made, not only about which technique to use when, but also about *how* they are to be introduced. Questions of who does what with whom; the sequence and duration of activities; and adjustments to the physical layout of the room(s) can often be all-important in sustaining the momentum and spirit of participative work.

For example groups can be formed in different ways – either to be as mixed as possible in their memberships or to be more homogeneous in terms of the interests or disciplines they represent. Also, it is possible to draw on approaches which combine elements of individual, sub-group and plenary work, not only to demonstrate how each participant can make a full contribution from the start, but also start to build on the contributions of others. These are choices which should not be made lightly because the outcomes can vary according to continually changing circumstances.

Extensions to process management skills

The various concepts, processes, techniques and methods presented in this chapter as extensions and adaptations to the strategic choice approach have been devised in response to the needs of those involved in extensive participatory projects. They cover, between them, all the aspects of the A-TOPP model – Approach, Technology, Organisation, Process and Products – often touching on two or more of these in combination. But they cannot be used all at the same time, and individually they are often not enough – so they have to be in some way 'orchestrated'. The all-important twin ideas of selectivity and adaptiveness which were introduced in Chapter 9 become a matter of even greater concern, and are seen as the central responsibility of the process manager.

An important point to recognise, especially for those who are accustomed to the management of more conventional projects, is that the management of extensive participatory projects calls not only for practical project management skills of the kind which are widely recognised as vital to the success of any large and complex project, but also for more subtle skills of *process management.* The more extensive the project in terms of the range of interests involved, the higher will be the premium on skills oriented towards the building of such invisible products as synergy, mutual understanding and commitment, alongside the incremental growth of more visible products.

Furthermore, it is important to recognise that process management in such a context involves much more than the skill of facilitating progress within a single working group – even though this has come to be regarded as the key to success in managing a more intensive 'one-off' strategic choice workshop. Serious attention must also be given to a range of complementary skills, to each of which the strategic choice approach is relevant to a different extent.

These skills cannot be dealt with in detail here, but there follow outline descriptions which are intended to give readers some idea of what is involved and of ways in which their own acquired skills might be extended and improved:

- **Organisational/group development skills.** The concept of the extended 'project organisation' – as expressed in Figures 84 and 85, and further developed in this chapter – provides plenty of scope for creative use of organisational and group design skills. The concept of *dynamic grouping* discussed on page 257 is highly relevant both at this level and at the level of designing sub-group work within a strategic discussion event.

- **Process design skills.** In the design of strategic discussion events on interreactive principles, the concept of *flexible scheduling* discussed on page 267 plays an important role. The use of 'flexitime' (time put aside for use when that use becomes more clear) and 'slop' (allowing more time than is technically necessary for each task) represent a recognition of process uncertainty and can provide vital opportunities for the facilitation team to respond to the needs of the participants as they are expressed.

- **Network management skills.** Recognition of people on the fringe of the regular project organisation, who nevertheless have a serious interest in the subject, can offer the basis for building a broader consensus than would otherwise be possible. The challenge is that, while setting up an extended project network as described on page 308 is not difficult, without proper maintenance it will just fade away.

  For this reason members of the network can become the main target audience for regular project newsletters, while innovative thinking in process design can provide occasional opportunities during strategic discussions to obtain input from the wider network. Two-way communication within the network can also be enabled by encouraging written inputs, using methods ranging from simple questionnaires to exercises using the Delphi method (Moore 1987).

- **Effective negotiation/participation skills.** These skills are sometimes thought of as useful mainly at the point of interaction; but it is now recognised that the way in which any negotiation or interaction is initiated, the amount of effort put into preparation, and the attention paid to follow-up actions can be just as critical, in the context of a wider understanding of process (Hawkins and Hudson 1986). The concept presented in earlier chapters of strategic choice as a continuous learning process is significant in this respect.

- **Skills in the management of information flows.** The effect of the strategic choice approach here is to introduce new perspectives on the type of information being communicated. Conventional approaches focus on what is known, and there is a strong emphasis on facts. Recognition of uncertainty, as in strategic choice, leads to an emphasis on what is not known and the range of assumptions which may have to be made. What is more, the focus changes from a concentration on uncertainties of type UE (ie data) to a more balanced approach in which peoples' values and intentions become equally important.

- **Project evaluation skills.** The more extensive a project, the more important it becomes to build in explicit methods for keeping track of progress at each stage. For the more any personal feelings of either satisfaction or dissatisfaction can be shared, the more opportunities will be created for the process manager to make adjustments in the subsequent process, as well as to demonstrate that it is being managed in a truly participatory way.

    Evaluation exercises may be either at a micro scale – involving quick checks taken during interactive workshops – or at a macro scale where the subject is the whole project and where it is leading. The latter type of evaluation is usually most relevant some way into the project, and can be used to switch the focus of the group to finishing the project as well as to obtain important process-related feedback.

    This principle applies to both the visible and the invisible products of the process. So far as the visible products are concerned, the division of the work into manageable 'work bites' within parallel streams of work can provide a useful basis for assessing progress. As discussed on page 277, it is not so easy to keep track of the development of invisible products: although they are often made a part of open evaluations within the project group, a more sensitive way is for core group members to check continuously with participants at a personal level.

- **Conflict mediation skills.** So far the principal 'third party' role discussed has been that of facilitator, which may be adopted by an individual or a team. The task is to enable effective utilisation of the time of people with diverse responsibilities and skills, with respect to the prevention of open conflict among the key objectives.

  However, it is only realistic to expect that unproductive conflict will occur from time to time and, when it does, it is helpful to have available the mediation skills to manage it. The main difference between mediation and facilitation is that the mediator will spend more time with the conflicting parties separately, helping them come to terms with the needs of the other side – especially with respect to the relationship with their constituents. He or she is also likely to be a little more involved in the substantive content, and the concept of 'options for mutual gain' can play a useful role.

  The use of a commitment package in resolving conflict is also significant here, as conflict is often based on differing opinions about the assumptions to be made. Use of the idea of a contingency plan in case of the assumption being wrong can provide just the breakthrough which is needed.

- **Project planning skills.** This can be viewed in terms of process design at the scale of the project as a whole rather than at that of the individual interactive event. The basic strategic choice concept of cyclic continuity is most relevant here, and the ISCRA process provides the framework for putting it into action.

  The more extensive the project, the more important too that process management should become seen as a team activity; for it can become a heavy load for any individual to carry alone, and the process can be much enriched when each member of a project management team has the opportunity to draw on the experience and resources of others.

Creating the context for success

However, experience has repeatedly shown that the success of an extensive participatory project does not depend on the quality of its project management alone, even when the importance of good process management is fully recognised and applied.

Such a project can only be expected to succeed if the context for it is right. The quality of such a context has been found to depend on the following conditions:

- a *significant set of issues* which is agreed to be of sufficient common concern;
- an *experienced project leader* with a clear understanding of process, as a focus for the project management team;

- an *internal sponsor* highly placed in the 'client' organisation, with a commitment to seeing the project conducted in an interactive participatory way.

While it may be difficult or impossible to create these conditions if they are not in place, it may be possible to influence them to some extent. Therefore, in the initial negotiations leading up to the launch of a project, it is important to discuss explicitly how far such conditions are fulfilled.

Where any doubts exist, it will pay to review ways in which they might be countered. If this proves impossible there are five complementary aspects of the context which are generally easier to influence; and it may be helpful to review them also with a view to providing some compensating features. These aspects are:

- a *committed project group* which believes, or is at least willing to suspend its disbelief, in the benefits of the proposed style of working;
- an *external sponsor* who plays a similar supporting role as the internal sponsor, but from outside the organisation;
- a *non-hostile culture* in the 'client' organisation or organisations, so that the work is not constantly under threat of being sabotaged;
- an *appropriate workplace* which is somewhat larger than normal, with good light, ventilation and blank walls;
- a *long enough project* in terms of the time available for developing the long-term 'added value' represented by the invisible products.

The absence of all these characteristics of an appropriate context is likely to make the successful conduct of an extensive participatory project impossible. However the practical question to be faced is one of how to adapt the approach to take into account the more negative characteristics.

Figure 96 illustrates the importance of investment in creating and maintaining an appropriate context. It does so by summarising all the stages that were involved in the design and management of an important extensive project – in this case, involving assistance to the government of Latvia from the governments of the Netherlands and Sweden in developing its first National Environmental Policy Plan.

This summary – taken from an official project document – begins at the time when it was agreed to set up the project in the spring of 1994, omitting details of various earlier exploratory discussions in 1993. However, the political complexity of the project is well reflected both in the arrangements preceding the series of three workshops held in the summer and autumn of 1994, and in the events leading up to the final adoption of agreed policy proposals. Also, the cross-cultural aspects of the project are reflected in the planned transition from Dutch to Latvian co-facilitators after the first workshop, supported by appropriate training events.

Figure 96   Managing an extensive environmental project: An illustration from practice

First National Environmental Policy Plan for Latvia (NEPP-L)

Autumn 1993

[Various preliminary meetings and arrangements involving senior representatives of Netherlands and Latvian Governments]

Spring 1994

Decision by Latvian Ministry of Environmental Protection and Regional Development to issue National Environmental Policy Plan (NEPP-L)

Setting up of project organization in Latvia, i.e. appointment of NEPP-L project leader, core group and project group.

Drafting of project plan in Latvia.

Meeting in the Netherlands of the Latvian Minister of Environmental Protection and Regional Development with the Dutch Minister of Housing, Spatial Planning and the Environment on the occasion of 1st conference of the International Network of Green Planners.

Meeting in the Netherlands of Director of the Environmental Protection Department, who is the NEPP-L project leader, and Deputy-Director with representatives of Dutch Directorate of International Environmental Affairs and representatives of Directorate of Strategic Planning

Preparation of Ministerial presentations on policy plan by State Minister of Environmental Protection, the NEPP-L project leader and the Dutch for approx. 50 representatives of the Ministry and another 50 key policy-makers in other ministries and institutions.

Visit to Stockholm of a representative of the Dutch Directorate for International

Environmental Affairs for meeting with Latvians at Swedish Environmental Protection Agency (EPA).

Involvement of process consultant.

Summer 1994

1st Workshop on policy plan for Latvian project group: approx. 50 people present. The workshop takes 3 days and is organized in a hotel in Jurmala. Facilitation by an external process consultant and Dutch representatives. Dutch representation from Directorates of Strategic Planning and International Environmental Affairs. Representation from the Swedish EPA. Formal reception offered by the State Minister of Environmental Protection. Information on the development of the NEPP-L is presented to the press. Tour through Latvian countryside by some of the Dutch representatives.

Involvement of communication experts from Latvian and Dutch Ministries on policy planning process.

Training of Latvians in workshop facilitation.

2nd workshop on policy plan for Latvian project group; approx. 70 people present. Workshop takes 2 days and is organized in a conference facility in Riga. Facilitation by an external process consultant and Latvian co-facilitators. Dutch representatives from Directorate of Strategic Planning and Department for Information and External Relations. Meeting with State Minister of Environmental Protection and communication experts.

Autumn 1994

Writing of the 1st draft of the policy plan by core group with the assistance of one Dutch representative of the Directorate of Strategic Planning.

Visit to Netherlands by Latvian core-group and communication expert. Discussions on 1st draft of the policy plan at the Directorate of Strategic Planning and with the Dutch informal advisory board for twinning. Discussions on communication strategy for the policy plan. Media training for core-group and communication expert by media consultant.

Redrafting of policy plan.

Further training of Latvians in workshop facilitation.

3rd workshop on the policy plan for Latvian project group. Approx. 70 people present during 2 days. Facilitation by an external process consultant and Latvian co-facilitators. Dutch representation from the Directorate of Strategic Planning and the Directorate of International Environmental Affairs. Discussion with the State Minister of Environmental Protection about the process of accepting the concept NEPP-L by the cabinet of Ministers.

Spring 1995

Redrafting of Policy Plan.

Notification in Inter-Ministerial Meeting of State Secretaries.

Review and comments by other Ministries.

Approval of Policy Plan in Cabinet of Ministers.

Issue of Newsletter

Evaluation of twinning

The success of this project was to lead in turn to another in which the focus is on the National Environmental Action Programme. This deals with implementation of the Policy Plan, and it is still in progress at the time of writing.

Similar projects have been launched in other Baltic and east European states, each of them providing important learning opportunities. The experience of each project is contributing to the design of further extensive projects in response to expressions of interest in other countries, relating to other fields of policy. So the process of development goes on, in pursuit of the 'holy grail' of any learning process – continuous improvement.

12 The developmental challenge

Strands of change

Over the ten years since since the first edition of this book went to press, the authors' views of the horizons for future development of the strategic choice approach have undergone a number of significant changes.

In the tenth and final chapter of the first edition, entitled 'Horizons', the prospects for change were surveyed under the following set of headings:

> State of the art
> Applications in public policy
> Applications to corporate strategy
> Applications in inter-organisational working
> Partisan strategic choice
> Eliciting problem perceptions
> The dynamics of the working group
> Developments in operational research and decision analysis
> The electronic resource
> The educational challenge

That there have been further developments in most of these directions over the last decade will be evident from a reading of the last two chapters. For the technological challenge of developing software to support processes of strategic choice, and the socio-political challenge of managing extensive projects with many and diverse participants, have together stimulated us to take a view of the opportunities for future development which is in some respects sharper, and in some respects wider than before.

The broader scene

We, the authors, have continued these last ten years to work closely alongside collaborators of many nationalities and many professional, organisational and political cultures. Yet it is important also to acknowledge those other people in many parts of the world who, with little or no reference to ourselves, have started to add the methods presented here to their own consulting, teaching or research repertoires, and have thereby contributed to the wider developmental process.

Some of these users first encountered the strategic choice approach by way of the first edition of this book, while others have been introduced to the principles through the STRAD software, or through attending training courses. The revised *Guide to further reading* which follows this chapter includes references to a number of recently published accounts of other people's experiences in applying strategic choice methods, in contexts ranging from that of the large commercial corporation to that of the informal community group.

Not all of these accounts describe the use of strategic choice methods in any depth. Of particular interest, however, is the spirit of creativity in which several of these users have experimented in combining methods from the strategic choice toolbox, as presented in earlier chapters, with methods from other sources which they have seen as capable of playing a complementary role.

For example, Ormerod (1996a, 1996b) describes how, in a consultancy role, he successfully introduced strategic choice methods in structuring the later phases of two five-phase projects each designed to help senior managers develop a new information systems strategy – one in a major supermarket chain, the other in an international mining group. In the earlier phases of these projects, he had introduced two other so-called 'soft operational research' approaches – Eden's Strategic Options Development Analysis and Checkland's Soft Systems Methodology – both of which are presented, alongside the strategic choice approach, in Rosenhead's *Rational Analysis for a Problematic World* (Checkland, 1989, Eden 1989).

A contrasting example is an account by White (1994) of his work with a co-operative in a Central American village. He chose first to develop an understanding of the lives of the villagers by introducing the method of Rapid Rural Appraisal (Chambers, 1983), before introducing strategic choice methods as a means of helping the members of the co-operative to agree on preferred ways forward. A different experience again was that of Kravatzky (1995) who, in organising a decision conference to develop an agreed conservation strategy for the Danube Delta in Romania, chose to introduce strategic choice methods as a means of agreeing on a preliminary structuring of the issues, before turning to more focussed decision analysis techniques (Phillips, 1990).

Such experiences in combining leading approaches to participatory decision-making have led some observers to ask some searching questions about the actual or potential relationships among them. In ascending order of the level of challenge presented, typical examples of such questions are:

- is it possible to advise a facilitator in what circumstances it might be advantageous to apply one approach rather than another?
- is it feasible to develop an integrated toolbox which combines the more valuable elements of different approaches?
- is there scope for closer integration between some or all of these approaches at the level of general management or planning theory?

In any survey of the shifting horizons for further development of the strategic choice approach, it is important to keep these broader questions in view. Not least, it is important to raise the question of whether there is scope for substantial progress at the level of articulating general theory as an underpinning for the evolution of future practice in supporting strategic decision processes. This will be the theme of the next two sections of this chapter, and will set a context for the discussion of more practical issues in the later sections.

So where's the theory?

Can the strategic choice approach, as presented here, claim to have any coherent basis in the realm of theory? This question was raised by Jackson (1991) in a review in the journal *Systems Practice* of Rosenhead's book *Rational Analysis for a Problematic World* (1989). Of the six contrasting approaches to problem-structuring presented in that book, Jackson expressed a preference for those of Checkland and Eden both of which, in his view, could demonstrate clear theoretical roots. In contrast, he saw the strategic choice approach as rooted more in applied common sense than in any recognisable domain of theory.

Jackson writes as a systems scientist, in a journal dedicated primarily to issues of systems theory and systems practice. The two approaches which he prefers can indeed be claimed to have identifiable theoretical roots, in the respective domains of systems theory and cognitive psychology. However, what gives them added significance is the way in which Checkland and Eden have developed innovative methods of working with clients drawing on these respective roots, deviating from yet enriching the relevant domains of theory in the process.

It is indeed not so easy to point to any acknowledged domain of theory as containing the seeds of the strategic choice approach. Historically, its origins can be traced to the experience of two major research projects in which the behaviour of groups engaged in complex real-time decision processes was observed over long periods by inter-disciplinary teams of Tavistock Institute staff. The topics of these two seminal projects were communications in the building industry and policy-making in city government, as reported briefly in Chapter 1 and discussed in more depth elsewhere (Higgin and Jessop, 1965; Crichton, 1966; Friend and Jessop 1977).

The research strategy of each of these projects was guided initially by systems concepts. However, the seminal experience in each case was one of observing and seeking to interpret processes of group *decision-making* within a complex web of interconnected meetings – formal and informal, public and private – with subtle and ever-shifting interfaces between political, operational and technical domains. In the city government project in particular, it was observed that issues of topical significance tended to move from one organisational agenda to another through diverse channels – in the process frequently converging or merging with other issues, and so changing shape in subtle and often unpredictable ways.

It became apparent that the course of these processes was deeply influenced by individual or collective judgements as to how to move forward in the face of many competing forms of *uncertainty*. So the project team found itself turning increasingly to a *decision-centred* as opposed to a *system-centred* view.

Subsequently, the strategic choice approach was to grow to maturity through over two decades of experience in facilitating decision-making groups within a succession of action research projects set within a variety of organisational – and often inter-organisational – fields. In these projects, the authors found themselves relating to diverse clients and collaborators – acting at times primarily in a research role and at times primarily in a facilitation role. Indeed, in retrospect, it is the *alternation* of these two types of role, rather than the maintenance at all times of a finely-judged balance between action and research, that has provided the platform for the progressive development of the theory that underpins the strategic choice approach.

Therefore, the strategic choice approach can be seen as an example of a body of methods built more on what is sometimes called *grounded theory* (Glaser and Strauss, 1967) than on any recognised body of *received theory* as taught in academic schools. During this process, reference was indeed made to a number of existing theoretical frameworks. However, often these had to be set aside, where they did not appear to have sufficient to offer in explaining the complex phenomena which were being observed.

In addition to the various strands of systems theory, there is a different yet equally well-established domain of *decision theory*, upon which the Tavistock research teams had the opportunity to draw – some of it building on mathematical foundations, and on probability theory in particular, while some of it draws more on the insights of behavioural scientists. The work of these two partially interwoven strands has been reviewed by Watson and Buede (1987).

However, most of the published work in decision theory, and in the related domain of *game theory* (Raiffa, 1968), tends to adopt a relatively localised focus on *episodes* in a decision process, without addressing its longer-term developmental character. The theory of games does introduce two or more interacting parties to the process; while the writings of Howard (1971), Bennett (1980), Bryant (1989) and their associates pursue broader issues arising from differing perceptions of the nature of the 'game' between the parties and the influence of what can be seen as non-rational behaviour. This work has gradually led them to forsake the metaphor of the *game* for that of the *drama* (Bryant, 1993).

An emergent scientific domain?

Is it possible to find a convenient phrase through which to describe the body of grounded theory, rooted more in decision theory than in systems theory, which has provided the motor for the subsequent evolution and widespread application of the strategic choice approach?

In searching for an appropriate phrase, it now appears wise to avoid the adjective *strategic*. For the two related words *strategic* and *strategy* have acquired a high profile over the last two decades in the world of business, and especially in the international business schools. In the business context, the concept of strategy has come to bear particular connotations of central guidance of the autonomous commercial enterprise, operating in what is usually seen as an essentially competitive environment. Such an emphasis, in our view, tends to bring simplifications of theory which can be helpful in the business context, but which lead some distance away from the foundations of grounded theory on which the strategic choice approach is built.

So an alternative phrase will now be proposed which does not carry this connotation: this phrase is *developmental decision theory*. As a description of an emergent body of theory within which the strategic choice approach can be located, this in turn can be seen as a springboard from which to speculate about a nascent field of academic study that might be called *developmental decision science*. Further, such a body of theory can be seen as providing conceptual foundations for a now quite well-established, if barely recognised, practice of *developmental decision support*: a practice which the two authors of this book – among others – can claim to have helped to pioneer.

Before going further, it is important to recognise that the adjective *developmental*, like such words as *strategy* and *system*, can invoke all kinds of differing associations for different people – not all of which may be helpful in seeking to identify the essence of this emergent field. Nevertheless, it is an adjective that has advantages compared with possible alternatives such as *evolutionary*, in that it does not carry any connotations of underlying forces or grand design. This in turn should make it potentially more useful in identifying the essential characteristics of an experience which is shared by many people, acting in many different roles in different contexts.

For the same person may become involved in developing a personal career; in developing new skills; in developing a role within an organisation; in developing significant personal relationships with relatives, partners, children and friends; and in developing contractual links with other parties. In a political capacity, she or he may become involved in developing the economic, social or physical fabric of a village, a city or a region, or in a commercial role, in developing the local, national or transnational policies of a business enterprise.

All these various developmental roles may become interlinked in subtle and ever-changing patterns. Such patterns can, however, become difficult to analyse from a systems perspective, because of the transience of many of the interpersonal and inter-organisational relationships involved, and the complex and volatile patterns of linkage among the issues and agendas to be addressed.

This observation helps to underline the differences between the methods of the strategic choice approach and those of most forms of systems analysis. Unlike a typical systems diagram, a typical decision graph – such as those of Figures 12, 38, 44 or 46 in this book – may have to be redrawn from scratch once enough time has passed for important decisions to have been taken and new issues to have emerged. No longer is it enough to see the modelling of the change as just a question of making successive adjustments to an enduring representation of relationships which can be assumed to take a more systemic form.

It would be rash to argue that this emergent perspective of developmental decision science should be considered superior to that of systems science, or that it should supersede it in all circumstances. However, it has been our experience that methods which reflect the perspective of developmental decision theory can offer a speedier and less demanding starting point when offering support to managers than most of the commonly taught organisation-centred methods of strategic planning.

This is especially the case in inter-organisational domains. Here, it is especially appropriate that the strategic choice approach treats objectives and values not so much as firm foundations to be agreed at the outset of a process, but rather as sources of uncertainty to be addressed as and when they emerge as relevant to the decisions to be made.

The value of identifying a potential scientific domain of developmental decision theory is that it enables an important distinction to be drawn between any *specific* set of working methods, and an emergent *generic* field within which they can be located. This makes it possible to stand back from any one body of concepts and methods such as those presented in Chapters 1 to 10, and to ask questions about their shortcomings. This in turn invites explorations as to how far these shortcomings might be addressed by drawing on the experiences of other people and the concepts of other scientists.

This broader perspective can help in exploring why some users of strategic choice methods have sought to combine them with methods drawn from other sources. In what circumstances, for example, can it be considered *sufficient* to begin a strategic choice workshop by building a shared listing of decision areas or issues, without some kind of prior preparation using other methods?

Pursuing this example, one initial hypothesis might be that it is sufficient to start with a straight listing of issues in any situation where people are accustomed to meeting periodically in order to address a shared yet ever-evolving agenda. Where there is no such foundation of a shared agenda, there may be value in starting with some other type of problem-structuring activity in order to help people explore each other's perceptions and build a basis of shared experience – as in the applications by Ormerod (1996a, 1996b) and White (1994) mentioned earlier.

Mapping the challenges ahead

So what of the implications for future practice? The theme of the final section of our first edition was the *educational challenge* – the challenge of transferring appropriate skills to new generations through the medium of educational systems.

Our experiences over the last decade have made it clear that this is a challenge which is intimately bound up with several other types of challenge – some of them with a more immediate bearing on the momentum of progress in methods for supporting developmental decision-making.

Agreement on the significance of some of these other challenges has emerged in the course of recent exploratory workshops to review ways of promoting the wider use of the strategic choice approach and related methods in such varied cultural settings as Japan, Scandanavia and Brazil. Among the priorities to emerge have been the training of consultants in relevant facilitation skills; the development of appropriate sponsorship structures; and various aspects of cross-cultural technology transfer – beginning with the translation of books and software, yet recognising that the transfer of appropriate skills and experience must always be viewed as a two-way process.

A potential starting point in exploring the cross-connections among these various challenges is offered in Figure 97. This presents what is in effect no more than a form of semi-structured checklist setting out several of the issues – 35 in all – that seem to be particularly relevant to the future advancement of the strategic choice approach; and indeed also to the wider advancement of the theory and the practice of developmental decision-making.

These issues are shown clustered into eight overlapping domains, concerned respectively with *research, methodology, facilitation, communication, technology, sponsorship, application* and *education*. The domain of *methodology* is here viewed as embodying the choice of specific analytical methods to support developmental decisions, as contrasted with the development of electronic and other *technologies* which can play a significant supporting role.

As a conceptual map, Figure 97 is intended merely to serve as a stimulus to further thought; it is not intended to be definitive in any way. Because our primary concern is with developing *methodology* for supporting *communication* among decision-makers, these two domains are placed in pivotal positions; the other six domains are positioned in such a way as to bring out some of the more significant areas of overlap – recognising these to be by no means the only ones. The domains of *facilitation* and *application* have been located within the central cluster to reflect our own primary concerns in our consulting roles – while the other four domains of *research, technology, sponsorship* and *education* appear in more peripheral positions, as these are domains in which we must look to other people to play the leading roles.

Although no attempt will be made to do so here, it would be feasible to use Figure 97 as a starting point for deeper analysis of the issues and their relationships. In so doing, it would be possible to adopt either the strategic choice language of interconnected decision areas or the conventions of any other problem-structuring method. Indeed, readers are encouraged to undertake such exercises for themselves – either on their own or in discussion with colleagues – starting from the areas of greatest concern to them in their own work and altering or extending the map of issues in whatever ways they may choose.

In order to identify the areas of development which we ourselves see as most critical as this edition goes to press, twelve of the 35 issues in Figure 97 have been picked out in bold typeface. It is these issues which have become of great-

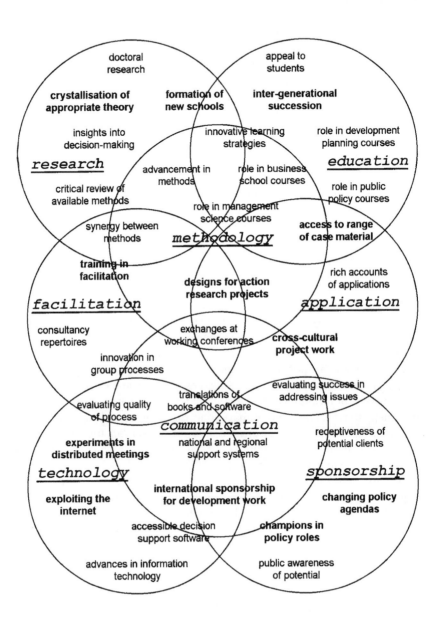

est concern to us in sustaining the future momentum of our own work, recognising that our future influence will be restricted by the reality that we operate primarily as consultants and facilitators rather than in academic or sponsorship roles; and recognising too that, now that we are both in our sixties, we must look primarily to others to sustain the momentum in the longer term.

The factors underlying our own particular concern with these twelve issues will be explained more fully in the brief guided tour of Figure 97 that follows. This tour will start in the top left corner, picking up the concerns with development of theory that have just been discussed. It will then progress in an anti-clockwise sequence, touching wherever relevant on the central themes of methodology and communication and concluding by revisiting the challenge to educational systems which provided the closing theme for our first edition.

A tour of some of the significant issues

Starting in the realm of *research*, it has already been argued that much of the strength of the strategic choice approach lies in its foundation of grounded theory, generated through successive applied research and consulting contracts. However, because the approach has so far evolved outside the setting of an academic school, it has not benefited as much as other comparable approaches from research of a more scholarly kind, in which doctoral and other postgraduate students can have a significant role to play. This has meant that there has been little critical comparison of its strengths and weaknesses with those of alternative approaches, and only modest progress so far towards broader synthesis of theory.

It is a recognition of the benefits of achieving such a critical mass of scholarly research that has prompted us to highlight the **formation of new schools** and **crystallisation of appropriate theory** in Figure 97. We are aware of isolated pieces of doctoral research in the strategic choice approach in several countries; yet initiatives to attract sponsorship for an academic centre focussed specifically on the strategic choice approach have not as yet borne fruit. The emergent concept of *developmental decision science* could now, in our view, offer a broader and more challenging focus for a research initiative of this kind.

The practice of *facilitation* of collaborative decision processes has emerged as a leading area of concern in many of the cultures and the policy fields in which we have worked. So, reflecting the priorities expressed in several recent cross-cultural discussions, the issue of **training in facilitation** appears highlighted in Figure 97.

Underlying the challenge of disseminating facilitation skills in different cultures are to be found the challenges of developing appropriate organisational contexts for interactive working. For, however evident may be the benefits of a process of face-to-face interaction under the guidance of an experienced facilitator, the process of setting up an informal workshop-style event tends to demand a considerable investment of organisational resources in advance, in which more formal and bureaucratic procedures tend to come into play. Dates have to be agreed in diaries; a suitable venue has to be negotiated (Hickling, 1990); the services of an experienced facilitator or facilitation team have to be secured; and supplies of essential materials (see Figure 83) must be arranged.

So it is that – somewhat paradoxically – even a small informal workshop can call for a high degree of relatively formal organisation in advance. This is especially likely if people from several different departments or organisations are involved, and lines of authority in convening the workshop are therefore not well-defined. So it is not perhaps surprising that it has been found far from easy to establish the 'workshop mode' of decision-making as an established and enduring feature of organisational arrangements for decision-making, except in circumstances where there has been a continuing commitment from people in powerful policy roles.

New technology to the rescue?

In overcoming such barriers to interactive working, it is now widely argued that new *technology* based on electronic media of communication can play an important and expanding role. Over the last decade, interest has grown rapidly in the use of *electronic meeting systems* (Mockler and Dologite, 1991, Nunamaker et al., 1991, Vogel, 1993) to overcome many of the perceived deficiencies of conventional management meetings, such as the biases resulting from the tendency of the views of some of the more forceful participants to overshadow the contributions of others.

Furthermore, the difficulty and expense of bringing busy people together for a conventional meeting, especially where considerable travel is involved, have led to a growing interest in *remote conferencing methods* – fuelled by recent rapid advances in the technology and the economics of global telecommunication networks.

As yet, electronic meeting systems have focussed largely on basic procedures for brainstorming, voting and recording within meetings, rather than on methods for building a shared appreciation of the *complexity* of the issues to be addressed. In several places, a modest start is now being made in exploring the potential for innovation in working with complexity through computer networks. For example, some simple trials have now been held in exchanging STRAD project files over the internet, enabling one user to comment on a problem formulation suggested by another and to propose changes.

One response to the receipt of a map of the issues that concern another user might be that none of the issues covered are of any significant concern to the recipient. Another response might be to identify connections between some of those issues and some of the issues on the recipient's own current agenda – connections which in some cases might be of sufficient importance as to lead to proposals for collaborative working on the development and comparison of options. An intermediate level of response might be to suggest changes in the formulation of some issues, so as to bring out more clearly matters of shared concern. Thus, patterns of interdependence would be expected to emerge more clearly, and groups of people in different locations might agree to come together – whether physically or through electronic channels – for periods of intensive workshop-style activity on issues of relatively intense joint concern. Inevitably, such a development will demand close attention to the evolution of sets of rules or protocols governing access to the information generated by others.

With such prospects in view, the two interrelated issues of **experiments in distributed meetings** and **exploiting the internet** are shown highlighted in the *technology* domain of Figure 97. It is, however, important that any development work in this field should be driven by the concerns of users rather than by technological imperatives. This raises concerns of appropriate *sponsorship* and, given the growing international dimensions of important environmental, social and economic issues, leads to the highlighting in the diagram of **international sponsorship for development work**.

Such sponsorship is only likely to be forthcoming if development work can keep pace with **changing policy agendas** and attract support from **champions in policy roles**. What can be achieved given such a level of commitment can be seen from the recent experiences of national and international collaboration within projects addressed to major environmental issues in Europe which have led to the extensions in process management discussed in Chapter 11.

A related realm of intense international policy concern in which strategic choice methods have been demonstrating their potential, as indicated in the Guide to further reading, is that of *sustainable development* in areas of rapid population growth yet sparse economic resources, as are to be found in many parts of Asia, Africa and Latin America.

At the time this edition goes to press, this is an area of direct concern to champions of the strategic choice approach of several nationalities who work in consulting and academic roles in these parts of the world. Consequently, a modest experiment has now been launched in the use of the internet to enable an informal 'club' of such people – hitherto working in isolation from each other – to communicate multilaterally, rather than through more conventional bilateral channels. Among the objects of this new network are to explore along what lines collaborative proposals might be designed, and in what ways international sponsors might be approached to support an increased momentum of development work in this field.

Within the domain of *application*, these concerns help to explain the emphasis given in Figure 97 to **cross-cultural project work** and to **designs for action research projects** – which can together be seen as important means of building a wider body of evidence as to the role that strategic choice and related collaborative planning methods can play in important realms of policy. Such evidence will only be convincing to the extent that performance in addressing issues of concern has been continuously *evaluated*. It is equally important that accounts of the applications should be widely published, written with a sufficient level of richness to reveal to others the nature of the learning experience for the participants as well as the nature and impact of the direct policy outcomes.

The educational challenge

Turning finally to the domain of *education*, the focus switches from ongoing applications of collaborative planning methods to a longer-term question: that of how the hard-won skills of practitioners and facilitators, built on cumulative experience in working under real-time pressures of complexity, uncertainty and conflict, can be made widely accessible to their successors in new generations.

When this question of **inter-generational succession** was posed in the concluding section of our first edition, it was argued that the world's educational systems have come to deploy substantial resources; yet, all too often, there remain obstinate gaps between the experience of those responsible for grappling with complex problems in the present and the resources of those responsible for helping new generations to profit from that experience.

Over the last ten years, there has been some encouraging progress in this direction. For the strategic choice approach and related methods have now become more widely taught in universities: especially in schools of management science and urban and regional planning, and to a lesser extent in schools of business and of public policy. Yet there are still many such schools whose staff remain either unaware of these methods, or unconvinced that their relevance is such as to justify a significant place on their courses.

Some of the most encouraging experiences have been in introducing the strategic choice approach to mature students. Among these have been part-time students on MBA course in business schools, most of whom have the direct management experience to be able to relate the concepts offered – such as the decision graph, the tripartite classification of uncertainty and the commitment package – to the issues with which they are currently engaged in their own organisational roles.

With such students, it has usually proved possible to set up a rich dialogue in which questions posed within a strategic choice framework are used to draw out the key characteristics of important and pressing issues on their own management agendas. The student's experience can then be 'mined' by questioning either from the course tutor or from another student; for this purpose, a simple checklist has been designed, drawing on strategic choice principles. It has proved especially effective to use this checklist within the context of a 'mutual facilitation' exercise in which the students work in threes, rotating through problem owner, consultant and reporter roles.

With undergraduate students or younger postgraduates, there is less scope for drawing on rich veins of personal management experience. So, to preserve the important principle of experiential learning, it becomes important to arrange **access to a range of case material** which is relevant to the theme of the course; and this is a demand that will be more readily met where there is a reservoir of rich accounts of practical applications on which to draw.

Often we have found ourselves working, in Britain or in other countries, alongside senior academic staff who are enthusiastic about the potential of the strategic choice approach, yet feel inhibited by a lack of personal experience in group facilitation roles. In universities, not all teaching staff find it easy to build experience in such roles – for reasons that may vary from the tyranny of teaching, supervision and examination timetables to a lack of consulting access to other organisations.

Much of the progress to date in the methodology of the strategic choice approach has been sustained through the willingness of governmental and other clients to sponsor experimental projects with a substantial action research content. Among these have been projects in which academics as well as consultants and action researchers – several of them with a background of work with the Tavistock Institute – have worked intensively alongside managers and planners, with complex yet often urgent matters of substance on the agenda.

Sustaining progress

In conclusion, we believe that sustainable progress in the practical business of supporting collaborative planning on important issues of shared concern will demand an underpinning of increasingly well-grounded theory – within the broad realm to which we have given the label of *developmental decision science*. The pace of future progress must also continue to depend – as it has over the last decade – on a rich fabric of interactions among people in consulting, academic, planning and management roles. For it is only in this way that the daunting barriers of national or professional culture, and of mother tongue, can be gradually surmounted, while important issues of deep complexity, uncertainty and potential for conflict are resolutely addressed.

The practical challenges to be faced in developing such a fabric of cross-connecting activities include in particular those which appear in the central *methodology* and *communication* domains of Figure 97. In our own work with associates in many countries, there is already a wealth of experience on which others can draw when designing action research projects, interchanges at working conferences and other such events.

The issue of sponsorship of such activities, as ever, remains a critical one; and the more this can be mobilised through international agencies, the wider the pool of human resources of experience and skill on which it will be possible to draw.

In sustaining this overall momentum, it is important not to forget the long-term significance of some of the issues that occupy more peripheral positions in the map of Figure 97. *Public awareness of the potential* of interactive styles of working must be raised and sustained; the *increasing capabilities of information technology* should be harnessed in imaginative ways; *doctoral research* in universities should play its role in advancing the frontiers of knowledge; and, last but not least, this broad field of knowledge and of practice should demonstrate an *appeal to students* on the threshold of their careers.

It is our belief that the influence and inspiration of people in many roles – managers, planners, academics, researchers, students, consultants and politicians – will be essential if future decision-makers are to be helped to make imaginative use, selectively and adaptively, of the ideas presented here.

For these ideas are built on many people's experiences in planning under pressure – people whose working lives are finite, even though there can be no respite in the challenges facing the many organisations, large and small, which share responsibility for the future of a troubled planet.

A guide to further reading

Introduction

In this section of the first edition, the observation was made that many of the things that had been written about the strategic choice approach and its applications were not very accessible to would-be readers, because they remained buried in conference proceedings, reports to government departments and other sponsors, and internal working papers.

It is satisfying now to be able to report that, over the last decade, this situation has started to change for the better. Therefore, while references to all the more accessible earlier publications will still be found in the bibliography, they will be mentioned more briefly in this revised guide, under headings similar to those used in the first edition.

The first of the sections that follow will review the principal general accounts of the strategic choice approach published in English. This will be followed by a section listing published applications of the approach; then by a section listing some publications and translations in other languages. Finally, a few suggestions are offered for reading to help set the approach in the context of other developments in decision support methods since the publication of the first edition.

Principal English language sources

The first book to introduce the basic concepts and methods of the strategic choice approach was *Local Government and Strategic Choice: An Operational Research Approach to the Processes of Public Planning*, by John Friend and the late Neil Jessop (Friend and Jessop, 1977) This was first published by Tavistock Publications of London in 1969 (ISBN 422 73050 5), a second edition (ISBN 0 08 021451 7) being published in 1977 by Pergamon of Oxford.

A subsequent book used the strategic choice framework to explore issues of inter-organisational planning in the public domain. This is *Public Planning: The Inter-Corporate Dimension* (Friend, Power and Yewlett, 1974) (London: Tavistock Publications, ISBN 0422 74450 6). Both this book and *Local Government and Strategic Choice* are now out of print, but should still be available through libraries.

The bibliography that follows this section also includes some early references to the logical design method of Analysis of Interconnected Decision Areas (AIDA), which is the basis of the analytical methods used in the shaping and designing modes of the strategic choice approach (Higgin and Jessop, 1965, Harary, Jessop, Luckman and Stringer, 1995, Crichton 1966, Luckman 1967, Morgan 1971).

More recently, the book *Rational Analysis for a Problematic World* (ed. Rosenhead, 1989) has presented the strategic choice approach as one of a set of six new interactive approaches to the structuring of complex problems. Chapter 6 by Friend introduces the basic methods, illustrated in this instance by an industrial case example, while Chapter 7 by Hickling describes an application to national policy development in the Netherlands.

Relevant journal articles and chapters in edited volumes include Friend, Norris and Stringer (1988), on the history of the Institute for Operational Research; and Stringer (1967) and Friend, (1993a) on multi-organisational decision-making. Separate contributions by Friend and Hickling will be found in another edited volume *Tackling Strategic Problems: The Role of Group Decision Support* (ed. Eden and Radford, 1990). The contribution by Friend discusses the handling of organisational complexity in group decision support, while that by Hickling discusses the practical art of designing appropriate 'decision spaces' for group decision-making.

Three general articles on the strategic choice approach addressed to different readerships will be found in Friend (1993b, 1993c, 1995); while Hickling has discussed recent developments in Breure and Hickling (1990) and in Hickling and de Jong (1990) – the latter being written in Dutch.

Brief discussions of the STRAD software will be found in Cartwright, (1992); Friend, (1992); and Friend, (1996).

Published applications

The limited number of published applications that could be quoted at the time the first edition went to press have been retained in the bibliography. The references are Friend, Wedgwood-Oppenheim et al (1970); Bunker (1974); Bather, Williams and Sutton (1976): Hickling (1978); Ferguson (1979); Dekker et al. (1978), Dekker and Mastop (1979); and van de Graf (1985). Other publications in this period which refer to at least some of the methods and concepts in an applied setting are Friend and Hunter (1970); Friend (1976); Floyd (1978); Friend (1977); Friend (1980); Friend, Laffin and Norris (1981); Hall (1980); Ormerod (1983) and Dello (1985).

Over the last ten years, the number of published applications has steadily increased, with considerable variation both in field of application and in level of description. Among the newer references to applied work that will be found in the bibliography are Hickling (1989) relating to governmental policy for transport of dangerous petrochemicals in the Netherlands; van Steenbergen (1990) on regional development planning in Indonesia; Ling (1990) on airport development in Hong Kong; Moullin (1991) on involvement of mothers in developing local maternity services; Thunhurst et al. (1992) on cooperative housing management; Khakee and Stromberg (1993) on hard-to-let housing in Sweden; Swanson (1994) on integrated transport planning; Holt (1994) on arms control negotiations; White (1994) on rural industry in Belize; and Ormerod (1995, 1996a, 1996b) on the design of information systems strategies for a major supermarket chain and an international mining corporation.

Publications in other languages

An abridged translation of *Local Government and Strategic Choice* into German was published in 1973 (Friend and Jessop, 1973), while the first edition of *Planning under Pressure* was translated into Japanese by Koike et al and published by Gihodo of Tokyo in 1991 (Friend and Hickling, 1991).

In addition, the following briefer handbooks on the strategic choice approach have been published in languages other than English. Several of these were adapted from an English language handbook by Allen Hickling, first published in Britain (Hickling, 1974) and subsequently in Canada in extended form (Hickling, 1976):

Dutch: Werken met Strategische Keuze by Hickling, A. Hartman, R. and Meester, J. Alpen aan den Rijn: Samson Uitverij, 1976.
Dutch: Mens en Beleid by Hickling, A. and de Jong, A. Leiden/Antwerpen: Stenfort Kroese, 1990.
French: Technologie de la Decision Complexe by Hickling, A., Wilkin, L. and Debreyne, F. Brussels: Universite Libre de Bruxelles, 1980.
Portuguese: Abordagem de Escolha Estrategica by Hickling A. Sao Paulo: Fundacao do Desenvolvimento Administrativo, 1985.
Swedish: Planera met Osakerheter! by Stromberg, K. Stockholm: Byggforskningsradet, 1986.
Bahasa Indonesia: Modul Pendekatan Pilihan Strategis by Ismail, M., Setiabudi, T. and van Steenbergen, F. Aceh: Bappeda Provinsi Daerah Istimewa Aceh, 1989.

Wider reading

During the late eighties and early nineties, a number of publications have appeared which help to set the strategic choice approach in the context of wider developments in such varied fields as strategic business management, problem structuring methods, urban and regional planning theory, operational research and participatory community development.

Reference has already been made earlier in this guide to the two edited books *Rational Analysis for a Problematic World* (ed. Rosenhead, 1989) and *Tackling Strategic Problems: The Role of Group Decision Support* (ed. Eden and Radford, 1990). Alongside our own chapters on the methods and applications of the strategic choice approach, the former book includes similar brief accounts of five other participative methods for the structuring of complex problems, all presented by British authors who have played a leading role in their development. These are, respectively, SODA (Strategic Options Development and Analysis (Eden); Soft Systems Methodology (Checkland); robustness analysis (Rosenhead); metagame analysis (Howard) and hypergame analysis (Bennett, Huxham and Cropper). Rosenhead as editor has set the context in opening and concluding chapters.

Tackling Strategic Problems (Eden and Radford, 1990) differs in focus by including North American as well as British contributions, and by being organised in terms of overall themes such as groups and organisations; support for groups; mixing methods; the use of computers; and the working environment. The book *Problem Management* by Bryant (1989) also touches on many of these themes, with the metaphor of drama well to the fore.

Various brief accounts of the use of problem-structuring methods, including the strategic choice approach, in working with community groups are offered in *Community Works* published by the Operational Research Society (Ritchie, Taket and Bryant, 1994). A useful overview of computer supported methods appears in a special issue of the *Environmental Professional* (15 (2), 1993), while strategic choice methods are set in the context of other developments in planning theory by Sagar (1993) in the journal *Planning Theory*.

A handbook on the use of consensus-building methods in environmental planning and decision-making, as discussed in Chapter 11, is obtainable from the Environment Council at the address given in the next section (*Beyond Compromise*, Environment Council, 1995).

Moving to the business field, *Change Everything at Once!* (Neumann, Holti and Standing, 1995) is a new guide to building a teamwork approach in manufacturing by staff of the Tavistock Institute's Organisational Change and Technological Innovation Group. This draws on many aspects of Tavistock experience including the strategic choice approach, demonstrating how they can be adapted to help organisations who feel themselves besieged by multiple pressures for change in such diverse areas as business strategy, job design, personnel policy, financial systems, information technology, manufacturing and quality assurance. Meanwhile, an important collection of writings related to the work of the Tavistock Institute over the years has appeared in three edited volumes (Trist and Murray 1990; Trist and Murray 1993; Trist, Emery and Murray 1997) with a review of the development of the strategic choice approach in the final volume.

In the first edition, readers were referred also to the seven issues of the *Linkage* periodical and various project reports produced by the Institute for Operational Research and its successor unit during the late seventies and the early eighties, and to a training video produced in Canada. The relevance of these has inevitably diminished with time, but reference can be made to John Friend on *Linkage*; to Allen Hickling on the video; and to either author on project reports and other IOR documents.

Points of contact

The authors can be contacted as follows:

John Friend   Stradspan Limited,
5 Bar Road North,
Beckingham,
DONCASTER, South Yorkshire
DN10 4NN   United Kingdom
Phone/fax (+44) (0)1427-848026
e-mail jfriend@syspace.co.uk

Allen Hickling   Allen Hickling and Associates,
2 The Old Bakery,
Church Road,
Long Itchington,
RUGBY, Warwickshire
CV23 8PW   United Kingdom
Phone (+44) (0)1926-817048
Fax (+44)(0)1926-815385
e-mail hickling@netcomuk.co.uk

Enquiries about **training, facilitation** and **consulting services** can be addressed to either author.

Enquiries about the **STRAD software** should be addressed to Stradspan Limited at the first address given above. Readers of *Planning under Pressure* are welcome to ask for a **free copy of the latest demonstration disk.** News on recent developments will be found on Stradspan's site on the world wide web at

http://www.fdgroup.co.uk/neo/strad/

Contact information follows for the Tavistock Institute; the Operational Research Society; the Environment Council; and various associates around the world who are active in the application or teaching of strategic choice methods.

The Tavistock Institute

30 Tabernacle Street, LONDON EC2A 4DE, UK
tel (+44) (0)171-417-0407 fax (+44) (0)171-417-0566

Contact points in Organisational Change and Technological Innovation pro-gramme: Dr. Jean Neumann (jean.neumann@tavinstitute.org) or Dr Richard Holti (rholti@tavinstitute.org).

The Operational Research Society

Seymour House, 12, Edward Street, BIRMINGHAM B1 2RX, UK
tel (+44) (0)121-233-9300   fax (+44) (0)121-233-0321

The Society's training programme includes periodic short courses in the strategic choice approach and other participative management science methods. E-mail enquiries via email@orsoc.org.uk.

The Environment Council

21 Elizabeth Street, LONDON SW1W 9RP, UK
tel (+44) (0)171-824-8111   fax (+44) (0)171-730-9941
e-mail environment.council@ukonline.co.uk

Allen Hickling is a member of the Council's Environmental Resolve committee, which provides training and consultancy services.

Associates in other countries

Abraham Breure, Netherlands	abreure@xs4all.nl
Tim Cartwright, Denmark	tjcman@carlbro.dk
Bolisomi Ebengo-Mbaku, Zaire	fax (+243) 884-0291
Gordon Erens, Australia	gordon@real.com.au
Jorge Giordani, Venezuela	jgiordani@eldish.lat.net
Rory Hunkin, South Africa	roryhunk@cis.co.za
Arnold de Jong, Greece	fax (+30) 1-973-2475
Detef Kammeier, Thailand	kammeier@ait.ac.th
Hirotaka Koike, Japan	koike@utsunomiya-u.ac.jp
Maria Angela Campelo de Melo, Brazil	macm@venus.rdc.puc-rio.br
John Russell-Hodge, Fiji	russellhodge@usp.ac
Nancy Sherman, Canada	nsherman@gbrownc.on.ca
Frank van Steenbergen, Netherlands	106523.1116@compuserve.com
Knut Stromberg, Sweden	knut@arch.chalmers.se

Many of these associates operate as consultants, facilitators and trainers not only in their own countries but worldwide; most of them also share an interest in the use of strategic choice methods in participatory planning and sustainable develop-ment in third world countries. New members continue to become associated with the network as it extends and evolves.

References

ACKOFF RL (1970) A Concept of Corporate Planning. New York: Wiley

ACKOFF RL (1974) Redesigning the Future. New York: Wiley

ACLAND, AF (1990) A Sudden Outbreak of Common Sense: Managing Conflict through Mediation. London: Hutchinson Business Books

ACLAND, AF (1995) Resolving Disputes without Going to Court. London: Business Books

ASHBY WR (1956) An introduction to Cybernetics. London: Chapman and Hall.

BALBO M (1975) La Pianificazione come Processo di Scelte Strategiche. In P Ceccarelli (ed) Potere e Piani Urbanistica. Milano: Franco Angeli Editore

BATHER NJ, WILLIAMS CM and SUTTON A (1976) Strategic Choice in Practice: The West Berkshire Structure Plan Experience. Reading, UK: University of Reading, Geographical Paper No 50

BATTY SE (1977) Game-Theoretic Approaches to Urban Planning and Design. In: Environment and Planning B 4, 211–39

BEER S (1966) Decision and Control. Chichester: Wiley

BENNETT P (1980) Hypergames: Developing a Model of Conflict. In: Futures, 12, 489–507

BENNETT P (1985) On Linking Approaches to Decision Aiding: Issues and Prospects. In: Journal of the Operational Research Society 36, 659-69

BENNETT P, CROPPER S and HUXHAM C (1989) Modelling Interactive Decisions: The Hypergame Focus. In: Rational Analysis for a Problematic World, ed. J.V. Rosenhead. Chichester: Wiley

BENNETT P and HUXHAM CS (1982) Hypergames and What They Do: A 'Soft OR' Approach. In: Journal of the Operational Research Society 33, 41–50

BION WR (1961) Experiences in Groups. London: Tavistock Publications

BREURE A and HICKLING A (1990) Coping with Unconventional Projects: a "Socio-Technical" Approach. In: Handbook of Management Projects, ed. R. Garies. Vienna: Manz

BRYANT JW (1989) Problem Management. Chichester/New York: Wiley

BRYANT JW (1993) OR Enactment: the Theatrical Metaphor as an Analytical Framework. In: Journal of the Operational Research Society 44, 551-561

BUNKER R (1974) Making Decisions in St Albans. In: Built Environment 1974, 316–8

CARTWRIGHT TJ (1992) STRAD: a New Role for Computers in Planning. In: Computers, Environment and Urban Systems, 16, 77–82

CHAMBERS R (1983) Rural Development: Putting the Last First. Harlow: Longman

CHECKLAND PB (1981) Systems Thinking, Systems Practice. Chichester: Wiley

CHECKLAND PB (1989) Soft Systems Methodology. In: Rational Analysis for a Problematic World, ed. J.V. Rosenhead. Chichester: Wiley

CHILD J (1972) Organisational Structure, Environment and Performance: The Role of Strategic Choice. In: Sociology 6, 2-22

CLARK AW (1976) Experimenting with Organisational Life: The Action Research Approach. New York: Plenum

CRICHTON (ed) (1966) Interdependence and Uncertainty: A Study of the Building Industry. London: Tavistock Publications

DALKEY NC (1969) The Delphi Method: An Experimental Study of Group Opinions. Memorandum RM–5888–PR. Santa Monica, Calif: Rand Corporation

DEKKER F and MASTOP P (1979) Strategic Choice: An Application in Dutch Planning Practice. In: Planning Outlook 22, 87–96

DEKKER F et al (1978) A Multi-Level Application of Strategic Choice at the Sub-Regional Level. In: Town Planning Review 49, 149-62

DELBECQ AL, VAN DE VEN AH and GUSTAFSON DH (1975) Group Techniques for Programme Planning. Glenview, Illinois: Scott Foresman and Company

DELLO P (1985) Strategic Choice and Evaluation: Some Methodological Considerations. In: Faludi A and Voogd H (eds) Evaluation of Complex Policy Problems. Delft: Delftsche Uitgevers Maatschappij

DOYLE M and STRAUS D (1976) How to Make Meetings Work: Jove

EDEN C (1989) Using Cognitive Mapping for Strategic Options Development and Analysis (SODA). In: Rational Analysis for a Problematic World, ed. J.V. Rosenhead. Chichester: Wiley

EDEN C and JONES S (1984) Using Repertory Grids for Problem Construction. In: Journal of the Operational Research Society 35, 779-90

EDEN C, JONES S and SIMS D (1983) Messing about in Problems. Oxford: Pergamon

EDEN C, JONES S, SIMS D and SMITHIN T (1981) The Intersubjectivity of Issues and Issues of Intersubjectivity. In: Journal of Management Studies 18, 34-47

EDEN C and RADFORD J (1990) Tackling Strategic Problems. London: Sage

EDEN C, WILLIAMS H and SMITHIN T (1986) Synthetic Wisdom: The Design of a Mixed Mode Modelling System for Organisational Decision Making. In: Journal of the Operational Research Society 37, 233-42

EMERY FE and TRIST EL (1972) Towards a Social Ecology: Contextual Appreciation of the Future in the Present. London: Plenium

ETZIONI A (1968) The Active Society: A Theory of Societal and Political Processes. New York: The Free Press

FALUDI A (1973) Planning Theory. Oxford: Pergamon

FALUDI A (1984) The Return of Rationality. In: Breheny MJ and Hooper AJ (eds) Rationality in Planning. London: Pion 1984

FALUDI A (1986) Critical Rationalism and Planning Methodology. London: Pion Press

FALUDI A (1987) A Decision Centred View of Environmental Planning. Oxford: Pergamon

FALUDI A and MASTOP JM (1982) The IOR School – The Development of a Planning Methodology. In: Environment and Planning B 9, 241–56

FERGUSON MJ (1979) A Strategic Choice Approach to Recreation Site Resource acquisition. In: Town Planning Review 50, 325–45

FISHER R and BROWN S (1989) Getting Together: Building a Relationship that Gets to Yes. London: Business Books

FISHER R and URY W (1982) Getting to Yes. London: Hutchinson

FLOOD RL and JACKSON MC (1991) Creative Problem Solving: Total Systems Intervention. Chichester: John Wiley

FLOYD M (1978) Structure Plan Monitoring: Looking to the Future. In: Town Planning Review 49, 476–85

FRIEND JK (1976) Planners, Policies and Organisational Boundaries: Some Recent Developments in Britain. In: Policy and Politics 5, 25–46

FRIEND JK (1977) The Dynamics of Policy Change. In: Long Range Planning 10, 40–7

FRIEND JK (1980) Planning in a Multi-Organisational Context. In: Town Planning Review 51, 261–9

FRIEND JK (1988) Building on Public Sector Wisdom. In:Management Development in the Public Sector: a European Perspective, ed. R. Kakabadse, P. Brovetto and R. Holzer. Aldershot: Avebury

FRIEND JK (1988) The Institute for Operational Research: an Initiative to Extend the Scope of OR. In: Journal of the Operational Research Society, 39, 705–13 (with M.E. Norris and J. Stringer)

FRIEND JK (1989) Planning as Responsible Scheming. In: Operational Research and the Social Sciences, ed. M.C. Jackson, P. Keys and S.A. Cropper. New York: Plenum

FRIEND JK (1989) The Strategic Choice Approach. In: Rational Analysis for a Problematic World, ed. J.V. Rosenhead. Chichester: Wiley

FRIEND JK (1990) Handling Organizational Complexity in Group Decision Support. In: Tackling Strategic Problems: the Role of Group Decision Support, ed. C.L. Eden and J. Radford. London: Sage

FRIEND JK (1990) Planning Concepts, Planning Contexts. In: Systems Practice, 3, 195–206

FRIEND JK (1992) New Directions in Software for Strategic Choice. In: European Journal of Operational Research, 61, 154–64

FRIEND JK (1993) Searching for Appropriate Theory and Practice in Multi-Organisational Fields. In: Journal of the Operational Research Society, 44, 585–98

FRIEND JK (1993) The Strategic Choice Approach in Environmental Policy-Making. In: The Environmental Professional, 15, 164–75

FRIEND JK (1993) Planning in the Presence of Uncertainty: Principles and Practice. In: Journal of Infrastructure Planning and Management (Japan), *476/IV-21*, 1–9

FRIEND JK (1994) Community Involvement in Health Strategy in Tower Hamlets. In: Community Works, eds. C. Ritchie, A. Taket, J. Bryant. Birmingham: Operational Research Society

FRIEND JK (1995) Supporting Developmental Decision Processes: the Evolution of an OR Approach. In: International Transactions in Operational Research. *2*, 225–232

FRIEND JK (1996) Strategy on the Run: Decision Support for Hard-Pressed Managers. In: IT Support in the Productive Workplace, ed. J Chapman. Cheltenham: Stanley Thornes

FRIEND JK (1997) Connective Planning: from Practice to Theory and Back. In: The Social Engagement of Social Science. Volume III: the Socio-Ecological Perspective, Eds. E.L. TRIST, F. EMERY,. and H. MURRAY. Philadelphia: The University of Pennsylvania Press

FRIEND JK and HICKLING A (1991) The Strategic Choice Approach. Japanese translation of Planning under Pressure by Koike, H. et al. Tokyo: Gihodo

FRIEND JK and HUNTER JMH (1970) Multi-Organisational Decision Processes in the Planned Expansion of Towns. In: Environment and Planning *2*, 33-54

FRIEND JK and JESSOP WN (1977) Local Government and Strategic Choice: An Operational Research Approach to the Processes of Public Planning (Second Edition). Oxford: Pergamon. [First Edition (1969) – London: Tavistock Publications]

FRIEND JK and JESSOP WN (1971) Hvad er Planlaegning. In: BYPLAN *23*, 134–40

FRIEND JK and JESSOP WN (1973) Entscheidungsstrategie in Stadtplanung und Verwaltung. German translation by Zwirner WGO. Dusseldorf: Bertelsmann

FRIEND JK, LAFFIN MJ and NORRIS ME (1981) Competition in Public Policy: The Structure Plan as Arena. In: Public Administration *59*, 441-63

FRIEND JK, NORRIS ME and STRINGER J (1988) The Institute for Operational Research: an Initiative to Extend the Scope of OR. In: Journal of the Operational Research Society, *39*. 705–713

FRIEND JK, POWER JM and YEWLETT CJL (1974) Public Planning: The Inter–Corporate Dimension. London: Tavistock Publications

FRIEND JK, WEDGWOOD-OPPENHEIM F et al (1970) The LOGIMP Experiment: A Collaborative Exercise in the Application of a New Approach to Local Planning Problems. London: Centre for Environmental Studies (refer to Tavistock Institute of Human Relations)

GLASER B and STRAUSS AL (1967) The Discovery of Grounded Theory. Chicago: Aldine

GTZ (1991) Methods and Instruments for Project Planning and Implementation. Eschborn: Gesellschaft für Technische Zusammenarbeit

GUPTA SK and ROSENHEAD J (1968) Robustness in Sequential Investment

Decisions. In: Management Science *15*, 13-18

HALL P (1980) Great Planning Disasters. London: Weidenfeld & Nicholson

HARARY F, JESSOP WN, LUCKMAN J and STRINGER S (1965) Analysis of Interconnected Decision Areas: An Algorithm for Project Development. In: Nature *206*, 118

HART DA, HICKLING DA, NORRIS ME and SKELCHER CK (1980) Regional Planning Methodology. London: Tavistock Institute of Human Relations. Internal Paper 2T/436

HAWKINS L and HUDSON M (1986) Effective Negotiation. Melbourne: Information Australia

HICKLING A (1974) Managing Decisions: The Strategic Choice Approach. Rugby: Mantec (refer to Tavistock Institute of Human Relations, London)

HICKLING A (1976) Aids to Strategic Choice (Second Edition). Vancouver: University of British Colombia, Centre for Continuing Education

HICKLING A (1978) AIDA and the Levels of Choice in Structure Plans. In: Town Planning Review *49*, 459-75

HICKLING A (1979) Aids to Strategic Choice Revisited. London: Tavistock Institute of Human Relations. Internal Paper 2T/226

HICKLING A (1981) Abordagem da Escolha Estrategica. Sao Paulo: Fundacao do Desenvolvimento Administrativo

HICKLING A (1982) Beyond a Linear Iterative Process. In: Evans B, Powell J and Ralbot R (eds) Changing Design. Chichester: Wiley

HICKLING A (1985) Evaluation is a Five Finger Exercise. In: Faludi A and Voogd H (eds) Evaluation of Complex Policy Problems. Delft: Delftsche Uitgevers Maatschappij

HICKLING A (1989) Gambling with Frozen Fire? In: Rational Analysis for a Problematic World, ed. J.V. Rosenhead, Chichester/New York: Wiley, pp 159–192

HICKLING A (1990) Decision Spaces. In: Tackling Strategic Problems, eds. C. Eden and J. Radford London: Sage

HICKLING A and DE JONG A (1990) Mens en Beleid. Leiden/Antwerpen: Stenfert Kroese Uitgevers

HICKLING A, HARTMAN R and MEESTER JG (1976) Werken met Strategische Keuze. Alpen aan den Rijn: Samson Uitgeverij

HICKLING A, WILKIN L and DEBREYNE F (1980) Technologie de la Decision Complexe: Des Aides pour l'Elaboration des Choix Strategiques. Bruxelles: Universite Libre de Bruxelles, Centre E Bernheim pour l'Etude des Affaires

HIGGIN G and JESSOP WN (1965) Communications in the Building Industry: The Report of a Pilot Study. London: Tavistock Publications

HILL M (1968) A Goals-Achievement Matrix for Evaluating Alternative Plans. In: Journal of the American Institute of Planners *34*, 19-28

HILL M (1985) Decision-Making Contexts and Strategies for Evaluation. In: Faludi A and Voogd H (eds) Evaluation of Complex Policy Problems. Delft: Delftsche Uitgevers Maatschappij

HOLT J (1994) Disarming Defences. In: OR Insight *7* (4), 19–26. Birmingham:

Operational Research Society

HOWARD N (1971) Paradoxes of Rationality: The Theory of Metagames. London: MIT Press

HOWARD N (1989) The Manager as Politician and General: the Metagame Approach to Analysing Cooperation and Conflict. In: Rational Analysis for a Problematic World, ed. J.V. Rosenhead. Chichester: Wiley

HUXHAM, C (Ed) (1996) Creating Collaborative Advantage. London: Sage

ISMAEL M, SETIABUDI T and VAN STEENBERGEN, F (1989) Modul Pendekatan Pilihan Strategis (in Bahasa Indonesia). Aceh:Bappeda Provinsi Daerah Istimewa Aceh

JACKSON MC (1991) Review of Rational Analysis for a Problematic World (ed. Rosenhead) in Systems Practice 4 (3), 258–260

JACKSON MC (1992) Systems Methodology for the Management Sciences. New York: Plenum

JAGO L and NORRIS M (1981) Training in inter-Organisational Working: An Experimental Course. In: LINKAGE SIX. London: Tavistock Institute of Human Relations

JAGO L et al (1983) Strategies for Working between Organisations: A Training Experience Reviewed. In: LINKAGE SEVEN. London: Tavistock Institute of Human Relations

JONES S and EDEN C (1980) OR in the Community. In: Journal of the Operational Research Society 32, 335-345

KELLY GA (1955) The Psychology of Personal Constructs. New York: Norton

KELLY GA (1972) A Theory of Personality. New York: Norton

KHAKEE A. and STROMBERG K (1993) Applying Futures Studies and the Strategic Choice Approach in Urban Planning. In: Journal of the Operational Research Society, 44 (3), 213–224

KRAVATZKY AJ (1995) Hiview and Equity: Decision Analysis for Environmental Management. In PARKS: The International Journal for Protected Area Managers, 5 (1), 32–45

LICHFIELD N (1966) Cost-Benefit Analysis in Town Planning. A Case Study—Swanley. In: Urban Studies 3, 215–49

LICHFIELD N, KETTLE P and WHITBREAD M (1975) Evaluation in the Planning Process. Oxford: Pergamon

LICHFIELD N (1985) From Impact Assessment to Impact Evaluation. In: Evaluation of Complex Policy Problems. Delft: Delftsche Uitgevers Maatschappij

LINDBLOM CE (1965) The Intelligence of Democracy: Decision Making through Mutual Agreement. New York: Free Press, London: Collier-MacMillan

LING M (1990) Making Sense of Planning Evaluations: a Critique of Some Methods. In: Planning and Development (Hong Kong), 6 (1), 14–20

LUCKMAN J (1967) An Approach to the Management of Design. In: Operational Research Quarterly 18, 345-58

MACHOL R (1976) Principles of Operations Research: The Sutton Effect. : Interfaces 7, 106-7

MASON RD and MITROFF II (1981) Challenging Strategic Planning Assumptions. New York: Wiley

MILLER EJ and RICE AK (1967) Systems of Organization. London: Tavistock Publications.

MOCKLER RJ and DOLOGITE DG (1991) Using Computer Software to Improve Group Decision-Making. In: Long Range Planning, *24*, 44–47

MOORE CM (1987) Group Techniques for Idea Building. London: Sage

MORGAN JR (1971) AIDA – A Technique for the Management of Design. IOR Monograph No 2. London: Tavistock Institute of Human Relations.

MOULLIN M (1991) Getting Planners to take Notice. In: OR Insight, *4* (1), 25–29. Birmingham: Operational Research Society

NEUMANN JE, HOLTI R and STANDING H. (1995) Change Everything at Once! Didcot: Management Books 2000

NORRIS ME (1985) Operational Research and the Social Sciences: Review of Local Government and Strategic Choice. In: Journal of the Operational Research Society *36*, 870-2

NUNAMAKER JF, DENNIS AR, VALACIO, JS, VOGEL DR and GEORGE, JF (1991) Electronic Meeting Systems to Support Group Work. Communications of the ACM, *34* (7), 40–61

OPEN SYSTEMS GROUP (1981) Systems Behaviour (Third Edition).London: Harper & Row

OPENSHAW S and WHITEHEAD P (1986) The Decision Optimising Technique: History, development and progress towards a future machine based planning system. In: Willis KG (ed) Contemporary Issues in Town Planning. Aldershot: Gower

ORMEROD R (1983) Corporate Planning and its use of OR in the NCB: A Personal View. In: Journal of the Operational Research Society *34*, 461-7

ORMEROD R (1995) Putting Soft OR Methods to Work: Information Systems Strategy Development at Sainsbury's. In: Journal of the Operational Research Society, *46*, 277–293

ORMEROD R (1996a) Information Systems Strategy Development at Sainsbury's Supermarkets using "Soft" OR. In: Interfaces, *26*, 102–130

ORMEROD R (1996b) Putting Soft OR Methods to Work: Information Systems Strategy Development at Richards Bay. In: Journal of the Operational Research Society, *47*, 1083–1097

PHILLIPS LD (1982) Requisite Decision Modelling. In: Journal of the Operational Research Society *33*, 303-12

PHILLIPS LD (1990) Decision Analysis for Group Decision Support. In: Tackling strategic problems: the Role of Group Decision Support ed. C. Eden and J. Radford. London: Sage

RAIFFA H (1968) Decision Analysis. Reading, Mass: Addison-Wesley

RICE AK (1965) Learning for Leadership – Inter-Personal and Inter-group Relations. London: Tavistock Publications

RICKARDS T (1974) Problem Solving through Creative Analysis. Epping: Gower Press

RITCHIE C, TAKET A and BRYANT J (1994) Community Works: 26 Case Studies of Community OR in Action. Birmingham: Operational Research Society

ROBINSON I (ed) (1972) Decision-Making in Urban Planning: An Introduction to New Methodologies. London: Sage

ROSENHEAD J (1978) An Education in Robustness. In: Journal of the Operational Research Society *29*, 105-11

ROSENHEAD J (1980) Planning under Uncertainty: II A Methodology for Robustness Analysis. In: Journal of the Operational Research Society *31*, 331–42

ROSENHEAD JV (ed.) (1989) Rational Analysis for a Problematic World. Chichester/New York: Wiley

SAATY T (1980) The Analytical Hierarchy Process. New York: McGraw-Hill

SAGAR T (1993) Paradigms for Planning: a Rationality-Based Classification. In: Planning Theory, *9*, 79–118

SCHARPF FW (1972) Komplexitat als Schranke der Politischen Planung. Politische Innovation und Gesellschafliche Wandel: Politische Vierteljahresschrift

SCHNELLE E (1973) Metaplan: Op Zoek naar Doelstellingen Leerproces an Medewerkers Betrokken. Amersfoort: DHV

SCHON DA (1971) Beyond the Stable State: Public and Private Learning in Changing Society. London: Temple Smith

SHAKUN MF (1995) Restructuring a Negotiation with Evolutionary Systems Design. In Negotiation Journal, *11* (2), 145–150

STRINGER J (1967) Operational Research for Multi-Organisations. In: Operational Research Quarterly *18*, 105-20

STROMBERG K (1986) Planera met Onsakerheter! (in Swedish) Stockholm: Byggforskningsradet

SUSSKIND A and CRUIKSHANK J (1987) Breaking the Impasse: Consensus Approaches to Resolving Public Disputes. New York: Basic Books

SUTTON A and WILKIN L (eds) (1986) Related Socio-Technical Approaches to the Management of Uncertainty. Dordrecht: Martinus Nijhoff

SWANSON J (1994) Sending out the Right Packages. In: The Surveyor (UK), 18 August

THUNHURST C, RITCHIE C, FRIEND JK and BOOKER P (1992) Housing in the Dearne Valley: Doing Community OR with the Thurnscoe Tenants Housing Co-operative. Part I – the Involvement of the Community OR Unit. In: Journal of the Operational Research Society, *43*, 81–94

TRIST EL, HIGGIN GW, MURRAY H and POLLOCK AB (1963) Organizational Choice. London: Tavistock

TRIST EL and MURRAY H (eds.) (1990) The Social Engagement of Social Science. Volume I: the Socio-Psychological Perspective. London: Free Association Books

TRIST EL and MURRAY H (eds.) (1993) The Social Engagement of Social Science. Volume II: the Socio-Technical Perspective. Philadelphia: The University of Pennsylvania Press

TRIST EL, EMERY, F. and MURRAY H (eds.) (1997) The Social Engagement of Social Science. Volume III: the Socio-Ecological Perspective. Philadelphia: The

University of Pennsylvania Press

URY W (1991) Getting Past No: Negotiating with Difficult People. London: Business Books

VAN DE GRAAF R (198S) Strategic Choice in LPG Policy. In: A Faludi and Voogd H (eds) Evaluation of Complex Policy Problems. Delft: Delftsche Uitgeres Maatschappij

VAN GRUNDY, AB (1981) Techniques of Structured Problem Solving. New York: Van Nostrand Reinhold

VAN STEENBERGEN F (1990) The Strategic Choice Approach in Regional Development Planning. In: Third World Planning Review, *12* (3), 301–304

VICKERS G (1965) The Art of Judgement. London: Chapman and Hall

VOGEL DR (1993) Electronic Meeting Support. In: The Environmental Professional, *15*, 198–206

WATSON, SR and BUEDE, DM (1987) Decision Synthesis. Cambridge: Cambridge University Press

WEDGWOOD-OPPENHEIM F (1972) Planning Under Uncertainty. In: Local Government Studies *2*, 53-65

WHITE L (1994) Development Options for a Rural Community in Belize – Alternative Development and Operational Research. In: International Transactions in Operational Research *1* (4), 453–462

WILCOX D (1994) The Guide to Effective Participation. Brighton: Partnership Books

WORLD BANK (1996) The World Bank Participation Sourcebook. Washington DC: The World Bank

Answers to exercises

Chapter 2 – Exercises: Answers and Comments

1. There would be 13 additional decision links. Figure 12 shows 8 decision links, out of a maximum possible of 21. As was mentioned in passing in the chapter, the maximum can be worked out by calculating that each of the seven decision areas could be connected to each of the other six – making 42 links in all, which reduces to 21 when double-counting is allowed for. Alternatively, you could draw in the thirteen extra links on a copy of the decision graph; which could help you in appreciating how confusing and lacking in structural information a fully connected decision graph becomes.

2. There are various possibilities for rearranging the graph after you have added the two additional links. For example, try redrawing it with GAS SITE? and GRIFF SCHL? out to the right; WEST ST? swung around to the top; and DIST LIFE? shifted to the centre of the ROAD LINE?/SHOP LOC'N?/CENT'L SITE? triangle. You should then be able to avoid crossovers between decision links – though this would not necessarily remain possible if still more decision links were added. This example illustrates how a little skill and judgement in positioning can make structural relationships more clear.

3. In the modified decision graph of question 2, you will find that there are five fully interconnected triads. They are:

> ROAD LINE?/WEST ST?/SHOP LOC'N?
> ROAD LINE?/SHOP LOC'N?/CENT'L SITE?
> ROAD LINE?/SHOP LOC'N?/DIST LIFE?
> SHOP LOC'N?/CENT'L SITE?/DIST LIFE?
> ROAD LINE?/CENT'L SITE?/DIST LIFE?

Note that ROAD LINE?/SHOP LOC'N?/DIST LIFE?/CENT'L SITE? also forms a fully connected cluster of four decision areas. You might decide to choose either this or any of the five triads listed above as a problem focus within which to explore what combinations of options were available: but you might wish to take other non-structural information into account in making this choice.

4. A quick glance at Figure 17 shows that schemes E, G and I are the only ones including the 40-year option in DIST LIFE?, so these three would be removed. This exercise illustrates how easy it can be to test the effect of removing specific options when decision schemes are presented in the form of a tree.

5. Schemes G and I in Figure 17 both involve the combination of 40YR in DIST LIFE? with OPEN in CENT'L SITE?, so would be eliminated. This again is not hard to see simply by inspecting the tree. Of course, you can do this kind of exercise very quickly with a computer – which can be useful if you have larger trees to handle and if you want to explore the effects of many different changes in assumptions.

6. These two extra option bars would eliminate schemes A, B, C, D and F, in addition to G, which was already ruled out by the option bar introduced in question 5. So, only schemes E and H would remain: in practice this would probably lead you to ask questions as to whether other option bars could be removed to open the range of choice up again.

7. Removal of the SOUTH – IND option bar in Figure 16 would allow two additional schemes to be introduced:

   SOUTH – GAS – IND – 20YR
   SOUTH – GAS – IND – 40YR

   The information to allow you to work this out is contained in the option graph of Figure 16; but you may have found it useful to refer to the tree in Figure 17 as well, to find out the answer quickly.

8. Looking at the map in Figure 18, you might wonder why there was no link shown in Figure 12 between the WEST ST? and CENT'L SITE? decision areas, given that the two sites are adjacent. However, you would be wise then to refer back to the fuller descriptions of these two decision areas in Figure 10. It is important to bear in mind that locational connections are not the *only* possible grounds for introducing links between decision areas: there may be no *decision* links at all between choices on adjoining sites while, conversely, choices relating to non-adjacent sites may be linked for financial, functional or other reasons. The map could also cause you to wonder whether there might be a direct link between DIST LIFE? and GRIFF SCHL?, given that the school looks as if it could serve the neighbourhood. However, the map on its own gives you far less information than would be available in practice to anyone with a detailed knowledge of the area, its people and its services. So, the point of this exercise is that there is not *necessarily* any relationship between a decision graph and a physical map: adjacency is only one of many kinds of relatedness which may (or may not) be reflected in a

decision graph.

4. The answer to this question is even more open than that to question 8, for similar reasons. You might wonder why Figure 16 shows an incompatibility between NORTH in ROAD LINE? and GAS in SHOP LOC'N?, given that the gasworks site seems to be so remote from the northern road line; or you might wonder why an option bar appears between SOUTH in ROAD LINE? and IND in CENT'L SITE?. And would not IND in CENT'L SITE? make it difficult to keep the shops in Main Street which runs alongside, suggesting a new option bar? But these again are questions rather than answers; questions that could be put to people with more specific knowledge of local circumstances, yet even then might not have clear cut answers. For option bars are essentially *working assumptions* about which combinations are possible and which are not.

Chapter 3 – Exercises: Answers and Comments

1. The CAPITAL: comparison area could, if desired, be split into two elements concerned with construction works and property acquisition; or the RESI-DENTS: comparison area into separate elements concerned with confidence and quality of life – though these could prove much harder to separate in practice. Other distinctions could be made between different types of employment within JOBS:, and between different sources of INCOME:. This is not to suggest that it will usually be a good thing to divide comparison areas into smaller and smaller elements: the point of the exercise is simply that there are differing levels of abstraction that can be thought about in formulating an appropriate set of comparison areas for working purposes.

2. You will probably have found this a hard question to answer because of the way ranges are used to express uncertainty in Figure 20. A statistician would tell you that there is no sound way of deducing the assessments for H compared to B in terms of numerical ranges for CAPITAL:, INCOME: and JOBS: without making further assumptions about whether the sources of variation in the B versus A and H versus A comparisons can be considered as independent. Working on mid-points of ranges, you might say that H was likely to cost about 350k more than B; to generate about 50k per annum less income than A; and to generate about 25 more jobs – but it is only in the case of INCOME: that you could be fairly confident that H will yield less than B, because the ranges do not overlap. A reasonable inference to make from the two RESIDENTS: assessments is that B will probably generate much more confidence than H.

3. B would now yield more income and jobs than A for the expenditure of less capital: so it is likely that the only hesitation in expressing a preference for B would lie in the assessment that it would 'probably' generate more confidence among residents. This suggests a *possibility*, however remote, that it might leave them feeling less rather than more confidence. So could the

conditions likely to lead to this outcome be at least briefly explored?

4. The changes proposed in question 3 would swing the INCOME: and JOBS: ranges over into corresponding positions on the right hand side of the advantage comparison chart. It now seems that any possible advantage to A in terms of the RESIDENTS: assessment could be at most marginal: this would be outweighed by the significant-to-considerable advantage to B in terms of CAPITAL:, even before taking the INCOME: and JOBS: advantage to B into account. This suggests there is no real risk in eliminating A as inferior to B – unless, of course, there could be advantages in other comparison areas not yet included in the list.

5. Comparing the 'best guess' points of the CAPITAL: and INCOME: ranges as presented in Figure 21, the balance of advantage is likely to be in favour of B because the CAPITAL: advantage to B appears as 'considerable' and the INCOME: advantage to A as only 'significant'. But the two ranges indicate that there is quite a lot of uncertainty in this judgement; there is at least a possibility that the net financial advantage could be to A if the capital advantage to B were on the low side of the range and the income advantage to B on the high side. Further examination of this could mean looking both into sources of uncertainty in the money amounts involved, and into any time discounting assumptions used to weigh income against capital.

6. The capital cost indices for schemes C, D, E, F and G would reduce by 200k each, becoming 1800k, 1900k, 1950k, 1750k and 1800k. The costs for H and I would reduce by 150k each, becoming 1900k and 1950k respectively. The new order of preference on capital cost would be B, F, (C, G), (D, H) and, lastly, (A, E, I), using brackets to indicate ties. The arguments for shortlisting B and E still apply as in Figure 22; but A is less attractive and might be replaced by D, C or G.

7. Figure 22 shows that there are two schemes – B and C – which differ *only* in the choice of location for the shopping centre. Because B is given a higher residents' confidence rating than C in Figure 22, it seems that residents' confidence will be higher if it is proposed to retain the MAIN shopping location rather than move it to KING.

8. The informal soundings in response to the ?VALJOB uncertainty area were assessed in Figure 24 as leading to a much greater gain in confidence in comparing A against B than the market survey aimed at the ?SITEJOBS uncertainty area; yet the delay is less and, instead of an estimated fee of 20k, the only resource demand is 'some demands' on the time of busy policy-makers. These demands would probably have to be very severe to outweigh the expenditure of 20,000 monetary units, so the second exploratory option appears to be very much more resource-effective than the first.

9. Rearranging the tree, there are three action schemes which leave open the choice of two alternative decision schemes in the longer term: these are 10YR-HOUS, 20YR-OPEN and 40YR-OPEN. The other three action schemes leave open no flexibility for the future. Of those mentioned above, however, cross-reference to Figure 22 shows that only the 10YR-HOUS action scheme leaves open more than one decision scheme scoring RRR or above on the residents' confidence index. So on these grounds 10YR-HOUS is the most *robust* of the six possible action schemes.

10. In the SHOP LOCATION? row of Figure 26, MAIN STREET would disappear from the first cell – though you could replace it by '*NOT* GASWORKS SITE'. You would now enter in the deferred choices column something like 'in x months decide shop location [Main Street or King Square]'. There are all kinds of steps you could consider – for example, consulting the local traders; detailed costing or design exercises; or discussions with a supermarket company which might help finance the development on King Square.

11. The figures in Figure 27 give you a little more information about the numbers of 'stakeholders' in some of the decisions that are being faced over the future of South Side in relation to the wider metropolitan area. But of course, the size of their stakes will differ and these differences would probably have to be weighed up politically. Note however there is no financial or economic information in Figure 27 (apart from a hint about the economic condition of existing traders). Some kinds of financial information might be easily obtained from municipal sources, while other kinds could be more inaccessible. Given the pressures on the South Side Working Party, they would have to make some quick judgements in the *value* of any such information to the decisions they face before deciding whether to invest time and resources in obtaining and processing it – which helps to illustrate the more general points about exploratory options discussed in Chapter 3.

Index

Bold text indicates definitions of core concepts